Western Music

Western Music and Its Others

Difference, Representation, and Appropriation in Music

EDITED BY

Georgina Born and
David Hesmondhalgh

UNIVERSITY OF CALIFORNIA PRESS

Berkeley   Los Angeles   London

All musical examples in this book are transcriptions by the authors
of the individual chapters, unless otherwise stated in the chapters.

University of California Press
Berkeley and Los Angeles, California

University of California Press, Ltd.
London, England

Library of Congress Cataloging-in-Publication Data

Western music and its others : difference, representation, and appropriation in music /
edited by Georgina Born and David Hesmondhalgh.
        p.   cm.
Includes bibliographical references and index.
ISBN 0-520-22083-8 (cloth : alk. paper)—ISBN 0-520-22084-6 (pbk. : alk. paper)
    1. Music—20th century—Social aspects.   I. Born, Georgina.   II. Hesmondhalgh,
David.
ML3795.W45   2000
781.6—dc21   00-029871

Manufactured in the United States of America

09   08   07   06   05   04   03   02   01   00

10   9   8   7   6   5   4   3   2   1

The paper used in this publication meets the minimum requirements of ANSI/NISO
Z39.48-1992 (R 1997) (*Permanence of Paper*). ♾

For Clara and Theo (GB) and Rosa and Joe (DH)
And in loving memory of George Mully (1925–1999)

CONTENTS

ACKNOWLEDGMENTS

This book has had a long genesis. The initial ideas came from two directions: from thoughts Georgina Born developed while writing a Ph.D. and an earlier book on music; and from a timely conference, called "The Debt to 'Other' Musics," held in July 1990 jointly by the Royal Anthropological Institute of Great Britain and Ireland with the Institute of Contemporary Arts in London. We would like to thank Jonathan Benthall, Michael Chanan and Judith Squires for organizing the conference which, as far as we know, was the first ever held on these themes; and Ragnar Farr and Helena Reckitt of the ICA for their early help in developing a book project following the conference.

Our authors have had to exercise enormous patience, since obstacle after obstacle arose to delay progress toward publication, always for unavoidable human and professional reasons. We want to express our heartfelt thanks to all the contributors for sticking with it, as well as for their creative and serious engagement with the book's themes. We hope they find the end product worth all the waiting. We thank also those who gave feedback on aspects of the manuscript. They include John Butt, Aaron Fox, Ralph P. Locke, Dominic Moran, Ato Quayson, Michael Stewart, Will Straw, Daniel Thompson, and three anonymous reviewers. Needless to say, they are not responsible for any errors or misjudgments that remain. Thanks too to Jan Spauschus Johnson at the University of California Press for all her hard work; Evan Camfield for his extremely skillful copyediting; and Lynne Withey for shepherding the project.

I want to thank Dave Hesmondhalgh for coming on board and helping to shape this book so well; his contributions have been essential for its completion. I was fortunate to be the Senior Research Fellow at King's College, Cambridge in 1997–98, for which I am grateful to the Provost, Professor Pat Bateson, and the Fellows of the College. Between 1996 and 1998 I also held the Visiting Professorship at the Institute of Musicology of the University of Aarhus, Denmark, for which I thank my friend and colleague Steen Neilsen. Both situations provided me with the mental space in which my work on this book was brought to fruition. The ideas have been presented over the years in seminars for the University of London Intercollegiate Anthropology seminar, Magdalen College, Oxford, the Queen's University, Belfast, and at the departments of Music or Anthropology of the University of Ottawa, the University of Rochester, New York University, the University of Chicago, and the University of California, Berkeley. My thinking in this area was stimulated by the teaching of Mike Gilsenan, to whom I remain grateful, and very early on, Richard Middleton kindly gave me useful criticisms.

The interest of my colleagues Philip Bohlman, Jonathan Burston, Steve Feld, Simon Frith, Antoine Hennion, George Lewis, Ralph P. Locke, Colin MacCabe, George Marcus, Martin Stokes, Marilyn Strathern, and Janet Wolff has provided me with the confidence to pursue these concerns, and—even though some of them may not admire this effort—I offer my gratitude. For his support, for refusing to limit life to academia, and for his wonderful dancing, I thank my partner Andrew Barry—whose musical tastes are way ahead of mine. On a very different note, just twenty-four hours after I completed work on this manuscript I was woken to the awful news that my beloved stepfather, George Mully, had died suddenly and unexpectedly. My pleasure in this book is thus tied inextricably with a sense of loss. George lived according to strong progressive convictions and was exceptionally talented, as a father and an artist (opera and theater director, filmmaker, writer, translator). As a child, I watched him produce and direct chamber opera and theater, and it left me with a lifelong interest in analyzing authorship and cultural production. This book, which Dave and I intended to dedicate to our children, is now dedicated also to his memory.

Georgina Born

Many people provided me with practical and emotional assistance during the period in which this book was being prepared. I would like to thank the following groups of friends in particular: colleagues and students at Goldsmiths College and at Coventry University; various members of the International Association for the Study of Popular Music for providing times and places in which musical culture can be discussed seriously and enjoyably; and the Accrington-Amsterdam posse for wonderful holidays away and for revitalization closer to home.

Thanks also to the following friends and colleagues for comments on and conversations about this book and/or about my chapter in it: Les Back, Bill Brewer, Patrick Costello, Nick Couldry, Kev Grant, Dai Griffiths, Arun Kundnani, Lorraine Leu, Caspar Melville, Richard Middleton, Jim Osborne, Kate Osborne, Sara Salih, Nilly Sarkar, Simon Underwood, and Tim Ward. Jim Osborne was a good friend, a music lover and nonacademic intellectual who saw academic work as a resource, not a threat. I shall miss him enormously and my chapter in this book is dedicated to his memory.

My special thanks to: Georgie Born for inviting me to participate in this project and for her generous, detailed comments on much of my work; Pete Playdon for help in preparing the manuscript; Teresa Gowan, Dave Swann, Steve Swann, and Graham Caveny for understanding, in various ways, how strange it is to have come from there and to get to here; and Jonathan Burston and Jason Toynbee for acts of rescue and intellectual stimulation inside the workplace and out. Most of all, thanks to Mum and Dad for everything they have done for me over the years; to Ernie and Cathy Steward; to Julie Hesmondhalgh, who is a star; to Rosa Hesmondhalgh, who will be one, I think; and to Helen Steward, who is just incredible. Finally, welcome to Joe, who was born just in time—a few days before this manuscript was dispatched to the publishers.

David Hesmondhalgh

Introduction:
On Difference, Representation,
and Appropriation in Music

Georgina Born and David Hesmondhalgh

The music of Asia and India is to be admired because it has reached a stage of perfection, and it is this stage of perfection that interests me. But otherwise the music is dead.
PIERRE BOULEZ

The least interesting form of influence, to my mind, is that of imitating the sound of some non-Western music. . . . Instead of imitation, the influences of non-Western musical structures on the thinking of a Western composer is likely to produce something genuinely new.
STEVE REICH

I got interested in world music as a failed drummer; I was able to look for fresher rhythms. It just seemed fresh, wonderful, more live and spiritual than most pop.
PETER GABRIEL

The study of world musics moved out of what would nowadays be called an Orientalist stance only in the 1960s. Till then, few people seriously questioned the notion that beyond the Western classical tradition there were three kinds of music to be studied: Oriental, folk, and primitive. . . . "Oriental" of course referred to those Asian "high cultures" that had long-term, accessible internal histories and that could be "compared" with similar European systems. "Primitive" encompassed all the "preliterate" peoples of the world, who had to rely on oral tradition for transmission and who had no highly professionalized "art musicians" in their midst. The "folk" were the internal primitives of Euro-America.
MARK SLOBIN

How should we conceive of difference in music? The kind of difference invoked when music, that quintessentially nonrepresentational medium, is employed (paradoxically) so as to represent, through musical figures, another music, another culture, an other? What is implied by attending to the *boundaries* of musical-aesthetic discourses inherent in this notion of representing or appropriating another music or culture *in* music? Or in the notion that a music's construction of its own identity may involve the exclusion or repudiation of another music? Or in the concept of hybridity as a process of mixing between erstwhile distinct and bounded musical cultures? How do we understand the differences embodied in the master meta-classification of music noted by Mark Slobin in the quotation above? Must all such classifications—that is, must the recognition of difference in music—necessarily be fictive and divisive, ideological and hierarchical? Or can it be allied to a reflexive, analytical project?

This book is an attempt to ask basic questions of this nature in relation to two related phenomena: musical borrowings or appropriations, and the way that music has been used to construct, evoke, or mark alterity of a musical or a sociocultural kind. The book begins on the theme, broadly, of the relationship between "Western" art music and "other" musics.[1] Focused primarily on the twentieth century, it examines the ways in which art musics have drawn upon, or repudiated, popular, non-Western, and ethnic musics, and what these relations mean in cultural and political terms. This requires an analysis of the particularity of musical constructions of alterity, of the techniques of the musical imaginary, whether in exoticist, Orientalist, or primitivist musics, and of how these musical signs come to bear meaning. This is to address the nature of specifically musical representation—a problem easily ignored given music's status as a nonrepresentational medium; given also the more obviously ideological propensities of denotative media, that is, the literary and visual arts.[2] The collection also pursues wider issues of representation through music: how other cultures are represented in music through the appropriation or imaginative figuration of their own music, and, conversely, how social and cultural identities and differences come to be constructed and articulated in music. In later essays, these issues are taken up in relation to mass-mediated and commercial popular musics: the representation of others in the narrative film music of Hollywood; how contemporary Third World musics come to be represented in the discourse of world music; and the politics of representation and appropriation in contemporary hybrid popular musics.

In some ways, this collection revisits the territory covered by a number of recent works addressing issues of musical exoticism and Orientalism,[3] the relations between Western musics and non-Western musics,[4] musicology and difference,[5] and world music.[6] Indeed, a common problematic across musicology, ethnomusicology, and popular music studies in recent years has been the theorization of music and identity and, by implication, difference.[7] But the aim of this book is to foster further conceptual development by thinking *across* a number of these questions, which have often been treated separately.[8] Importantly, it addresses them in relation to both art musics and popular musics, proposing that we may learn from the comparative exercise of tracing exoticism through the practices of early-twentieth-century French composers (see Pasler's essay) to those of late-twentieth-century world dance fusion groups (see Hesmondhalgh's essay).

The collection is also a departure in its attempt to think through these issues in relation to several music disciplines: musicology, ethnomusicology, popular music studies, and film music studies. Each discipline brings a characteristic focus and set of analytical tools to bear on the material, and together they offer a comparative sense of analytical possibilities. We intend this to be useful for scholars and students from each discipline who may want to become familiar with other approaches. From film music studies, Claudia Gorbman focuses on the relations between music and filmic and dramatic texts in the genre of the western. From popular music studies, Simon Frith and David Hesmondhalgh examine the political, industrial, organizational, and discursive dimensions of world music and dance fusion musics, with emphasis on how these dimensions condition musical representations. From ethnomusicology, Philip V. Bohlman and Martin Stokes examine, with reference to Jewish cantors in nineteenth-century Austria and arabesk popular music in late-twentieth-century Turkey, how musical representations are inserted into wider sociocultural processes, in particular the changing contours of collective cultural identities. From musicology, Julie Brown, Peter Franklin, Richard Middleton and Jann Pasler give composer-, music-, and text-centered accounts of the complexities of musical authorship and agency. This enables them to explore the ideologies and musical imaginaries of a range of composers, the nature of the hybrids resulting from their musical borrowings, and how certain musics are constituted through the purposive or ambivalent absenting or mastery of other musics and cultures. Yet many of the essays confound neat disciplinary divisions and attest to the increasing mutual influence and shared problematics between the disciplines. In the face of the historical fragmentation of music scholarship into its several disciplines, it is these kinds of intellectual and methodological crossovers that today yield some of the most interesting findings. But, emphatically, this book is not an exercise in methodological relativism. In this introduction, we attempt to show that it is precisely an interdisciplinary perspective that makes it possible to advance some central conceptual problems.

I. POSTCOLONIAL ANALYSIS AND MUSIC STUDIES

To examine musical borrowing and appropriation is necessarily to consider the relations between culture, power, ethnicity, and class; and these relations are always further entangled in the dynamics of gender and sexuality, as certain essays in this volume indicate. In recent years, the political importance and complexity of these matters has been argued for with great vigor in literary and cultural studies. An important subfield of literary studies focused particularly on the connections between culture, race, and empire has crystallized in the 1980s and 1990s around the theme of postcolonialism. We begin by pointing to some ways in which postcolonial analysis provides a starting point for the consideration of musical appropriation in this collection. Productive aspects of postcolonial theory and criticism have been neglected in music studies; but, while we want to argue for their value here, we also want to suggest the need for qualification.

The attention paid by postcolonial analysis to the politics of culture and colonialism is not without precedent. According to Williams and Chrisman, the contributions of black nationalist intellectuals and liberation thinkers from the late nineteenth century and earlier twentieth century tend to be "overlooked by academics intent on identifying Frantz Fanon as the founding father of Third World liberationist discourse."[9] But aside from the work of Fanon, most commentators agree that, if there is a distinctive field of postcolonial analysis, it developed in the wake of Edward Said's *Orientalism* (1978).[10] Said employed the insights of French poststructuralism, in particular those of Foucault, to analyze nineteenth-century European writings on non-European cultures with the aim of illuminating the discursive operations of colonialism. By examining a range of representational practices—the work of geographers, historians, travellers, and early anthropologists, as well as literary high culture and memoirs—Said highlighted the forms of language and knowledge that were intimately connected to, and colluded with, the history of European colonialism, while granting these cultural forms a certain autonomy. In Foucauldian manner, Said portrayed the development of Orientalist colonial discourses and representational practices as resulting in a construction that determined both what could be said and what could count as truth. For Said, Orientalism was the academic study of "the East" (the original meaning of the term); it was also, more broadly, the attempt by various writers (including Aeschylus, Dante, Hugo, and Marx) to engage with and understand "Eastern" cultures. Above all it was a discourse, in the Foucauldian sense, which, through the complicity of knowledge systems, politics, and government, not only constructed but was instrumental in administering and subjugating "the Orient."

In the 1980s, as other writers took up Said's project, colonial discourse analysis became a burgeoning field of literary theory and criticism, and by the 1990s it was increasingly incorporated into the domain of postcolonial studies. As a whole, this field now subsumes a range of distinctive aims and methods: the analysis of literary works produced in colonizing countries and of how they treat, or ignore, the issue of colonization; the analysis of writing (and cultural production in general) about colonized countries, reflecting an increasing concern to expand the object of literary study beyond fiction, drama, and poetry; the analysis of writing that emerged from colonized countries during and after the formal colonial period; and scrutiny of the relations in the postcolonial period between Western theories, institutions, and intellectuals and those of the formerly colonized countries (including the implications of using poststructuralist critical method itself).[11]

Yet however internally heterogeneous it may be, postcolonial studies can be demarcated from other modes of cultural analysis, and its contribution to the project of developing the history and theory of "race," culture, and power are considerable.

An initial way that postcolonial studies is relevant for an analysis of the musical treatment of sociocultural difference, and of the power-imbued nature of musical appropriation, is that it refuses to treat culture as an autonomous and politically innocent domain of social life. Rather, there is a relentless insistence on the importance of culture and knowledge in understanding social power. As has been well-established by recent work in critical musicology, postwar music scholarship has been particularly prone to the view that an analysis of social and political processes is irrelevant for an understanding of culture.[12] It is true that much music scholarship has sought to avoid out-and-out formalism by addressing music's various "contexts"; paradoxically, the very treatment of these contexts as explanatory factors in understanding musical texts can reinforce the tendency to privilege the text itself. What is lost here is any sense of the dialectical relationship between acts of musical communication on the one hand and political, economic, and cultural power-relations on the other. Postcolonial analysis, then, sets a fruitful example for music studies in that it pays meticulous attention to textual detail, but always sees such analysis as subsidiary to the larger project of thinking through the implications of cultural expression for understanding asymmetrical power relations and concomitant processes of marginalization and denigration.

Like the poststructuralist thought to which it is often indebted, postcolonial analysis seeks to enhance the conceptualization of cultural politics. Much recent work has attempted to move beyond the neo-Gramscian concepts of hegemony and resistance, which have become reified into simplistic binaries. This means avoiding the racist conception of colonizers as civilizing agents and the colonized as beneficiaries; but equally, it means avoiding any anticolonialist reversal of these categories, which would homogenize the colonizing practice and conceive of the colonized as victims. Gayatri Chakravorty Spivak's work, for example, is marked by an insistence on heterogeneity and contradiction, stressing variations in the historical experience and expression of oppression and differences within the colonizing formations, and the impossibility of a process of subject-formation that can evade the effects of logocentrism, phallocentrism, and colonialism. In passing, Spivak has evoked the combined destructive and productive impacts of imperialism in the concept of an "enabling violence,"[13] a concept that summarizes beautifully the paradoxes of the material in the present book.

Postcolonial studies, like cultural studies as a whole, has been characterized by a marked interdisciplinarity. It has, for example, developed productive interfaces with historical studies of colonialism and the analysis of representation in cultural anthropology.[14] One important nexus has focused on psychoanalysis following the work of Homi Bhabha. Bhabha attempts to understand the colonial encounter by bringing together the reading of Lacanian psychoanalysis with theories of ideology inaugurated by 1970s film theory, the earlier work of Fanon, and a Foucauldian theory of subjectification. His essay "The Other Question," for example, explicitly challenges functionalist and determinist accounts of colonialism by pointing to a lack that is central to the constitution of colonial subjectivity, a lack suggested by the necessity of repetition for the reproduction of discursive stereotypes.[15]

Postcolonial analysis is thus an ambitious field that foregrounds the racial and ethnic power dynamics of global cultural relations. It does so historically, through analysis of the discourses of colonialism; it attempts to understand the legacies and repercussions of colonialist culture in the contemporary world; and it strives also to reveal how identities and epistemologies characteristic of the West continue to be underpinned by the legacies of racism and colonialism. Some of the basic questions raised by the field are shared by the essays that follow, even where they address apparently noncolonialist forms of racism and class inequality, such as the treatment of "internal others" (Brown, Bohlman, Stokes) and "Low-others" (Middleton). The questions include: How is it possible to represent other cultures? What techniques are available for representation, and what implicit meanings do they bear? What is the relationship between political domination and cultural- and knowledge-production? What forms of subversion of dominant representational practices are possible? What role do Western and non-Western cultural producers and intellectuals play, wittingly and unwittingly, in various processes of representation?

In spite of its myriad strengths, however, postcolonial theory has been criticized for certain limitations as a mode of cultural analysis, even on its home terrain of culture and colonialism. While constantly alert to the racialized nature of cultural power, it tends to treat such power almost entirely in terms of textuality and epistemology. Material conditions and the possibility of political practices oriented toward changing material conditions are sidelined. This has been the cause of some bitter Marxist polemics against the field, but it is a point made also by sympathetic critics such as Benita Parry.[16] Indeed, a major debate concerns the degree to which the postcolonial project is compatible with epistemologies and accounts of agency characteristic of Marxism. Sociological, political, and economic issues tend to be unintegrated or neglected. Again, even sympathetic proponents have noted this feature. Stuart Hall, for example, has described the failure in postcolonial studies to consider the relationship between postcolonialism and global capitalism as "seriously damaging and disabling for everything positive which the postcolonial paradigm can, and has the ambition to, accomplish."[17] Moreover, postcolonial analysis has tended to concentrate on "official" and high-art discourses at the expense of a systematic account of the prominent role of commercial popular culture within systems of colonialism and neocolonialism (as it can operate both to reinforce and, on occasion, to subvert these processes).[18]

More generally, perhaps under the influence of poststructuralism, postcolonial analysis has tended to avoid questions of agency. One response to this neglect has been formulated by the anthropologist Nicholas Thomas, who calls for a plural account of colonial formations and strategies adequate to the variety of their historical forms and, relatedly, for an analysis of agency and of the complexities of the "practical expression of discourse." Thomas's aim is to develop a "productive analytical tension, a reading that is stretched between regimes of [representation and] truth and their moments of mediation, reformulation and contestation in practice."[19] Later, in sections IV and V of the introduction, we advocate a more complex account of agency, one that addresses both its individual and collective modalities and that, in considering individual agency, can address the core problem of the interface between (collective) discourse and individual subjectivities. It is, nonetheless, the kind of perspective opened up by Thomas that allows for analyses such as we offer in this book: of specific moments and forms of musical representations of others, of their variability in context, of the complexities of authorial agency and practice in relation to wider discursive formations, and of the changing contours of discursive debate and conflict as they are projected into musical forms.

Given the productive example and the substantial cultural impact in recent years of postcolonial analysis, the relative lack of attention in music studies to the relationships between musical cultures, race, and colonialism is striking.[20] There are a number of possible reasons. First, there is music's apparent status as a nonrepresentational medium, referred to above and probed throughout this volume. There is the continuing reluctance in the core music disciplines to consider the political dimensions of musical cultures and of music scholarship. The last twenty years have seen attempts to alter this state of affairs by politicizing music scholarship in various ways. The delayed impacts of neo-Marxism, critical theory, and poststructuralism have inspired a number of studies that, whatever their differences, portray music as inextricably bound to the exercise and interrogation of power. These studies have been particularly successful in generating greater attention to issues of gender and sexuality, both in the analysis of musical cultures and as they affect musicology.[21] In this context, it is even more unfortunate that the new critical music scholarship has, on the whole, neglected to engage with the issues raised by postcolonial studies.

There are, of course, exceptions. As Martin Stokes points out in his contribution, ethnomusicology has always attended to questions of how music represents, and how music and musicians are represented. This has helped to pave the way for a relatively swift response from ethnomusicology to the concern with practices of representation central to both postcolonial analysis and poststructuralism; and in section III of this introduction we trace how debates about appropriation, globalization, and hybridity have been configured in popular music studies and some recent ethnomusicology.[22] But in the study of Western art music, still the privileged domain of academic music scholarship, the impact of postcolonial analysis has as yet been minimal. There is no lack of studies of Western music's long history of borrowing from and evoking non-Western cultures and musics. Commonly, however, the main analytical issue has been the accuracy and authenticity of the appropriated material.[23] Elsewhere, the act of borrowing from other musical cultures has been portrayed as primarily an open-minded and empathic gesture of interest in and fascination with marginalized musics.[24] Such a perspective holds the danger of treating non-Western cultures purely as a resource for the reinvigoration of Western culture.

The present volume does not apply postcolonial theory to music, but it does take initial steps in the direction of exploring the relations between structured inequalities of race/class power and the history, theory, and analysis of music.[25] Its main predecessors are a number of valuable essays that took the lead from postcolonial studies, primarily through engagement with the legacy of Said.[26] Ralph P. Locke, for example, has assessed a group of nineteenth- and twentieth-century Orientalist operas in terms of recurring structures of plot and character, and the musical means employed by composers to carry out or "undercut" such characterization. In an essay on Saint-Saëns's *Samson et Dalila* (begun 1868), Locke identifies a prototypical narrative of Orientalist opera, which the Saint-Saëns work knowingly complexifies:

> Young, tolerant, brave, possibly naïve, white-European tenor-hero intrudes, at risk of disloyalty to his own people and colonialist ethic, into mysterious, dark-skinned, colonized territory represented by alluring dancing girls and deeply affectionate, sensitive lyric soprano, incurring wrath of brutal, intransigent tribal chieftain (bass or bass-baritone) and blindly obedient chorus of male savages.[27]

The Orientalist paradigm thus revolves around the gendered binary opposition of "a morally superior 'us' (or 'collective Self') and an appealing but dangerous 'them' ('collective other'),"[28] an eroticized encounter in which "they" come close to causing "our" downfall. The other is figured as a highly sexual female (Delilah in this opera) who is both desirable and desiring and represents both temptation and threat. Locke, exploring the wider context of Orientalism in nineteenth-century France, suggests that given the general silencing of women's sexuality in this period, Orientalist images of woman operated as an "exotic mask [whereby] much that was otherwise repressed could be smuggled into the art gallery and opera house."[29] In both articles, Locke examines the way that pentatonicism and other unusual or purposefully constrained musical procedures are used in Orientalist operas to suggest "Easternness," in relation to both female and male characters. In the later essay, he stresses the importance of distinguishing representations of Easternness from the composers' and librettists' intentions to make allegorical statements about events closer to home.[30] Yet Locke's is no mechanistic reading; citing Saint-Saëns's anti-imperialist leanings, he argues that the characteristically Orientalist binarisms of *Samson et Dalila* are subverted in places by the music, and that the work remixes its own apparent ideological terms by portraying the Hebrews (the self, the West, the male) in a less enticing, less vital and animated way than the Philistines (the other, Delilah's tribe). In this way Locke brings a subtle hermeneutics, attentive to internal contradiction, to the textual reading of musical Orientalism.

In a similarly rich essay stemming from debates around Borodin's *Prince Igor*, Richard Taruskin pursues the social, political, and intellectual contexts of nineteenth-century Russian musical Orientalism, noting the variations of the genre and yet also its semiotic coherence. Taruskin argues that this Orientalism can only be understood in the context of Russian imperialist ventures of the time. He charges *Prince Igor* with aggressive nationalism and with making overt Russian Orientalism's subtext: "The racially justified endorsement of Russia's militaristic expansion to the east." In support, he notes that both Borodin and Mussorgsky were enrolled to compose works for the celebration of Tsar Alexander II's silver jubilee in 1880, works intended "to glorify Alexander's expansionist policy."[31] Taruskin even asserts that Russian musical Orientalism can be periodized by reference to corresponding phases of Russian imperial adventure. His main concern, however, is to demonstrate the development of the particular set of musical tropes that came to be understood as connoting Easternness. Taruskin brings out the many paradoxes composing Russian Orientalism that reveal it as an essentially arbitrary musical sign, a set of conventions that developed through a lineage of composers, as he shows through the example of successive, increasingly Orientalist settings of a Pushkin lyric by Glinka, Balakirev, and Rachmaninov. These conventions, consolidated in *Prince Igor*, associate oriental cultures with an erotic and exotic languorous hedonism which serves to suggest the decadence and powerlessness of the East when faced by Russian might and efficiency. By the time Rachmaninov reworks the conventions, Taruskin comments, his Pushkin setting "speaks the sign language of Russian Orientalism in a highly developed form."[32] Condensed in the Orientalist trope of *nega*—"a flexible amalgam of ethnic verisimilitude, sensual iconicity, characteristic vocal or instrumental timbres and Glinka-esque harmony"—the other is represented as a degenerate counterpart to manly Russian virtues; *nega* "marked the other . . . for justified conquest."[33] As an ultimate irony, Taruskin notes how Russian musical Orientalism's greatest conquest was perhaps that of artistic Paris, in the guise of Diaghilev's ballet company and its seduction of the audience by sex-drenched Eastern fantasy. Henceforth, for the French, and thence for the West, Russian musical Orientalism *was* Russian music, and Russia *was* the East. Diaghilev's ploy prevented him "from presenting to the West the musical artifacts of European Russia with which he personally identified."[34] Through Taruskin's analysis, the sheer relativity of Orientalist positioning becomes apparent.

Taruskin and Locke open up great vistas of interpretive possibility. As yet, there has been less attention to the twentieth-century musical practices that are the focus of this book. In the next section, we outline the essays that address issues of representation and appropriation in musical modernism and postmodernism. Other contributions extend the analysis of Orientalist, primitivist, and exoticist musical discourses beyond the realm of art music, revealing new problematics and calling for more adequate theorization of musical representation. Steven Feld addresses the remarkable variety of ways in which the musics of the equatorial forest peoples of Central Africa have been mediated by jazz, jazz-fusion, new age, and other Western popular musics over the last thirty years; while David Hesmondhalgh discusses the ethical and aesthetic problems raised by the use of digital sampling to appropriate non-Western and ethnic musics in the work of contemporary dance and fusion popular musicians with a commitment to internationalist politics (see section III below). John Corbett traces the legacy of the American experimental tradition's attitudes toward cultural borrowing in the work of a number of musicians and composers existing often on the boundaries of art-music institutions, including Asian composers who attempt to "answer back" to such appropriation. These authors are all concerned to extend a critical analysis of tropes of difference beyond the Western canon, or to question the boundedness of that canon.

Claudia Gorbman takes these issues to the analysis of representation in film music. In a previous study, Gorbman argued that the "unheard melodies" of movie soundtracks are particularly powerful disseminators of meaning because of the way they pervade the interpretive work of film audiences in a semiconscious way. Here, she extends these insights by examining a fraught area of cinematic representation: the portrayal of the native American in the western.[35] In that central genre of America's "mythic self-definition," we see exemplified the kinds of processes to which postcolonial criticism has directed attention: the formation of a hegemonic national identity through reiterated representations (in painting, drama, fiction, and television, as well as cinema) of a despised other—in the western genre, an other that was the subject of internal colonialism. Film studies have pointed out how, as American national identity became more provisional in the decades after the Second World War, Indians began to be represented in increasingly complex and sometimes sympathetic ways. Gorbman traces corresponding shifts in the musical scores of key westerns and, in doing so, reveals the way that musical meaning is intensely bound up with visual and narrative texts. Yet Gorbman also points to disjunctures between events on screen and in the score; in particular, "the humanization of the Indian occurred more slowly in music than in on-screen characterization," suggesting a resilient racism at work in the film-musical subconscious that worked against changing narratives.

Gorbman analyzes some later scores to show how efforts to produce a more liberal, "progressive" representation of Indians brought contradictory results. The attempts of *A Man Called Horse* (directed by Elliot Silverstein, 1969) to convey the sense of "really being in an alien culture" are matched by the musical integration of diegetic[36] Sioux drumming within a (white) modernist, atonal score. As Gorbman puts it, the score "de-alienates the Indians," but this happens on white terms. The diegetic Sioux music is framed within the modernist score, and through this frame the viewing/listening subject is invited musically to "enter" the represented other. *Dances with Wolves* (directed by Kevin Costner, 1990), perhaps the most significant western of recent decades, continues the attempt to figure allegorically a process of "understanding" native American culture, and the narrative drive is reinforced by John Barry's score. The score even suggests that the U.S. army are the "real savages" by borrowing tropes from the traditional western's musical representation of Indians and using them to figure the army: a fascinating reversal of representational and ideological norms. Yet once the hero begins to associate with the Sioux, the Indians are assigned music that evades tom-tom clichés in favor of "Western-sounding themes," indicating that, in these liberal westerns, efforts at "understanding" result in nostalgic assimilation into the universal Western subject. Gorbman's essay thus explores the difficulties involved in humanist attempts to treat other cultures with sympathy, but it also indicates the potential representational gains that may derive from reflexive and imaginative film music.

This volume's relationship to postcolonial analysis can be summarized in terms of a shared lack and a contribution. Like postcolonial studies, and due no doubt to the magnitude of the challenge set by the material, the collection is perhaps susceptible to the charge of being insufficiently attentive to integrating analysis of the aesthetic and discursive with analysis of the social, political, and economic contexts of representation. But by addressing elements of popular music and culture in depth, the collection also makes an offering to postcolonial debate. As certain essays show, the centrality of discourses of race and ethnicity and the continuing prominence of Orientalist, primitivist, and exoticist tropes in popular music make music a particularly productive locus in the task of bringing postcolonial analysis to bear on popular culture per se.

II. MUSICAL MODERNISM, POSTMODERNISM, AND OTHERS

A second route into this book stems from consideration of musical modernism and postmodernism, and their contrasting relations with other musics. In modernism, the relationship of Western cultural forms to their others takes on a new significance. The development of modernism was simultaneous with the rise, from the mid–nineteenth century, of the commercial popular culture and entertainment industries, including new forms of commodified and urban popular musics. The early modernist period was also the height of the British and French empire; and in Europe it saw the continuation of a rural, agrarian peasant society alongside a small, increasingly cosmopolitan intelligentsia, among them the various artistic avant-gardes. With these coexistences in mind, we have a framework within which to theorize the relations between musical modernism and its several others: not just the musical and cultural influences that *have* been drawn upon but—as importantly—those that have rarely been referenced, and indeed those that have been neglected or denied.

Musical modernism emerged out of the expansion of tonality in late romanticism and the break into atonality in the early decades of the twentieth century. It took a number of forms. One of the most historically powerful was the serialism or twelve-tone technique of composers Schoenberg, Webern, and Berg—the Second Viennese School. Schoenberg conceived serialism as a new compositional technique based on the structural negation of the pitch hierarchies and forms associated with tonality. Schoenberg himself embodied the antinomies of modernism: wishing to encompass both rupture and continuity of tradition; employing both the rationalist methods of serialism and more expressionist and, occasionally, tonal idioms. Given that tonality and modality are the aesthetic bases of many popular musics, serialist principles prescribe an aesthetic that is completely antithetical to these other musics. Serialism thus stands as the musical equivalent of the negation of representation and figuration in modernist abstract visual art.

However, if we look at other developments in early-twentieth-century musical modernism, before and concurrent with Schoenberg's development of serialism, different aesthetic strategies become evident: not absolute and autonomous formal negation, but various attempts to draw upon other musics, to represent the other, to bring into the orbit of modernist music the sounds of the other. In literature and the visual arts as well as music, these strategies combined explorations in form with the representation of popular and everyday content or subject matter. The different aesthetic properties of non-Western and popular arts became sources of experiment and innovation. Picasso's admiration for African sculpture is well-known; Debussy's fascination with the music of Indonesia and Japan, and Ives's admiration for and emulation of New England popular musics, are musical counterparts.

These developments involved major composers who, unlike the serialists, failed to found a general technique or school. Among them, both the aesthetic form of reference to the other and the conception of the other differ in characteristic ways. Initially, we can note two related tendencies: the desire to reinvigorate the present by reference to principles of earlier musics, for example in the neo-classicisms of Stravinsky or Hindemith; and the turn to other musics—urban popular musics, Western and non-Western folk and ethnic musics—as sources of new sounds and rhythms, musical forms and ideas. The early decades of the century saw a reference to jazz on the part of Krenek, Poulenc, Milhaud, Copland, Antheil, and Gershwin. By contrast, in this same period a number of European composers, including Bartók, Kodály, Stravinsky, Falla, and Vaughan Williams, turned to the folk musics that were increasingly available from ethnographic studies and archives as influences on their distinctive nationalist modernisms.[37] Non-art musics were therefore conceived by these composers as others to be drawn in a variety of ways into their compositional practice.

It is the relationship of influence by or reference to other musics that is interrogated by Julie Brown and Jann Pasler in their analyses of modernist composers' attempts to renew their musical language, and that John Corbett illuminates in his discussion of composers from the postmodern experimental music tradition. Building on the studies of nineteenth- and early-twentieth-century musical Orientalism, Pasler analyzes the evolving varieties of Orientalism in French art music following France's Entente Cordiale with Britain in 1904, as composers came into increasing contact with Indian music and culture via field visits and early recordings. Pasler contrasts two composers, Albert Roussel and Maurice Delage, who engaged differently with Indian music following their travels to India in 1909 and 1912. She sets musical analysis within an account of the cultural and ideological milieux of the two, who came from rival French schools. Roussel, from the culturally and politically conservative Schola Cantorum, was drawn to the "simplicity" of Indian folk music, mediated through the Schola's association of *chansons populaires* (folk song) with nature, immutable racial qualities, national identity, and spirituality. On the basis of memory and sketches, Roussel used this music freely as a basis for his *Evocations* (1910). In the context of the Schola's conservative Catholicism and its base in the landowning aristocracy, Roussel's "empathic" rendering of Indian poverty and spirituality is a projection entirely consonant with the Schola's religious and racist ideological mission. Roussel's notebooks appear inattentive to the subtleties of Indian music, and his stance is that the Indian "impressions" should be subordinate to his own musical development, causing Pasler to cite Said: "The last traces of the particular have been rubbed out."[38] Yet, Pasler argues, sections of *Evocations* suggest a deeper engagement with the specificities of Indian music, such as its improvisatory qualities.

In contrast, Delage was an enthusiastic modernist who focused in his travels on Indian classical music. He idealized Indian music as audacious, authentic, pure, and as a means of transcending Western musical constraints. Mediated through the French modernist commitment to the primacy of sound color over syntax (the opposite of Scholist doctrine), Delage was enraptured by Indian music's timbral richness, its non-European tuning systems, improvised rhythms, and vocal and instrumental techniques. By studying these aesthetic components, Delage created an intercultural soundworld that, Pasler argues, went beyond a superficial impressionism and enabled him to subvert Western practices, while retaining elements of conventional Orientalism. Pasler stresses Delage's use, unlike Roussel, of early sound recordings, which gave him continuing aural access to Indian music's timbral and microtonal subtleties. Delage used almost unchanged transcriptions of certain recordings in sections of his *Quatre poèmes hindous* (1912–13) and *Ragamalika* (1912–22), thus raising issues of intellectual property in relation to such musical appropriations, as well as the irony whereby, while Delage valued Indian music's "purity" and "authenticity," he was precisely an agent of its subsumption by Western idioms. Pasler throws light here on the important role of technologies of sound reproduction in the burgeoning of twentieth-century practices of musical appropriation.

Like Pasler, Brown explores the complexities of authorial subjectivity and its influence by wider cultural and discursive forces. She examines the place of Bartók's evolving conceptions of gypsy and peasant musics in his Hungarian nationalist cultural project. Brown's analysis shows that they exhibit a classic instance of splitting between an idealized, pure, and authentic peasantry, conceived as the norm, and a degenerate, deviant, impure gypsy culture, a splitting imbued with racist fear of contamination by the gypsy "Orientals within" and their "foreign" cultural elements. Brown proposes that this ideological and psychic configuration, articulated in Bartók's writings and modified over the years, was inherent in Bartók's aesthetic project of founding a Hungarian modernism that was allied to a progressive Western modernity and progressive nationalist elements, and which must therefore be doubly purged of the putatively non-Western, antimodern, inauthentic marks of Hungarian gypsy music. The thrust of her case is that Bartók's idealizing aesthetic embrace of peasant musics must be understood as immanently linked with these negative racist projections and prohibitions, which themselves evidence Bartók's subjectification by the racist cultural and nationalist doctrines of the late nineteenth and early twentieth centuries. Brown traces the concept of "hybridity" through Bartók's later essays, noting that, as his understanding of peasant and gypsy musics developed, and as he began to accept that peasant music was not without its own syncretisms, so his classification shifted to center on an opposition between the "bad hybridity" of gypsy music versus the "good hybridity" of peasant music. In this opposition, influenced by the Left mass culture critique, the gypsies were associated with the taint of urban and commercial music-making, while the peasantry were emblematic of a rural, natural state of musical grace. By the early 1930s, the threat of Americanization brought a reconfiguration in which Bartók came to value gypsy music as a specifically *Hungarian* urban popular music. In this same period, Brown argues, Bartók would have been aware of the rise of ultranationalist fascist parties in central Europe, and would have seen the parallels between his own original views of the gypsies and the extreme racist rhetoric and acts of oppression being enacted in Germany. In his late writings, Bartók developed a discourse of deracialized nationalism and portrayed gypsy music as a product of social oppression; while, Brown proposes, his *Concerto for Orchestra* (1942) enacted a kind of psychocultural reconciliation through its integration of gypsy and peasant musical elements.

In the aftermath of the Second World War, aided by Schoenberg's substantial influence and pedagogic writings, it was the serialist lineage of musical modernism that became dominant in the institutions and the teaching of new music. The earlier modernist (or proto-postmodernist) experiments with representations of others—whether exotic, nationalistic, or populist— gave way to an increasingly abstract, scientistic, and rationalist formalism based still on the near or total negation of tonality. Postwar high modernist composition powerfully asserted musical autonomy, refusing the representation of ethnic or popular musics in the name of formal innovation and rigor; and the modernisms of Bartók and Stravinsky, which engaged with folk and ethnic musics, failed to achieve hegemony in the face of the systematic serialisms of Boulez, Stockhausen, and Babbitt. The lineage that became institutionally and ideologically dominant in musical modernism—serialism and its aftermath[39]—and which is defined as an absolute and autonomous aesthetic development, won out over the eclecticism of other early modernist experiments, including the various forms of aesthetic reference to other musics.[40] Despite the apparent freeing up of art music in the plural, postmodern environment of the late 1960s and 1970s, until recently serialism has remained the dominant technique in the academic training of many Western composers; and other, nonserialist forms of academic and institutionalized high modernism in music remain resolutely distant from tonality.

It is perhaps a truism to point out that those modernist and postmodernist composers who have drawn upon or made reference to other musics (non-Western, folk, or urban popular) are not producing that music but drawing upon it in order to enrich their own compositional frame. They are transforming that music through incorporation into their own aesthetic: appropriating and re-presenting it. Crucially, in doing so, they intend not only to evoke that other music, but to create a distance from it and transcend it. This raises an issue that informs many essays in this collection: whether the structure of representation of the other constructs an unequal relation between aesthetic subject (the composer, and later the audience identifying with the composer) and object (the music or culture being represented); that is, the question of the extent to which this relation of musical representation must inevitably involve the attempt aesthetically and discursively to subsume and control the other.

We can now discern two basic, structural relations-of-difference to the musical other at work in musical modernism and postmodernism. The first, as in those composers who drew on other musics, is one of recognition of difference yet attempted aesthetic incorporation or subsumption. The second, as with serialism and other high-modernist tendencies, is the attempt to construct a "relation" of absolute difference, nonrecognition, and nonreference. With the coexistence of modernism and commercial, folk and non-Western musics in mind, it becomes apparent that a defining discursive and aesthetic characteristic of the dominant high modernist tradition has been its assertion, under the guise of a self-referential, formal autonomy, of its absolute difference from popular musics. This has the character of a defensive maneuver against the vitality of those popular forms, as though out of a fear of aesthetic and social contagion. The continuity of this tradition has, then, involved the sustained suppression or denial, under the ideology of formal autonomy, of the vagaries of its existence: competition with the market; the struggle for legitimacy and to gain cultural hegemony and an audience; and nonrecognition of other musics. This "nonrecognition" becomes less innocent in the hands of the major culture critics who were exegetes and apologists for formalist modernism: Adorno for music, and Greenberg for painting. Adorno's infamous attacks on the "primitive" and degraded nature of mass culture, and writings by Greenberg such as "Avant-Garde and Kitsch," reveal an underlying hostility to and repudiation of the culture of the "masses" that are latent in the claims of "absolute otherness."[41] This is a discourse that, far from being extinct, has continued to be reproduced in the writings of influential figures such as Boulez.[42] Thus, as others have argued,[43] mass culture is modernism's other in music as in the other arts, while reference to "authentic" folk and ethnic musics, primitive and exotic constructions, have remained more enduring and acceptable as forms of appropriation and projection in music.

Following the scholarship that has uncovered the immanent hybridity and syncretism, the aesthetic "impurity,"[44] of earlier Western high musics, one thing is now clear. It is postwar musical modernism's attempts to construct aesthetic *autarchy* and self-enclosure, through the negation or denial of reference to other musics and cultures, that is historically aberrant and that contrasts with the early eclectic modernisms and musical postmodernism, in both of which reference to other musics is a common defining trope. Serialist and analogous modernisms thus evince an intriguing omnipotent fantasy of aesthetic autarchy—the fantasy that one could invent a new musical language without reference to other musics, without recourse to syncretism, stripped of representational intent, and through a process of pure conceptual invention.

In his essay "Modernism, Deception, and Musical Others," Peter Franklin examines the cultural historical conditions that gave rise to and supported this fantasy structure. Franklin sketches a history replete with denial, a history that has itself been denied in what he identifies as the "institutionalized history of twentieth century music." He focuses on a "network of contradictions" that ensnared a disparate group of composers—Rachmaninov, Stravinsky, Schoenberg, and Korngold—and a theorist—Adorno—who fetched up in close proximity as émigrés in Los Angeles in the 1930s and 1940s, representatives of a high culture on the defensive in the face of its increasingly significant other, the American entertainment industry. Franklin charts the different responses of the four composers to the uneasy coexistence of the art-music tradition alongside popular music and culture. The "deception" in his title refers both to the title of Korngold's last original film score (1946) and to the complexities of the composerly subject-positions, in particular the ambivalences and deceptions of the composers' discourses regarding their own music, as well as Adorno's thesis on Schoenberg. Rachmaninov, alienated from his Russian homeland and his compositional achievements and style, was haunted by a musical direction—the "new"—that he could not emulate. Chastised by antipopulist American music critics for epitomizing the "latent realist tendencies" of tonal music, posthumously absorbed into the film industry through the frequent imitation of his style in film scores, Rachmaninov had internalized his fellow Russian émigré Stravinsky's abhorrence of his own music; he felt it was inferior to the modernists'.

While Stravinsky denied that programmatic or representational elements existed in his music, and famously denied music's capacity to "express" anything, Franklin shows the strains of this position. He quotes Stravinsky's passing admission that his *Symphony in Three Movements* (1945) was "activated" by concrete, often cinematographic, impressions of war and contained the "genesis of a war plot." Stravinsky's denial of representation in his work was paralleled by his hostility to entertainment film—a hostility that speaks of his desire to repudiate and avoid contamination by the other of mass culture. Franklin similarly interprets Schoenberg's avowal of secret realist representational intent in his *String Trio* (1946). Against the entire thrust of Adorno's reading of Schoenberg, and of the discourse of autonomous music, Franklin highlights Schoenberg's repressed representational tendencies, arguing that the composer revealed on occasion "that his own music was indeed representing all the things [i.e., physical and mental pain, angst and insanity] with which an 'uninformed' popular audience might have associated it." Franklin points to Schoenberg's craving for reconciliation and stresses "the gap between discursive constructions of Schoenberg's compositional practice—particularly Adorno's—and his actual aesthetic and political views."

Korngold, meanwhile, achieved mass popular success with his film scores. Yet, like Rachmaninov, he was profoundly ambivalent about this success and considered the music "not serious," not "for himself," simply a way of earning money. Franklin reads these dynamics into the music and narrative of *Deception* (1946). Korngold's score, combining diegetic classical music, his own nondiegetic late romantic style, and the sounds of urban life, creates an "almost Ivesian montage" that attests to Korngold's ability to conjure with multiple musical subject-positions or identifications in the score. The film's musical climax is an "autonomous" cello concerto which, in the narrative, is the work of a European composer character, but which Korngold also published as his own work. The film culminates in Bette Davis's *femme fatale*—the feminine "other" of mass culture—murdering the patriarchal composer, signifying American mass culture's ascendance over a decaying European culture. Korngold here scores the murder of the "composer" with whom part of himself is powerfully identified. Franklin thus probes the "deceptions" of the dominant discourse of twentieth-century music history, which, he contends, has tended to occlude its own vicissitudes, ideological character, contradictions, and social elitism, all of which emerge when attending to its constructions of difference from its others, its founding ambivalences and denials.

From the early century, one tradition took on the role of musical and ideological antithesis to serialism. This was the experimental music movement, which grew from the work of American composers Ives, Cowell, and Cage, and which also engaged in different ways with musical and cultural others. Experimental music drew on vernacular, non-Western, "primitive," and "oriental" musics and philosophies to challenge and negate the complex abstractions of serialism and other high modernist approaches. The experimental music tradition branched in the postwar period into minimalism, systems, environmental, and ambient musics, and has existed in tense proximity with avant-garde developments in jazz and improvised musics. It has become a focus for practices of, and debates around, crossovers between art and popular musics, and thus for the analysis of postmodernism in music.

At the same time, postmodern cultural theory, with its assertion that the old divisions between high and low, art and popular culture, the "autonomous" and the commercial in culture, are now redundant and superseded, has commonly taken music as its exemplar. Certain experimental composers (John Cage, Philip Glass, Steve Reich, Michael Nyman) and rock artists (David Byrne, Elvis Costello) are often portrayed as emblematic of postmodernity and of the collapsing divisions. This deceptively simple assertion conflates several issues. The first is the notion that we are witnessing an end to the univocal hierarchies of musical value and authority characteristic of an earlier modernism, themselves rooted in the universalism of post-Enlightenment Western aesthetic discourses. A related argument is that there is an ever less clear distinction to be found between the economic and institutional foundations of commercial and art musics. With the decline in public funding and subsidy for the arts, all musics have increasingly to find ways to survive on the basis of substantial markets; all are increasingly dependent on the dynamics of the recording and entertainment industries; and marketing and market-oriented thinking have become prevalent in concert organizations, music education, and new music institutions. A third, unifying proposition in this perspective is that we are witnessing unparalleled and intensifying aesthetic crossovers between popular, non-Western, and art musics, a relativizing and decentered "will to hybridity" evident in the transglobal movements of musicians and sounds. The implication is that these hybrid aesthetics and movements are free of the earlier hierarchical consciousness and practice, that there are no significant "core-periphery" structures at work, and thus that these aesthetics are free also of the asymmetrical relations of representation and the seductions of the exoticisms, primitivisms, and Orientalisms that paralleled colonial and neocolonial relations. In this view, then, "all the differences" are being levelled. Hybridity can rebound from its discursive origins in colonial fantasies and oppressions and can become instead a practical and creative means of cultural rearticulation and resurgence from the margins.[45]

The essays presented here open out aspects of this postmodern reasoning and reveal the complexity that may be obscured in these assertions. The institutional and economic assumptions are questionable; despite changes, the field of contemporary art music is still structured by divisions of status and discourses of differential value that are reproduced by subsidized, public, and authoritative institutions that continue to play a leading role in the legitimation and canonization of certain musics.[46] Moreover, the aesthetic analysis ignores the differences attendant on who is doing the hybridity, from which position and with what intention and result, and the astonishing resilience of exoticisms and primitivisms.

Indeed, John Corbett's essay demonstrates that while experimental and related postmodern musics have encompassed a range of forms of musical influence and representation, and have claimed to inhabit a plural and relativist musical universe, they have nonetheless made repeated returns to exoticist and primitivist aesthetic tropes. Corbett is concerned to uncover experimental music's discursive foundations, which have enabled these aesthetics to recur over the century in the output of musicians and composers from Henry Cowell and John Cage, through Steve Reich and Toru Takemitsu, to Brian Eno and John Zorn. Under the concept of "experimentation," with its scientistic connotations and its appeal to exploration, discovery of the new, and undetermined outcomes, Corbett finds a unifying evacuation of any potential political and ideological critique of musical or cultural appropriation.

Pointing to a mechanism central also to Richard Middleton's essay, and citing Said on Orientalism's dependence on a strategy of flexible positional superiority, Corbett argues that the essentialized Oriental object is represented in experimental music through a combined "projection of Western desires and anxieties and a reassertion of Western control." Corbett defines two basic forms of musical Orientalism in this tradition. The first, stemming from Cage and differently inflected by Steve Reich, is "conceptual Orientalism." Here, the music is obliquely, conceptually indebted to a non-Western inspiration, but the aim is not at all musical semblance or sounding non-Western. The second Corbett terms "decorative Orientalism." This more common strategy is exemplified by Cowell's *Persian Set*, which, Corbett argues, is a "contemporary chinoiserie" bordering on pastiche and "world-music kitsch."

Corbett traces these lines into a new phase in the 1980s and 1990s, and notes the move of experimental musicians such as Jon Hassell into early world-jazz fusion. Hassell in his *Possible Musics: Fourth World Vol. 1* (1980) inaugurates a "fantasy of new hybrid transculturation," a utopian imaginary universe (the "Fourth World") in which all musics and cultures "mingle freely without concern for authenticity or propriety." Corbett asks to what extent these "utopian" mergings should be seen as continuous with the imaginary forms of Orientalism, "as a mere extension of [Orientalism's] imperialist mapping of a fantasy space of otherness into the electronic telecommunications era?" He perceives an important potential space of difference in the work of some Asian experimentalist composers. For Corbett, a number of these composers—among them Toru Takemitsu and Tan Dun—collude in Cageian Orientalism and employ a musical idiom derived from Western modernism or late romanticism, sometimes even stooping to chinoiserie, even if these aesthetics are refracted through their own Asian identities. Yet Corbett notes exceptions, such as the Koreans Isang Yun and Younghi Pagh-Pann, arguing that the latter integrates Western postserialism with a distinctly Korean aesthetic, achieving a new aesthetic free of those definitive historical tropes and of pastiche. Corbett sums up the multiple refractions of the contemporary cultural condition with this comment on the music of Tan Dun: "An Asian composer in the West uses techniques devised by a Western composer [Cage] inspired by Asian philosophy; the work is played for an Asian audience which hears it as an artifact of the bizarre West. Orientalism is reflected back-and-forth like a music-cultural *mise-en-abyme.*"

Corbett's essay indicates how exoticisms and Orientalisms continue to proliferate and mutate in the imaginaries and aesthetics of many contemporary art musics of West and East, and particularly in the now-global Cageian experimental movement. He argues that these remain characteristic of recent attempts to create interstitial aesthetic zones between art, popular, and non-Western musics, crossover musics that generally proliferate in the avant-gardist and specialist niches of the music industry. We must ask why it is that these discourses remain so resilient and seductive. One point to note is that the apparent pluralism and relativism of Cage and his *confrères* never precluded quite conscious bids to establish an American/experimental counter- (or complementary) hegemony to European modernism, a hegemony that for Cage was predicated on the ideological conflation of "America" with "the world."[47] American cultural postmodernism, at least in the mid–twentieth century, as evidenced in its exemplary musical manifestations, has thus been founded on a curious "plural-universalism." We might also speculate whether similar mechanisms to those involved in reproducing the hegemony of post-serialist modernism—that is, the way that aesthetic movements lay down deep historical tracks through the cumulative momentum of their institution-alization, cultural authority, power, and, given the internationalization of twentieth-century avant-gardes, their wide geographical dispersal[48]—whether these mechanisms may not also have affected that rival and antagonist of modernism, experimental music. Through their negative mutuality and com-plementarity the two traditions effectively dominate twentieth-century art musics. Those seeking an alternative "universal" tradition to modernism with which to engage have been impelled toward, and subsumed by, the Cage tra-dition. The fact that globalization is not only a property of the music industry but is also a tendency of the institutional framework of contemporary art music means that a discursive universalism has for decades been central to the socialization of composers of both East and West. The global art music network thus risks "aesthetic (as opposed to epistemic) violence" through the tyrannies and closures of its universalizing discourses.

It is in the postmodern "resolution" of issues of appropriation into un-problematic notions of crossover and pluralism in both art and popular mu-sics that we find the dominant expression today of the idea that cross-cul-tural empathy and its attendant aesthetic "reconciliation" equalizes musics of formerly unequal status and power, and erases erstwhile differences of le-gitimacy. As Born has argued elsewhere, pluralism is central to the way that postmodern intellectuals experience the aesthetic imaginatively as progres-sive; aesthetic pluralism is divorced from extant socioeconomic differences and held to be an autonomous and effective force for transforming those differences. The aesthetic is held to portend social change; it can stand in psychically for wider social change.[49] In this sense, cultural postmodernism can be seen as an ideology *tout court* in the classic sense of a cultural system that conceals domination and inequality.

III. OTHERING, HYBRIDITY, AND FUSION
IN TRANSNATIONAL POPULAR MUSICS

A third way into the material in this book concerns a new relationship be-tween popular music studies and ethnomusicology and how these disciplines have been inflected by postcolonial theory and black cultural studies, as well as by wider socioeconomic and cultural transformations associated with globalization.

Public debate about cultural appropriation has been particularly vigorous with regard to the African American expressive tradition. At the heart of debates about cultural identity, property, and belonging in popular music have been controversies over "black musics," largely because African American music (and other Afro-diasporic forms such as reggae) have been so popular and significant throughout much of the world. Charles Keil wrote in 1966 that "it is simply incontestable that year by year, American popular music has come to sound more and more like African popular music."[50] For Keil, each time an African American genre (such as ragtime, jazz, the blues, rhythm and blues) was appropriated into the mainstream of American musical life, African Americans responded by turning their creativity toward sounds and practices that showed even more clearly the African legacy of the descendants of the slaves. Whatever the merits of Keil's case, many other critics have noted that, in music, "African-Americans invert the expected relationship between hegemonic superculture and subculture."[51] Richard Middleton, for example, has written of the "astonishing confluence, in a twin triumph, of global capital circulation in the political economy, African musical diaspora in the sign economy."[52]

Do the worldwide popularity and significance of musics of black origin represent a triumph for African American culture? Or a cultural consolation for political suppression and economic inequality? Is the "borrowing" by white musicians of putatively black forms, and the vast profits generated by the recording industry on the basis of such traffic in sounds, merely another form of racist exploitation? The existing debates often take simplistic, polarized forms, reliant on overly bounded notions of the relation of musical form or style to social grouping. Nevertheless, they raise crucial issues about music, identity, and difference.

Some writers have seen black musics as cultural spaces in which intercultural dialogue between ethnic groups can take place. George Lipsitz, for example, interpreted the postwar history of rock and roll in this way in his *Time Passages* (1990). Studies by Dick Hebdige and Simon Jones celebrated the popularity of the Caribbean musical diaspora in Britain among white, working-class youth as a sign of opposition to popular racism and state nationalisms. Gregory Stephens has interpreted the popularity of rap among white American youth as showing that, at least culturally, black and white America are in contact.[53] Others, however, have detected exoticism and primitivism in the way that black musics and black musicians have been treated in the commercial popular music industry. Jazz, in particular, has provided the raw material for a critique of the attitudes of white musicians, critics, and listeners drawn to black music culture.[54] In his essay "Jazz and the White Critic," first published in *Downbeat* in 1963, Amiri Baraka (then Leroi Jones) complained that the formalism of white critics prevented them from understanding the social conditions of jazz, resulting in two kinds of distortion: the treatment of jazz as an equivalent to European high culture, or as natural, untutored and "primitive."[55] In line with this interpretation, a number of writers have researched primitivist discourses about jazz.[56]

Other critiques of the treatment of black popular musics have revolved around the degree to which white musicians and listeners have brought about a "dilution" of black music, and the extent to which the recording industry (in general, white-owned) has exploited black culture and black musicians in particular. Again, jazz is a key genre here. While nearly all informed critics view it as an urban field of production that includes black and white sensibilities and practices, the greater rewards and prestige granted to white jazz musicians such as Paul Whiteman have often been the subject of bitter recriminations. Similarly, rock and roll's status as an urban fusion of black and white influences should not obscure the fact that its white stars have generally been paid much more attention than significant black innovators such as Chuck Berry. These debates are just as intense with regard to hip hop; the enormous popularity of rap among white American youth has been portrayed as the reason for its gradual diminution as a powerful public medium, and as a sign that white-owned labels have been out to exploit the latest black innovations in cultural expression.[57]

Richard Middleton's chapter builds on these debates and traditions of critique. Using Stallybrass and White's analysis in *The Politics and Poetics of Transgression* (1986),[58] Middleton identifies a twin strategy of assimilation and projection as characteristic of post-Renaissance Europe's way of confronting difference. With the rising popularity of African American styles during the 1920s, Middleton claims, the "Low-other" becomes conflated with blackness in music in new ways; and he offers an analysis of how George Gershwin's *Porgy and Bess* represents a particular version of assimilation/projection, "a New Yorker's Eden," in which Gershwin exerts a powerful monological control over his eclectic material via Wagnerian leitmotifs. In Gershwin's modernism, which takes seriously its encounter with urban black popular musics, despite the chromatic richness of some passages, black characters are commonly represented as "simple," either by folky pentatonics or the banjo tunes of "I Got Plenty o' Nuttin'." "Low-life" is figured through the picturesque; we see this world entirely through Gershwin's eyes, according to Middleton. Such strategies are not confined to the jazz age. Middleton also identifies them at work in Paul Simon's *Graceland* album: "The South African sound becomes a support for Simon's elliptical lyrics, and by the end it is swamped by the predominantly synthesized texture."

However, in black America and South Africa there is evidence of more complex negotiation between high and low, Europe and Africa, assimilation and resistance. Here, Middleton draws on the growing emphasis in black cultural studies on an affirmative portrayal of black expressive culture as "a counterculture of modernity."[59] This has received its best-known expressions in African American literary criticism and black British cultural studies. James Snead, for example, has argued that the importance of repetition in black culture represents a challenge to the teleological thinking and logics of Western rationalism.[60] Henry Louis Gates's now-famous notion of "Signifyin(g)," derived from Houston Baker, also builds on the presence of repetition and difference in vernacular culture (the transformation of stock material in stories and songs) to build an aesthetic theory that sees black popular culture as a challenge to conventional aesthetics, with its overemphasis on both realism and innovation—on "the mimetic representation of novel content," as Gates puts it.[61]

Middleton adopts Houston Baker's concept of "deformation of mastery"[62] to suggest how the music of Duke Ellington (criticized by some Harlem Renaissance intellectuals for its primitivism) and the contemporary South African jazz musician Abdullah Ibrahim (formerly Dollar Brand) might contribute to a "politics of reappropriation," by "answering back" to the assimilation/projection evident in *Porgy and Bess* and *Graceland*. Much of Ellington's music demonstrates an acceptance of difference within black music, which contrasts with Gershwin's and Simon's monological mastery. In Ellington's work, says Middleton, we see a pluralist envisioning of new possibilities, a rejection of simple notions of authenticity. And in the work of Abdullah Ibrahim there is a double-conscious use of repetition, recalling the use of pitch cycles in rural South African musics but employing chord structures commonly used to suggest closure and resolution in European music. So "closure is rewritten as process, cadence as endless chain," in a musical space both South African and "European," and yet neither. Middleton's response to these productive theoretical developments in black cultural studies, and his concern with the ways in which black music culture can provide a critique of hegemonic forms of music, suggest important directions in recent popular music theory.

The movement of musical styles and instruments across the world is nothing new, as the diasporic nature of African American music itself suggests. This mobility has intensified in the twentieth century, in part because of the activity of transnational corporations seeking markets for musical reproduction equipment and for recordings abroad. One result has been a spectacular inequality in the economic rewards and prestige accorded to Western pop products outside the West when compared with how non-Western recordings are rewarded and viewed in the West. The dissemination of Western commercial popular music throughout the world has traditionally been a cause of great concern to ethnomusicologists and writers on cultural imperialism.[63]

Recent years have seen paradigm shifts in popular music studies and ethnomusicology away from a cultural imperialism approach to global cultural flows and toward theories of postcoloniality and globalization. Some researchers have produced impressive evidence that the export of Western sounds and technologies has not led to the kind of cultural "grey-out" and homogenization that some ethnomusicologists and cultural imperialism analysts feared.[64] With vast movements of peoples from the economic disaster zones of global capitalism to the cities of the North, new musical syncretisms have emerged from the encounter of North and South, East and West. The very complexity of global musical-cultural flows has meant the abandonment of what was the dominant paradigm in ethnomusicology and anthropology during the 1970s and 1980s: acculturation. This was an attempt to understand the nature of change in what were presumed to be otherwise discrete and relatively stable, authentic, and self-reproducing traditional cultures and musics. In music, the term implied processes of cultural contact between two or more distinct musical cultures that resulted in musical mixes or syncretisms. Just a decade ago, Manuel used this perspective with acuity and subtlety in the opening of his survey of mass-mediated popular musics of the non-Western world.[65] By the late 1990s, acculturation theory had been banished to the conceptual dark ages, for unacceptable essentialism and lack of sufficient attention to global-historical structures of power. Influenced by theories of globalization and by the emphasis on transnational cultural flows and deterritorialization in cultural theory, postcolonial studies, and anthropology, writers such as Slobin, Gilroy, and Lipsitz have ushered in a new, still-current discourse centered on notions of musical hybridity and interaction, and oriented toward new kinds of musical objects.[66] In contrast with ethnomusicology's former object of study—"traditional musics"—it is diasporic music that has moved to the center of attention.

Such complex interactions are not as recent a phenomenon as many commentators have implied. Throughout the twentieth century, even in the era when Anglo-American repertoire seemed to be dominating the world market, some non-Western popular musics have been successful in the West, whether in the guise of styles adopted by Western musicians, or in the importation by record companies and promoters of recordings and stars which could then be repackaged and sold on to consumers. A series of Latin dance musics have crossed the world, from the *habañera* popular in Bizet's France in the nineteenth century, to the tango in the first decades of the twentieth century, to the *lambada* in the 1980s. Country music, on the surface a musical form with deep roots in the southern United States, has a long history of borrowings, drawing on sources as diverse as Swiss yodelling and Hawaiian guitar. Famously, a number of British and American musicians incorporated Indian styles and instrumentation into their work in the 1960s, including the Beatles, the Kinks, and the Byrds.[67] In the 1970s, African Americans picked up ethnomusicological recordings of traditional African musics and the resulting fusions circulated the globe, as Steven Feld shows in his essay for this volume. There is little doubt, though, that the 1980s saw an increasing presence of non-Western popular musics (and, to some extent, non-Western "traditional" musics) in the West. The consequences of this new stage in the transnationalization of sound have been complex and ambiguous, and some of the most important recent debates concerning appropriation and difference in music center on this moment.

The increasing impact of non-Western popular forms and styles in the West was in part the result of well-meaning efforts on the part of independent entrepreneurs to promote and distribute these musics more widely, in an attempt to counter the ethnocentrism of the major Western markets. Record shops, magazines, independent labels and distributors sprang up devoted to the promotion of non-Western musics in Europe, North America, and Australia. The terms "world music" and "world beat" were coined in order to create a marketing niche in industry discourse for non-Western acts and genres.[68] At about the same time, certain Western pop stars, most notably Paul Simon, Peter Gabriel, and David Byrne, were making increasing use of non-Western sounds in their music, and this helped to popularize certain African and Latin styles. Ethnomusicologists and popular music scholars have, in general, been critical of the use of non-Western musics by Western superstars. Steven Feld, among others, has examined the politics of Paul Simon's *Graceland*, stressing Simon's genuinely respectful intentions, but drawing attention to questions of ownership:

> All of the performance styles, grooves, beats, sounds, and genres are South African in identity. . . . [But] the [South African] musicians fill the role of wage laborers. . . . That no significant ownership of the product is shared with them beyond base royalties and their wages for recording . . . reflects the rule of elite artistry. What statement does this make about the role of Paul Simon vis-à-vis the roles of the musicians without whom the record would have been impossible? It seems to draw the boundary line between participation and collaboration at *ownership*. Whose music? Paul Simon's music.[69]

George Lipsitz, meanwhile, writes disapprovingly of the unwillingness of Paul Simon and David Byrne to "examine their own relationship to power or to allow for reciprocal subjectivities between and among cultures."[70]

Popular music studies, in contrast to its critical treatment of the borrowing by Western pop superstars of non-Western styles, has tended to celebrate the proliferation of new musical forms based on the encounter of non-Western migrants with Western musical languages and technologies. Here the assumption is that globally, in recent decades at least, musical creativity has been marked by incessant and frenetic activities of musical dialogue and syncretism. The key words are "difference, diversity and dialogue."[71] George Lip-

sitz, in his compelling study *Dangerous Crossroads* (1994), provides a celebration of musical hybridity. The musics of a vast range of artists, united only
by their provenance in "aggrieved communities," are interpreted by Lipsitz
as illustrations of a new kind of politics which "takes commodity culture for
granted," but which produces "an immanent critique of contemporary social relations" and has the power to illuminate "affinities, resemblances and
potentials for alliances among a world population that now must be as dynamic and as mobile as the forces of capital."[72]

Lipsitz's optimism is, however, worryingly overdetermined by an insistent
internationalist class politics, as though musical and cultural forms have no
validity or meaning outside their signification of these other, now-global politics of class and race; and as though there are no problematic antagonisms,
or essentialisms, or nationalisms being expressed in these musical forms.
For another approach, we might turn to Martin Stokes's essay in this volume, in which he analyzes the upsurge of hybrid urban popular musics in
Turkey and other Middle Eastern contexts in the 1980s as conditioned by
three related forces: economic liberalization, the end of statist promotions
of a unified national culture, and the increasing penetration of multinational
capitalism, leading to a "proliferation of transnational information and images [and sounds] . . . [which are] impossible (or extremely difficult) to censor or control." Mark Slobin has offered a theoretical schema which may
account for such a range of forces and which is irreducible to an external
political function. It conceives of three levels—superculture, interculture,
and subculture in relation to music—by which to analyze different spaces
and forms of musical interaction.[73] This perspective, uniting ethnomusicology with popular music studies by way of cultural studies, is itself conceptually a fertile hybrid. And yet, in the desire to read these hybrid musics as embodiments of a new and effective cultural politics from the margins, as
productive ways of "writing back" against the center, writers such as Lipsitz
and Slobin perhaps overstate the relative cultural power and visibility of these
musics, and neglect the extent to which they are structured by an increasingly global and flexible industrial complex. In our view, Paul Gilroy's work
promises the richest reading of diasporic musics. Gilroy's careful tracing of
the integrity, the historical structures and lineages of Black Atlantic expressive traditions, as well as his attention to new forms of hybridity, make conceptual allowance both for the fluidity of syncretisms and hybrids and for
the continuing existence of bounded cultural traditions.[74] What emerges is
an analysis of the *differential* permeability of the boundaries of various cultural lineages and forms.

Others have been less sanguine about the consequences of the intensified
transnationalization of music. Veit Erlmann, for example, in a reading
influenced by Luhmann's system theory and Baudrillard's postmodern pessimism, portrays world music not as a sign of resistance or opposition, but

as a "new aesthetic form of the global imagination."[75] For Erlmann, world music is a postmodern pastiche where distinctions between tradition, authenticity, and modernity dissolve, demonstrating the "loss of referentiality" and the triumph of the culture of the simulacrum. This is a stimulating interpretation, but it also risks functionalism. Erlmann treats "the market" as a homogeneous system and, by taking as an analytical category the industry's own notoriously vague term "world music," he fails adequately to differentiate the discourses and practices subsumed by this term.

The contributions to this book that deal with transnational popular musics probe the recent optimism about the flows of commodified musical sounds across the world in other ways, without assuming the end of history. Often, they suggest that there is a certain continuity in industrial practices, in spite of claims that we have entered a new era of transnationalization.[76] Steven Feld, for example, follows a seminal article on the discourses and commodification practices of world music[77] by undertaking a survey of the remarkable array of uses to which Western popular and postmodern musicians have put the music of the peoples of the equatorial forests of Central Africa, and especially the "pygmy music" of the Mbuti, Aka, and Binga peoples. Feld traces what we might call the social life (or life history) of pygmy musics:[78] a series of aesthetic appropriations and reappropriations or relays via evocation, mimesis, and concrete sampling. One such lineage, for example, connects the 1966 ethnomusicological recordings of Simha Arom and Geneviève Taurelle, through their imitation in the Herbie Hancock hit "Watermelon Man" of 1973, to Madonna's sampling of the Hancock copy in her song "Sanctuary" from the 1994 CD *Bedtime Stories*.

At the same time, Feld deploys the history of "pygmy pop" to understand what happens when sounds become split from their sources: a process that, following F. Murray Schaffer, he labels "schizophonia." The outcomes of this process cannot be condemned or praised in advance. But the escalating process of splitting-from-origins as musicians increasingly engage in intertextual borrowings, accompanied by an escalation of "difference, power, rights, control, ownership, authority[,] politicizes the schizophonic practices artists could once claim more innocently as matters of inspiration, or as a purely artistic dialogue of imitation and inspiration." Feld detects romanticism and anxious nostalgia behind these new patterns of mediation, and he insists on the importance of the asymmetrical power relations between the corporations who record and distribute Western jazz and pop, on the one hand, and the pygmy peoples, on the other. In the astonishing range of appropriations Feld collates, only a "caricatured image" survives the borrowings by popular musicians from ethnomusicological recordings, usually a "single untexted vocalization or falsetto yodel"—an aural analogue of the representational reductionism noted by Said. Ethnomusicologists, though thanked by Western musicians for providing raw materials for such appropriations, are lambasted by the music press and represented as purist voyeurs, while the fusion practices of groups like Zap Mama and Deep Forest are celebrated by the press as exciting hybrids which do creative justice to the original musics. Ethnomusicologists thus play an ambiguous and unwittingly enabling role in this drama of mimesis and alterity, splitting and escalation. Only a tiny fraction of the vast range of musical practices they record is lifted into popular commodity circulation.

Feld's analysis, like Corbett's, suggests that sampler technologies have added critical new dimensions to the politics of musical appropriation in an era when many writers are celebrating hybridity. This brings up to the present the question of the role of sound recording and simulation technologies in musical appropriation. David Hesmondhalgh's essay pursues the issue through an examination of the practices of a number of "diasporic" acts based at Nation Records. Nation is a successful British independent label committed to the kind of hybrid oppositional musical politics that Lipsitz praises throughout his book. Hesmondhalgh examines the politics and aesthetics of bands attached to Nation. He argues that those bands developing a multicultural dance fusion aesthetic indulge in questionable forms of exoticism and simulate ethnic hybridity both aurally—through sampling practices—and visually or iconographically in their performance practices and publicity. Hesmondhalgh contrasts this with those Nation bands deploying a range of black nationalist, African and Asian aesthetics and politics: from fundamentalist Islamic and Sikh nationalist politics married to hip hop sounds, to Asian bands producing experimental, cross-generic musical forms. However, it is the international success of one of its exoticist bands, Transglobal Underground, that has provided the label with secure financial foundations.

Hesmondhalgh explores the complex interplay between the reflexive ethical debates over sampling and the economic dynamics of sampling within the label. The debates rest on Nation musicians' opposed positions regarding the substitution of live non-Western and ethnic musicians' labor for digital samples as a way of mitigating the grosser exploitations of musical appropriation. This exploitation is amply demonstrated by the way Nation and Transglobal Underground were directly responsible, through a hit record, for the appropriation by Coca-Cola and its allies, the multinationals BMG and Warner-Chappell, of the singing of a Tahitian women's gospel choir as the core musical figure in a Coke advertisement. We see here enacted the global-corporate exploitation of non-Western others' intellectual and artistic property through the mediation of a Western multicultural label and band, with no recompense whatsoever going to the Tahitian musicians. One issue raised is the received view that it is impossible and/or futile to trace the origins of such a sample—a view sometimes enunciated in the Nation debates, as though the aim to find the origins of a sample is buying into an essentialist error about musical authorship. Indeed, certain multicultural Nation acts espouse a quasi-poststructuralist discourse of the benefits of "getting rid of the authorial ego" as their own convenient variant of Barthes' philosophy of the "death of the author."[79] Ironically, a putatively "critical" discourse of the end of authorship here becomes an ideology of cultural practice and is used to legitimize acts of musical appropriation. Yet as Hesmondhalgh says, in cases like the Tahitian sample there are British agencies close at hand, such as the National Sound Archive, willing to work through the ethnomusicological archives to try to identify the original recording, the musicians or the culture from which samples have been taken. Thus it is not so much that the question of origins here takes the form of an essentialist ideology of the non-Western musician, but, on the contrary, that the myth of obscured or impossible or irrelevant origins is itself highly ideological: as in the Tahitian case, it can conceal and naturalize domination, both economic and aesthetic, in the cultural sphere.

Simon Frith's essay, finally, provides a wide-ranging overview of recent work on transnational popular musics. He too perceives a shift toward hybridity as a governing concept. If acculturation was the key term for a previous generation in ethnomusicology, in an earlier phase of popular music studies the buzzword was authenticity, and this has also been consigned to the intellectual dust-heap. Academics have been quick to point out that the focus on authenticity in world music discourse has served to exoticize non-Western musics; as Frith puts it, non-Western musicians are treated in the authenticity-talk of the world music industry "as raw materials to be processed into commodities for the West." Frith surveys a number of recent contributions, teasing out a range of attitudes toward globalization and postmodernity. Ironically, he suggests, hybridity has been reinflected by popular music scholars as a new form of authenticity: whether writing about Caribbean musicians' consciousness of their position within a global industry, or the way that non-Western musicians have been drawn to rock, that seemingly most Western of popular forms, these writers suggest that music in an era of globalization powerfully affirms the syncretic nature of contemporary cultural identity. Frith sets Erlmann's pessimistic reading of this situation against Timothy Taylor's more optimistic interpretation, which argues that world musicians provide an authentic expression of the most creative dimensions of the postmodern condition.[80] But Frith resists either pole, preferring particularistic analyses of the ways in which music articulates identity in specific local contexts. For, as recent studies of musical changes in Central and Eastern Europe show, such close readings reveal the enormous importance of music in constructing national and ethnic identities. For Frith, the significance of transnational popular music derives not from its potential use as a sign of a new era of globalization (whether read optimistically or pessimistically), but from the lives and practices of musicians and music-industry workers and their formations of networks of activity. In such microlevel practices, Frith detects evidence of the negotiation of new cultural alliances, a kind of "globalization from below." His reading implies that much of the work carried out in this area is overambitious in its attempts to "read off" from musical forms the meaning of cultural practices. His own approach suggests instead the fruitfulness of attending to how understandings of transnational music are created through a set of intertwined vernacular and academic discourses.

IV. MUSIC AND THE REPRESENTATION/ ARTICULATION OF SOCIOCULTURAL IDENTITIES

Where the papers just discussed center primarily on interpreting appropriation and hybridity in contemporary popular musics, those by Philip V. Bohlman and Martin Stokes pursue the analysis of subaltern musics within larger social and cultural formations, examining how these musics come to represent changing collective identities. The problematic being addressed here and by other papers in the volume is how particular social and cultural identities may be evoked, articulated, and represented in music, whether in processes of composition, performance, or consumption.

The theorization of music and sociocultural identity is presently a major preoccupation. An older model, given new life in certain versions of subculture theory, argues that music reflects or enunciates underlying social relations and structures. The problem is to trace the links between a musical form or practice and its production or consumption by particular social groups. This "homology" model has often been discredited for a mechanical, deterministic mapping of the relation between social base and cultural superstructure, whether in Marxian or Durkheimian formulations. It is accused of reifying and hypostatizing what are more accurately conceived as fluid and processual dynamics in the formation and change of social and cultural identities. A new model has emerged based on these criticisms, which amounts to a current orthodoxy. It proposes that music "reflects" nothing; rather, music has a formative role in the construction, negotiation, and transformation of sociocultural identities.[81] In this view, music engenders communities or "scenes";[82] it allows a play with, a performance of, and an imaginary exploration of identities. Its aesthetic pleasure has much to do with this vicarious exploration of identities.

How do we reconcile these contending models? In its rejection of the essentialist "dangers" of the homology model, the process model introduces new dangers of reductionism; processual analysis, as it currently exists, cannot generate the conceptual complexity adequate to the challenge of theorizing music and sociocultural identity. Rather than seeing these explanatory schemes as mutually exclusive, it bears pointing out that each brings insight in relation to different sociomusical phenomena. There is a need to acknowledge that music can variably *both* construct new identities *and* reflect existing ones. Sociocultural identities are not simply constructed in music; there are "prior" identities that come to be embodied dynamically in musical cultures, which then also *form* the reproduction of those identities—no passive process of reflection. We cannot afford to jettison completely a reflectionist model when, for example, as Stokes has shown in relation to the role of marching bands in Northern Ireland, or Parkes for song performance among the Kalasha of northwest Pakistan, or Mach for the role of Chopin's music in the changing face of Polish nationalisms,[83] in certain circumstances music does function primarily and powerfully to articulate the boundaries defining the collective identities or mutual antagonisms of pre-existing sociocultural groups, groups defined by shared cultural systems quite distinct from music. In his important discussion of ethnicity, identity, and music, Stokes mentions in passing the discomfort of thinking music and violence together;[84] and yet, as he agrees, music has often played a leading role in the disciplinary socialization and ideological conditioning fostered by extremely repressive regimes.[85] This capacity of music tends itself to be suppressed under the sunny terms of postmodern cultural theory. Thus, against prevailing views that music is primarily a means for the imagining of emergent and labile identities, we stress that music is equally at times a medium for marking and reinforcing the boundaries of existing sociocultural categories and groups. Again as Stokes has argued, "Music is intensely involved in the propagation of dominant classifications" of ethnicity, class, and gender, and notably, too, in the cultural articulation of nationalism.[86] Indeed, "the violence which enforces dominant classifications is seldom far away from musical performances in many situations."[87]

But the point is that the two perspectives are not contradictory. It is precisely music's extraordinary powers of imaginary evocation of identity and of cross-cultural and intersubjective empathy that render it a primary means of both marking and transforming individual and collective identities. As Born has argued previously, it is because music lacks denotative meaning, in contrast with the visual and literary arts, that it has particular powers of connotation.[88] Music's *hyperconnotative* character, its intense cognitive, cultural, and emotional associations, and its abstraction, are perhaps what give it a unique role in the imaginary constitution of cross-cultural and intersubjective desire, of exotic/erotic charge for the other culture or music in social fantasy.[89] But these qualities are also means for *self*-idealization and, through repetition of the existing tropes and genres of identity-in-music (national anthems, patriotic songs), for the reinforcement of extant collective identities.

How, then, can we account for movement across and between identities? Here it becomes critically important to distinguish between individual self-identity and collective identity in relation to music. Because of the ubiquity of music in the mass-mediated world, and individuals' subjectification and socialization by a number of different musics, each bearing different dimensions of both their existing and desired, potential identities, rather than musical subjectivity being fixed and unitary, several musical "identities" may inhabit the same individual. These are expressed in different musical tastes and practices, some of them in tension with each other or in contradiction with other parts of the self. Thus states of both "authentic," "essential" musical identity and more playful, postmodern relations of desire and protoidentification through music coexist in many individuals, producing a state of fragmentary and multiple imaginary musical identification. Rather than conceiving of individual subjectivities as fully self-transparent and coherent, then, and in contrast to the apparent "unities" of collective experience, we should adopt the insights of poststructuralism and psychoanalysis and develop an awareness of the multiple musical identifications or subject positions to which individuals are susceptible as producers and consumers.[90] This conception allows an understanding of the complexities of mobile, conflicting, and changing musical identifications. Without such a distinction between individual and collective forms of musical identity, we cannot understand individual agency on the part of musicians and composers as it bears on wider musical-cultural changes. Above all, we cannot address the potential disjunctures and conflicts between individual and collective musical identities, the way that cultural expectations and norms, or dominant musical discourses, may be in tension with individual identities and may exert powerful pressures of musical subjectification.[91] Indeed, as Hall has argued, the problem of conceiving the relationship between individual subjectivities and discursive formations or dominant cultural systems remains the main challenge to theories of identity in general.[92] Certain essays in this collection respond to these challenges by developing a more complex account of musical subjectivity than is common in music scholarship. For example, Brown on Bartók, Franklin on Rachmaninov, Schoenberg, and Korngold, and Hesmondhalgh on the dilemmas of some Nation musicians offer close readings of authorial subjectivities that reveal the intrasubjective conflicts and fragmentations manifest in dynamics of idealization and denigration, splitting, ambivalence, and denial, as they are experienced in relation to different musical selves or projected onto musical others.

The process model of musical identity tends to focus on the microsociality of musical performance, practice, and bodily gesture, and how these condense the signification of identity. In this view, musical practice and bodily experience are microcosmic and effective of identity formation.[93] Yet this emphasis on the microsocial, while fruitful, risks evacuating a sense of how individual and collective musical identifications may be powerfully formed and influenced by larger discursive, ideological, social, and generic forces—as Brown suggests in relation to Bartók's susceptibility to contemporary racist and nationalist discourses; as Pasler indicates for Roussel and Delage through their subjectification by rival French compositional and cultural philosophies; as Corbett shows regarding the post-Cageian turn to Eastern philosophies; and as Feld indicates for the influence of pan-Africanist discourses on African American musicians. It is, however, Stokes's paper that develops this approach most fully, through an analysis of the contesting discourses struggling for interpretive primacy around Turkish arabesk. Stokes's insistence on the "openness" of arabesk musical culture as a space of profuse discursive projections of identity thus makes more complex our understanding of music and identity, difference and appropriation. Here, the appropriation at issue is emphatically *discursive:* the apparent need of the Turkish statist and Left intelligentsia, through interpretation and critique, to subsume and master this socially and culturally pervasive musical other.[94]

But arabesk represents more than just a musical other. Both Stokes's and Bohlman's essays concern centrally the changing boundaries between a dominant national culture, its representatives and guardians, and internal subalterns, as manifest in the successes and incursions of the subalterns' musical culture. For some Turkish intellectuals, arabesk is associated with a peasant underclass that inhabits the squatter settlements on the peripheries of the major cities, an underclass that is the unwelcome, disowned, and yet inevitable social by-product of Turkish modernization. Arabesk is also associated with the insurgent Kurdish people, the focus of Turkey's crisis of internal insurrection. Musically and textually, arabesk is a hybrid cosmopolitan genre incorporating Arabic (especially Egyptian) influences with profane elements of Western popular culture. Its sentimental lyrics center on disorder, despair, and pain. Arabesk's formal and musical character is thus highly problematic for the guardians and proponents of a modern, Western-leaning national culture; it connotes for its critics a subversive internal orient, a subaltern eastern Turkey resistant to secularized modernity. For some years the genre was banned from state radio and television. Arabesk's role in drawing the fire of state-identified intellectuals must be understood in the context of the state project, from the 1930s to the present, to foster an authentic Anatolian folk music purged of any urban, Ottoman, or foreign influences, a project in which Bartók played a part. This musical state-planning resulted in a music unpopular among peasants and urbanites, in contrast to the messily hybrid and massively popular arabesk. Significantly, the denigration by Turkish state and intellectuals of arabesk and its constituency, complemented by their invention of an idealized authentic folk tradition, replicates Bartók's own splitting between an impure, degenerate gypsy music and folk music, its idealized other.

Stokes traces the discursive lines into recent decades, showing how the 1980s brought economic liberalization and political populism under a Center-Right Turkish government and their attempted co-option of arabesk. In response, the Left produced in the early 1990s a new, counterhegemonic reading of this powerful, interstitial popular cultural form. In this discourse, indebted to the cultural theory of Raymond Williams and Stuart Hall, arabesk is seen to represent opposition and resistance, a utopian element in popular culture. In sum, for Stokes, all the prominent discourses around arabesk exhibit "reverse essentialism," an internal Orientalism in which the genre represents an "east" within to be either expelled or reintegrated. And yet, through a reading of a song by the major arabesk star, Orhan Gencebay, Stokes shows how arabesk's music and lyrics, its "dissonant multitextuality," can themselves work through internal contradiction to ironize and under-mine the simplistic east/west binaries they are supposed to encode. Arabesk's hybridity thus resiliently insists on the genre's own sociocultural complex-ity, its foundation in processes of cultural hybridity and social change, in the face of highly politicized discursive reductions.

To account for the range of musical representations of identity, we can ini-tially make an ideal-typical distinction between musical constructions of identity and difference that are *primarily* experiences of the cultural imagi-nary, what Born has termed "musically-imagined communities,"[95] and music that is driven by sociocultural identities that are *ontologically and sociologically prior,* even if their enhancement and enactment in musical practice and per-formance produces effects on those identity formations. But we can develop further this simple polarity by conceiving of music's articulation of sociocul-tural identity in terms of a *quasi-temporality,* a series of distinct potential mo-ments or forms. We would distinguish four such structural articulations:

(1) When music works to create a *purely imaginary identification,* an imag-inary figuration of sociocultural identities, with no intent to actualize those identities: a kind of psychic tourism through music. This is an identification that only ever exists in collective or individual fantasy, and thus acts surrep-titiously but powerfully to inscribe and reinscribe existing boundaries of self and other, as well as the hierarchies and stratifications between those cate-gories. This moment may be a precondition for the emergence or negotia-tion of new identities (as in 2, below); but it also commonly operates as a *substitute* for such real identifications. Much of the scholarship and most of the papers in this volume dealing with musical primitivism, exoticism, and Orientalism address these kinds of purely imaginary projections that are fan-tasy-imbued, act primarily as imaginary extensions of the subject, and are never enacted in real cultural transformations of individual or collective self.

(2) When the musical imaginary works to *prefigure,* crystallize or poten-tialize *emergent, real* forms of sociocultural identity or alliance; and thus how labile or emergent sociocultural identities come to be prefigured, negoti-ated, and constructed in music, so *re-forming* (or reconstructing) the bound-aries between social categories, between self and other. This is the moment encapsulated by the process model.

(3) When the musical imaginary works to *reproduce,* reinforce, actualize,

or memorialize *extant* sociocultural identities, in some cases also forcefully *repressing* both transformation and alternatives. Here, musical representations may potentially be hypostatized by such a "burden of representation"; they may be strongly bounded, highly redundant, prevented from engaging in the "promiscuity" of hybridity. This is the moment summed up by the homology model.

(4) When the musical representations of sociocultural identity come, *after the fact,* to be reinterpreted and debated discursively and, out of this process, "reinserted" as representations into the changing social-cultural formation (as Stokes shows for arabesk, and Brown for Bartók's reading of gypsy musics). This form also sums up the primary *macrohistorical,* transformative dynamic to which all musics are subject: that is, how musics become subject to inevitable historical processes of reinterpretation and then reinsertion into the changing sociocultural formation—a kind of discursive and practical reflexivity around music.

Our intention here is to expand theoretically on the dictum that identification is always imaginary,[96] as well as the assumption of a metaphorical and substantive equation between identity and music per se,[97] by clarifying that not all forms of musically articulated "identity" are the same. Instead, we should distinguish these four kinds of imaginary identification or discursive subjectification through music, their distinctive articulations and effects. Bohlman's paper, which explores the dynamics surrounding the music of one of Europe's foremost "internal others," the Jews, in some ways exemplifies a temporal conception of the (trans)formation of collective identities through music. In his study of the place of Jewish cantors in Viennese society from the mid-nineteenth to the early twentieth centuries, Bohlman portrays the cantors' musical culture both as embedded in a preexistent Jewish community and tradition, and as coming to play a significant role in forming the new boundaries and contours of an inclusive Viennese public sphere. He shows how, in this period, profound cultural differences within the Jewish community (as Vienna experienced waves of immigration of eastern European Jews), and between the Jews and Austrian society, were met by changes in musical culture. These involved a professionalization and popularization of the cantor's role and an expansion of the practices of Jewish musics, first within the Jewish community and then into the public spaces of the host society.

The development of print media, enabling the wide dissemination of the cantors' repertoires and of Jewish popular broadsides, was one condition for the changes. Another was the passing in nineteenth-century Austria of increasingly liberal laws, which allowed Jews to enter for the first time the "free professions" of Austrian society. Changes of aesthetic and of language made the music more attractive and "open" to the Viennese public. Bohlman stresses the collective and individual agency of the Jewish community and of particular cantors in these transformations of Viennese public culture. Through music, difference was composed, performed, and enacted; and yet, through music's powers of pleasing and unifying, differences were also lessened, effecting, through cultural practice, a rapprochement with the Jewish other within. Bohlman shows how historically vulnerable were these processes, for by the 1930s absolute boundaries between Jewish and Austrian societies were reasserted with ever more persecutory intent, as the internal other became a target for annihilation. Bohlman thus confirms music's powers to articulate and transform the contours of collective sociocultural identity. But he suggests too that, under conditions of internal otherness and when driven by the subaltern group, what might appear as musical "appropriation" can be a conscious practice *by* that group of musical integration and merging, with the aim of effecting sociocultural integration.

V. TECHNIQUES OF THE MUSICAL IMAGINARY

How should we think the *specificity of music* in the various processes outlined? Far from forcing the various arguments in play into a spurious unity, we want in this last section simply to gather thoughts on significant issues that arise.

A first comment is methodological and ontological: it concerns the multitextuality of music as culture and the irreducible complexity of musical signification. Music exists and generates meaning in a number of different, simultaneous forms: as musical sound, and this as mediated by notations, by technological and visual forms, by the practices and sociality of performance, by social institutions and socioeconomic arrangements, by language in different guises (lyrics and dramatic narratives, theoretical and critical exegeses, and other discourses) and, relatedly, by conceptual and knowledge systems. The essays demonstrate repeatedly how the key questions raised by this book can only be addressed by attending to music's mediations as well as to the musical sound, often by reading a number of different levels or forms of musical signification as a—sometimes contradictory—constellation. As Born has proposed, this requires a social semiotics of music adequate to the analysis of music as culture, as a complex multitextual object in history.[98]

Gorbman's revelation of the ideological tensions generated between film narrative and music in the evolution of the western genre; Brown's focus on Bartók's positioning by wider discourses of nationalism and race as evidenced through his writings; Franklin's reading of the contradictory and ambivalent presentations of self of émigré European composers in Los Angeles in the face of the dominance of American mass culture as revealed in their public and private statements, his analysis of the disjunctures between discursive accounts of Schoenberg and the composer's actual aesthetics and politics, and his account of Korngold's split musical subjectivity through the allegory of the film *Deception;* Feld's and Hesmondhalgh's analyses of how contemporary primitivisms and exoticisms are augmented by the visual iconography, marketing, and lyrics of world and fusion music acts; the prime place accorded by Pasler, Bohlman, Stokes, Hesmondhalgh, and Feld to technologies of sound reproduction (early recordings, print media, cassettes, samplers) in appropriative and representational strategies: all of these speak to the methodological necessity of attending to music's mediations and their complex juxtapositions and disjunctures. That this is more than a dry analytical proposal and can inflect an urgent politics is shown by Hesmondhalgh's account of critique circulating between the Nation bands. Reflecting on what would mitigate the objectionable exoticism of the multicultural act Transglobal Underground, a musician from the more experimental Asian Dub Foundation explained that, if TGU will not change their music and visuals, they might at least temper the exoticism by dialoguing with their audience on antiracist politics in a new performance practice. Here we see how musicians' awareness of the complexities of musical signification forms a calculus that can inform agency. Stokes's and Brown's essays, which center on tracing discursive fields around music, confirm another core methodological precept: music's extraordinary capacity to generate commentary and to absorb theoretical and other discursive projections, and the need to analyze these for their parallel, sometimes autonomous effects, as well as for their influence on the musicians' agency.

Here it is instructive to revisit the question of *authorial agency,* retheorized after the poststructuralist critique of authorship. In this introduction we have suggested the need to integrate an account of discursive formations, cultural and ideological systems, including those systems specific to music history, with an analysis of musicians' subjectivities.[99] Most of the essays adopt this perspective: Pasler depicts Delage and Roussel as conditioned by their cultural contexts, but artistically as relatively autonomous; Corbett and Feld portray musicians and composers as caught up in the ongoing momentum of dominant discursive fields, though with the possibility of variation and of resisting that momentum; while Hesmondhalgh examines agency by attending to the play of position-taking by Nation musicians. We have employed psychoanalytic concepts to elucidate the material, arguing that psychic dynamics, notably splitting and denial, are immanently at work in processes of the musical imaginary. We have noted the projection onto others and into the self of combined extremes of idealization and denigration, an emotional binarism encapsulated in the concept of splitting; the coexistence in the musical self of contradictory states and multiple subject positions, invoking the concept of intrasubjective fragmentation; and the attempt to absent or exclude an other aesthetic or music, which amounts to denial in musical subjectivity or cultural system. We are not alone in turning to psychoanalysis; as we have mentioned, historians of colonialism and postcolonial theorists engaged in the analysis of representation and appropriation have also shown how these processes may be imbued with projection and splitting.[100] This is no call for a return to humanist conceptions of sovereign agency or intentionality. We propose instead a theoretical hybrid, combining Foucauldian concepts of the production of subjectivity in discourse and psychoanalytic perspectives on the psychic forms immanent in individual subjectivity and cultural processes. Nor does such a hybrid commit us to abandoning all possibility of conscious agency. We would differ, for example, from Judith Butler's recent attempt to combine Foucauldian and psychoanalytic perspectives, in which she theorizes agency as a form of iteration, "an uneasy practice of repetition and its risks."[101] Butler's resolution of the agency problem risks, in its excessive structuralism, being insufficiently attuned to historical differences in the expression and outcome of agency.

Another aim of this introduction is to enhance the classification of different modes of appropriating and representing other musical cultures, different techniques of the musical imaginary. Earlier writers have developed their own classifications, partly in order to legitimize certain techniques. Bartók, expounding on his and Kodály's compositional practices, outlined three ways in which peasant musics may be "transmuted into" modern art music: by taking over a folk melody unchanged and writing an accompaniment, the closest to direct quotation; by simulating folk music, to produce an imaginative musical imitation or extension; and by absorbing completely the idiom of peasant music or using it as a basis for analysis, the results of which are used in original ways and incorporated into the composer's own style.[102] Leonard Meyer, writing on the crisis of teleological models of progress in music history, offers a classification for what he considers productive uses of past musics in a "radically pluralistic" present.[103] He distinguishes paraphrase, borrowing, allusion, simulation, and modelling, ranged along a spectrum between more and less freely modelled or imitative, and more and less formal-structural or thematic uses. He writes cannily of these techniques as "aesthetically self-reflective,"[104] yet apart from noting allusion's quality of "reminiscence," his interpretation focuses on formal qualities and eschews the techniques' different self-reflective cultural, psychological, and affective properties.

For an improved semiotics adequate to the complexities of musical practice, these earlier classifications need augmenting. Additional techniques that demand to be theorized include pastiche, parody, juxtaposition, and montage in music; and because of their rich extramusical implications, these techniques require analysis in more than formal terms. We might explore pastiche as an apparently affectionate and humorous mimesis, a mode of musical obeisance to the "original"; parody, by contrast, as a satirical, darkly humorous imitation that produces a critical distanciation from the original; and juxtaposition as a musical collage that creates perspectival distance, fragmentation, and relativism between each musical object alluded to.[105]

There is the question of whether it is possible for musical imitation to function as an aural analogue of stereotype or caricature, a question to which Feld responds with a resounding "yes" by arguing that musical caricature is definitive of the entire repertoire of popular appropriations of pygmy musics. The earlier schemes also require modernizing in order to address the now-ubiquitous techniques of electronic and computer music media, notably the varieties of technologically mediated sound montage and simulation. In principle, an adequate classification would address also the aural and aesthetic complexity of film, television, and advertising soundtracks, which combine music with diegetic dialogue, nondiegetic voice-over, and ambient sound, and thus require analysis of the aural effect of the complex simultaneity and shifting hierarchical interrelations of these different tracks.

There exists in addition a distinct species of reference involving nonmusical or extramusical discursive, cultural, and social associations derived from other musics and cultures, which replace, override, or determine musical reference. Corbett, for example, exemplifies this with the Eastern philosophical imperatives, unaccompanied by direct musical influence, of Cageian "conceptual Orientalism." But there are equally appropriations that derive their impetus from the ideological connotations or political identifications attached to particular musical cultures, for example when reference to popular music or song is made for its political associations, as in nationalists' uses of folk music, or in the appropriation of socialist songs for their revolutionary affiliation. Reference is also sometimes made to other musics through the imitation of their social forms or performance modes. Experimental and improvised musics have been particularly susceptible to these kinds of extramusical associations, for example in their mimicry of the collectivism of non-Western musical cultures or jazz.[106]

Perhaps the most theoretically challenging mode of musical representation is the kind of concrete quotation or "objectification" of another music found in forms such as musical montage, juxtaposition, pastiche, and parody. Here, representation of the other music is set within the bounded "identity" of the encompassing style; this is always a knowing (and in this sense self-reflective) allusion, a purely musical representation of another, distinct musical style or culture. These are forms which, through musical figuration of other musics, paradoxically defy music's status as essentially nonrepresentational. It is as though, while in music's abstract and asemantic first order of signification there is an absence of denotation or literal representation, and while profuse, ramifying fields of connotation and association constitute music's second, semantic order of signification, we need to conceive of a semantic third order consisting of *intermusical representations figured intramusically*, and thus a return of "denotation" of a purely intermusical kind, as it were, after the detour through connotation.[107] This technique is simply one concrete end of the spectrum of potential modes of subsumption of different musical styles within a musical "identity."

We must leave the further pursuit of the classificatory project for another time. Nonetheless, interesting questions arise. We might ask, first, whether there is a significant gulf between "realist" musical representations of other musics, those that intend "faithfully" to represent some aspect of another musical culture, and representations that are conceived purely imaginatively, set within the boundaries of existing genres and tropes, and thus have little concern for "faithfulness." Does the different degree of engagement with the other exhibited in these strategies matter? Is the latter—being less grounded, less researched, more purely fantasized, more an intrasubjective and intracultural phenomenon of projection/assimilation, and so likely more exoticist, Orientalist, primitivist—is it thus less defensible? This would provide a grounds for evaluating between, say, Roussel, whose representations of Indian music were more projective and self-oriented, and Delage, whose music contained moments of "realist" accuracy and who transcribed the details of Indian music's difference perceptively and with empathy. It would make plausible a cultural politics attuned to the difference between Madonna's careless invocation of pygmy musical sound bites via Herbie Hancock, and those artists—Zap Mama, Francis Bebey, Martin Cradick—who attempt to approach very close to the subtleties of pygmy techniques and musics. However it is Feld, on the multiple appropriations of pygmy musics, who voices strong cynicism on the politics of empathy: "Everyone—no matter how exoticizing, how patronizing, how romanticizing, how essentializing in their rhetoric or packaging—declares their fundamental respect, even affection, for the original music and its makers. Concern for the future of the rainforests and their inhabitants is now central to the genre." Moreover, the conditions for a politics of empathy have surely changed when "faithful" representations of other musics are a mere flick of a button away through the instant cut-and-paste of sampler technologies. This may explain the emphasis in recent political debate among musicians, as evidenced by Feld and Hesmondhalgh, on developing relatively unmediated and social engagements with the "musical other" through attention to modes of performance and practice, and even to playing with those musicians, as opposed to sheer musical results and sound surfaces.

Yet, resisting the tendency to read domination and subsumption into any and all musical appropriation, we should surely also ask whether, or under what conditions, musical otherness can be simple aesthetic difference? Is it possible to discern intramusical constructions of otherness that are intended as "pure" aesthetic play with other sounds and are thus, crucially, unburdened by ideological associations and the psychic dynamics of projection and splitting? Hesmondhalgh, for example, describes this as the position of

Nation band Loop Guru, who defend the notion that their non-Western and ethnic samples amount to an apolitical, nonappropriative engagement backed up by contacts with musicians through their travels. Despite musicians' intentions, can this hold? In a similar spirit of skepticism, following the earlier critique of serialist modernism's strategy of aesthetic autarchy,[108] we might reverse that critique and consider whether there is value in the attempt to shore up the boundaries and differences between distinct musical systems and aesthetic traditions, not in the cause of some questionable ideological embrace of, or nostalgia for, musical autonomy, authenticity, or essentialism, but as a productive tactic of "strategic essentialism" in music to stimulate cultural diversity and mark distinct social identities.[109] Where the current trend is toward the celebration of hybridities without end, and in the face of the global circulation of the entire archive of music history promised by the internet, a "postpostmodern" interest in musical boundaries, embeddedness, and location may have increasing creative salience.[110]

The classification of techniques of the musical imaginary can become an overly formalistic project that evades the analysis of power. But that is not a necessary property of all formal analysis. One potentially fruitful approach is to follow the lead of cultural theorists engaged in analyzing the discursive hierarchies at work in narrative structures, so as to theorize, by analogy, intramusical subsumptions of musical difference and how they articulate power and its subversion. An influential model is provided by MacCabe, who, in the Brechtian tradition of critique, has analyzed the existence of a hierarchy of discourses at work in the "classic realist text."[111] In this hierarchy, the framing narrative prose acts as a metalanguage which, in its transparency, denies its own discursivity and assumes the status of the "real" (or subject speaking truth). At the same time, the metalanguage subsumes a number of other narratives or object languages, which are perceived *as* discourses, *as* representations, while the identity of the metalanguage is obscured. For MacCabe, the ideological truth-effect produced by the discursive hierarchy is definitive of classic realism in both the novel and film.[112] This approach is similar to that pioneered by Susan McClary in her deconstructive studies of the narrative and social-discursive structures immanent in certain canonic Western musical works.[113] Her essay on Bach, for example, analyzes Bach's appropriations and juxtapositions of the then-dominant, "widely divergent, ideologically antagonistic" Italian and French styles in the Fifth Brandenburg Concerto. McClary argues that he incorporates them within a discursive hierarchy in which the Germanic Lutheran tradition remains "musical king"[114]—that is, acts as a metalanguage that finally subsumes the Italian and French idioms.

McClary's approach appears more open than MacCabe's on the question of whether such narrative forms must inevitably be ideologically reactionary. Her thesis is that Bach was working from the margins and was uncomfortable in any one lingua franca, preferring to effect dynamic syntheses of all musical languages at hand. Nonetheless, in her analysis of Cantata 140, *Wachet auf*, McClary argues that "the cantata enacts a synthesis of all available national styles in such a way as to appropriate them all and put them in the service of an expressly Lutheran agenda. The monad that contains the whole world is located, significantly, on German soil."[115] She equates this musical-narrative hierarchy, at least in its nineteenth-century reinterpretation in the service of Bach's canonization as inaugurator of "absolute music," with claims to the music's universalism and "extra-human truth."[116] McClary ends by herself equating Bach with "the postmodern eclectic . . . the ideologically marginalized artist empowering himself to appropriate, reinterpret, and manipulate to his own ends the signs and forms of dominant culture."[117] Here Bach appears almost as the prophet of "Signifyin(g)," and McClary's call for a careful elucidation of sociohistorical context risks being compromised by her desire to claim him for today's cultural politics of hybridity.[118]

Hirschkop has developed a similar perspective by introducing social context into linguistic theories of music through Mikhail Bakhtin's politicized sociolinguistics. The Bakhtinian concept of the poetic text, which Hirschkop treats as analogous to dominant forms of classical and popular music, is defined, again, by a hierarchy of discourses, a universalizing strategy that Bakhtin termed monological: "Poetic texts 'erase any sense of the boundedness, the historicity, the social determination and specificity of one's own language.'"[119] Against this, citing Bakhtin's concept of dialogism, Hirschkop poses those musical forms that re-use and recontextualize diverse musical languages without bringing them under the closure of a hierarchy of "truth" and universality. "External dialogism," found in Beethoven's late style and Mahler's symphonic work, is a form in which there is estrangement from dominant musical conventions through "the work's inability to 'take itself seriously'. . . . The music refers implicitly to its own historical limits." By contrast, "internal dialogism" stages a confrontation between different musics; other, "socially alien languages"—in classical music, popular or folk musics—are cited in the body of the work and thereby produce distanciation. But Hirschkop argues from music's immanent sociality that "to really dialogize music [it is necessary] to bring in not just musical language from popular social contexts but actual institutional elements of those social contexts themselves: forms of performance, reception and composition."[120] A different productive use of Bakhtin is Brown's analysis of parody, play, and the grotesque in a number of Bartók's works that synthesize modernism and folk musics.[121] These include dramatic pieces (*The Miraculous Mandarin, The Wooden Prince,* and *Bluebeard's Castle*), but also the supposedly nonreferential *Third String Quartet.* Drawing on Bakhtin's and Wolfgang Kayser's theories of the grotesque, Brown argues that Bartók does not merely assimilate other musical voices but, by emphasizing their difference, uses them to challenge prevailing national

(Habsburg) canons through "lively dialogue." She draws connections between the "elemental vitality" of the indestructible mandarin and the mechanical wooden prince in the dramas, whose hybrid bodies challenge "life/death" binarisms, and the Third String Quartet's affront to the genre's exalted status as the epitome of absolute music, and hence to its social exclusivity, through Bartók's use of folk musics and of "grotesque," extreme instrumental techniques.

Yet for all the fruitful examination of intramusical forms of power and subversion, there remains a danger of formalism unless they are thought ultimately in relation to the macro-socioeconomic processes within which techniques of representation and appropriation take place. Here we might recall Taruskin's uncompromising linking of Russian musical Orientalism with Russian imperialism. It is Feld who pursues this question most fully in this volume, summing up his essay on the exponential expansion of the pygmy pop industry:

> The primary circulation of small-scale, low-budget, and largely nonprofit ethnomusicological records is now directly linked to a secondary circulation of several million dollars' worth of contemporary record sales, copyrights, royalties and ownership claims, many of them held by the largest music entertainment conglomerates in the world. Hardly any of this money circulation returns to or benefits the originators of the cultural and intellectual property in question. It is this basic inequity, coupled with the reproduction of negative caricature, that creates the current ethnomusicological reality: discourses on world music are inseparable from discourses on indigeneity and domination.

Feld stresses, after Adorno and Derrida, the need to theorize the mimesis (or imitation/appropriation) that forms the basis of the world music industry from a perspective

> at the double-edge of affirmation and critique. . . . [Thus, in Adorno's aesthetic theory,] mimesis makes a theatrical appearance cloaked as the warped logic of domination, [yet] dialectically unleashing repressed desire, a longing for the other. . . . Adorno repeatedly insists that as distance, separation, and isolation are illuminated as the products of domination, so too do they glow as signals of a desire to reach out of subjection and into connection.

What is distinctive, then, about the political-economy of musical globalization as it is fuelled by the twin motors of capital accumulation and desire, as Feld and Hesmondhalgh imply, is that the economic and cultural correlates of aesthetic appropriation through commodification are very highly developed in music in comparison with such fields as postcolonial literature or the globalization of ethnic visual arts. Given music's suitability to mass, global commodification, and given the profitability of the music industry, the stakes in the exploitation of indigenous and marginalized groups' cultural property are very high. At the same time, due to commodified music's boundless capacity to create and corral desire, the capacity of these other musics to generate new aesthetic forms of identification, new modes of the global musical imaginary, are also great.[122] Taken as a whole, Feld's material suggests that, speeded on by ever more efficient technologies of appropriation and objectification of music and by the profit-augmenting imperatives of the multinational conglomerates, we are witnessing a new phase of neocolonial relations in culture, *definitively extractive* in their economic dynamics whatever the complex and two-way flows of aesthetic hybridity. The stark question arises: was musical appropriation *before* expanded commodification really a form of domination? The essays by Pasler, Brown, Franklin, and Middleton indicate that early twentieth-century musical appropriations and repudiations, while they may have been economically extractive in less developed ways, were imbued with the psychic dynamics of projection/assimilation, splitting, and subsumption that inhere in the social and discursive asymmetries of colonialism. Characterized by a dialectic of repression/denigration and desire/empathy, whatever the spaces of individual agency carved out from these dynamics, the musical subsumptions and splittings of the earlier twentieth century resonate with colonialist cultural domination. It is when the combined dynamics of commodification and technological objectification gain pace, as it becomes possible for enormously profitable uses to be made out of "original sources," that musical appropriation tips over into an expanded, dual economic-and-cultural extraction. While this may be no revolutionary conclusion, it yields a temporary closure.

Yet finally, there remain a series of questions concerning reception and history that demand attention. We should ask: is there some special way that, because of its lack of denotation, and compared with the visual and literary arts, music hides the traces of its appropriations, hybridities, and representations, so that they come over time to be *naturalized and aestheticized*? Does this make these structures of representation historically evanescent, and does this in turn render them unproblematic? If musical representation is entirely conventional and coded—again, because of the absence of denotative meaning—does this make the anchoring of meaning dependent only on reception? Similarly, whatever the intentions of the composer, aren't the original conditions of and connotations attached to musical appropriations erased—don't they disappear eventually—in reception? Aren't such influences also commonly misrecognized in reception? What does this imply for the original appropriation? Does it matter, then, that relatively powerless and immobile musical cultures have historically been appropriated in order to revitalize Western art and popular music traditions? These questions touch on the wider debate in cultural theory regarding the relations between reception, production, and the text. In music, these issues are particularly critical.

The questions appear to throw doubt on the need to be concerned at all with the historical moments of composition and production as they form the text. However, we suggest that there is an ontological argument to be made concerning the movement of the musical object (or text) through a series of states: imagination, composition, and production; dissemination and performance; reception. Each has a role in conditioning subsequent states. In this view, the characteristics of production, including authorial intention or compositional agency, themselves have a historical specificity and require understanding. Moreover, they come to be immanent in the text and set limits to the text, which, in turn, because of its finitude, sets certain limits to and forms reception.[123] Rather than the traces of musical appropriation simply being erased in time and in reception, they become, as with all musical elements, the object of changing discursive projections and interpretations, reinterpretations that in turn may become productive of new musical possibilities. Whatever the original sociocultural and ideological connotations such borrowings may have carried will fade in due course, unless they are reproduced as a projection into the musical object by other, nonmusical forces. In this sense, music's representational meanings, lacking any denotative "back-up," need always to be established, buttressed, through other sociocultural dynamics. The connotations attached to musical representations and appropriations are potentially more labile and unfixed, and perhaps at the same time more aesthetically and discursively fertile, than those of the visual and literary arts. Thus, a stress on reception as the final phase in the production of meaning does not wipe out the need to pursue the history of musical representations, but rather opens up the need to trace the "social life of sounds" through their several states ever more attentively. We might refer to Norris's paraphrase of Ernst Bloch, who wrote of the need for a constant effort of demystification of "nature" in music: "For Bloch . . . music is allegorical through and through . . . Musical works take on their significance through time in a history of successive re-encounters whose meaning can never be exhausted."[124] It is, we suggest, another naturalistic fallacy to believe that the musical object arrives fully formed in the world without the mediation of the author/musician/composer and the corresponding state/stage of production.

If, in this volume, greater attention has been paid to the semiotic character of musical representations of difference, to the forms of appropriation, and to the complexities of authorial subjectivities and production agencies than to their material and social contexts, this indicates what we acknowledge are the limitations of our project rather than a lack of commitment to the importance of analyzing the relations between those forms, agencies, and contexts. It bears repeating that our aim has not been to conduct an exercise in cultural relativism but to contribute to a reflexive critique of Western music and music history. Others are now writing analyses of musics and hybridities that are *not* dominant forms or centered in the West, sketching the outlines of a history that traces different roots/routes and spaces and in this way answers back to Western dominance.[125] While the present book does not contribute much to that project, this does not imply a view on our part that only the stories told here matter. We accept that writing even a self-critical account focused on the West might tend to reproduce the very hegemony, the very binary oppositions, it sets out to deconstruct. But we believe that developing greater critical acuity about the techniques and forms through which power is deployed in Western music contributes in a complementary way to the larger project of questioning and unsettling those modes of power. The limits remain; this volume indubitably raises questions for further research. It is a call awaiting a response.

NOTES

The epigraphs to this introduction are to be found in Pierre Boulez, "Oriental Music: A Lost Paradise?" in *Orientations* (London: Faber, 1986), 421; Steve Reich, *Writings about Music* (Halifax, Nova Scotia: Nove Scotia College of Art and Design, 1974), 40; Peter Gabriel, quoted in Timothy D. Taylor, *Global Pop: World Music, World Markets* (New York: Routledge, 1997), 50; Mark Slobin, *Subcultural Sounds: Micromusics of the West* (Hanover, N.H.: Wesleyan University Press, 1993), 4.

1. We want to signal our difficulties with the terms "Western" and "other" while arguing for their retention. We use "Western" to denote Europe and North America. Many people now prefer the divisions "North" and "South" as a means of referring to the division between relatively rich and poor areas of the world. But, given that this is a book about music, we need to refer to the longstanding concept of "Western music" while distancing ourselves from those traditions of analysis which have taken such a category for granted, or which have privileged it, or both. This means also using the even more unfortunate but still widely used term "non-Western," which makes it sound as though the rest of the world is a kind of residue of the West. As we have worked on this book, "Euro-American" has emerged as a more accurate term for the geographical area that has dominated so much of the world's politics and culture. The term "other," meanwhile, has been widely used in a number of critical fields, especially feminism and postcolonial studies, to denote those groups of people that white Western heterosexual men have usually defined themselves against, and whose selfhood they have tended to deny. Unlike many writers, however, we have chosen not to capitalize the word "other." Given that our critical intentions are hopefully evident, scare quotation marks have not been used after the initial appearance of "Western" and "other" in each chapter.

2. By denotative media we refer to Barthes's distinction between denotation and connotation as two forms of signification comprising the "imitative" arts. See Roland Barthes, "The Photographic Message" and "Rhetoric of the Image," in *Image-Music-Text*, trans. Stephen Heath (London: Fontana, 1977). Music, in its immanent abstraction, is different from these arts in lacking a level of denotation, or literal, analogical representation.

3. See Ralph P. Locke, "Constructing the Oriental 'Other': Saint-Saëns's *Samson et Dalila*," *Cambridge Opera Journal* 3, no. 3 (1991): 261–302; Ralph P. Locke, "Reflec-

tions on Orientalism in Opera and Musical Theatre," *Opera Quarterly* 10, no. 1 (1993): 49–73; Susan McClary, *Georges Bizet: Carmen* (Cambridge: Cambridge University Press, 1992); Richard Taruskin, "'Entoiling the Falconet': Russian Musical Orientalism in Context," *Cambridge Opera Journal* 4 (1992): 253–80; Jonathan Bellman, ed., *The Exotic in Western Music* (Boston: Northeastern University Press, 1998); and Philip Hayward, ed., *Widening the Horizon: Exoticism in Post-War Popular Music* (Bloomington: Indiana University Press, 1999). Miriam K. Whaples, "Early Exoticism Revisited," in *The Exotic in Western Music*, ed. Bellman, 3–4, provides a useful survey of major works in orthodox musicology on the subject of exoticism, including an important German tradition of research.

4. See, for example, Gerry Farrell, *Indian Music and the West* (Oxford: Clarendon Press, 1997).

5. See Ruth Solie, ed., *Musicology and Difference: Gender and Sexuality in Music Scholarship* (Berkeley: University of California Press, 1993); Lawrence Kramer, *Classical Music and Postmodern Knowledge* (Berkeley: University of California Press, 1995); and Richard Dellamora and Daniel Fischlin, eds., *The Work of Opera: Genre, Nationhood, and Sexual Difference* (New York: Columbia University Press, 1997). The work of Gary Tomlinson has also been influential in this area. In *Music in Renaissance Magic: Toward a Historiography of Others* (Chicago: University of Chicago Press, 1993) and "Musical Pasts and Postmodern Musicologies: A Response to Lawrence Kramer," *Current Musicology* 53 (summer 1994): 18–24, Tomlinson applies poststructuralist concerns with representation to questions of music history, asking, "How can we construct ways of seeing others that do not aggressively familiarize (colonize, terrorize) them?" (ibid., 23).

6. See Simon Frith, ed., *World Music, Politics, and Social Change* (Manchester: Manchester University Press, 1989); Tony Mitchell, *Popular Music and Local Identity: Rock, Pop and Rap in Europe and Oceania* (London: Leicester University Press, 1996); and Timothy D. Taylor, *Global Pop: World Music, World Markets* (New York: Routledge, 1997).

7. See Will Straw, "Systems of Articulation, Logics of Change: Communities and Scenes in Popular Music," *Cultural Studies* 5, no. 3 (1991): 368–88; Will Straw et al., eds., *Popular Music—Style and Identity* (Montreal: International Association for the Study of Popular Music, 1995); Martin Stokes, ed., *Ethnicity, Identity and Music* (Oxford: Berg, 1994); Simon Frith, "Music and Identity," in *Questions of Cultural Identity*, ed. Stuart Hall and Paul du Gay (London: Sage, 1996); and Simon Frith, *Performing Rites: On the Value of Popular Music* (Cambridge, Mass.: Harvard University Press, 1996).

8. Line Grenier, in "From 'Diversity' to 'Difference': The Case of Socio-Cultural Studies of Music," *New Formations* 9 (winter 1989): 125–42, traces the historical development of discourses on music and difference, and argues for the importance of this history to cultural studies in general. Grenier's study is an innovative precursor to this essay and this collection.

9. Patrick Williams and Laura Chrisman, eds., *Colonial Discourse and Post-Colonial Theory: A Reader* (Hemel Hempstead, U.K.: Harvester Wheatsheaf, 1993), 15. Similarly, the early postcolonial criticism of writers such as Wilson Harris, Chinua Achebe, and Wole Soyinka has often been disregarded in the attention paid in recent years to postcolonial theory. Bart Moore-Gilbert has argued eloquently for the reintegration of these two major strands of postcolonial analysis (i.e., criticism and theory). See Bart Moore-Gilbert, *Postcolonial Theory* (London: Verso, 1997): 169–84.

10. Frantz Fanon, *The Wretched of the Earth*, trans. Constance Farrington (1961;

reprint, Harmondsworth: Penguin, 1983); Edward Said, *Orientalism* (New York: Pantheon, 1978).

11. These ramifying concerns have been conjoined with attempts to understand racial dynamics in other contexts that can only be called "postcolonial" in very loose or metaphorical ways, such as the work of African American cultural critics. Moreover, some of the work that might most comfortably be brought under the rubric "postcolonial," in the sense that it aims at a poststructuralist, antifoundational analysis of colonial and postcolonial discourses, argues that the term "postcolonial" is itself problematic due to its assumption of a radical break between the colonial period and the era that followed. See, for example, Ella Shohat, "Notes on 'The Post-Colonial,'" *Social Text* 31/32 (1992): 99–113, and Anne McClintock, "The Angel of Progress: Pitfalls in the Term 'Post-Colonialism,'" *Social Text* 31/32 (1992): 1–15.

12. See, for example, Richard Leppert and Susan McClary, eds., *Music and Society: The Politics of Composition, Performance and Reception* (Cambridge: Cambridge University Press, 1987); Philip V. Bohlman, "Musicology as a Political Act," *Journal of Musicology* 11, no. 4 (1993): 411–36; and Kramer, *Classical Music and Postmodern Knowledge.*

13. Gayatri Chakravorty Spivak, *The Spivak Reader* (New York: Routledge, 1996), 19. The general arguments are evident throughout Spivak's work; see, among many examples, Spivak, "Negotiating the Structures of Violence," in *The Post Colonial Critic: Interviews, Strategies, Dialogues,* ed. Sarah Harasym (New York: Routledge, 1990); and Spivak, *Outside in the Teaching Machine* (New York: Routledge, 1993).

14. See, for example, Timothy Mitchell, *Colonizing Egypt* (Cambridge: Cambridge University Press, 1988), and James Clifford, *The Predicament of Culture: Ethnography, Art, and Literature in the Twentieth Century* (Cambridge, Mass.: Harvard University Press, 1989).

15. Homi Bhabha, "The Other Question: Stereotype, Discrimination and the Discourse of Colonialism," in *The Location of Culture* (1983; New York: Routledge, 1994).

16. Benita Parry, "Problems in Current Theories of Colonial Discourse," *Oxford Literary Review* 9 (1987): 27–58. Marxist criticism of postcolonial studies includes Aijaz Ahmad, *In Theory: Classes, Nations, Literatures* (London: Verso, 1992), and Arif Dirlik, "The Postcolonial Aura: Third World Criticism in the Age of Global Capitalism," *Critical Inquiry* 20 (1994): 329–56.

17. See Stuart Hall, "When Was 'The Post-Colonial'? Thinking at the Limit," in *The Post-Colonial Question: Common Skies, Divided Horizons,* ed. Iain Chambers and Lidia Curti (New York: Routledge, 1996), 257. There have, however, been robust replies to these critiques of postcolonial studies. Robert Young, for example, answers persuasively that "the investigation of the discursive construction of colonialism does not seek to replace or exclude other forms of analysis, whether they be historical, geographical, economic, military or political." Moreover, in this view, the importance of colonial discourse analysis lies in the way it emphasizes how "colonialism involved not just a military or economic activity, but permeated forms of knowledge which, if unchallenged, may continue to be the very ones through which we try to understand colonialism itself." See Robert Young, *Colonial Desire* (London: Routledge, 1995), 163.

18. Exceptions to the lack of consideration of popular culture are writers such

as Paul Gilroy and bell hooks, who are generally considered more marginal than the three central figures of postcolonial studies, Said, Spivak, and Bhabha. See, for example, Paul Gilroy, *Small Acts: Thoughts on the Politics of Black Cultures* (London: Serpent's Tail, 1993), and bell hooks, *Yearning: Race, Gender and Cultural Politics* (London: Turnaround, 1991). The neglect of popular culture in the work of the three central writers mentioned is almost total.

19. Both quotations from Nicholas Thomas, *Colonialism's Culture: Anthropology, Travel and Government* (Cambridge, England: Polity Press, 1994), 58. In theorizing agency and practice, Thomas draws on Pierre Bourdieu, *Outline of a Theory of Practice* (Cambridge: Cambridge University Press, 1977).

20. Art history, for example, has been considerably more responsive to these issues. See Susan Hiller, ed., *The Myth of Primitivism* (London: Routledge, 1991), and Hal Foster, "Primitive Scenes," *Critical Inquiry* 20, no. 1 (1993): 69–102.

21. See, for example, Susan McClary, *Feminine Endings: Music, Gender and Sexuality* (Minneapolis: University of Minnesota Press, 1991), and Solie, ed., *Musicology and Difference.*

22. Recent decades have seen an expanding literature focused on ethnomusicology's growing self-critical reflexivity about its historical role in positioning the relations between Western music and its others. Studies include Bruno Nettl, *The Western Impact on World Music* (New York: Schirmer Books, 1985); Bruno Nettl and Philip V. Bohlman, eds., *Comparative Musicology and Anthropology of Music* (Chicago: University of Chicago Press, 1991); and Stephen Blum, Philip V. Bohlman, and Daniel Neuman, eds., *Ethnomusicology and Modern Music History* (Urbana: University of Illinois Press, 1991). Given the difficulty of including so many areas of scholarship in this introduction, and despite the importance of this development within ethnomusicology (to which some of our contributors attest—see the essays by Bohlman and Stokes), we have not pursued the ethnomusicological perspective as a central theme in this essay and we acknowledge this as a limitation.

23. Locke, in "Reflections on Orientalism in Opera and Musical Theatre," 62–63, lists a large number of such works. See section V of this introduction for a critical reflection on the implications of the "accuracy" or otherwise of appropriated materials in relation to their sources.

24. See, for example, Neil Sorrell, *The Gamelan* (London: Faber, 1990), for a discussion of Western composers' (such as Debussy's) borrowings from gamelan music.

25. Other recent attempts to address issues of race, ethnicity, and music/musicology are Ronald Radano and Philip V. Bohlman, eds., *Music and the Racial Imagination* (Chicago: University of Chicago Press, forthcoming); and Stokes, ed., *Ethnicity, Identity and Music.*

26. Said himself discusses Verdi's *Aida* in his *Culture and Imperialism* (London: Chatto and Windus, 1993): 133–59, although his analysis has been subject to critique. See, for instance, Bart Moore-Gilbert, *Postcolonial Theory* (London: Verso, 1997), 68–69. It is interesting, in relation to the concerns of this book, that in his main work of music criticism, *Musical Elaborations* (London: Chatto and Windus, 1991), Said applies his critical armory to music only very schematically, which suggests that music has the status of a significant lacuna in his work. While he writes appreciatively of new directions in the sociocultural study of music, and raises issues of difference and representation, ideology and authority, orthodoxy and its others, and so on, his think-

ing almost exclusively concerns Western classical music. In a telling late passage, Said remembers his first concert as a small boy growing up in Egypt, a concert by Umm Kalthoum of classical Arabic song. He reflects that the music seemed "puzzling" with its aesthetic of repetition and "almost total absence of development"; and adds that, because of his "preponderantly Western education (both musical and academic), the kind of art practiced by Umm Kalthoum receded in importance for me" (98). Here we sense, through this intimate anecdote, Said's awareness of the hierarchical ordering and jostling for place between different musical traditions, how this is affected by large-scale cultural historical processes, and its embodiment in the most private and "local" musical experiences. His own cultural biography speaks to these central issues. Yet rather than interpret in this way, Said returns to classical music as unquestioned norm: "But of course it [i.e., music such as Umm Kalthoum's] only went beneath the surface of my conscious awareness until, in recent years, I returned to an interest in Arabic culture, where I rediscovered her, and was able to associate what she did musically with some features of Western classical music" (98).

27. Locke, "Constructing the Oriental 'Other,'" 263. Locke's wider analysis of Orientalist operas is given in his "Reflections on Orientalism."

28. Locke, "Constructing the Oriental 'Other,'" 263.

29. Ibid., 271.

30. Locke, "Reflections on Orientalism," 61–2. See also Paul Robinson, "Is *Aida* an Orientalist Opera?" *Cambridge Opera Journal* 5 (1993): 133–40.

31. Both quotations, Taruskin, "'Entoiling the Falconet,'" 255.

32. Ibid., 259.

33. Both quotations, ibid., 279.

34. Ibid., 280.

35. Claudia Gorbman, *Unheard Melodies: Narrative Film Music* (London and Bloomington, Indiana: British Film Institute/Indiana University Press, 1987). Gorbman clearly took literally our request for a paper about *Western* music and its others.

36. In film, diegesis is the "narratively implied spatiotemporal world of the actions and characters" (Gorbman, *Unheard Melodies*, 21); it is the universe of the narrated story. Diegetic music is that which appears to issue from or belong to this narrative world. By contrast, nondiegetic music is all that which does *not* belong to the story and exists apart from it, commenting on it. For a fuller discussion of diegesis as well as diegetic and nondiegetic film music, see Gorbman, *Unheard Melodies*, 20–30.

37. See Georgina Born, *Rationalizing Culture: IRCAM, Boulez, and the Institutionalization of the Musical Avant-Garde* (Berkeley: University of California Press, 1995), 49, for an analysis of the eclectic early modernist tendencies that drew on "other" musics as "'proto' postmodern."

38. Said, *Orientalism*, 179.

39. For an account of aspects of the later development of serialist modernism, see Born, *Rationalizing Culture*.

40. This analysis has interesting analogies with Crow on modernist visual art. See Thomas Crow, "Modernism and Mass Culture in the Visual Arts," in *Modernism and Modernity*, ed. Benjamin Buchloh et al. (Halifax, Canada: 1983).

41. See, for instance, Theodor Adorno, "On the Fetish Character in Music and the Regression of Listening" and "Culture Industry Reconsidered," in *The Culture Industry: Selected Essays on Mass Culture*, ed. Jay Bernstein (New York: Routledge, 1991),

26–52, 85–92; Clement Greenberg, "Avant-Garde and Kitsch," in *Pollock and After: The Critical Debate,* ed. Francis Frascina (1939; London: Harper and Row, 1985).

42. Pierre Boulez, "On New Music," *New York Review of Books,* 28 June 1984, 14–15; Pierre Boulez and Michel Foucault, "Contemporary Music and the Public," *Perspectives of New Music* 24, no. 1 (1985): 6–12.

43. Crow, "Modernism and Mass Culture"; Andreas Huyssen, *After the Great Divide: Modernism, Mass Culture, Postmodernism* (Bloomington, Ind.: Indiana University Press, 1986).

44. Guy Scarpetta, *L'Impureté* (Paris: Bernard Grasset, 1985).

45. See, for example, Robert Young, *Colonial Desire* (New York: Routledge, 1995).

46. See Born, *Rationalizing Culture,* for a detailed account of exactly these processes in the international circuits of contemporary art music.

47. See John Cage, *Silence* (Cambridge, Mass.: MIT Press, 1969): 74–75, in which Cage argues that American experimentalism will supersede the European modernist avant-garde, and then equates American developments with the universal—with "the world."

48. For an analysis of these processes in relation to postserialism see Born, *Rationalizing Culture,* chapters 2, 10, and 11.

49. Born, *Rationalizing Culture,* especially 305–6.

50. Charles Keil, *Urban Blues* (1966; reprint, Chicago: University of Chicago Press, 1991), 45.

51. Ingrid Monson, "Doubleness and Jazz Improvisation: Irony, Parody and Ethnomusicology," *Critical Inquiry* 20 (1994): 286.

52. Richard Middleton, "Repeat Performance," in *Music on Show: Issues of Performance,* ed. Tarja Hautamäki and Helmi Järviluoma (Tampere, Finland: Department of Folk Tradition, 1998), 211. A debate persists about whether it is possible to talk about a distinctive set of musical practices that can be labelled "black music" or "African American" music: see David Hatch and Stephen Millward, *From Blues to Rock* (Manchester: Manchester University Press, 1987): 116–29; Philip Tagg, "Open Letter: Black Music, Afro-American Music and European Music," *Popular Music* 8 (1989): 285–98; and see David Brackett, *Interpreting Popular Music* (Cambridge: Cambridge University Press, 1995): 108–19 for an impressive defense of the concept.

53. George Lipsitz, *Time Passages: Collective Memory and American Popular Culture* (Minneapolis: University of Minnesota Press, 1990); Dick Hebdige, *Subculture: The Meaning of Style* (London: Methuen, 1979); Simon Jones, *Black Youth, White Culture: The Reggae Tradition from JA to UK* (Basingstoke: Macmillan, 1988); and Gregory Stephens, "Rap Music's Double-Voiced Discourse: A Crossroads for Inter-Racial Communication," *Journal of Communication Inquiry* 15, no. 2 (1991): 100–115.

54. There are important resonances between such black music criticism and postcolonial theory. Ben Sidran is one writer who makes explicit such links in his *Black Talk* (1971; reprint, Edinburgh: Payback Press, 1995), when he cites that key progenitor of postcolonial analysis, Frantz Fanon. The contribution of black writers on music such as Sidran and Leroi Jones/Amiri Baraka is rarely acknowledged in postcolonial studies.

55. Leroi Jones/Amiri Baraka, "Jazz and the White Critic," in *Black Music* (New York: William Morrow, 1967): 11–20. Baraka often directs his criticisms at the "black elite" as well as at white folk. The dangers and difficulties associated with construct-

ing a jazz canon in parallel to those in existence for European music are discussed eloquently by Gary Tomlinson, "Cultural Dialogics and Jazz: A White Historian Signifies," in *Disciplining Music: Musicology and Its Canons,* ed. Katherine Bergeron and Philip V. Bohlman (Chicago: University of Chicago Press, 1992): 64–94.

56. Ted Gioia, *The Imperfect Art: Reflections on Jazz and Modern Culture* (New York: Oxford University Press, 1988); Bernard Gendron, "Jamming at La Boeuf: Jazz and the Paris Avant-Garde," *Discourse* 12, no. 1 (1989/90).

57. S. H. Fernando Jr., *The New Beats: Exploring the Music, Culture and Attitudes of Hip-Hop* (New York: Doubleday, 1994): xx–xxiii.

58. Peter Stallybrass and Allon White, *The Politics and Poetics of Transgression* (London: Methuen, 1986).

59. Paul Gilroy, *The Black Atlantic: Modernity and Double Consciousness* (London: Verso, 1993).

60. James Snead, "Repetition as a Figure of Black Culture," in *Black Literature and Literary Theory,* ed. Henry Louis Gates (New York: Routledge, 1984), 59–80.

61. Henry Louis Gates, *The Signifying Monkey: A Theory of African-American Literary Criticism* (New York: Oxford University Press, 1988), 79.

62. See Houston A. Baker Jr., *Modernism and the Harlem Renaissance* (Chicago: University of Chicago Press, 1987).

63. See, for example, Alan Lomax, *Folk Song: Style and Structure* (New Brunswick, N.J.: Transaction Books, 1978); Cees J. Hamelink, *Cultural Autonomy in Global Communication* (New York: Longmans, 1983).

64. For example, Martin Hatch, "Popular Music in Indonesia," in *World Music, Politics and Social Change,* ed. Simon Frith (Manchester: Manchester University Press, 1989), and Peter Manuel, *Popular Musics of the Non-Western World* (New York: Oxford University Press, 1993).

65. Manuel, *Popular Musics of the Non-Western World,* 19–23.

66. Mark Slobin, *Subcultural Sounds: Micromusics of the West* (Hanover, N.H.: Wesleyan University Press, 1993); Gilroy, *The Black Atlantic;* George Lipsitz, *Dangerous Crossroads: Popular Music, Postmodernism, and the Poetics of Place* (London: Verso, 1994).

67. See Jonathan Bellman, "Indian Resonances in the British Invasion, 1965–1968," in *The Exotic in Western Music,* ed. Bellman, 292–306.

68. The terms "world music" and "world beat" are very confusing and have shifting meanings. In Britain, the term "world beat" is not used, and "world music" is generally used to mean:

(a) The music of Western stars who have shown an interest in non-Western pop;
(b) Non-Western and/or nonrock popular musics distributed in the West, especially commercial, hybrid forms such as salsa, zydeco, rai, soca, highlife, jújù, etc.;
(c) Supposedly "traditional" musical forms such as Balkan a capella choirs.

In the United States, on the other hand, "world beat" is used to mean (a) and (b) in this classification, while "world music" has tended to denote (c). As is so often the case with generic terms, things have gotten more complicated still. According to Feld the two terms are merging—perhaps as the success of the marketing term "world music" gains popularity outside the U.K.; see Steven Feld, "From Schizophonia to Schismogenesis: On the Discourses and Commodification Practices of 'World Music' and 'World Beat,'" in Charles Keil and Steven Feld, *Music Grooves: Essays and Dialogues* (Chicago: University of Chicago Press, 1994): 265–68.

69. Steven Feld, "Notes on 'World Beat,'" in Keil and Feld, *Music Grooves,* 242. Other critical commentaries on Simon's *Graceland* include Charles Hamm, "*Graceland* Revisited," *Popular Music* 8, no. 3 (1989): 299–304; Charles Hamm, "African-American Music, South Africa and Apartheid," in *Putting Popular Music in Its Place* (Cambridge: Cambridge University Press, 1995): 167–209; and Louise Meintjes, "Paul Simon's *Graceland,* South Africa, and the Mediation of Musical Meaning," *Ethnomusicology* 34 (1990): 37–73. Hesmondhalgh, in his essay for this collection, also examines the politics of ownership in music.

70. Lipsitz, *Dangerous Crossroads,* 63.

71. Ibid., 132.

72. Ibid., 7, 12, and 17.

73. Slobin, *Subcultural Sounds.*

74. Gilroy, *The Black Atlantic.*

75. Veit Erlmann, "The Aesthetics of the Global Imagination: Reflections on World Music in the 1990s," *Public Culture* 8 (1996): 467.

76. Simon Frith, "Anglo-America and Its Discontents," *Cultural Studies* 5, no. 3 (1991).

77. Feld, "From Schizophonia to Schismogenesis."

78. The reference is to Arjun Appadurai, ed., *The Social Life of Things: Commodities in Cultural Perspective* (Cambridge: Cambridge University Press, 1986).

79. Roland Barthes, "The Death of the Author," in *Image-Music-Text* (London: Fontana, 1977).

80. Erlmann, "The Aesthetics of the Global Imagination"; Taylor, *Global Pop.*

81. See Martin Stokes, "Introduction: Ethnicity, Identity and Music," in *Ethnicity, Identity and Music,* ed. Stokes; and Frith, "Music and Identity."

82. See Straw, "Systems of Articulation, Logics of Change."

83. Stokes, "Introduction," 8–10; Peter Parkes, "Personal and Collective Identity in Kalasha Song Performance: The Significance of Music-Making in a Minority Enclave," in *Ethnicity, Identity and Music,* ed. Stokes; Zdzislaw Mach, "National Anthems: The Case of Chopin as a National Composer," in *Ethnicity, Identity and Music,* ed. Stokes.

84. Stokes, "Introduction," 8.

85. Erik Levi, "Music and National Socialism: The Politicisation of Criticism, Composition and Performance," in *The Nazification of Art,* ed. Brandon Taylor and Wilfried van der Will (Winchester, England: Winchester Press, 1990); Sabine Meier, "A Generation Led Astray: Community Singing as a Means of National Socialist Indoctrination of the Youth" (Ph.D. thesis, Goldsmiths' College, University of London, 1992).

86. Stokes, "Introduction," 10. Recent scholarship on music and nationalism includes Jane Fulcher, *The Nation's Image: French Grand Opera as Politics and Politicised Art* (Cambridge: Cambridge University Press, 1987); Anthony Arblaster, *Viva la Libertà! Politics in Opera* (London: Verso, 1992); and Dellamora and Fischlin, *The Work of Opera: Genre, Nationhood and Sexual Difference.* Arblaster puts a convincing and productive case for the relationship between music, specifically opera, and nationalism, arguing that "It is impossible to think of any other ideological force or creed that has had a more profound and lasting impact on music in the past two centuries than nationalism. From Weber to Vaughan Williams, from Berlioz to Bartok, from Chopin

to Shostakovitch, there is a long list of composers whose musical achievement is bound up with their involvement with nationalism [and who] in discovering their nation and its music discovered their musical selves. . . . Often, because explicitly political activities were prohibited, the opera house became a forum for the expression of subversive political sentiments [and for] political demonstration" (64).

87. Stokes, "Introduction," 8.

88. Georgina Born, "Understanding Music as Culture: Contributions from Popular Music Studies to a Social Semiotics of Music," in *Tendenze e metodi nella ricerca musicologica*, ed. Raffaele Pozzi (Florence: Olschki, 1993); Born, *Rationalizing Culture*, chapter 1. There are of course occasional (primarily modernist) exceptions to the denotational character of the visual and literary arts, such as abstract painting and dadaistic verse.

89. On the place of social fantasy in colonial and postcolonial cultures, see Robert Young, *Colonial Desire* (and see note 100 below).

90. See also Stokes, "Introduction," 3–4.

91. See Born, *Rationalizing Culture*, chapters 4, 5, 6, and 10; Georgina Born, "Modernist Discourse, Psychic Forms, and Agency: Aesthetic Subjectivities at IRCAM," *Cultural Anthropology* 12, no. 4 (1997); and Georgina Born, "Anthropology, Kleinian Psychoanalysis, and the Subject in Discourse," *American Anthropologist* 100 (summer 1998).

92. Stuart Hall, "Introduction: Who Needs Identity?" in *Questions of Cultural Identity*, ed. Stuart Hall and Paul du Gay (London: Sage, 1996).

93. Frith, "Music and Identity," 123–24, exemplifies this principle by reference to Paul Gilroy, "Sounds Authentic: Black Music, Ethnicity, and the Challenge of a *Changing* Same," *Black Music Research Journal* 10, no. 2 (1990). Gilroy (127) argues that black identity formation "remains the outcome of practical activity: language, gesture, bodily significations, desires. . . . These significations are condensed in musical performance, although it does not, of course, monopolise them. In this context, they produce the imaginary effect of an internal racial core or essence by acting on the body through the specific mechanisms of identification and recognition that are produced in the intimate interaction of performer and crowd."

94. The discursive subsumption of other musics, as an attempt to exert control, parallels the more commonly noted subsumption of other musics by Western notation as a key historical technique of reduction and attempted mastery. See, for example, Farrell, *Indian Music and the West*, chapter 2, on the place of notation in European encounters with Indian musics.

95. Georgina Born, "Afterword: Music Policy, Aesthetic and Social Difference," in *Rock and Popular Music: Politics, Policies, Institutions*, ed. Tony Bennett et al. (New York: Routledge, 1993), 286.

96. Hall, "Introduction: Who Needs Identity?" 16, cites Judith Butler on identification, who in her own way introduces a kind of temporality into the concept: "Identifications belong to the imaginary; they are phantasmic efforts of alignment, loyalty, ambiguous and cross-corporeal cohabitations. . . . Identifications are never fully and finally made; they are incessantly reconstituted. . . . They are that which is constantly marshalled, consolidated, retrenched, contested and, on occasion, compelled to give way." Quotation from Judith Butler, *Bodies That Matter* (London: Routledge, 1993), 105.

97. See Frith, "Music and Identity," 108–10.

98. Georgina Born, "Music, Modernism, and Signification," in *Thinking Art: Beyond Traditional Aesthetics,* ed. Andrew Benjamin and Peter Osborne (London: Institute of Contemporary Arts, 1991); Born, "Understanding Music as Culture"; Born, *Rationalizing Culture.*

99. On the necessity of theorizing agency in cultural production, specifically in relation to music and musicians' subjectivities, see Born, "Afterword: Music Policy, Aesthetic and Social Difference," especially 271–83.

100. The central place of the psychoanalytic concept of ambivalence in Bhabha's work resonates with our use of splitting; indeed, Bhabha also continually has recourse to the concept of splitting. See Homi Bhabha, *The Location of Culture* (New York: Routledge, 1994). Robert Young in *Colonial Desire,* for another example, develops from the work of Deleuze and Guattari the notion of group fantasy (169), or social or collective fantasy (98), in his attempt to delineate a "social theory of desire." He uses this to understand racism as the core dynamic of colonialism: "Racism is perhaps the best example through which we can immediately grasp the form of desire, and its antithesis, repulsion, as a social production, [a] *group fantasy*" (169). Young's idea of the mutuality of desire and repulsion echoes with the concept of splitting.

101. Judith Butler, *The Psychic Life of Power* (Stanford: Stanford University Press, 1997), 30. For a fuller argument concerning the retheorization of agency within a combined Foucauldian and Kleinian psychoanalytic framework, see Born, "Modernist Discourse, Psychic Forms, and Agency" and Born, "Anthropology, Kleinian Psychoanalysis, and the Subject in Discourse."

102. Bela Bartók, "The Influence of Peasant Music on Modern Music," in *Bela Bartok Essays,* ed. Benjamin Suchoff (1931; reprint, New York: St. Martin's Press, 1976).

103. Leonard B. Meyer, *Music, The Arts, and Ideas* (Chicago: University of Chicago Press, 1967), 208.

104. Ibid., 194.

105. This technique of juxtaposition is exemplified by some of Ives's major orchestral works, such as *Central Park in the Dark* (1906) and *Decoration Day* (1912), in which the floating musical objects also have the quality of affectionate pastiche. But it is equally a quality of the collage-techniques central to hip-hop–influenced forms; listen, for example, to the music of DJ Shadow.

106. The groups fostered by the British experimental composer Cornelius Cardew were particularly interesting in this regard. Cardew's Scratch Orchestra was driven essentially by a social philosophy of music-making, summarized by Nyman as "a regularly meeting large experimental ensemble, a flexible social unit with written and unwritten 'laws' of community and musical behavior." See Michael Nyman, *Experimental Music: Cage and Beyond* (New York: Schirmer, 1974), 115. Initially motivated by the principles of Confucius, the Scratch Orchestra moved towards revolutionary Maoist politics. People's Liberation Music, Cardew's last band, self-consciously took as its social and performative model the "rock group" in a blatant attempt to engage a youth audience in revolutionary Marxism through the knowing simulation of a popular musical form to which they would readily relate.

107. The term "detour" here is ironic since, as we have stressed, connotation is undoubtedly the dominant mode of musical signification. There may be parallels, in this idea of a third, denotative level of musical signification, with aspects of John

Shepherd and Peter Wicke's attempt, in *Music and Cultural Theory* (Cambridge: Polity Press, 1997), to produce an encompassing theory of musical signification; see for example their Figure 1 (157).

108. As evidence of high musical modernism's aesthetic autarchy we might refer to Robert Samuels, "The Other of Invention: Modernist and Postmodernist Moments in the Works of Harrison Birtwistle" (unpublished ms., 1996). Samuels argues that the British postserialist composer Birtwistle, rather than evoking alterity in his music through reference to other musics, sets out to produce figures of alterity as a core component of his own aesthetic. Samuels portrays this as central to Birtwistle's larger project of constructing an autonomous musical imaginary that is without predecessors or kinship to other musical systems.

109. On the concept of "strategic essentialism," its qualifications and problems, see Spivak, *Outside in the Teaching Machine*, 3–4; Gilroy, *The Black Atlantic*, 31–40; and on related issues of essentialism and antiessentialism in relation to music, Gilroy, *The Black Atlantic*, chapter 3, and Lipsitz, *Dangerous Crossroads*, chapter 3.

110. For a fuller discussion of these issues, see Georgina Born, "Music and the Internet: Globalization or Pluralisation?" *New Media and Society* (forthcoming).

111. Colin MacCabe, "Realism and the Cinema: Notes on Some Brechtian Theses," *Screen* 15, no. 2 (1974).

112. For a debate concerning MacCabe's theory of classic realism, see Colin McArthur, "*Days of Hope*," *Screen* 16, no. 4 (1975/6), and MacCabe's response, "*Days of Hope*: A Response to Colin McArthur," *Screen* 17, no. 1 (1976), collected in *Popular Television and Film*, ed. Tony Bennett et al. (London: BFI, 1985).

113. See Susan McClary, "The Blasphemy of Talking Politics During Bach Year," in *Music and Society*, ed. Leppert and McClary; McClary, *Feminine Endings;* and Susan McClary, "Narrative Agendas in 'Absolute' Music: Identity and Difference in Brahms's Third Symphony," in *Musicology and Difference*, ed. Solie.

114. McClary, "The Blasphemy of Talking Politics During Bach Year," 47.

115. Ibid., 51.

116. Ibid., 57.

117. Ibid., 62.

118. A similar problem is raised by McClary's insistent return in her oeuvre to gender as it is coded in musical signification. The question is whether she is sufficiently attuned to cultural and historical differences in gender discourses as they are coded in musical texts. Relatedly, there is a sense of contemporary political overdetermination in her work which prompts one to question whether she is privileging gender vis-à-vis other classificatory, ideological, and narrative structures in music, so that gender risks coming to stand for any and all intramusical forms of difference. If gender becomes a metaphor for theorizing all kinds of difference, its specificity is lost. McClary's own recognition of these problems is hinted at in "Narrative Agendas in 'Absolute' Music," her essay on narrative structures in Brahms's Third Symphony (1993). First she introduces gender as a way of analyzing the ideological dimensions of narrative organization (330–34). Then she proceeds to analyze the symphony (334–40), admitting finally, however, that "in a sense, the 'feminine' Other here is gratuitous, a mere narrative pretext. For the principal dilemma in the symphony is finally oedipal: the archetypal struggle of the rebellious son against the conventional Law of the Father" (340). Later still she portrays the main semiotic conflicts

within the piece as stemming from the restrictions of nineteenth-century tonal and formal conventions (342), and in this way she returns to standard, formalistic musicological ground. The detour through gender seems unnecessary and unconvincing in light of this quite convincing denouement.

119. Ken Hirschkop, "The Classical and the Popular: Musical Form and Social Context," in *Music and the Politics of Culture,* ed. Christopher Norris (London: Lawrence and Wishart, 1989), 286, quoting Mikhail Bakhtin, "Discourse in the Novel," in *The Dialogical Imagination* (Austin: University of Texas Press, 1981), 291.

120. All quotations from Hirschkop, "The Classical and the Popular," 294–95.

121. Julie Brown, *Bartok's Third String Quartet: Interpretative Perspectives* (Royal Musical Association Monographs, forthcoming).

122. For an analysis of the dynamics of identification, pleasure, and desire, but also omnipotence and tyranny, immanent in a global imaginary in music, see Born, "Afterword: Music Policy, Aesthetic and Social Difference," 281–83, 286.

123. For a quite different perspective on composers' intentionality, a perspective, however, in accord with the argument made here that there are definite "marks" of composers' intentionality and experience in the musical text (as score and as performance), see John Butt, "Rewriting Intention in the Historical Performance of Music" (forthcoming).

124. Christopher Norris, "Utopian Deconstruction: Ernst Bloch, Paul de Man and the Politics of Music," in *Music and the Politics of Culture,* ed. Norris, 341.

125. Gilroy, *The Black Atlantic;* Lipsitz, *Dangerous Crossroads.* Another argument for this kind of approach, one "that [would dispute] the very nature of centre-periphery distinctions," is given abstractly in Iain Chambers, "Travelling Sounds: Whose Centre, Whose Periphery?" in *Otherness and the Media: The Ethnography of the Imagined and the Imaged,* ed. Hamid Naficy and Teshome H. Gabriel (Chur, Switzerland: Harwood Academic, 1993).

Musical Belongings:
Western Music and Its Low-Other

Richard Middleton

Music can never "belong" (to me).[1] It is always already "other," always located elsewhere (than here), in the matrix of dialogically constructed codes and historical debris responsible for its specific forms. Its interiority—in one sense real enough, because it is grounded in a sense of the bodily processes of sound production—has been turned into a myth of origination and possession. This is a hard argument for cultural property-owners to accept, but taking that step is—paradoxically—a precondition for any possibility of superseding musical alienation, of losing ourselves in the music, as the phrase goes. The price of any reconciliation between subjectivity and (musical) nature is an acknowledgment of the irreducible mediated sociality of both; for to belong to music (to *a* music)—as distinct from treating it as a belonging—must mean not some pseudoatavistic regression but a reflexive acceptance of the self's dependencies.

The sense of music's "autonomy" intensified in the late eighteenth century, setting off a development in Western music which resulted in the growth of that monstrous superstructure of meaning surrounding musical processes today. An increasingly powerful awareness of music's specificity, set within wider tendencies of rationalization in post-Enlightenment culture, had the effect of reformulating music's position in the cultural field as, first and foremost, a vehicle of expression and representation, and an object of interpretation and discursive elaboration. The nineteenth-century history is well known.[2] But at the same time, this fullness produced a lack. In a complementary movement, there is located "below" the sphere of meaning and reflexivity an image, or a kind of memory, of musical immediacy—of prediscursive musical practices, or musics of nature, often identified with a range of others (archaic, folk, popular, foreign, exotic), whose musics are taken to really, authentically, belong to them. Ironically, it is the development of elaborate alienating meaning systems in the Western musical culture that makes possible the depiction and annexation of these others: only when a sophisticated method of manipulating (mediating) semiotic difference is in place can immediacy be portrayed. At the same time, the fact that in the deconstructive late twentieth century the peculiarities of this apparatus are increasingly visible suggests the start of a new historical phase in which it is becoming clear that only when others are freed to pursue their own trajectories can Western music properly acknowledge the multiplicity of differences lying beneath its authoritarian binaries and become productively other to itself.

This new phase, if such it is, cannot be fully understood outside of a knowledge of the previous history. That in turn demands that we grasp the continuous interplay between the ways in which Western music has treated its others and the broader issue of how difference is articulated in all music. Music as such, it can be said, works by manipulating difference, both structurally—in terms of degrees of repetition, variation, and change—and semiotically, in terms of the dialogues coded into the polyphonies of both musical practice and repertory. In the music-historical field under consideration here, however, these processes are articulated to the network of interests active within social and ideological formations which are structured in dominance. Exploring this interplay between difference-in-general and difference-in-particular, we need to consider how it works within, and connects to, the whole sweep of Western musical developments taking place under the sign of the post-Enlightenment "modernity project." Of special interest are the configurations of what Paul Gilroy has called the "Black Atlantic"—the black other conceived as an active constituent in modernity itself;[3] though I want to think more broadly of a "Low Atlantic," which poses popular against elite, and of how, within that, "low" and black relate to each other.

Nineteenth-century discourses around the philosophy of music continually display the effects of the basic contradiction outlined above: between awareness of music's expanding meaningfulness, on the one hand, and, on the other, a quest for its essential immediacy (sometimes manifesting itself in an unwillingness to shift music as such out of a sphere of pure spontaneity). This tension tracks a parallel one in the contemporary musical practice: an exponential growth in talk about music—from criticism to compositional programs—proceeding alongside the romantic intuition that the "real" meaning of music lies *beyond* words (an intuition formalized by Schopenhauer in his doctrine that music directly embodies the primordial, inarticulate movements of Will, free from any attachments to external objects or rational thought). Nietzsche pointed out that the very idea of the prereflective in music (the naïve, to use Schiller's formulation) is the product precisely of an advanced stage of intellectual reflection. Nevertheless, he himself constructs a history in which music is progressively enveloped by symbolisms and

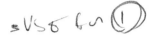

systems of interpretation of various kinds, and he seems to see a level (a "primitive stage of music") that is prior to this history—a level where music operates directly, "of and in itself," "before" the imposition of meaning.[4] This historical model harks back to Rousseau, for whom the origins of both music and language lay in a kind of primitive speech-song which, without recourse to any semiotic convention or conscious manipulation, directly expressed the movements of "spontaneous desire." This "voice of nature," Rousseau argued, was gradually overwhelmed by the growth of harmony, counterpoint and the other "civilized" complexities of compositional technique.[5]

Rousseau's theory, the subject of postmodern critiques by Derrida and De Man,[6] is the most important source for the romantic myth of musical authenticity. It can be felt, for example, behind Kant's more measured tones. Kant places music relatively low in his typology of the arts precisely because it "speaks . . . without concepts," leaving no "food for reflection"; it is thus "more . . . enjoyment than . . . culture."[7] Kant is concerned to distinguish beauty from mere enjoyment, and to some extent he can rescue classical music by means of an appeal to the beauties of its formal coherence—though at the expense of a fastidious demotion of sensuous pleasures, such that, as Lawrence Kramer suggests, he seems to be responding "less to an absence of thought than to the presence of danger";[8] but the attraction as well as the threat of this sensuous underside is palpable. Hegel reformulates and historicizes the Kantian critique, seeing the triumph of "independent" (i.e., instrumental) music as directing music's content increasingly into areas of abstract, "sterile" technique. Paradoxically, by describing music in terms of "sounding inwardness," representing subjectivity directly to itself,[9] Hegel can account for music's centrality in nineteenth-century culture—it is the cutting edge of Spirit—but only in such a way that the resulting sterility inevitably leads to the "end of art," as its function within his historical schema is taken over by philosophical reflection. The prereflective, as summoned up by reflexivity, can only function either as myth (as in Rousseau) or by transmuting into reflexivity (as in Hegel) and self-destructing. Small wonder that Hegel saw the "unreflective" culture of Africa as lying quite outside history, entirely fitted to be "slave" to the Western "master."[10]

It is this sterility, in a culture which he saw as ruled by "criticism," "historicism," and "academicism," that is the starting motivation behind Nietzsche's search for the roots of the "Dionysian spirit," in which "nature itself . . . rises again to celebrate the reconciliation with her prodigal son, man."[11] Richard Wagner, Nietzsche's favored vessel (at least at first) for the longed-for rebirth of a Hellenic fusion of Dionysian and Apollonian tendencies, found the sources of his primitive other in Nordic myths. Ironically, however, he could only clothe it in the most up-to-date compositional and orchestral technique. In an immense, egotistic assimilative move (which is repeated elsewhere, as we shall see), one version of the drama of modernity and its others is played out within the self-contained Wagnerian music-world.

This is one strategy. Its complement is that of projection, where the other, far from being assimilated, is externalized in a sphere of apparent social difference. It is this strategy which explains the attractions of the many thousands of "peasant dances," "Volkslieder," "bohemian rhapsodies," "Scottish" or "Slavic" character pieces, "plantation melodies," and so forth which throng the nineteenth-century repertory. A parallel development is the emergence of musical folklore and anthropology—with their typical romanticizing and exoticizing tendencies—from Herder, the Grimms, Ossian and Scott through to Vaughan Williams and Bartók. Sometimes the two strategies intersect, as at the 1932 Congress of Arab Music in Cairo,[12] where Europeans, including Bartók (who drew on "exotic" folk musics in his own compositions), begged the Arab musicians not to "modernize"; or in the involvement of English Musical Renaissance composers—Vaughan Williams among others—in folk song collection;[13] or in the influence of the early German folk song collectors, such as Herder, on Schubert. In all three of these cases (and many others) it is interesting that the approved other is defined as a defense against a threatening usurper: for Bartók this was city music; for the English composers and collectors, music hall; and for Herder, "the mob of the streets, who never sing or compose but shriek and mutilate."[14] We see that the differentiated sphere can be coded either positive or negative, and many tactical moves, on the part of composers or theorists, concern the interplay that can result.

However divergent their tactics, the aim of both assimilation and projection strategies is to manage the threat posed by potentially infinite difference to the authority of the bourgeois self, by reducing such difference to a stable hierarchy. This may be configured either through binary distinctions, dividing center from periphery, or through co-option of the peripheries into the center's sphere of influence. But the cast of others contains a range of characters and is rarely entirely passive; hierarchic closure is difficult to maintain. I shall be concentrating here on the relationship between Western music and what has been called its "low-other";[15] but, as we shall see, the various types have been to some extent interchangeable, and from the first, the whole range (peasants, primitives, exotics, women, bohemians, lumpen) are liable to be slipped into, connected to, conflated with each other. Yet this in turn only increases the chance that something will not fit—that control will break down.

SHACKLING PAPAGENO

What is at issue here is what Stallybrass and White have called "the formation of the cultural Imaginary [the forbidden zones, denied but desired] of the middle class in post-Renaissance Europe," a process involving "an internal distancing from the popular which was complex and often contradictory in its effects."[16] As mid-eighteenth-century musical style developed a range of internally more differentiated forms, together with the ability to portray a range of social types, behavioral characters and emotional gestures, so the twin strategies of assimilation and projection emerged. Comic low figures, differentiated musically, were a feature of opera from the beginning of the eighteenth century; and "exotics" also appeared, clothed for example in "Turkish" music, or in the pseudobarbaric strains given to the Scythians in Gluck's *Iphigénie en Tauride* (1779). In the famous ballroom scene in *Don Giovanni*, Mozart has three orchestras play simultaneously three dances: a minuet for the aristocracy, a *contre-danse* (urbanized "country dance") for the bourgeoisie, a waltz for the peasants. In instrumental music, such differentiated realms could be assimilated into the composer's controlling vision, as with the popular tunes used by Haydn, or—above all perhaps—through the refining treatment of dance rhythms. The concert use of minuet, then waltz, is especially interesting, enabling the rational bourgeois to deal with the disturbing fascination of the degenerate aristocracy on the one hand, the earthy peasantry on the other.[17]

The new structural principle of sonata was particularly conducive to the depiction of "other" spheres, either through differentiation of themes (for instance, the second theme of a sonata-principle movement was routinely described as "feminine," by contrast with the "masculine" first theme), or differentiation of keys. In 1755 Joseph Riepel published a treatise on key structure,[18] in which the interrelationships of the keys to which a piece was most likely to modulate were portrayed in terms of the social structure of the (high) bourgeois household. The tonic was the "master" key, while dominant, subdominant, and their relative minors represented various grades of servant; thus distant parts of the social sphere could be visited, but in the end they owed their meaning, and must give way to, the hegemony of the paterfamilias. (It is interesting that the relationships of masters and servants is a pervasive theme in Mozart's operas. The figure of the servant [especially female: nurses, maids], both as a marker of social distinction and as a route to forbidden, low-cultural zones, remains a common one into and throughout the nineteenth century.[19]) Fascinatingly, the tonic minor, a much more distant key, and one always suggesting something disturbing, foreign, an outburst of irrationality, is personified by Riepel as *Die schwarze Gredel* ("Black Maggie," Queen Margaret of Sweden, who was notorious for her swarthy complexion). While it seems unlikely that Riepel had heard any black music, it is significant that systemic disturbance to the established musical language is already associated with "blackness." Much later, the minor-ish tendencies of African American "blue notes," and the minor-pentatonic tonality of many blues, would give this association more substance.

Eighteenth- and nineteenth-century techniques of structurally differentiating areas of otherness, through thematic, tonal, or expressive means, have been discussed by several musicologists, notably Susan McClary and Lawrence Kramer.[20] For the romantics such moments are often marked by qualities of lyrical "inwardness" and "immediacy"; they offer a glimpse of something constructed as beyond the grip of bourgeois rationality. While they may be projected on to social others, especially in opera and program music, in absolute music, as Kramer points out, they are usually integrated within the orbit of the monologic gaze of the controlling authorial intent. Where this control is weakened—in some works by Tchaikovsky and Mahler, for example—the form may threaten to fall apart. But this carries our story into the moment of the modernist crisis; for illustration of the more balanced approach to the low-other characteristic of the high-bourgeois phase of European music, we need to move back historically, and no better example can be found than Mozart's opera *The Magic Flute* (1791).

It is a commonplace that this work, a *Singspiel* with Enlightenment and Masonic themes, effects a marvelous interplay and fusion of high and popular elements. What is less often remarked is the *range* of others deployed (women; blacks, in the persons of the "moorish" Monostatos and the slaves; and plebeians, in the form of the comic birdcatcher, Papageno). Of special interest is Mozart's handling of Papageno. This Enlightenment Caliban is, as he tells us himself, a "child of nature," a happy simpleton, whose longings reach no further than food, drink, a good woman, and floods of children. And his music, drawing on the popular ballad style of the *Singspiel* tradition, certainly sets him apart from the high characters. At the same time, however, his simplicity sounds mechanical (see example 1.1): the tick-tock rhythms, the elementary tonic-dominant progressions, the predictable melodic sequences, the banal phrase-structure, produce an effect less like folk song than like rational classicism reduced to its nuts and bolts; or rather, like an image of "folk song" from above. This is a vision of what folk song *ought* to be (i.e., simple) and at the same time what it has become (i.e., rationalized, enchained—just as Papageno's birdcatcher's panpipes rationalize the vagaries of birdsong into the first five notes of the major scale). Conflating the "people" with a Newtonian clockwork nature, this presents the Enlightenment's idea of the low: *under control,* at once a caricature of the other and a mirror-image of the rational self.

When Papageno and Monostatos come face to face, they terrify each other equally ("that is surely the Devil!"); and they are equated musically, singing their halting, frightened phrases in parallel. Later, in the finale of act 1, when the princely hero Tamino charms (Orfeo-like) the birds and beasts with his magic flute, his tune is in a refined *Singspiel* ballad style; and then, when he hears Papageno's pipes, he imitates their scalic figure: thus culture draws on nature, high on low. Immediately, in an echoing invocation of music's magical possessive power, Papageno, with an almost parodically simple tune on

Example 1.1 Mozart, "Der Vogelfänger bin ich ja," from *The Magic Flute*

his magic bells, enchants Monostatos and his slaves, so that they leave off their pursuit and withdraw. A hierarchy of projections is set up, with Papageno as its mediating focus: as the low is to Tamino (i.e., "natural"), so blacks are to Papageno. (Monostatos's later aria, "Alles fühlt der Liebe Freuden," is about as "Turkish" as Papageno's songs are "folky": in both cases, then, the other is heavily mediated by High-Western refinement.)

A parallel structure of relationships links Papageno and Woman.[21] Papageno is woefully lacking in courage ("Be a man!" Tamino says to the terrified birdcatcher; "I wish I were a girl," he replies). He is a "chatterer." The first of the Masonic initiation tests for him and Tamino is that they stay silent, resisting the blandishments of the Three Ladies; "a man thinks before he speaks," he "seeks proof," whereas women are associated with bewitchment, treachery, gossip, and falsehood. But Papageno cannot hold his tongue, and he survives only with Tamino's help (the high solicitously lifting up the low). Early in the opera, Papageno lies to Tamino, and his punishment is to have his mouth padlocked (a scold's bridle?!). The link between his femininity and his "natural" qualities appears musically in the clockwork style of his songs, for, as Huyssen has suggested, the eighteenth century's love of automata quickly developed in such a way that the threat of the robotic machine was conflated with the threat of Woman: the automaton, seen in terms of a clockwork theory of Nature, became coded as feminine (since Woman represented Nature).[22] Mozart himself composed pieces for mechanical musical toys, and the music he wrote for Papageno's magic bells (especially in his act 2 aria and the subsequent Finale) reminds us of this, as it fuses together the magical and the mechanical: the childlike Papageno (unreflective, easily amused) plays at rationality.

So simple is this child of nature that, in the act 2 Finale, united at last with his Papagena, the two of them can only stutter ("Pa—pa—pa"), as if relearning the power of speech.[23] But Papageno can be *taught*. In act 1, as he struggles to speak through his padlocked lips, his musically basic lines to "hm" are echoed and filled out by the tutelary Tamino. In the ensemble that follows (padlock removed), his line becomes somewhat more complex, for musically he is now captured and under guidance. Similarly, in his duet with the heroine Pamina ("Bei Männern, welche Liebe fühlen"), he copies her first phrase; it is simple, but rather too hymnlike, too elevated, for his normal style. Her second phrase gets too difficult for him, and he just adds to it a straightforward bass. By the time the final stages of the opera are reached, this tutoring process enables Papageno, in despair at apparently losing his Papagena, to move from his usual simplicity (tonic-dominant movement, scalic pipe interpolations) into music which is emotionally and harmonically more complex. This final assimilative gesture, its "humanizing" warmth limited by the underlying comedy (of course Papageno lacks the courage to hang himself), marks the boundary beyond which the Enlightenment's anthropology could not push, at the same time as the subtlety and complexity of Mozart's work represent one of that anthropology's high points.

CRIPPLING PORGY

After *The Magic Flute,* it is often argued,[24] the balance of high and popular elements achieved there was unrepeatable; they tended to split apart. What is more interesting to consider is the myriad strategies that evolved for dealing with this situation. Projective exoticism and assimilative self-assertion (for example, in theories of popular music as nothing more than *gesunkenes Kulturgut*—"cultured" musical materials that have descended, diluted, to be taken up by the uncreative masses) chased each other around the nineteenth-century musical field. And these tendencies continued to energize twentieth-century developments, taking ever new forms. With the spread of African American styles, notably jazz, conflations of black and low took on a greater intensity, resulting in complex, two-way negotiations within white popular music.[25] Indeed, it is increasingly in white responses (musical and verbal) to "black" styles that the clearest musical and discursive representations of bourgeois feelings about subterranean cultural experience are to be found. Depictions of early jazz as "primitive"—both positively and negatively charged— have been well researched;[26] just as characteristic were *denials* of the music's particularity, assuming their most sophisticated form in Adorno's reduction of jazz to "diluted romanticism," its internal differences to "pseudo-individualization."[27] It is clear too in Adorno's discussions how the historical context—the emergence of monopoly capitalism, the rise of mass culture, artistic modernism—gave these impulses a new sharpness. In the shadow both of World War I and of emerging Depression and totalitarianism, the bourgeoisie and intelligentsia of the 1920s and early 1930s readily located a challenge to "civilization," welcome or not, in the threat posed by the new popular musics.

In the U.S., the period was highly racially charged as well; and George Gershwin's opera *Porgy and Bess,* with its all-black cast and its use of "black" musical idioms, excited controversy from its very first performance in 1935. It is a kind of *Carmen* set in a folk South, in which the heroic but naive Porgy is physically crippled: he is never going to succeed in the "real world." The relationship in the opera between the "folk" world of Catfish Row—innocent and arcadian—and the values of a modernizing America—grown-up, sophisticated, corrupt—which are forever intruding can be linked to the central debates which have surrounded the work, focusing as they do either on the question of exploitation (does Gershwin steal from black music? does he patronize his characters?) or on that of aesthetic status (does the piece succeed in the grown-up world of opera?).[28] *Porgy and Bess* also reminds us of *The Magic Flute.* We feel Gershwin striving after a Mozartian encompassing balance of styles and social layers. At the same time, compared with the earlier work, his opera does move its center of gravity significantly toward the low: virtually all the characters are black and poor, and their important moments of musical otherness are painted in stand-out colors. Against this, telling the story not in speech but in florid recitative (as neither Mozart nor Bizet in *Carmen* does) yanks the aesthetic fulcrum back toward high art convention.

David Horn, in an attractive argument,[29] has suggested that we relax the critical pressure on Gershwin and allow the characters to speak in their varied specificity. Yet for all the musical eclecticism of *Porgy and Bess* and the tensions that result, one feels that the authorial Gershwin is always pulling at the strings. The characters are allowed a range of idioms, which, in the context of the overall stylistic location of the work, are not difficult to interpret; they range from Sportin' Life's slithery sensual chromatics to Porgy's folky-cum-heroic lyricism, from the "ecstasy" of the religious pieces to the neoprimitive abandon of the picnic scene. Yet in the end this differentiation of the other is circumscribed by the framework of genre: the black idioms are encased, put in their place, by the style, orchestration, and structural conventions of late-romantic opera. By choosing to write in this genre, Gershwin is unavoidably constrained by received power-relationships between high and low; his attempt to unify the work through use of the Wagnerian leitmotif technique is symptomatic of his hope that "the element within him that was Porgy might one day come to terms with the element that was Sportin' Life."[30] Thus the Gershwin psyche is the chief character. Against the pull, perhaps, of his own marginal status (his Jewishness, his Tin Pan Alley background, both of which must have motivated his identification with his low-others), he has situated himself where he is inevitably heir to the nineteenth-century strategy of imposing monologic authorial control on disparate materials, and where the only method available to him of representing "low-life" is through the code of the picturesque.

Like Neil Leonard's description of Gershwin's *Rhapsody in Blue* as "Liszt in blackface," Rudi Blesh's criticism of *Porgy and Bess* is cruel but revealing: "It is Negroesque. . . . [Like] the earlier travesty of minstrelsy . . . the Negro . . . is set forth as an entertainer singing a music that the white public finds to be just like *its own*."[31] This catches the work's dilution of "authenticity" in the picturesque, and at the same time the tension set up between appropriation and assimilation, difference and control. Gershwin himself insisted that he had composed "folk music"; but he also explained that he "decided against the use of traditional folk materials because I wanted the music to be all of one piece. Therefore I wrote my own spirituals and folk songs." His 1927 comment relating to *Rhapsody in Blue* is in similar vein: "Certain types of it [jazz] are in bad taste, but I do think it has certain elements which can be developed. I do not know whether it will be jazz when it is finished."[32]

The clearest examples of otherness, projected on to black characters, are the folky set-pieces: the children's song (act 3, scene 3); the prayers and shouts of the religious Serena; the chorus "I Ain't Got No Shame" (act 2, scene 2—the picnic scene), with its frenzied pseudoprimitive drumming; the fishermen's spiritual/work song (act 2, scene 1); the street-sellers' cries ("Here come the honeyman," for example). Even here, however, the authentic is *presented* to us; we see through Gershwin's eyes. Thus the honeyman's haunting pentatonic cry is surrounded by a harmonic "haze" created by drones and ostinatos, which has the effect of magically placing the scene in a distant landscape within the composer's mind—a place of trance and lost innocence. Porgy's minstrelized "I Got Plenty o' Nuttin'" draws on a different stereotype. But the musical differences between its simple scalic tune, with rag-style syncopations and banjo-strum accompaniment, and the pentatonics and blue notes of the other pieces mentioned does not disguise the ideological link, which lies in the picturing of simplicity.

"I Got Plenty" is an equivalent to the Enlightened folk songs that Mozart wrote for Papageno: civilization's parody of the precultured. And this assimilative impulse comprises the other pole in Gershwin's aesthetic strategy. At the beginning of the opera, the orchestral Introduction, with its repetitive pentatonic figurations over static harmonies and ostinati, is meant to transport us to an imagined Eden, as Mellers writes;[33] but it is a New Yorker's

Example 1.2 Gershwin, Porgy's theme, from *Porgy and Bess*

Eden, mediated through glittery symphonic sound—a canvas of exotic colors and showy rhythmic oomph. Jazzbo Brown's "lowdown blues," which follows, encases its bluesy phrases in fashionable (at the time) Tin Pan Alley piano chromatics (the style of Gershwin the nightclub pianist, in fact). "Roll Dem Bones," the chorus which then introduces the crap game, is an imitation spiritual—but the orchestration (string tremolandos and high-register violins doubled at the octave) turn this into melodrama. Similarly, when Porgy enters, he is announced by his orchestral leitmotif, a blues cliché (example 1.2). But this is delivered in Puccinian violin octaves, accompanied by "modernistic" parallel-sliding triads: the folk-hero is romanticized (in more than one sense—he is both folklorized and elevated).

As in *The Magic Flute*, assimilation slips into paternalism. The marvelous love songs for Porgy and Bess work by extending their bluesy modal starting ideas into long-breathed, upward-straining Puccinian lyricism, complete with lump-in-the-throat chromatic modulations. Porgy and Bess have to learn that, while "black" idioms are fine for Eden, grown-up emotions like personal love require the manner of European late romanticism. Bess's "divorce" from Crown turns her "from woman to lady" (act 2, scene 1), and Porgy, who buys her release, turns from innocent beggar to patriarchal provider. As they imagine leaving the folk, their music crosses the class-cultural barrier.

Like *The Magic Flute*, Gershwin's opera both exposes and exploits to the utmost the limits imposed on its project by genre convention and cultural situation. In large part its terrific power arises from the resulting tension, in particular the tension associated with the effort to bring musical (and social) multiplicity into line with the simpler structure of a high/low binary. Working on the composition, Gershwin made a research trip to South Carolina. It represented less an "exploration," wrote Dubose Heyward (author of the original novel and part librettist of the opera) than a "homecoming." One day, Gershwin heard a prayer-meeting of "shouting Negroes." He joined in—but he outshouted them: he "stole the show."[34] He loved what he heard, as what perhaps seemed to him to encapsulate an important part of himself; but—and here is the strategy of *Porgy and Bess* in a nutshell—difference was effaced, as projection and assimilation merged in the assertion of authority: he had to be master.

PAPAGENO/PORGY ANSWERS BACK

The composer Virgil Thomson commented acutely on the strategy of Porgy and Bess: "Folklore subjects recounted by an outsider are only valid as long as the folk in question is unable to speak for itself, which is certainly not true of the American Negro in 1935."[35] How, then, did this other speak? Can the low answer back?

Much of George Gershwin's education in low-life and black music took place in the nightclubs of Harlem, increasingly at that time a playground for affluent white slummers.[36] This white invasion was connected to a broader crisis in, and restructuring of, white bourgeois values evident since the turn of the century, but in the context of the jazz age, it took on a new intensity and meaning, focusing its exploration of low culture on "the Negro"—who at the same time could be kept conveniently at arm's length in the ghetto.[37] For Nathan Huggins, "Harlem seemed a cultural enclave that had magically survived the psychic fetters of Puritanism." "White folks," wrote Claude McKay, "discovered black magic there." James Weldon Johnson observed the visitors "seeking to recapture a state of primitive joy in life and living; trying to work their way back into that jungle which was the original Garden of Eden; in a word, doing their best to pass for colored." Rudolph Fisher remarked that "Now Negroes go to their own cabarets to see how white people act. And what do we see? Why, we see them actually playing Negro games . . . and they do them all better than I!"[38] Nowhere was this ersatz exoticism more in evidence than at Harlem's Cotton Club, where black dancers and musicians performed for all-white audiences, against a "jungle" decor, putting on shows with "a primitive naked quality that was supposed to make a civilized audience lose its inhibitions."[39] A typical program from 1929 advertised a "Congo Jamboree . . . an exhibition of unrestrained Nubian abandon."[40] Here Duke Ellington's "Jungle Band," in residence from 1927 to 1932, was responsible for the pseudoprimitive musical ambience (which was relayed across the U.S. on network radio).

Ellington was to criticize the "lamp-black Negroisms" of *Porgy and Bess*.[41] Criticisms of a similar sort, applied more widely to the whole phenomenon of black popular music's new-found appeal, came from many Harlem Renaissance intellectuals, who saw the songs, dances and shows as a new minstrelsy, simply updating stereotypes.[42] Ellington, master of the "pure put-on,"[43] seems to have played his role at the Cotton Club with equanimity; yet he was intensely serious about his music, rejecting the "jazz" label and claiming that African American musical forms "are as much an art medium as are the most profound works of the famous classical composers."[44] Ellington the man was equally as complex as the situation in which he and other black musicians found themselves, and there are no simple ways to resolve this apparent contradiction. We can start to understand its dynamics, though, by looking first at his upbringing in black middle-class Washington, D.C., and second at his working methods.

The Washington black bourgeoisie was proper and ambitious, its ideology of betterment centered on a sense of racial aspiration. Ellington never lost the combination of courtesy (which could include an ironic use of the minstrel's mask) and drive, nor the ambition of writing (and extending) the story of "his people." At the same time, he mixed easily with other classes, and his musical training mostly came, informally, from low-class musicians. Yet many of these—Will Marion Cook, for instance—were working for a serious popular music, insisting on the need for respectability in order to counter destructive stereotyping.[45] Working within this mix of social and ideological forces enabled Ellington to play off the different strategies against one another. Of course, this does not rule out the possibility of simply assimilating to white bourgeois norms; and arguably this sometimes happens—in some of the later large-scale concert works, for example.[46] More commonly, I would say, the cultural context that nurtured Ellington, marked by awareness of multiple black histories, could make available a "jungle to Harlem" narrative capable of *relocating* the jungle into a modern here and now—a narrative, then, which, rather than assimilating completely to Darwinian models of social and racial progress, worked to inscribe them in a project organized around the laying out of a quite "new territory."[47] Central to this strategy was an acceptance of difference within black music. Just as Duke mixed easily in different class spheres, so he both brought together disparate ideas and idioms and treated his band as a source of *collective* composition, encouraging and learning from his players' contributions.[48] It is possible to exaggerate Ellington's easy-going tolerance of diversity; yet even in pieces that demonstrate the imprint of his structural planning, the content rarely succumbs to a Gershwinian single-mindedness. This is not to say that the authorial Ellington just relinquishes control. Given the legacy of "double consciousness" deeply imprinted within African American culture, the constellations of self/other relations must in fact take on peculiarly complex forms here—a point with important implications for interpretation of the music, as we shall see.

Jazz historians have generally neglected Ellington's Cotton Club period, treating it at best as formative for later, more important developments.[49] This is rather unfair to some excellent music and, more important here, ignores the light it can cast on ways in which subaltern others can "answer back." Inheriting the nineteenth-century disposition to musical pictorialism,[50] Ellington was easily capable of meeting the demand for fashionable Orientalism (e.g., in "Japanese Dream" and "Arabian Lover," both 1929—replete with gongs, tinkly piano, woodblocks, etc.); and of transferring this exoticizing aesthetic to the strand in his own music that was becoming known as his "jungle style." In "Diga-Diga-Doo" (1928), the clichéd phrases over tonic drone chord come over now as comically simplified, the cymbal crashes as extravagant, the heavily strummed beat as "primitive" and the growled trumpet solo as melodramatically "barbaric"; is this Papageno/Porgy, tongue firmly in cheek, performing for his betters?[51] But the jungle style was an autonomous development, emerging some years before the Cotton Club residency,[52] and for other reasons. It was in large part the creation of trumpeter Bubber Miley and trombonist Joe Nanton, whose "talking" plunger-mute techniques derived from New Orleans sources; and when Ellington heard Miley's "gutbucket" stuff, he said (with slight exaggeration), he forgot all about "sweet music": "As a student of Negro history I had, in any case, a natural inclination in this direction."[53] In the 1927 "Black and Tan Fantasy" (credited to Miley and Ellington),[54] all the ingredients of the style—"growling" brass, heavy stomping four-beat rhythm, minor key with blues inflections—are used to intensely serious effect; but the "jungle" sections are cobbled together with an alto sax solo of nightclub sensuality and a piano bridge in cabaret style—with no attempt to finesse the differences into a single perspective.

Definitive interpretation of Ellington's "jungle" music is impossible, however. No doubt contemporary response varied, in part along lines driven by racial and class divisions and by differing cultural-political sympathies. One might nevertheless hear in Ellington's output from this period something of a passage between (to use the words of a contemporary critic) "stunts" on the one hand, and, on the other, "'effects' that are effects" (that is, which effect something "original and striking").[55] Even so, it is still possible to hear many recordings in more than one way, as they resist ideological closure. "Jungle Blues" (1930), for example, frames its growled solos with an introduction and coda which superimpose dissonant horn chords ("modernistic"?—or "comically braying"?) over a drone-like open fifth ("powerful"?—or "pointedly crude"?) in the rhythm section. "Jungle Nights in Harlem" (1930) collects together the usual growled trumpet solo, with stuttering ("pre-linguistic"?) repeated notes, extravagant screeches and swoops from Johnny Hodges's alto, and scale figurations from Barny Bigard's clarinet which might sound almost manic; background unison sax riffs outline the atmosphere, popular in jazz at the time, of melodramatic, minor-key foreboding, while Sonny Greer's continuous whiplash rim-shots could easily suggest barbaric ritual. The result, arguably, is an almost garish jungle evocation, delivered however with a gloss which distances the musicians from the message: "Man, look how terribly primitive we are!" they seem to say.[56]

There are other pieces, however, where, leaving the mask where it is, their gaze seems to swivel round, now pointing inward, into the new territory that the style makes available. "Echoes of the Jungle" (1931; credited to trumpeter Cootie Williams) draws on the same mixture of (basically simple) elements, but welds them into a richly elaborate variety of textures which capture the listener, pulling us into a quite new sound-world, functioning on its own terms. "Old Man Blues" (1930) pursues the same line of development, at faster tempo: pounding open fifths and talking muted-trumpet chords leave behind any purely "stunt"-like quality they might once have had, and now strike one as marks of cultural self-confidence.[57] This is a line that in one direction decisively colored Ellington's particular variant of 1930s big-band swing, and in another was to lead to his large-scale concert work of 1943, *Black, Brown and Beige*, "A Tone Parallel to the History of the Negro in America."[58] Nineteen years earlier, Paul Whiteman's famous Aeolian Hall concert, at which Gershwin's *Rhapsody in Blue* was premiered, had highlighted the assimilation of a tamed jazz to a middle-class white agenda (or, to put it in Whiteman's words, had signalled "that it was a great deal more than savage rhythm from the jungle"[59]). Ellington's badly received Carnegie Hall performance, criticized ever since for pretentiousness and formal incoherence, may on the contrary be taken to mark not any "jungle to concert hall" (minstrelsy to assimilationism) career move but an experiment whose indulgence of pluralism envisions a new world: a world conceived not as "populated by endangered authenticities—pure products always going crazy. Rather it makes space for specific [and diverse] paths through modernity."[60]

From 1926 to 1939 Ellington was managed by Irving Mills—a man who made his initial reputation in the music business, typically for of the 1920s, by buying "blues," *any* blues, from their composers, for flat $20 fees, and whose efforts as promoter, publisher, and agent certainly played a large part in Ellington's commercial success, particularly with white audiences, at the Cotton Club and more widely. Mills's other star performer was singer, bandleader, and showman extraordinaire Cab Calloway (who followed Ellington into the Cotton Club). Calloway's mixture of "scat" singing, "jive" lingo and "freak" instrumental effects, set in the context of pieces that conjured up a hepster's Harlem (complete with arcane references to weird characters and drug-filled lifestyles), might offer a clue to interpretation of Ellington's jungle style, on which Calloway drew. Both coupled an exotic appeal to captivated whites (probably engineered to a considerable extent by Mills) with a new and quite specific "path through modernity"—an urban-jungle subculturalism, rooted in black popular tastes but routed toward the hip, hybrid modernistic art of bebop.[61]

STRATEGIES OF SIGNIFYING

Henry Louis Gates identifies "Signifyin(g)"—continual reworking of a "changing same"—as the master-trope of black cultural practice.[62] Drawing on a distinction (and on terms) introduced by Houston Baker in his discussion of African American modernism and the Harlem Renaissance, we can identify two different yet overlapping strategies of Signifyin(g). On the one hand, *mastery of form* denotes the minstrelesque "liberating manipulation of masks," while on the other, *deformation of mastery*, by counterposing to the norms a knowingly alien discourse, performs an act of territorialization, an assertion of self which is "never simply a coming into being, but always, also, a release from a BEING POSSESSED."[63] As we have seen, both strategies would seem to be exemplified in Duke Ellington's music. Baker stresses that they are not mutually exclusive alternatives but continuously interacting possibilities, sliding between each other; and we can actually observe such a slide in one critic's response to Ellington's "Black and Tan Fantasy." Writing in 1932, R. D. Darrell recounts that "I laughed like everyone else over its instrumental wa-waing and garbling and gobbling. . . . But as I continued to play the record . . . I laughed less heartily and with less zest. In my ears the whinnies and wa-was began to resolve into new tone colors, distorted and tortured, but agonizingly expressive. The piece took on a surprising individuality . . . a twisted beauty that grew on me more and more and could not be shaken off."[64] As the music is heard as freeing itself from the demands of the mask, so Darrell, freed in turn from the burden of his controlling gaze, is able to accede to the *music's* demands, to *belong* to it.

Twentieth-century popular music has continued to be strung between the various discursive and ideological forces sketched in the previous two sections—drawn in particular between the pull of authenticity on the one hand and of legitimation on the other—while on occasion essaying momentary "deformations of mastery." Of course, white popular styles are (as was Gershwin) in a peculiarly complex position. Not only do they stand as other to the "high" cultural levels in our society, but they often act at the same time as the hegemonic self in relation to the other of black music.[65] African American culture has remained at the point of maximum sensitivity—"He who would enter the twenty-first century, must come by way of me," said James Baldwin[66]—but in recent decades, as the global economy and postcolonial politics have expanded the cast of characters available to the Western cultural drama, the category of "world music" has entered the field of debate as well. Nowhere have the effects been more dramatic than in South Africa.

Fueled by racial oppression and latterly by the structures of apartheid, minstrelsy has been a constant presence.[67] The very terms of discourse (civilization on the one hand, roots on the other) were set by the master-culture, and many of the available models came from European and U.S. (especially African American) sources. "Tribal" musics were easily linked with the "homeland" ideology. Apparently simple "township jazz" styles—jive, *kwela*—

could offer an image of colorful, dancing, happy-go-lucky blacks, show-cased also in musical shows like *Ipi Tombi* (1974). Working against this histori-cal background, neotraditional musicians of the 1980s—*mbaqanga* star Mahlathini, *mbube* vocal group Ladysmith Black Mambazo, for example— inevitably faced the criticism that they were acceding to the projections con-structed in white myths of black music (and the "ethnic" stations of the South African Broadcasting Corporation certainly had no difficulty in aligning them with their own "separate development" ideology). In both cases, however, there is also the possibility that Signifyin(g) on received elements was tak-ing place. Ladysmith Black Mambazo, for instance, cooled the extravagant "bombing" style of *mbube* which they inherited (as if to say, look, we blacks may be reassuringly primitive but we can sing these ethnic riffs sweetly, and in tune!),[68] while Mahlathini set the call-and-response and growled vocals of rural Zulu tradition in an aggressive (electrified) township context (the jun-gle urbanized). Behind the mask, then, moves of "liberating manipulation" could perhaps be found.[69]

Assimilationism has an equally long history, in the hands both of whites and middle-class blacks (for example, the hymns and refined "ragtime" of Reuben Caluza[70]—or indeed, the anthem of the African National Congress, and now of the new South African state as well, "Nkosi Sikele iAfrica"). A re-vealing moment is represented by Paul Simon's 1986 album *Graceland,* which uses compositions, performers, and recordings with a variety of origins (American and South African—including Ladysmith Black Mambazo), mix-ing them together in New York. Many songs fuse aspects of different genres and styles. Yet, like Gershwin in *Porgy and Bess,* Simon clearly dominates, both musically and commercially (he takes the lion's share of royalties), cleaning up and interpreting his ethnic sources so that they support the visions of a white, middle-class American singer-songwriter. "The Boy in the Bubble" is representative, overdubbing an existing record by Tao Ea Matsekha in the driving, accordion-dominated *sheshwe* style with Simon's vocals and new gui-tar and synthesizer parts. The South African sound becomes a support for Simon's elliptical lyrics, and by the end it is swamped by the predominantly synthesized texture. Andrew Tracey complains that "Africa provides the rhythm section, the body of the pop music world, while Europe provides the melody, the head. . . . It is the Black man's job to help the White man do his thing. . . . Is African music only good for backings, not frontings?"[71] The fit Simon effects is powerful and imaginative, and certainly is a technological "miracle and wonder," as the lyrics have it; but, again as in *Porgy,* the limita-tions imposed by genre and by context (here economic as well as ideologi-cal) seem to me decisive, for, while "these are [indeed] the days of lasers in the jungle," the end result here is that the jungle is beamed back home, do-mesticated, to our New York loft.[72]

Example 1.3 John Knox Bokwe, "Ulo thix'o mkhulu" (The Great Hymn). Transcribed by Veit Erlmann from a recording by the Zwelitsha Choral Society of Kingwilliamstown, Cape Province, directed by S. T. Bokwe (the soloist), recorded by Hugh Tracey (International Library of African Music AMA TR-26, 1957).

The South African history, however, displays patterns of far more complex negotiation than the simple schema sketched above indicates.[73] Thus, for instance, John Knox Bokwe's "Great Hymn" (c. 1880), a cornerstone of early middle-class black nationalist culture, is already couching its Europeanized triads and simple triple meter in overlapping call-and-response textures and an alternating two-chord structure derived from Xhosa sources (example 1.3).[74] And a later variant, "Ilezwe Ngelethu," sung by trade union choirs in the 1980s, gives it a political rather than religious text and a vigorous, syncopated rhythm, carrying it clearly into "new territory."[75]

Such "deformations of mastery" have become more common in recent years: they can often be found, for example, in the work of pianist-composer Abdullah Ibrahim. In his *Soweto Is Where It's At,*[76] the basic material—a four-chord sequence repeated virtually unbroken for the whole twenty-minute

Example 1.4 Theme from Abdullah Ibrahim, *Soweto Is Where It's At* (*Tintinyana,* Kaz LP 103, 1988 [track recorded 1975]). Transcription by author.

performance—could easily have become stereotypically other: the sequence, and its structural use in this way, derive from earlier black urban styles (*marabi, kwela, mbube*) and before that from the use of pitch cycles in rural South African musics; and "endless repetition" is endemic throughout the region. But the variety of textures used, the mixture of improvising styles in the superimposed solos, and the jazz phrasings in the horn theme and backings rule out any single, "authentic" cultural location. However, the chord sequence (example 1.4) actually points, culturally, both ways: while the I-IV-I$^6_4$-V^7 progression is a classic of South African popular styles, it is also a classical music cliché—typically Mozartian (or, even more, Rossinian). In that European context it functions as a cadence figure—a way of signaling closure, exerting control. Indeed, Rossini uses it, as part of the notorious "Rossini crescendo," to build a final climax, inciting his audience to tumultuous applause. What happens in Ibrahim's piece, then, is that closure is rewritten as process, cadence as endless chain—an open-endedness energized by rhythmic drive and constant rhythmic, melodic, and textural shifts. The monologic gaze is rejected, perspective opened out. The people, pictured by Rossini (according to some critics) as puppets, mindlessly clapping at what they have been given, are refigured as a participating body—a body politic.

The "double consciousness" implicit in Ibrahim's piece has been associated with the African American experience ever since W. E. B. Dubois wrote about its quality of "second sight . . . this sense of always looking at oneself through the eyes of others"; and Dubois already extended the idea to postcolonial peoples in general: it figures, for example, in Aimé Césaire's conception of *négritude*.[77] It may be characteristic of *all* others who become conscious of their position, and are enabled to open up the internal dialogics inherent in their cultural miscegeny.[78] And such consciousness may be a precondition of productive strategies of Signifyin(g) (or "answering back"); as Baker puts it, today "any conceivable global modernism . . . must be articulated through Caliban's [Papageno's, Porgy's] expressive traditions—traditions that sing a joyful song on the far side of an acknowledgment of the fictional character of 'self' and 'other.'"[79]

In such strategies, the demands of meaning are inescapable. No retreat is available from the increasingly intense play of representations so characteristic of the cultural sphere under the conditions of modernity. Thus struggles over music's meaning—for particular discursive translations of musical signifiers—cannot but be fought. Yet there have been arguments that much of music's power stems from a capacity to slip the leash of these discursive mechanisms, engaging us on a less reflective level—a level that, elsewhere, I have conceptualized as one of "gesture."[80] It is possible that it is in this arena where the most radical attempts at "deformation of mastery" take place: where, for example, Abdullah Ibrahim's treatment of his four-chord sequence does not so much contest its meaning as redesign its implications for our sense of the body's location in time and space. The result is to produce a sense of a particular "gestural habitus"—a place where, as an embodied organism rather than a reflecting consciousness, one can *feel at home.*[81]

There is a danger here of reinstating romantic myths of immediacy. Yet such myths misrecognize a truth. If we conceive the gestural sphere not as that of some kind of mystical unmediated "presence" but as simply that of practical, as opposed to discursive, consciousness, we see that what the romantic theories get wrong is the structure of possession. While music can never belong to us (as myths of authenticity would wish), belonging *to* a music (making ourselves at home within its territory) is distinctly possible.[82] As we have seen, however, for low-others this sort of possession normally functions as a kind of tenancy, for they themselves are possessed—their home belongs to the master. Deformation makes possible strategies which, because they break down binaries, freeing the other to express his or her internal differences, also free the master-discourse to accept its own differences to itself (rather than projecting them outwards or assimilating them into false identity). Needless to say, this can never guarantee the new position against a further move of projection or assimilation. Short of utopia—or at least an end to gross social hierarchies—a permanent condition of negotiation represents the limit of the musical politics available to the low-other.

NOTES

1. Whatever faults might remain, this chapter owes a good deal to helpful comments made not only by the editors but also by Dave Laing and David Horn.

2. The usual historical image of the eighteenth century, which sees the rise of Viennese Classicism as signalling a move *away* from explicit meaningfulness into "pure form," is misleading. As Agawu has shown (*Playing with Signs* [Princeton: Princeton

University Press, 1991]), this music is ruled by an elaborate semiotics of musical "topics." Neither can nineteenth-century formalism be offered as a counterargument. Whether Kantian or Hanslichian, such formalism does not deny meaning, but is concerned just to distinguish external associations from what is taken to be the untranslatable significance of "the music itself."

3. See Paul Gilroy, *The Black Atlantic: Modernity and Double Consciousness* (London: Verso, 1993).

4. Friedrich Nietzsche, *Human, All Too Human*, trans. R. J. Hollindale (Cambridge: Cambridge University Press, 1986), 99.

5. Jean-Jacques Rousseau, "On the Origin of Language" (extracts), in *Music and Aesthetics in the Eighteenth and Early-Nineteenth Centuries*, ed. Peter Le Huray and James Day (Cambridge: Cambridge University Press, 1981), 92, 105.

6. Summarized in the contributions by Alastair Williams and Christopher Norris to *Music and the Politics of Culture*, ed. Christopher Norris (London: Lawrence and Wishart, 1989).

7. Immanuel Kant, *The Critique of Judgement*, trans. James Creed Meredith (Oxford: Oxford University Press, 1952), 193, 194.

8. Lawrence Kramer, *Music as Cultural Practice 1800–1900* (Berkeley: University of California Press, 1991), 4.

9. There is an incisive critique of Hegel's theory of musical immediacy in Lucy Green, *Music on Deaf Ears* (Manchester: Manchester University Press, 1988), 12–16.

10. G. W. F. Hegel, *Lectures on the Philosophy of World History*, trans. H. B. Nisbet (Cambridge: Cambridge University Press, 1975), 173–90.

11. Friedrich Nietzsche, *The Birth of Tragedy*, trans. Francis Golffing (New York: Doubleday, 1956), 23.

12. See Ali Jihad Racy, "Historical Worldviews of Early Ethnomusicologists: An East-West Encounter in Cairo, 1932," in *Ethnomusicology and Modern Music History*, ed. Stephen Blum, Philip V. Bohlman, and Daniel M. Neuman (Urbana: University of Illinois Press, 1991), 68–91.

13. Vic Gammon has dissected the ideology behind this moment; see his "Folk Song Collecting in Sussex and Surrey, 1843–1914," *History Workshop Journal* 10 (1980): 61–89.

14. Herder quoted in Peter Burke, *Popular Culture in Early Modern Europe* (London: Temple Smith, 1978), 22.

15. Peter Stallybrass and Allon White, *The Politics and Poetics of Transgression* (London: Methuen, 1986).

16. Ibid., 193.

17. On the parallels constructed in the eighteenth-century bourgeois mind between these higher and lower groups, see ibid., chapter 2.

18. *Grundregeln zur Tonordnung insgemein* (1755).

19. For example, in Victorian Britain, Arthur Munby secretly married his servant Hannah Cullwick. She had to abase herself for his voyeuristic pleasure, black up and dress as a slave, but also take him on her knee like a child. See Stallybrass and White, *Politics and Poetics*, 151, 154–56. Only a few years after Mozart's operas were written, Hegel, in his celebrated and influential discourse on "masters and slaves," was laying out the terms with which the relationship between the self/other dialectic and the structure of bourgeois consciousness could be discussed; see *The Phenomenology*

of Mind, trans. J. B. Baillie (New York: Harper and Row, 1967; first published 1807), chapter 4.

20. Kramer, *Music as Cultural Practice*, especially chapter 6; Susan McClary, "Pitches, Expression, Ideology: A Exercise in Mediation," *Enclitic* 7 (1983): 76–86, and "A Musical Dialectic from the Enlightenment: Mozart's *Piano Concerto in G Major, K.453*, Movement 2," *Cultural Critique* 4 (1986): 129–69.

21. For a feminist reading of *The Magic Flute*, see Catherine Clement, *Opera, or the Undoing of Women*, trans. Betsy Wing (Minneapolis: University of Minnesota Press, 1988), 70–76. Clement also remarks on the importance of class relationships in the opera but does not pursue the musical implications of this point.

22. Andreas Huyssen, "The Vamp and the Machine: Fritz Lang's *Metropolis*," in *After the Great Divide* (Bloomington: University of Indiana Press, 1986), 65–81. Popular culture also became coded as feminine (passive, irrational, garrulous, repetitive, etc.) in the nineteenth century, creating a threefold system of equations: Machine–Woman–People. See Huyssen, "Mass Culture as Woman: Modernism's Other," in ibid., 44–62; Tania Modleski, "Femininity as Mas(s)querade: A Feminist Approach to Mass Culture," in *High Theory, Low Culture: Analysing Popular Television and Film*, ed. Colin McCabe (Manchester: Manchester University Press, 1986), 37–52.

23. Would it be far-fetched to think of this reinitiation into the symbolic order of language as invoking the Lacanian Law of the Father ("pa-pa")?

24. For example, in Theodor W. Adorno, *Introduction to the Sociology of Music*, trans. E. B. Ashton (New York: Seabury Press, 1976), 22.

25. On the black-low relationship, see e.g. Gilroy, *The Black Atlantic*.

26. E.g., in Neil Leonard, *Jazz and the White Americans: The Acceptance of a New Art Form* (Chicago: University of Chicago Press, 1962).

27. This view can be found in any of Adorno's writings on jazz; for a survey, see J. Bradford Robinson, "The Jazz Essays of Theodor Adorno: Some Thoughts on Jazz Reception in Weimar Germany," *Popular Music* 13 (1994): 1–25.

28. On the debates surrounding *Porgy and Bess*, see Richard Crawford, "It Ain't Necessarily Soul: Gershwin's 'Porgy and Bess' as a Symbol," *Yearbook of Inter-American Musical Research* (1972): 17–38; David Horn, "Who Loves You Porgy?" in *The American Musical in Context*, ed. Robert Lawson-Peebles (Exeter: University of Exeter Press, 1994), 109–26; David Horn, "From Catfish Row to Granby Street: Contesting Meaning in *Porgy and Bess*," *Popular Music* 13 (1994): 165–74.

29. Horn, "Who Loves You Porgy?"

30. Wilfrid Mellers, *Music in a New Found Land: Themes and Developments in the History of American Music* (London: Barrie and Rockcliff, 1964), 412. On leitmotif technique in *Porgy*, see Lawrence Starr, "Toward a Re-evaluation of Gershwin's 'Porgy and Bess,'" *American Music* 2, no. 2 (1984): 25–37.

31. Leonard, *Jazz*, 84; Blesh, quoted in Crawford, "It Ain't Necessarily Soul," 33. Emphasis in original.

32. Gershwin, quoted in Crawford, "It Ain't Necessarily Soul," 26; in Hollis Alpert, *The Life and Times of Porgy and Bess: The Story of an American Classic* (London: Nick Hern Books, 1990), 81; and in Leonard, *Jazz*, 84. Amusingly, just as Gershwin arguably condescends to his musical sources, so some of the critics condescended to him. A series of displacements is set up as Virgil Thomson describes *Porgy*'s "freshness . . .

the hall-mark of *les grandes natures.* . . . I like its lack of respectability, the way it can be popular and vulgar. . . . He didn't know much . . . but his musical heart was really pure." (Quoted in Crawford, "It Ain't Necessarily Soul," 25–26.)

33. Mellers, *Music in a New Found Land,* 393.

34. Quoted in Edward Jablonski, *Gershwin* (Garden City: Doubleday, 1987), 273. For an account of Gershwin's trip to South Carolina, see Alpert, *Life and Times,* 88–90.

35. Virgil Thomson, quoted in Crawford, "It Ain't Necessarily Soul," 30.

36. Ed Kirkeby documents this aspect of Gershwin's life; see the quotation from him in Samuel A. Floyd Jr., "Music in the Harlem Renaissance: An Overview," in *Black Music in the Harlem Renaissance: A Collection of Essays,* ed. Samuel A. Floyd Jr. (Westport, Conn.: Greenwood Press, 1990), 22. (Floyd also argues that "Summertime," from *Porgy and Bess,* is derived from the spiritual "Sometimes I Feel Like a Motherless Child"; see Floyd, "Troping the Blues: From Spirituals to Concert Hall," *Black Music Research Journal* 13, no. 1 [1993]: 31–51.) Gershwin was also apparently present at the notorious party given by white author, socialite, and black culture propagandist Carl Van Vechten at which blues singer Bessie Smith performed: see Chris Albertson, *Bessie* (London: Barrie and Jenkins, 1972), 139–45; Nat Shapiro and Nat Hentoff, *Hear Me Talkin' to Ya* (Harmondsworth: Penguin, 1962), 241–42.

37. Lewis A. Erenberg, *Steppin' Out: New York Nightlife and the Transformation of American Culture 1890–1930* (Westport, Conn.: Greenwood Press, 1981) explores the broader context admirably. On white slumming in Harlem, see also Leonard, *Jazz;* Nathan I. Huggins, *Harlem Renaissance* (New York: Oxford University Press, 1971); Gilbert Osofsky, *Harlem: The Making of a Ghetto* (New York: Harper and Row, 1968).

38. Huggins, *Harlem Renaissance,* 89; McKay quoted in Osofsky, *Harlem,* 184; James Weldon Johnson, *Along This Way* (New York: Viking Press, 1968), 328; Rudolph Fisher, "The Caucasian Storms Harlem," *American Mercury* 11 (1927): 398.

39. Lena Horne, quoted in Jim Haskins, *The Cotton Club* (New York: Random House, 1977), 132. Haskins's book has a good feel for the Cotton Club primitivism, as well as giving details of the musical policy and repertory.

40. Quoted in Mark Tucker, "The Genesis of *Black, Brown and Beige,*" *Black Music Research Journal* 13, no. 2 (1993): 71. A much-quoted description of a typical Cotton Club "jungle sketch" can be found in Marshall Stearns, *The Story of Jazz,* rev. ed. (New York: Oxford University Press, 1970), 183–84.

41. A phrase used in a 1935 interview with Ellington, carried in *New Theatre* magazine; see Mark Tucker, *The Duke Ellington Reader* (New York: Oxford University Press, 1993), 114–17. There is some question about the credibility of this interview; Ellington certainly objected to the appearance of some of the phrases attributed to him. However, there seems no doubt that he did criticize *Porgy and Bess,* nor that his grounds were that it exploited and stereotyped rather than genuinely represented "Negro music."

42. See Floyd, "Music in the Harlem Renaissance"; Haskins, *The Cotton Club,* 21. The Harlem Renaissance was a movement of African American artists and intellectuals in the 1920s.

43. Mark Tucker, *Ellington: The Early Years* (Urbana: University of Illinois Press, 1991), 3.

44. Quoted in Mark Tucker, "The Renaissance Education of Duke Ellington," in *Black Music in the Harlem Renaissance,* ed. Samuel A. Floyd Jr. (Westport, Conn.: Greenwood Press, 1990), 122.

45. On Ellington's upbringing and its cultural context, see Tucker, "The Renaissance Education," and Tucker, *Ellington: The Early Years.*

46. Similarly, many Renaissance intellectuals saw black folk music as raw material for the production of high art. See Floyd, "Music in the Harlem Renaissance," 1–9.

47. The phrase comes from Houston Baker Jr., *Modernism and the Harlem Renaissance* (Chicago: University of Chicago Press, 1987). Interestingly, black history was a central object of study in the Washington schools of Ellington's boyhood. Also shows (theatrical and musical) with a "jungle to Harlem" theme were common in the 1920s; several were staged at the Cotton Club. See Tucker, *Ellington: The Early Years,* 69–72. Of course, *Porgy and Bess* has a kind of "jungle to New York" story too—though here New York represents not a relocated jungle but *escape.* The contrast is instructive.

48. Almost any book by or about Ellington casts light on his working methods, but Shapiro and Hentoff, *Hear Me,* 222, and Tucker, *The Duke Ellington Reader,* 96–102, are especially revealing.

49. The best discussion is Gunther Schuller's in *Early Jazz* (New York: Oxford University Press, 1968), 318–57, esp. 339ff. But even he stresses most of all the Cotton Club's role in Ellington's career: "The need for new background music for constantly changing acts . . . *required* Ellington to investigate composition (rather than arranging) as a medium of expression" (340). Schuller, a "schooled" composer himself, is wanting to push Ellington toward an ideology of compositional integration.

50. "Painting a picture, or having a story to go with what you were going to play, was of vital importance": Duke Ellington, *Music Is My Mistress* (London: Quartet Books, 1973), 47. On his pictorialism, see also Tucker, *Ellington: The Early Years,* 231–37.

51. Duke Ellington, "Japanese Dream" and "Arabian Lover," *The Works of Duke,* vol. 3 (RCA 741 029); "Diga-Diga-Doo," *The Works of Duke,* vol. 2 (RCA 741 028).

52. As early as 1924 ("Choo Choo"). Duke's use of the minstrelsy mask also predates the Cotton Club: see Tucker's discussion (*Duke Ellington: The Early Years,* 122–23) of his 1925 song "Jim Dandy (A Strut Dance)."

53. Ellington, quoted in Shapiro and Hentoff, *Hear Me,* 228; and in Haskins, *The Cotton Club,* 53. Interviews with the young Ellington and reviews of his work, reprinted in Tucker, *The Duke Ellington Reader,* confirm the impression of a man who identified his ambition of developing a serious black music with the cultivation of black historical difference; he "believe[s] that in the heart of the Africa a man can travel into today there lies a great secret of music" (1930; quoted in ibid., 43).

54. Duke Ellington, "Black and Tan Fantasy," *The Works of Duke,* vol. 1 (RCA 731 043).

55. The critic was R. G. Darrell, reprinted in Tucker, *The Duke Ellington Reader,* 34.

56. Duke Ellington, "Jungle Blues," *The Complete Duke Ellington,* vol. 3 (CBS 88000); "Jungle Nights in Harlem," *The Works of Duke,* vol. 4 (RCA 741 039).

57. Duke Ellington, "Echoes of the Jungle," *The Works of Duke*, vol. 6 (RCA 741 068); "Old Man Blues," *The Works of Duke*, vol. 5 (RCA 741 048).

58. Duke Ellington, *Black, Brown and Beige* (live recording of first performance, Prestige P-34004).

59. Whiteman speaking about *Rhapsody in Blue*, quoted in Leonard, *Jazz*, 80. Leonard is good on the significance of the concert, and so is Crawford ("It Ain't Necessarily Soul," 19).

60. James Clifford, *The Predicament of Culture: Twentieth-Century Ethnography, Literature, and Art* (Cambridge, Mass.: Harvard University Press, 1988), 5. For the reception of *Black, Brown and Beige*, see Tucker, *The Duke Ellington Reader*, 153–204; *Black Music Research Journal* 13, no. 2 (1993).

61. On Calloway's "popular modernism," see Gunther Schuller, *The Swing Era* (New York: Oxford University Press, 1989), 326–50. From 1939 to 1941 the young bebop pioneer-to-be, Dizzy Gillespie, played with (and wrote for) the Calloway Band. At the core of bebop, of Ellington's "jungle" style, and of a great deal of hot Harlem jazz of the 1930s, including Calloway's, was blues; and it is worth noting Ellington's 1930 declaration on the subject: "The Negro is the blues. Blues is the rage in popular music. And popular music is the good music of tomorrow." (Quoted in Tucker, *The Duke Ellington Reader*, 45.)

62. Henry Louis Gates, *The Signifying Monkey: A Theory of African-American Literary Criticism* (New York: Oxford University Press, 1988). "The absent *g* is a figure for the Signifyin(g) black difference" (46).

63. Baker, *Modernism*, 25, 56, and passim.

64. In *disques,* June 1932, reprinted in Tucker, *The Duke Ellington Reader*, 58. We can follow the evolution of Darrell's Ellington criticism between 1927 and 1931, in extracts included in ibid. 33–40 (from which I quoted earlier).

65. Usually these complexities are implicit and have to be teased out, but occasionally they are more obvious—as in the case of the British house/hip-hop offshoot called "jungle"; practiced and enjoyed by both blacks and whites, this style displays allusions to itself as a primitive other in lyrics and in discourse about the music, and it has become an object of debate in questions of racial musical politics.

66. In a Sunday afternoon church performance! Quoted in Baker, *Modernism*, 61. There is further complexity here, however. Baldwin's blasphemous aphorism certainly catches the centrality of the African American experience for postcolonial modernity; but on another level it perhaps also points towards the way in which African American music has been assimilated into the hegemonic global designs of the U.S. music industry. "Double consciousness" indeed!

67. American minstrel troupes visited South Africa as early as the 1850s. See Veit Erlmann, *African Stars: Studies in Black South African Performance* (Chicago: University of Chicago Press, 1991), 21–53. African American influences remained crucial.

68. See Veit Erlmann, "Conversation with Joseph Shabalala of Ladysmith Black Mambazo," *World of Music* 31, no. 1 (1989): 31–58.

69. For one earlier example of creative manipulation of the mask, see Erlmann's discussion of the development of the Zulu *ingoma* dance: Veit Erlmann, "'Horses in the Race Course': The Domestication of Ingoma Dancing in South Africa 1929–39," *Popular Music* 8 (1989): 259–73. Rich documentation of complex responses to received models, stereotypes, and pressures can be found in Christopher Ballantine,

"Concert and Dance: The Foundations of Black Jazz in South Africa Between the Twenties and the Early Forties," *Popular Music* 10 (1991): 121–45.

70. See Erlmann, *African Stars,* 112–55.

71. Andrew Tracey, "A Word from the Editor," *African Music* 6, no. 4 (1987): 3.

72. Louise Meintjes argues persuasively ("Paul Simon's *Graceland,* South Africa, and the Mediation of Musical Meaning," *Ethnomusicology* 34, no. 1 [1990]: 37–74) that *Graceland* is open to a variety of readings, relating to a variety of political positions. No doubt *Porgy and Bess* and *The Magic Flute* are open to varied readings too, and we saw how difficult it is to provide definitive interpretations of the politics of Duke Ellington's music. Here, though, the question of *dominant* readings becomes inescapable, assuming that the dimension of power is to be taken at all seriously.

73. In addition to the works cited in notes 67 and 69, see David Coplan, *In Township Tonight! South Africa's Black City Music and Theatre* (Johannesburg: Ravan Press, 1985); Richard Middleton, "The Politics of Cultural Expression: African Musics and the World Market," in *Poverty and Development in the 1990s,* ed. Tim Allen and Alan Thomas (Oxford: Oxford University Press, 1992), 362–78.

74. The "Great Hymn" had been derived from an earlier, probably very *un*-European piece by the early Christian Xhosa convert Nkitsana Gaba. See Veit Erlmann, "Black Political Song in South Africa—Some Research Perspectives," in *Popular Music Perspectives 2,* ed. David Horn (Gothenburg, Sweden: IASPM, 1985), 187–209. Richard Middleton and the editors would like to thank Veit Erlmann for permission to reproduce this transcription from his "Black Political Song in South Africa—Some Research Perspectives," in *Popular Music Perspectives* 2, ed. David Horn (Gothenberg: International Association for the Study of Popular Music, 1985), 203.

75. Braitex Workers, "Ilezwe Ngelethu," *South African Trade Union Worker Choirs* (Rounder 5020, 1986).

76. Abdullah Ibrahim, *Soweto Is Where It's At,* on *Tintinyana* (Kaz LP 103, 1988).

77. W. E. B. Dubois, *The Souls of Black Folk* (Chicago: McClurg, 1903), 3. On Césaire's *négritude,* see Clifford, *The Predicament of Culture,* 6. On "double consciousness," see also Gilroy, *The Black Atlantic.*

78. The implications of this for white Western popular music history have hardly been investigated, let alone theorized. It is worth noting that Baker, in principle, does not limit Signifyin(g) to African and Afro-diasporic cultures.

79. Baker, *Modernism,* 61. For a similar view, see Huggins, *Harlem Renaissance,* 244–45.

80. Some arguments of this kind are summarized in Richard Middleton, *Studying Popular Music* (Buckingham: Open University Press, 1990), 239–44, 261–67. For "gesture" see Richard Middleton, "Popular Music Analysis and Musicology: Bridging the Gap," *Popular Music* 12 (1993): 175–90.

81. The concept of "habitus" and the idea of a practice-based "disposition" come from Pierre Bourdieu, *Outline of a Theory of Practice* (Cambridge: Cambridge University Press, 1977).

82. In the sleeve notes to *Buena Vista Social Club,* an album of Cuban music he produced (World Circuit WCD050, 1997), Ry Cooder puts this beautifully; this music, he writes, "takes care of you and rebuilds you from the inside out." Cooder's

participation in the performances, captivated yet modest and supportive, may be fruitfully compared with Paul Simon's role in *Graceland:* the intricately variegated styles of this Caribbean/Spanish/African/American hybrid music culture survive intact, both "very refined and deeply funky" (as Cooder says), "different" yet also "modern."

Race, Orientalism, and Distinction in the Wake of the "Yellow Peril"

Jann Pasler

By 1904, the French began to understand the Orient as something besides a vague, mostly passive "other," seductive as it might be, that served in the arts as the pretext for Western dreaming, escape, and an opportunity to foreground self-assertion. A fear of *le péril jaune* (the "yellow peril") set fire in French imagination when, after agreeing in 1902 to side with the Russians in their Far Eastern imperialism, they watched in horror as the Japanese unexpectedly took on their ally, beginning a "war about race." "It's the yellow race threatening the white race for the first time since Genghis Khan and his band of Tartars," a French critic wrote. If the Chinese should join the Japanese, as some predicted, their power would be "colossal," a "threat to the rest of the universe."[1]

French attitudes toward the East were in flux. With Turkey sympathetic to Germany and the Franco-Russian alliance encouraging the French to fund Russian imperialism, France's other expanded beyond North Africa and the Middle East to encompass her ally's other, the Far East.[2] But when the Far East proved to be a force with military power and the capacity to defeat the West, the discourses about it became complicated. Edward Said and others have taught us to associate Orientalism with narratives of national identity as well as struggles concerning gender, class, and race, always focused on the "positional superiority"[3] of one group vis-à-vis another. But after 1905, it was no longer unambiguous who was the stronger and who the weaker in the Orientalist's conventional binary constructions. Those who stood to profit from the growing interconnectedness of the international economy found it important to diffuse these binarisms, to reinterpret them in view of coexistence, at least from a Western perspective. Those who did not responded to this threat to Western hegemony by redefining the West and what was distinctive about it in new journals like *L'Occident* and *La Renaissance latine.*

French writers argued that since civilization "marched westward," they, the French, the "*extrême-occidentaux*," were the ultimate representatives of the West, its "resolution," and their culture its "harmonious or bold conclusion."[4]

French political leaders likewise began to feel that "consolidation" among European countries was necessary to match the East's potential force. In 1904, this led to the Entente Cordiale, an alliance with Britain, the other major power there. Struggles with Germany in North Africa in 1905–1906 resulted in even closer ties and in 1907 led to the Triple Entente between France, Russia, and Britain. The politics of these agreements, an increasing fear of the Far East, and an interest in exploring the origins of Aryan Westerners may well have encouraged French artists to turn to Britain's other, India, as a safer, more neutral terrain for their Orientalist fantasies.

In this chapter, I examine two composers' responses to this Orient. Both traveled to India between 1909 and 1912, Albert Roussel (1869–1936) on his honeymoon after visits with the French navy, and Maurice Delage (1879–1961) on tour with his parents to the family's shoe-polish factories. Both went on to the Far East, Roussel to Indochina and Delage to Japan, though what they chose to write home, keep journals, and later write music about were their experiences in India. After retracing their footsteps and locating some of their sources in fall 1988, I was astounded to find such variance in the musical experiences they describe and in the influence of Indian music and culture on the music they composed after these trips, especially since they visited many of the same places. Subsequently I wrote about the relation of self and other as represented in this music.[5] What interests me here are two other conclusions: first, how after 1904 India became a repository for new kinds of Orientalist projections, based on acknowledging power in the other, and second, how these composers' interest in India was rooted in their own essentially Western preoccupations.

These attitudes were not so Western as to deny the influence of Indian music on their own composition,[6] but rather were shaped by their contrasting backgrounds, professional situations, aesthetics, and political orientations. A heightened awareness of the world at large, with its globally interdependent concerns and highly mobile capital, and the self-critical frameworks of modernism predisposed Delage to acknowledge the value of foreign resources and to engage with the culture on its own terms more so than did the royalist nationalism and the conservative aesthetics of the Schola Cantorum, the Parisian music school where Roussel taught. Like other modernists, Delage sought to innovate in an international context and shared with global industrialists a desire for access to ever-new resources. Indian music provided him with new sounds with which to enrich a composer's palette. Scholists, by contrast, primarily landowners from the provinces, were caught more in the debates about French music and influenced by the rhetoric of the nationalist *ligues*. The Schola's religious philosophy prepared Roussel for a spiritually enriching experience of India, though one distanced from material culture (including its music) and resulting from a projection rather than an induction of value in its culture. That these two composers could respond so differently to Indian music forces us to reexamine our understanding of Orientalism during this period and to accept the plurality of its meanings and functions in French culture after 1904.

INDIAN MUSIC, UNDERSTOOD FROM AFAR

In the early nineteenth century, at a time when Paris was "a hub of Orientalist study," India was perceived as "the scene of many cultural confrontations, the ground of an East-West meeting."[7] The Belgian painter François Solvyns published four volumes of *Les Hindous* in Paris between 1808 and 1812,[8] and the French missionary Abbé Dubois (c. 1770–1848) left largely reliable analyses of Hindu life in his *Moeurs, institutions, et cérémonies des peuples de l'Inde* (1825). Writers too, especially Lamartine, Hugo, Vigny, and Michelet, were "enchanted" by India's religion and famous epics. Until the end of the century, however, "no major French Indic scholar visited India."[9] Of course, there were the memoirs of a few French visitors, occasional articles,[10] and, throughout spring 1902, *Le Matin*'s serial publication of Kipling's novel *Kim* (based on the author's travels in India). But the country remained for most French something vague, largely a function of their own hunger for escape.

Music was a classic means of making this point, with vague references to India serving as ideal opportunities to coax audiences into dreaming. One has only to think of Bizet's *Les Pêcheurs des perles* (1863), a love triangle in ancient Ceylon; Massenet's *Le Roi de Lahore* (1872–77), also set in ancient India; and Delibes' *Lakmé* (1883), a love story between an Indian priestess and a contemporary colonialist.[11] Each of these works explores the "enchanting Orient" as a "charming memory" or "sweet dream" of seduction, intoxication, and loss of self. Each serves as a pretext for composers to write fluid melismas, use drones, and feature delicate orchestration with harps and flutes. This suggests that, dangerous as this freedom might have been to the hegemony of late nineteenth-century musical conventions, this release from various musical constraints was as important to composers as the exotic locale.

What attracted nineteenth-century French musicians most to Indian music was the melodic character of the modes. This rendered it distinctive. The rebirth of interest in modality, composers' use of scales other than the major and minor, parallels the colonial curiosity and acquisitiveness of the late nineteenth century. In France, the imperialist government of the Third Republic (1871–1940) saw music as an opportunity to expand its cultural horizons while asserting its cultural superiority.[12] In the 1870s, 1880s, and 1890s, the government gave grants to collect *chansons populaires*, indigenous folk music known for modal variety, in the French provinces and abroad. Eventually this vogue extended to Indian music.[13] Some composers even borrowed Indian scales to use in their own music;[14] however, when it came to understanding the nature of these scales, their use of quarter tones, and their meaning, there was serious confusion.

Other kinds of knowledge about Indian music were even more limited. The Solvyns portraits, the first systematic study of Indian musical instruments, were virtually never cited.[15] Fétis, who dedicated the fifth volume of his *Histoire générale de la musique* (1869–76) to Indian music, bemoans the little he had been able to learn. Pierre Loti's description of what he heard in India and Edmond Bailly's explanation of Indian musical philosophy go into little detail.[16]

The most thorough French study of Indian music from this period is chapter 5 of Julien Tiersot's *Notes d'ethnologie musicale* (1905). Tiersot identifies "Hindu melodies" in *Le Roi de Lahore* and *Lakmé*, though he notes they are indistinguishable from other themes in the work. But mostly he criticizes Fétis and borrows from recent studies by J. Grosset (1888), C. R. Day (1891), and the Bengali musicologist S. M. Tagore (1874–1896).[17] Tiersot includes musical examples and describes the Indian instruments at the Conservatoire museum. Still, he too makes mistakes, such as asserting that this music is "purely melodic" and that "the vīnā only doubles the voice." Tiersot concludes that "the problem of Hindu music offers [even] more uncertainty than that of Greek music . . . it remains for us, in large measure, a dead relic [*lettre morte*]."[18]

There is, in fact, little record of Indian musicians in Paris before 1910. Folk musicians took part in the 1900 Universal Exhibition, but Tiersot dismisses them: "We heard no song of high style or some development from their mouths . . . in general only very short rhythmic formulas." After giving musical examples, he writes, "One cannot deny that this music is simple, simple to an extreme. . . . The negroes of Africa often have richer and less elementary musical forms. Decadence, or the remnants of a primitive art from the low classes of the Hindu society?"[19] Another opportunity to hear Indian musicians apparently did not arise until Edwin Evans[20] led "an orchestra composed of pure-blooded Indians" on a European tour in summer 1910, hailed in the *Courrier musical* as an "Indian invasion." In 1913 and 1914, the sitar player Inayat Khan (1895–1938) visited Paris.[21]

With the growth of interest in so-called primitive or ancient societies and the notion of India as the "cradle of civilization"[22] came an important reason for the French to be interested in Indian music, one that both related to their own origins and allowed them to fantasize about the Orient as separate from the colonial present. In his 1907 correspondence with the modernist writer Victor Segalen, who had served as a student interpreter in the French navy, Debussy, considering a collaboration, questions: "You must be solidly versed on Hindu music? If you so please . . . you would render a great service to musicology—so awful on these wonderful subjects." Segalen responded,

> Of course there is a lot to say about Hindu musics that has never been said. First of all, [we must] rid ourselves of all our prejudices about sound. But . . . India [is] vast and tumultuous like a continent, with two or three hundred separate dialects and different rhythms. It would be better to focus on a music assumed to be beautiful and homogeneous by reason of caste and ritual necessity: the music of the Aryans of Vedic India. . . . One would have for one's material an epoch of very noble allure, not too strange to our thinkers because Aryan, not too familiar because distant in space and time.[23]

In the long section on Indian music in his *Histoire de la musique,* the Scholist Henri Woollett also proposed this notion of India as originally Aryan (also meaning aristocratic). Even though there has "never been any resemblance between the music of our period and that of ancient India," he reminds French readers, "don't let us forget that we [too] are Aryans."[24] By 1910 then, especially for French nationalists, Indian music came to signify the music of the distant (and aristocratic) ancestors of the French—in this context, its relative imperviousness to Western influences could appear as a strength. Confronting India in this period thus must have been a complex endeavor based on little knowledge and a variety of self-serving projections.

ALBERT ROUSSEL

Albert Roussel was the among the few who travelled to India. Then a professor at the Schola Cantorum, he left with his new wife on 22 September 1909. After disembarking at Bombay, the newlyweds toured the country whose shores he had often visited as a naval officer.[25] In a letter of 29 October 1909 to Henri Woollett—who was just finishing his music history book— he described his impressions of the country's music:

> I just traveled through Hindustan from Bombay to Calcutta and everything I saw impressed me profoundly. From the musical point of view, however, I haven't heard anything up until this moment that is really curious. The Hindu music that I have heard, stripped of harmony and very different from Javanese or Japanese music, consisted uniquely of several folk songs [*chansons populaires*] in our ordinary tonalities. Maybe there is something else that I haven't yet encountered?[26]

Such a statement suggests what predispositions Roussel brought with him and how he processed his experiences. Surprisingly, while he admits to having been visually impressed, Roussel denies finding anything particularly interesting in what he heard. He describes the music as a form of absence, "stripped of harmony." It is not even "really curious"—"curious" being a category in which music periodicals at the turn of the century published exotic music, *chansons populaires*, early music, and even some contemporary music (i.e., Satie). Roussel conceptualizes this music as if Western (*chansons populaires*) but without recognizing that it has more than "our ordinary tonalities" to speak for it.

Indian music had come to signify the origins of Aryan civilization, but there was more underlying Roussel's apparent denial of exoticism and his attempt to classify Indian music as a variant of Western music—specifically, the institutional politics of the Schola Cantorum, where Roussel studied beginning in 1898 and taught from 1902 to 1914, and his colleagues' conception of *chansons populaires*. Founded by a group of aristocrats, ecclesiastics, and musicians, the Schola Cantorum began in 1894 as a school to reform church music and encourage new compositions inspired by Gregorian chant and predecessors like Palestrina. Cardinal Richard, archbishop of Paris, was its first and most important patron. In 1898 it became affiliated with the Institut Catholique and in 1900 moved to what had been a Benedictine church and became an Ecole supérieure de musique. As such, it became an alternative to the Paris Conservatoire, politically challenging the republican government's hegemony in the field of music education. Musically, with its emphasis on counterpoint and instrumental music, it also challenged the Conservatoire's historic emphasis on opera and virtuosity.

Many of the Schola's teachers and students were from the French provinces, landowners who believed in decentralization and a return to what we might call "basic values." They were not, for the most part, part of the emerging rich industrialist class centered in Paris. Many of them, after studying in Paris, returned to the provinces to start branches of the Schola there (Roussel's friend Woollett founded one in Le Havre). The Schola's director after 1904, Vincent d'Indy, came from the province of Ardèche, was staunchly Catholic and a member of the reactionary Ligue des patriotes, which espoused and promoted an antirepublican nationalism. They hoped for a return to enlightened monarchy. Some of this same group started the journal *L'Occident,* which, as mentioned earlier, promoted a glorified sense of the French as the "harmonious conclusion" of the West. In one of its first issues, d'Indy articulated one of their main tenets: the idea of progress not as linear, as many republicans defined it, but as a "spiral," that is, one that based forward movement on incorporating the past, especially traditions that predated the French revolution.[27] In his lectures at the Schola, *Cours de composition,* d'Indy presents a history of compositional style and method as intertwined. This *Cours* not only exemplifies his spiral notion of progress but also reflects the author's desire to codify Western syntax, defining Western heritage from his distinct point of view.

D'Indy and his colleagues at the Schola considered *chansons populaires*, especially those of the French provinces, to be a "collective inspiration," an important repository of their past and, as such, emblematic in some way of their character (which meant their race).[28] Like the republican scholars of this music, Bourgault-Ducoudray and Tiersot,[29] they argued that what distinguished the *chansons populaires* from modern music were its modes, remnants of Greek and old church modes. Through their modes, Scholists insisted, these songs bear some resemblance to early liturgical music, a central interest of the Schola's founders. Unlike republican scholars of the genre, however, Scholists were not drawn to this music as part of a colonialist agenda to expand the boundaries of musical expression by assimilating forgotten modes. Politically much of the aristocracy preferred regaining Alsace and Lorraine to acquiring new land elsewhere. Neither did they wish to use it, as Prime Minister Jules Ferry did in the 1880s, to help unify the country or argue for music's universalism,[30] though they agreed that its relatively unchanging character over time was essential to its identity. Scholists focused on what they could learn from this music about the immutable racial qualities of the French. They also considered this genre an easy way "to inculcate a love of nature," this being another Scholist doctrine reflecting their roots in the French provinces.[31]

Study of French *chansons populaires* was considered very important at the Schola. D'Indy collected and published a volume of such songs from Ardèche, his *Chansons populaires de Vivarais,* and included a section about *chansons populaires* in his *Cours de composition.* Under his direction, the Schola offered an annual course on the genre. Another Schola founder, Charles Bordes, published a volume of Basque *chansons populaires,* organized a conference on the genre in 1905, and founded a journal, *Chansons de France,* to publish such songs from all over the country.

Perhaps because of their underlying political agenda and their association of *chansons populaires* with their aristocratic past, national identity, and nature, Scholists considered this music to be good, healthy "nourishment." Like Bourgault-Ducoudray, they believed certain of its modes "full of vigor and health," "very virile" and "so masculine."[32] Scholists claimed that this music was capable of inspiring "moral renewal" in the world. But when *la musique populaire et exotique* began to appear in the same category in music journals[33]—in part because it became increasingly difficult to separate them—the Scholists became anxious. They associated exoticism with facility, impressionism, and a lack of solid construction, and increasingly feared an "abuse of the picturesque"—traits they associated with "impressionist" composers trained at the Conservatoire. Scholists were reluctant to treat the *chansons populaires* of most other countries with the same respect as their own.

The diary and musical sketchbook Roussel kept during his journey to India suggest the strength of the Schola's influence on how and what he perceived in Indian music.[34] In the forty-five-page sketchbook, the absence of complex melodic and rhythmic structures, ornaments (*gamaka*), and microtones (*śrutis*)—otherwise characterizing the ragas and talas of Indian classical music—suggests that the composer may not have gained access to the courts and temples where classical music was regularly performed. Were his musical experiences limited principally, if not exclusively, to indigenous *chansons populaires* not performed by artful singers, as Day (1891) suggested was often the case?[35] Or were the subtleties of Indian music simply unimportant to him? A. H. Fox-Strangways also kept a musical diary during his 1910–11 trip there but bemoaned his inability to record timbral and intonation variations.[36] Unlike him, Roussel does not suggest in his diary or sketchbook that the melodies he noted were only partial transcriptions of what he heard. Although they capture the two-part structure and duple meter characteristic of much folk dance music in India, Roussel's sketches do not reflect the rhythmic acceleration and excessively rapid ornamentation that he otherwise describes in his diary. Furthermore, the F sharp at the beginning of two of the melodies suggests that Roussel heard these tunes in G major, one of the "ordinary tonalities" of which he wrote to Woollett, even though he consistently uses F sharp or C sharp in ascending lines and F natural or C natural in descending ones, which might otherwise imply the presence of ragas.

One sketch, an unmetered tune again with a key signature of F sharp (example 2.1), is Roussel's "translation" of the litany he heard sung without stopping by a "fakir[37] on the banks of the Ganges" at sunset. His "vision of this half-naked young man addressing the gods and stars" greatly impressed the composer even if the words were incomprehensible. In many ways, this tune is typical of many in his sketchbook. (Tiersot describes similar ones in Tagore's *A Few Specimens of Indian Songs.*)[38] It is in two parts, each formed of a very short period which, according to Roussel, the singer repeated many times. Its range is a sixth and its contour that of two sine waves. This is the only tune that appears more than once in the sketchbook; in its first recurrence it is transposed up a step, and in its fourth, it is elongated and its highest note reached by a fourth rather than a second.

The evolution of musical thinking in this notebook suggests that Roussel was more interested in writing a composition during his trip than in recording what Indian music he heard. From page eighteen on, one finds melodies, chord structures, short passages in four-part harmony, and even music on three and four staves. From the horns, trombones, bassoons, winds, and strings indicated, it is clear that Roussel was conceiving a piece for a Western ensemble. The occasional subtitles—adagio, allegretto, and lent—suggest that he was contemplating one with three movements. "Ellora," "Udaipur," and the letter "B" (for Benares) point to the three movements of his *Evocations,* "Les Dieux dans l'ombre des cavernes" (The gods in the shadow of the caves), "La Ville rose" (The pink city), and "Au bord du fleuve sacrée" (On the banks of the sacred river). He finished this upon his return to France in 1910.

Of course, there was a tradition of writing music based on one's travels—his teacher Vincent d'Indy wrote a set of piano pieces, *Tableaux de voyage* (1888), as did many of those who traveled as part of their Prix de Rome. In writing his *Evocations,* Roussel was concerned to maintain the nonprogrammatic quality of much of this genre. As he began work in March 1910, he explained to the critic Georges Jean-Aubry, "This will not be Far-Eastern music, but simply the sensations I felt over there translated into our ordinary musical language."[39] On 21 July 1910, as he was completing its first movement, he noted d'Indy's advice:

> So write your Hindu symphony without thinking about this or that, nor even about including too much local color; believe me, a simple indication (like the discreet trumpets in the Agnus of the Mass in D) is perfectly sufficient to put us in the mood, even better than a sound photograph of "national noises." . . .
>
> Look then at your India much more for the impressions it made on the man named Albert Roussel—impressions that, taken together, are a lot more European than Hindu—instead of for the orchestral imitation you might make of observed sounds; this procedure in art, inferior as it is, is becoming so commonplace that a mind such as yours could never be satisfied with it.[40]

Two years later, in another letter to Jean-Aubry, he made it clear that "even though these *Evocations* were inspired by India, I am anxious that the country remain vague. India, Tibet, Indochina, China, Persia, it doesn't matter."[41] In a 1928 essay, he is more explicit:

> If I haven't specified these places in the titles, it's because I don't want to impose any kind of limitation on the musical expression. However, if one absolutely must discover some bit of local color, I can point to a theme in "The Pink City" that was suggested to me by a scene I saw, the entry of the rajah into his palace, and in the third *Evocation,* the reminiscence of a melody that I heard sung on the banks of the Ganges by a young enlightened fakir.[42]

These words, even if written in retrospect, suggest how Roussel thought about his Indian experiences vis-à-vis his composition of *Evocations.* As in Lamartine's Orient, in which, as Said puts it, "the last traces of particularity have been rubbed out,"[43] they were not to "limit" his expression in any way. He might use a theme or two inspired by what he heard, but only in the tradition of local color, that is, as a signal for Western listeners to dream. The themes used in *Evocations* then were not meant to appear as actual transcriptions of Indian melodies, but rather as those "suggested" by what he "saw" or by "the reminiscence of a melody" he heard in India. This would be music that respects the intervening filter of time and space and that appropriates the foreign material not to vaunt it, but for other purposes. In describing music this way, Roussel draws attention to the important role his memory and creative imagination played in "translating" the Indian materials "into our ordinary musical language."

Example 2.1 Roussel's sketchbook, "Fakir au bord du Ganges"

Example 2.2 Roussel, *Evocation*, third movement, baritone solo

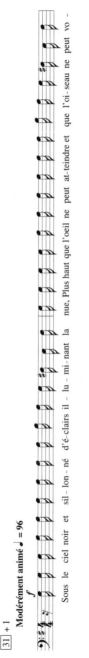

31 + 1

Modérément animé ♩ = 96

f

Sous le ciel noir et sil-lon- né d'é-clairs il - lu - mi-nant la nue, Plus haut que l'oeil ne peut at-teindre et que l'oi-seau ne peut vo -

ler, Son front ma-jes- tu-eux mon-tant jusqu'aux-pa-lais des im-mor-tels, Se dres—— se la mon - ta-gne sou-ve-rai - ne.

Such statements give one pause in interpreting the musical sketches Roussel made during his trip. If the tunes transcribed were meant to serve as a reminder of what he had heard, an invitation to reminiscence at some point later, Roussel might not have considered it important to try to capture the idiosyncrasies of another musical language, not even its different concepts of timbre and intonation. And there would be nothing wrong with being reductive of its aesthetic.

Examining the music of *Evocations* contributes a somewhat different sense of Roussel's perceptions of India than what his sketchbook or the letter to Woollett suggest. In many ways, the piece creates for the Western listener an evolving relationship with the differences represented by India. The first movement, virtually devoid of Indian musical influences, translates what Roussel calls his feelings of "grandeur and mystery" before the temples of Ellora. The sounds he describes in his diary—only water droplets and bird cries—may have inspired the musical opening, which resembles Debussy's and Ravel's music with its impressionist harmonies, arabesque arpeggiations, and pedal tone in the basses. In the second movement, Roussel creates a more generally Eastern sound with his delicate instrumentation and the static, oscillating nature of his motives.

The third movement shows the most Indian influence, even an engagement with Indian music. The sliding to and away from neighbor tones in the first measures recalls the *gamakas* of Indian music. The rapid ornaments, syncopations, and long sweeping line of the flute melody in 7 show an awareness of the improvisatory qualities in Indian music not otherwise accounted for in his sketchbook. The grace notes and glissandi, played by instruments of varied timbres, reflect the composer's attempts to translate the unison sound that so impressed him, while respecting the timbral complexity that must have accompanied these unisons.

In the middle of this movement (31 to 36), Roussel sets verbatim his "reminiscence" of the fakir melody (example 2.2), using it to spin out a long ballade-like setting of six four-line stanzas written at his request by the French critic M.-D. Calvocoressi.[44] When I played a recording of this music for various Indian musicians during my visit in 1988, most told me they found it totally lacking in Indian elements. In Benares, however, when I sang the tune myself after playing the recording, one of my drivers instantly recognized part of it as fakirs' devotional music; the eminent Indian music scholar I had come to interview concurred.[45] As in Roussel's sketch, their version of the melody centered on the reiteration of one pitch surrounded by an ascending and descending pattern; but, in contrast to the Roussel version, the opening of their tune spanned a third rather than a second, did not repeat the initial pitch, and, what they found particularly significant, included an odd number of the repeated pitch in its middle section, thereby allowing the natural accent to fall on *that* pitch rather than on the next higher one as in Roussel's version. Roussel had shifted the placement of the accent. By contrast, they found the second part of Roussel's tune totally unrecognizable: there was no consequent phrase in the music they knew. Roussel, with his classical Western training, evidently felt this tune needed one. In his sketch, he took his "reminiscence," or altered version of the Indian tune, as the antecedent of a theme and then completed it, giving it "consequence," that is, a goal, a point of arrival, as well as closure.

Repeating this theme over and over as the fakir himself did, Roussel respects the way the original melody might be performed even today. Because this is devotional music, the fakirs may sing the same text and music for hours, stretching the tempo at will, giving it different colors and expressing different feelings through it: according to Dr. Prem Lata Sharma, they think they will derive some spiritual benefit from this singing.[46] In sections 31 to 36, Roussel likewise sets the tune, with some variations, for virtually ten minutes. The only deviation in the antecedent phrase concerns whether it will begin on G (as in the first two stanzas) or on A-flat (as in the second two). The consequent phrase, by contrast, appears in different rhythmic and intervallic forms each time, depending on the number of syllables in the verse and which syllable the composer wishes to stress. This variation technique together with the timbral effects in *Evocations* suggest that Roussel heard more than he actually noted in his sketchbook. He evidently felt more comfortable in manipulating what he added to the music—the orchestration and the consequent of the baritone's theme—than in tampering with his transcriptions.

ROUSSEL'S CHALLENGE TO NINETEENTH-CENTURY ORIENTALISM

To explain what Roussel drew on from his Indian experiences, it is helpful to consider *Evocations* as embodying a new kind of musical Orientalism, one that departs from the conventions of the genre in the nineteenth century. First, it is the male voice that represents the other, a baritone rather than a soprano or mezzo as had long been the norm in earlier French works like *Lakmé*. Throughout the nineteenth century, the Republic used females as metaphors for the country and Conservatoire composers such as Massenet associated music with the feminine. This shift in the gender identity of the composer's voice is consonant with the new way the East was viewed after the Japanese defeat of Russia. It also signals a change in French identity itself, at least in the identity Roussel wished to explore.

Second, Roussel sets the text of this baritone syllabically rather than melismatically, that is, with one clearly articulated note per syllable rather than a string of fluidly meandering notes on vowel sounds. As such his text can be easily understood; indeed, the repetition of the melodic line draws attention to the changing stanzas of text. What appears as improvisatory is the text. Rational discourse draws more attention than musical discourse;

again, one might say, the conventionally masculine is more prominent than the conventionally feminine.

The charm of such music is not erotic but almost shamanistic, for, with the magic of repetition, it lures the listener to initiate transformation. This points to a third difference between *Evocations* and most nineteenth-century Orientalist music. The male here is neither despotic nor violent but devotional.[47] He is also, perhaps ironically, not a leader (as in works like *Samson et Dalila*) but a poor beggar. His power comes from his relationship to God— a theme that would have resonated with his Catholic peers at the Schola. Already in the notebook he had kept during his first trip overseas twenty years earlier, Roussel had expressed interest in the religion of nature and in non-Christian religions as "teaching man admiration for all that is beautiful, grand, heroic." Eastern civilization, for him, was intimately connected with "the luminous environment."[48] The fakir was the embodiment of this relationship to the divine through nature.

Calvocoressi develops these themes in his lyrics for the third movement of *Evocations* in a way that draws attention to the musical structure. The movement begins with what Roussel calls "an evocation of the night." After a long choral section of homorhythmic chords followed by rich counterpoint, it ends with a contralto summing up the meaning of the musical metaphor as in a poem by Baudelaire, "More sweet than the perfumes of the night, more ardent is my love." To prepare for the dawn, to reflect on the impending magnificent change in nature marking the end of the night, Roussel then calls on the shamanistic fakir.

Music and text play complementary roles in the fakir's section. The music's relentless thematic repetition, pulsating sixteenth notes, and gradually ascending melodic line suggest the irreversibility of change just before the sun rises. At the same time, the text unfolds visions in which the fakir focuses on his ecstasy. Each of the stanzas echoes the musical structure. Like the musical antecedent and consequent, the initial images of each stanza prepare for understanding the final ones. For example, after the lines "Under the black sky cut by lightning, higher than the eye can see and the bird can fly," the stanza culminates at "the supreme mountain," the zenith of the image. At this point, the baritone sings the longest, highest note of the musical period. The other stanzas work similarly:

> Its shade terrifies timid hearts . . .
> > it's a God whose voice descends among us;
> In the thick shade of the forests . . .
> > O river which reflects the luminous sky;
> Happy he whose face extinguishes on this shore . . .
> > leaving the soul free to rise towards the innumerable stars;
> Sacred river that washes the temples of the holy city . . .
> > let the sky of a new day be reborn.

After the baritone solo, the chorus returns to sing the "hymn of the sun" as if speaking directly to God. Including a chorus allowed Roussel to frame the Indian material in an interesting way. While the chorus both begins and ends the piece, the baritone functions as an antecedent to the final chorus much as the antecedent of the fakir's melody does to its consequent. That is, the Indian fakir prepares for and leads to a transformation in the chorus. This transformation takes place in the music the chorus sings, their shift from counterpoint (as in the beginning of the movement) to non-harmonized, homorhythmic singing resembling Western devotional music. Afterwards, in a dynamic climax, they praise God as the ultimate synthesis of masculine power and feminine beauty: "You hunt the immense army of the stars / And your passionate beauty reigns alone over the Ocean of heavens in your embrace."

This relationship of antecedent to consequent (or preparation to arrival) in the theme, the poetry, the vocal forces, and the devotion suggests a similar interpretation of how Roussel understood his Indian experiences vis-à-vis his composition. Numerous times Roussel refers to the feelings and visions he had there, and in a letter of 20 May 1920,[49] he insists that listeners have the *argument* (text) before them at any concert performances of the work. The fakir and these experiences may in fact represent an India that transformed Roussel, initiating him not only to new visions of life and nature (such as those described in Calvocoressi's text), but also to a "new day" in his own spirituality, a deeper understanding of the ultimate other.

This interpretation suggests that we consider India, and not its musical exoticism, as the crucial catalyst, and transformation as the goal of each kind of antecedent in the work. Roussel later writes about both art and life as "a series of continuous transformations" and the function of a work of art as "provoking in the listener a response that, if it is not identical, at least answers in some way the call of the composer."[50] From this perspective, perhaps the composer hoped his *Evocations* would likewise serve as an antecedent for his audiences, eliciting an experience of spiritual transformation that the founders of the Schola Cantorum would have enthusiastically endorsed.

MAURICE DELAGE

Maurice Delage, by contrast, was not yet a fully formed composer when he embarked on his voyage to India. He played the cello as an amateur and had studied composition with Ravel for about ten years. Otherwise, he was self-taught. Friends describe him as someone with a fine ear, "impatient with the weary discipline of technical training."[51] Friend of Stravinsky and host to the weekly meetings of Ravel's group, les Apaches,[52] Delage was an adventurer in many ways. In his first orchestral work, *Conté par la mer* (1909),[53] he wrote a note for horn outside its usual range. When, under d'Indy's leadership, the Société Nationale refused to perform it, his colleagues showed their esteem by breaking and forming a rival performance organization, the Société Musicale Indépendente (SMI).

The severity of this action suggests that by 1910 differences between Scholists and so-called impressionist composers from the Conservatoire had developed into a serious conflict, but one full of ironies, in part because some had sympathies in both directions and Apaches included representatives of both. Leaders at the Schola, founded to allow composers more individual freedom (especially from the constraints of state competitions), were increasingly preoccupied with issues of control and structure, even in their music; those inspired by Debussy's use of unresolved, "impressionist" harmonies were intent on taking full advantage of this liberation from conventional syntax. And whereas it was d'Indy who turned to Wagner for inspiration and in 1890 argued for more inclusion of music by foreign composers at the Société Nationale, by the turn of the century it was the young modernists trained at the Conservatoire who looked beyond national borders for new ideas. Debussy's innovations, some inspired by Javanese and Vietnamese music, were crucial to these composers, even though after 1902, like the Scholists, Debussy focused increasingly on a nationalist agenda. In their first concerts, the SMI premiered not only music by Delage but also Koechlin's transcriptions of Javanese "gamalang." In 1913 Ravel solicited Schoenberg's permission to perform *Pierrot Lunaire*,[54] a work whose novel instrumentation impressed both him and Stravinsky.

Delage did not study at the Conservatoire but he associated with those who did, though he had little interest in writing opera, took part in no competitions, and shared very little socially with the conservative republicans who ran the institution, many of whom, like Debussy, came from very modest backgrounds. Like most Apaches, he was born into a family with money made in the industrial world of the late nineteenth century. His father owned Lion Noir, a shoe polish still sold today. It is difficult to say what Delage's politics were, but one thing is clear: he had a life of ease spent helping friends, especially Ravel. In spring 1912, his parents used their factories in India and Japan as an excuse to travel to the Far East; Maurice went along.[55] According to Léon-Paul Fargue, Delage left with the fervor of a pilgrim; he was not the kind who "brings along his slippers." Although their travels took them to many of the same places as Roussel, Delage's impressions were quite different, as was the compositional form which later emerged.

In a letter from Ceylon published in the Parisian music journal *S.I.M.,* Delage admits that he had never read anything about Indian music before his trip.[56] Yet his comments in this letter, subsequent published interviews, and a radio program on Indian music he gave in April 1948[57] show remarkable perceptiveness. From what he writes, especially about instruments and performance practices, it is clear that Delage was exposed to Indian classical music.

Many of Delage's attitudes toward Indian music are rooted in his modernist inclinations. These differ from the concerns of Roussel and other Scholists in four ways. First, there is a tone of resistance and critique, perhaps inspired by Debussy's and Ravel's attitudes toward their Conservatoire training. Delage can't help but refer to Western musical practices and concepts; however, his focus is on their limitations. Indian improvisations, he writes, had an audacity that "escaped all organization, according to our logic, of course. . . . With my poor ear accustomed to the almost artificial subtleties of our Western polyphony,[58] I felt something that was beyond the notes." The vīnā player's use of parallel fifths led him to exclaim "Severe Academy . . . What could analysis and criticism do here, great gods! One must desire [only] to feel and love." Delage admits he "ignores what one must normally know" to speak of Indian culture. Using the other as a site for self-criticism is a typical Orientalist tactic, but he does not do this to reify the differences between the two or to demonstrate the strength and relative power of Western music. Rather, Delage hopes to set the terms for his own "naïve efforts towards novelty," his search to get beyond Western constraints, perhaps to appropriate some of the power inherent in Indian music.

Second, Delage supported Indians' resistance to foreign contamination in their musical traditions.[59] Underlying this was his respect for authenticity. Like Segalen, who proposed "salvaging the purity of the exotic by thinking it anew" for the sake of art and fantasized about India's distant past as a distraction from its colonialist present,[60] Delage was most impressed with genres that seemed purely Hindu (performance of the vīnā and South Indian vocal music). He railed against European influences on Indian music, especially phonographs, the harmonium, and, in South India, the violin.[61] Had he had access to the sultans' or maharajas' palaces, he might also have been shocked by the presence of pianos in their midst. He worried about how the "relative perfection" of Western tuning might endanger the "purity" of not so much the syntax of Indian music but its sound.[62] This was a complicated issue for Indians too. A writer in *Modern Review,* from Calcutta, claimed in 1912 that "the greatest problem of India . . . is how we can modernize ourselves and become progressive, without losing our heritage—without losing that spiritual power and wealth which made India great in the past."[63] Delage was also bothered by other non-Hindu influences, such as the disappearance of instruments after the Muslim invasion. But even if such criticism may have stemmed from racial prejudice, he appreciated the music of Kishori Lal, a singer from Punjab, enough to play a recording of it during his radio broadcast. Delage was especially sensitive to the importance of individual performers in maintaining musical traditions in India.[64]

With this focus on indigenous authenticity and performers, Delage differed from both Scholists (who tended to overlook the specificity of these traditions outside of France) and French republican scholars (who were more interested in the modal particularities of foreign music). In the context of the increased global contact which threatened the continuity of both Western and Eastern cultures, however, Delage and Roussel shared something crucial: both believed in preserving the "racial integrity" of musical traditions, be they Indian or French.

Delage's preoccupation with the timbral richness of Indian music is a third reflection of his modernist aesthetics. Eastern music represented for French modernists a way of validating their belief in the primacy of sound over syntax and a means of exploring the origins of music (as opposed to the origins of the French race). An interest in sound vibrations, nuance, fluidity, and spontaneity underlies the impressionist style and differs markedly from the Scholist focus on solid construction, linear clarity, and rigorous logic. Delage's attention to the immensely varied sound qualities produced on Indian instruments led him to take precise note of what he heard. Performance on the vīnā, the oldest multistringed Indian instrument used in both northern and southern India and the "most popular" one,[65] fascinated him. The slow glissandi, the striking of the strings and the case, and the staccato of the performer's left-hand fingers produced effects that the composer would later attempt to imitate.[66] Likewise, he was drawn to the vocal techniques of South Indian contraltos, especially the "voluptuous tension" of those who sang "with almost closed mouths, a high-pitched prosody involving strange nasal sonorities, cries, and breathing" and "the warm roughness of their low register where the rushed and feverish rhythms suddenly relax into a murmur full of caresses."[67] Not only in France but also in Vienna, modernists were increasingly defining research in timbre as the newest form of musical progress (for example, Schoenberg in his *Harmonielehre*). Delage's desire to "discover" such riches thus has a future-oriented, even utopian aspect.

Fourth, Delage's essays suggest that he, unlike Roussel, was more engaged by the musical traditions of India's contemporary elite—his peers—than by Indian folk or popular music. His attraction to the vīnā—what he calls the "noble instrument of modern India"—is a case in point. This instrument was associated with the upper classes.[68] Day points out that playing the vīnā, considered an "imitation of the human voice," was restricted to professional skilled musicians in northern India. In southern India it was a favorite among amateurs of the higher classes, perhaps those with whom Delage identified.[69]

To solve the problem of access to a wide variety of Indian music, Delage resorted to buying recordings.[70] On 23 October 1912, he wrote to Stravinsky, "You will see that I have been working and I will make you listen to the Hindu records, a kind of music of which you have no idea."[71] The Indian classical music preserved on these recordings, as opposed to the folk songs he might have heard or collected on records, are the key to the works Delage wrote upon his return. In these compositions is a highly original approach to Indian materials, an intercultural influence that goes far beyond that of superficial impressionism, and a re-presentation of Indian music that

Example 2.3 Imdad Khan, "Raga Jaunpuri Todika Alap" (beginning). Transcribed by Paul Smith.

original tonic: F♯
transposed to B

TRANSCRIBER'S NOTE:
All slurred notes are played as glissandi. Portamento indicates that the marked notes are lingered on briefly in the midst of the glissando passage. A broader, more accented pause is indicated with a tenuto mark.

empowers him to subvert traditional Western music practices. "Trying to find those Hindu sounds that send chills up my spine," as he explained to Stravinsky,[72] Delage experimented with unusual timbres produced by altered tunings and vocal techniques, special kinds of ornaments that modify the Western sense of interval and pitch, improvisatory rhythms, new forms, and especially novel performance techniques. The works that resulted from such exploration spanned much of his career, beginning with the *Quatre poèmes hindous* (Four Hindu Poems) for soprano and small chamber orchestra (written from spring 1912 through fall 1913) and *Ragamalika* (1912 to 1922).

The most interesting of these, from the perspective of Indian influence, is the second of the *Quatre poèmes hindous,* "Un Sapin isolé" (An Isolated Fir Tree), subtitled "Lahore." The text is a poem by Heinrich Heine. Its images invite the listener into reverie: one tree, covered with snow "on a bare mountain in the North," dreams of another, a "solitary" palm clinging to the edge of a scorched rock "in the distant East"—a metaphor for the human condition. For the opening cello solo, Delage inserted his transcription of a performance on the surbahār of "Jaunpuri Todika Alap" by Imdad Khan (1848–1920), probably recorded in 1905 (see examples 2.3 and 2.4a).[73] The performance instructions indicate that while the right hand plucks the first note, the cellist should use the same finger of the left hand to slide between the two adjacent notes. This use of ornaments and glissandi to prolong a

Example 2.4a   Delage, "Un Sapin isolé," from *Quatre poèmes hindous*, opening, cello/violin solo, m. 1–19

Example 2.4b Delage, "Un Sapin isolé," from *Quatre poèmes hindous,* vocalise, m. 10–16

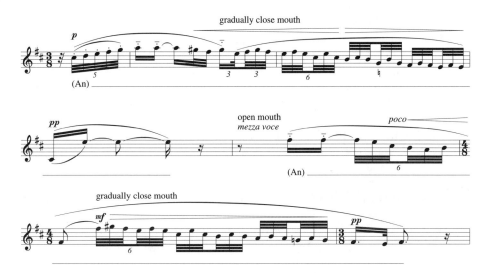

note, stress one, or slide from one to another results in a pitch continuum, microtonal shadings, and a timbre like those produced by sitar and vīnā play-ers.[74] After the first few bars of music, however, the transcription is no longer exact. Khan elaborates on the raga for almost three minutes, while Delage cuts some of the recurring passages and condenses the overall shape. He also alters the complex rhythms, and indicates a slower tempo—perhaps to give the cellist the time to execute the difficult techniques.

The vocal part dominates in the rest of the piece. Most of it is unequivo-cally Western though conventionally Orientalist. The final solo (example 2.4b) recalls two gestures from the opening of the "Bell Song" from *Lakmé.* Still, an Indian influence prevails. The Indian-type scale (built on D with three sharps), the quickly ascending scale of six notes, and gradually descending span of a thirteenth resemble the middle of the same Khan recording. Be-sides the low register, the quick, delicate staccatos throughout, and the or-naments that color the descending lines, Delage also calls for an Indian-in-spired closed-mouth singing in numerous places. This technique of open- and closed-mouth singing[75] shows Delage's first attempts to forge a personal style inspired by the vocal techniques he heard in India and on his record-ings, yet without attempting to retrain Western singers to produce their sounds in an Indian manner. It became a favorite in all his subsequent In-dian-inspired pieces, especially the Vocalise he wrote for a Paris Conserva-toire competition in the 1920s.

In the third Hindu poem, the "Naissance de Bouddha" (Birth of Buddha), subtitled "Benares," Delage borrows much of his thematic material from the flip side of the Khan recording discussed above, "Sohni." Delage transcribes this raga for English horn, giving it the same rhythms as in the recording. He then repeats the exposition as on the recording, has the clarinet respond with a similar virtuoso chromatic descent, and expands on these two ideas throughout the piece. The cello's ostinato recreates the sound of the accompanying strings on Kahn's surbahār. The plucking of the two open fifths, B♭F/DA, recalls what he thought might offend the "severe Academy" of the West. As on the recording, these open fifths function in this piece as a drone. The text, probably written by the composer, evokes the time when the gods and all of nature rejoiced at the news of Buddha's coming.

The first and last of the *Quatre poèmes hindous* frame the middle two and assure unity and coherence in the set. Although they set texts by Bhartrihari, an Indian king who became an ascetic, musically they express the Westerner's perspective which must frame his/her perception of Indian culture. Both have the same tempo and bear much less Indian musical influence. The first is dedicated to Ravel, the fourth to Stravinsky, both composers whose approach to orchestration may have influenced his chamber setting of these songs. Both songs begin with chromatic flute arabesques à la Debussy and conclude with the same gesture. The end of the first incorporates the opening motive of the last, and the closing measures of the last song incorporate the opening motive of the first one; the final measures of both pieces are the same.

These two songs are conventionally Orientalist in two ways. First, India is feminized, likened to a beautiful woman. The first depicts her wandering the forest—the object of the poet's contemplation; the last refers to her as a troubled but well-cherished memory: "If you think of her, you feel an aching torment. If you set eyes on her, your mind is troubled. If you touch her, you lose all reason. How can one call her the beloved?" Second, in setting the last two phrases, the music breaks into a Western-style climax, the apex of the song's vocal line. Outside of occasional moments in the cello solo of the second song, this is the only *forte* in the whole set. Such a moment captures the pinnacle of the composer's emotional response to his Indian experiences, one that obviously needs Western means for its full expression.

Ragamalika, perhaps his most Indian-sounding piece, is indeed a transcription of almost an entire recording, "Rāgamālikā, Ramalinga swamis arulpa," sung in Tamil by Coimbatore Thayi and probably recorded in 1909 (see example 2.5).[76] Thayi was a famous *devadasi* singer whom Delage had the pleasure of hearing live during a visit to the temples at Mahabalipurnam.[77] *Arulpa* are devotional songs that the *devadasis* sang for the entertainment and pleasure of the gods at the temples to which they were attached. Thayi recorded many of them.[78] Her recordings are full of elaborate passages of closed- and open-mouthed singing, microtonal ornaments, and long stretches in which she might change the timbre but not the pitch of important notes.

Example 2.5 Delage, *Ragamalika*

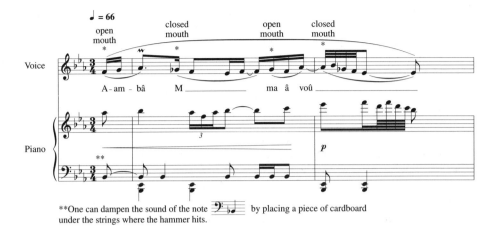

**One can dampen the sound of the note [♪] by placing a piece of cardboard under the strings where the hammer hits.

In every way, *Ragamalika* reflects its model—in its changing modes (*rāgamālikā* means "a garland of ragas"), its recurring refrain, its multipartite form, and its tempo relationships. The piano takes the place of the tabla and the droning string accompaniment. Its ostinati octaves serve principally to support the vocal line, except in one very important instance. To articulate the system tonic, B flat,[79] and to bring attention to the change of mode in the middle of the piece, Delage asks that one note on the *inside* of the piano be muted. This creates an unusual, otherworldly effect for the drone. It is perhaps the first example of "prepared piano" in European music. The publisher Durand was so "enchanted" by this music that on 20 June 1914 he paid Delage five hundred francs to orchestrate it.

With the help of these recordings, Delage succeeded better than his contemporaries in reproducing the spirit and the style of North and South Indian music. With its emphasis on self-criticism, sound for its own sake, and respect for traditions on their own terms, the modernist aesthetic prepared Delage to hear Indian music in its own terms. The industrialist relationship to other—based on recognizing the importance of foreign natural resources and using them for one's own purposes—inclined him to want to re-present it in his own way.

CONCLUSIONS: COMPOSITIONAL DISTINCTION

This chapter looks at two French composers' relationship with India, a country that, without any French military presence, remained an "Orient of memories."[80] Both fell under the spell of something so different and so dependent on their own sensibilities that they referred to it as a dream. Both appropriated tunes and stories, but not for domination. Both became fascinated with religious characters as intermediaries with the divine. Both wrote pieces inserting French singers, French texts, and an explicit French framework to preserve their memories and, through the catalyst of their music, stimulate similar experiences in others. And both used Indian influences in their first major work to help achieve distinction in their compositional careers.

For Scholists like Roussel, imagining another world was important. Their need to dream was a desire not for escape but for alternative power structures. The heroism and grandeur of ancient India presented these largely Catholic landowners, royalist aristocrats, and conservative traditionalists with a vision of what they sought and could not have under the anticlerical Republic. Their nationalism and fear of dealing with others, however, kept them anxious about outside influences on French culture. In response to a 1909 interview on Wagner's influence on French composers, Roussel sounds like d'Indy: "In this question of influences, it is difficult to leave aside the question of races and it would be very good if French music would tend to embody [*personnifier*] the genius of our race in an increasingly affirmative, vigorous way—the qualities of clarity, mind, sensibility, luminous and frank joy that form our artistic heritage."[81] This is the context for understanding Roussel's challenge to conventional notions of the musically exotic. The Scholists could not accept any artistic limitations that might compromise their own racial "genius" and an art they increasingly defined as masculine, that is, resistant to the notion of subsuming anything external to itself.

Roussel's resistance to others' influence made sense from another perspective as well. Typically it was important for a composer to move beyond his/her education and demonstrate a "personality." With *Evocations,* Roussel found a sly way to earn widely recognized distinction (in Bourdieu's sense). After its first performance on 18 May 1912 by the Société Nationale and on 30 March 1913 by Lamoureux's orchestra, a debate emerged. Non-Scholist critics saw Roussel breaking with Scholist principles. Jean Marnold, perhaps thinking about the first movement, said Roussel was "contaminated by Debussysme" even before he got to the Schola and did not assimilate all their "pedagogical influences."[82] In response, A. Sériyx vigorously reclaimed Roussel as a Scholist. Stressing the Western frame Roussel creates for the exotic locale, he points out specifically Scholist (and conventionally masculine) principles in the work:

> What gives the magnificent triptych "Evocations" great value, above all, is the impeccable equilibrium and the strength of the thematic and tonal construction. . . . It is no longer these unhealthy and ornate visions of some Orient with opium and folding screens: instead it's the magistral "evocation" of India, framed in the most pure form, blinding in its melodic clarity, infinitely rich in

rhythm without any effort, vigorous and passionate in expression without anything disturbing the integrity of the traditional construction.[83]

Jean-Aubry too pointed not to the Orientalism of the music but to the suave and voluptuous "quality of the dream" and hailed Roussel as "one of the most truly French souls in music today."[84] The nationalist Pierre Lalo praised it as "one of the principal works of our time."[85] In his review of a 1919 performance at which Debussy's *Nocturnes* was also performed, Antoine Mariotte points to truth in both Scholist and non-Scholist views. He sees Roussel's music as delicate, colorful, and powerful as Debussy's, but also calls it "cerebral and willful. . . . With M. Roussel, we are no longer in the clouds; we are in India." Mariotte argues that Roussel's Indian "impressions" are the pretext for demonstrating his ability to build and control large musical forms, to "logically order considerable developments," to express his mind and will as well as his sensibility.[86] In this sense, he is a colonialist, though his realm is music.

Taking India as his subject thus provided Roussel with a way to challenge musical impressionists on their own terrain (nature) and to demonstrate the strength of Scholist principles on new territory. This was surely the ultimate distinction for a young composer. Its success led to two of his most important commissions from Opéra director Jacques Rouché—the ballet *Le Festin de l'araignée* and his second Indian-inspired work, the opera-ballet *Padmâvatî*.[87]

For Delage, as we have seen, India was far more than a catalyst of visions and feelings. It had what Edward Said has called "separate sovereignty"; its natives were not "subservient nor sullenly uncooperative" as many a colonialist or visitor imagined them, but music-makers whom Delage admired, perhaps even envied.[88] For Delage as for his father the industrialist, India was a land of natural resources. Delage's success, like his father's, was based on understanding the value of these resources, particularly their use-value in the West. Self-taught, perhaps inspired by his father's entrepreneurial spirit, and aware of the marketability of the new, the composer took what he needed from his recordings. Incorporating the sound of Indian music—new to his contemporaries—Delage built the form of capital his world traded on, distinction and prestige.[89]

One could compare Delage's works with transcriptions of Indian recordings to his father's shoe polish—something partially made in India, but packaged and sold in France, something still selling today. But this would be to reduce his music to these transcriptions, to downplay his interest in Indian music as a means of criticizing Western practices, and to ignore his integration of Western and Eastern materials. Like Roussel's *Evocations,* Delage's *Quatre poèmes hindous* is, ultimately, a hybrid form, what Said calls a "narrative of integration."[90] In this set of songs, the integration is effected not only by giving the borrowed Indian passages to Western instruments and elaborating on Indian gestures, but also by juxtaposing and suggesting the interpenetration of the different materials. This allows each style to maintain, at least momentarily, its own integrity. In "Lahore," the text juxtaposes a fir tree on a snowy mountain with a palm on a hot rock, a vision possible only in an imaginary space. Sections of the Khan and Thayi recordings give the context for this dream, as Delage's trip helps explain his music. Placed within the same piece, these transcriptions of North and South Indian music, instrumental and vocal music, testify to their juxtaposition in Delage's Indian experience. The set as a whole also works by juxtaposition. The outer songs with their Orientalist gestures and similar structure frame the inner ones with their Indian citations. The traditional Indian music serves as the basis, even the inspiration, for the experimental use of the voice, strings, and piano. To the extent that Eastern and Western musical materials coexist and interpenetrate without conflict, this multifaceted integration of musical materials suggests the global interdependence, mobility of resources, and continued fascination with the new on which international capitalism depends.

Delage did not go unrewarded. *Quatre poèmes hindous* was premiered at the SMI on 14 January 1914, alongside first performances of Ravel's *Trois poèmes de Mallarmé* and Stravinsky's *Trois lyriques japonaises*.[91] Like them, it uses a chamber orchestra in part inspired by Schoenberg's *Pierrot lunaire*. Even though the audience had little idea of the work's secret—in his 1 February 1914 review in *S.I.M.*, Jean Poueigh makes reference to the "funny peculiarity" of the closed-mouth singing which he thought Delage had borrowed from its use in choruses—they demanded an encore of "Lahore." According to Georges Auric,[92] Delage's music stole the show, upstaging Ravel and Stravinsky. The composer knew he had found a personal voice worthy of a career.[93]

Despite their different perspectives, Roussel and Delage found in their attempts to reproduce Indian culture a means of expanding the territory over which they could demonstrate their compositional control. Neither created Orientalist works about their "positional superiority" or the feminine erotic, in part because, for them, race was a positive attribute of a people, a key to understanding them. Still, through their integration of Western and Eastern materials—Roussel to effect spiritual transformation and argue for a certain kind of French music, Delage to introduce new musical sounds and participate in the international modernist movement—both nonetheless had Orientalist aims couched within personal hopes. Both wished to escape the constraints of their times through an exotic other, appeal through something universal, and in doing so make a name for themselves.

NOTES

1. "Le Péril jaune," opinions of diverse French leaders, *La Revue russe* (9 June 1904): 7. Other revolutions in Persia (1905) and later Turkey (1908), China (1912), and Mexico (1911–1912) increased the ominousness of such a threat. The concur-

rent revolution in Russia also threatened the Franco-Russian alliance based on French confidence in Russian military forces.

2. In their essays in the *Revue internationale de musique française* 6, special issue on "L'Exotisme musical français" (November 1981): 22, 67–76, D. Pistone and G. Balardelle argue similarly.

3. Edward Said, *Orientalism* (New York: Vintage, 1979), 7.

4. "Déclaration," *L'Occident* (1902): 116.

5. Jann Pasler, "Reinterpreting Indian Music: Albert Roussel and Maurice Delage," in *Music-Cultures in Contact: Convergences and Collisions,* ed. Margaret Kartomi and Stephen Blum (Sydney: Currency Press, 1994), 122–57.

6. In his "Albert Roussel et l'exotisme musical," in *Albert Roussel: Musique et esthétique,* ed. Manfred Kelkel (Paris: Vrin, 1989), 77, Kelkel speaks incorrectly of "the absence of any recourse to authentic Hindu music."

7. Raymond Schwab makes this point in *The Oriental Renaissance: Europe's Rediscovery of India and the East, 1660–1880,* trans. Gene Patterson-Black and Victor Reinking (New York: Columbia University Press, 1984; first published in French in 1950 as *La Renaissance orientale*), 45. For a discussion of the musical scholarship of the period and for a very extensive bibliography of Westerners who published on Indian music, see Joep Bor, "The Rise of Ethnomusicology: Sources on Indian Music c. 1780–1890," *Yearbook for Traditional Music* (1988): 55ff. I am grateful to an anonymous reviewer for leading me to recent ethnomusicological work relevant to this subject.

8. For an analysis of Section 11 of this work on Indian music and musical instruments, see Robert Hardgrave Jr. and Stephen Slawek, "Instruments and Music Culture in 18th Century India: The Solvyns Portraits," *Asian Music* 20, no. 1 (fall-winter 1988–89): 1–92.

9. Schwab, *The Oriental Renaissance,* 47.

10. For example, Pierre Loti's *L'Inde sans les anglais* (Paris: Calmann-Lévy, 1903); P.-J. Toulet's *Journal et voyages* (Paris: Le Divan, 1955), documenting his trip there in spring 1903; René Puaux's *Ce fut le beau voyage* (1911–12), from which *Le Temps* published excerpts and Debussy was inspired to name his piano prelude, "La terrasse des audiences du clair de lune"; and Antoine Mathivet, "La vie populaire dans l'Inde d'après les Hindous," *Revue des deux mondes* 131 (15 September 1895): 407–23.

11. Other, lesser-known works from the period based on Indian subjects include Chausson's meditation on Hindu philosophy, *Hymne védique* (1886); Gabriel Pierné's incidental music for an "Indian drama in four acts," *Izeyl* (1894); Florent Schmitt's *La Danse des devadasis* (1900–08); and Bertelin's *Danses hindous.* For a discussion of colonialism and the exotic woman as representing escape in *Lakmé,* see James Parakilas, "The Soldier and the Exotic: Operatic Variations on a Theme of Racial Encounter: Part 1," *Opera Quarterly* 10, no. 2 (winter 1993–94): 33–56. For further discussion and a list of Indian-inspired French works from the period, see my "India and Its Music in the French Imagination before 1913," *Journal of the Indian Musicological Society* 27 (1996): 27–51.

12. So important did the government consider this project that, after a persuasive lecture on the topic by Bourgault-Ducoudray at the 1878 Exhibition, he was appointed Professor of Music History at the Paris Conservatory. Bourgault-Ducoudray, *Conférence sur la modalité dans la musique grecque (7 September 1878)* (Paris: Imprimerie nationale, 1879).

13. The popular domestic publication *Figaro musical* published two "Airs indiens" transcribed by G. Pfeiffer in its March 1893 issue, including one with a "Sanskrit text."

14. For example, see the use of the modes Varati and Bhairavi in Pierné's *Izeyl*, the modes Hindola and Asaveri in Déodat de Séverac's *Héliogabale* (1910), as well as the modes used in Debussy's *La Boîte à joujoux*. In these cases, the composers explicitly notate the names of the ragas on their scores. During this period, however, because of the enormous number of pieces called "Oriental," it is impossible to determine how many compositions incorporate Indian influence, be it the use of ragas or some other attribute of this music.

15. Hardgrave and Slawek, "The Solvyns Portraits."

16. Loti describes the Indian classical music he heard at a maharajah's court in 1899–1900 in his *L'Inde sans les anglais* (1903); Bailly writes on Hindu musical philosophy in his *Le Son dans la nature* (1900). According to his article "La Musique hindoue," *Musica* (March 1909): 43–44, Bailly spent much time with a Hindu singer, Nagenda Nath Roy, who spent six months in Paris in 1896.

17. Jacques Grosset, *Contribution à l'étude de la musique hindoue* (Paris: Ernest Leroux, 1888); C. R. Day, *Music and Musical Instruments of Southern India and the Deccan* (London: Novello, Ewer & Co., 1891). Grosset's book includes discussion of Indian music theory and musical instruments. Sourindro Muhan Tagore was a wealthy intellectual dedicated to reviving interest in classical music in India and to promoting it in the West. See Bor, "The Rise of Ethnomusicology," 63. Tiersot (62) acknowledges his use of several Tagore volumes, including *Six Principal Ragas with a Brief View of Hindu Music* (2nd ed.; Calcutta, 1877), *Hindu Music from Various Authors* (Calcutta, 1875), *A Few Specimens of Indian Songs* (Calcutta, 1879), *The Musical Scales of the Hindus* (Calcutta, 1884), and *The Twenty-Two Musical Srutis of the Hindus* (Calcutta, 1886).

18. Julien Tiersot, *Notes d'ethnologie musicale* (Paris: Fischbacher, 1905), 57, 64, 73–74, 78–79.

19. Ibid., 68–71.

20. According to Albert Roussel in his *Lettres et écrits,* ed. Nicole Labelle (Paris: Flammarion, 1987), 82–84, this is the same man who organized a concert of Roussel's music in London on 24 March 1909, which Roussel attended. Evans was also to do the English translation of Calvocoressi's text for his *Evocations,* though there is no record that he completed it. He was also a friend of Delage, possibly the person who arranged Delage's meeting with Kipling in 1913.

21. Edmond Bailly arranged his first concert; Khan later gave several lectures on music and philosophy. In 1914 he addressed the Congress of the Société Internationale de Musique. These visits made a significant impact on many, including Isadora Duncan, Jules Bois, Jules Echorcheville (who organized the Congress), and Debussy, whom Khan remembers as "very much interested in our ragas." Inayat Khan, *[Auto]Biography of Pir-O-Murshsid Inayat Khan* (London and The Hague: East-West Publications, 1979), 129.

22. Henry Woollett, *Histoire de la musique depuis l'antiquité jusqu'à nos jours* (1909; 3d ed., Paris: Eschig, 1925), 1:37. In his article "La Musique archaïque," *Revue bleue* (15 November 1924): 757–60, Inayat Khan concurs with this idea: "If anything can give an idea about the ancient music of the human race, it is oriental music, which still preserves traces of older traditions in it."

23. Annie Joly-Segalen and André Schaeffner, *Segalen et Debussy* (Monaco: Edi-

tions du rocher, 1961), 59–60. In his "Debussy et les musiques de l'Inde," in *Cahiers Debussy* (1988): 141–52, Roy Howat mentions an unfinished sketch on the life of Buddha, "Siddhartha." Howat dates it from 1906–09. We find the origins of this work discussed in the correspondence between Debussy and Segalen (*Segalen et Debussy*, 59–68).

24. Woollett, *Histoire de la musique*, 43.

25. Roussel was admitted into the Naval Academy in 1887 and, after many voyages abroad, resigned to concentrate on music in 1894.

26. Roussel, *Lettres et écrits*, 35.

27. For a fuller discussion of this idea, see my article "Paris: Conflicting Notions of Progress," in *The Late Romantic Era*, ed. Jim Samson (London: Macmillan, 1991), 389–416.

28. In this way, they resembled the comparative musicologists of the early part of this century. As Ali Jihad Racy writes in his article, "Historic Worldviews of Early Ethnomusicologists: An East-West Encounter in Cairo, 1932," in *Ethnomusicology and Modern Music History*, ed. Stephen Blum, Philip Bohlman, and Daniel Neuman (Urbana: University of Illinois Press, 1991), these scholars considered "folk music to be the purest manifestation of history and a living embodiment of the collective 'spirit' of the people" (87).

29. See Julien Tiersot's *Histoire de la chanson populaire en France* (Paris: Plon, 1889). For more on the differences between what the genre represented to different factions of the French musical world, see my "The Chanson Populaire as Malleable Symbol in Turn-of-the-Century France," in *Tradition and Its Future in Music*, ed. Y. Tokumaru et al. (Tokyo: Mita Press, 1991), 203–10.

30. In his *Histoire de la chanson populaire*, Tiersot concluded that "the sum total of the *chansons populaires* is identical from one end of the country to the other." Of course, there are variations, but "one always and everywhere gathers the same songs" (356–57). Moreover, in the chapter on "Tonality in popular melody," Tiersot poses as an axiom that "whatever the tonality at hand, antique, modern, French or Chinese, all agree on one fundamental principle: the existence of a tonic and dominant in each scale" (287).

31. Charles Bordes, "Résumé des doctrines esthétiques de la Schola Cantorum," *La Tribune de Saint-Gervais* 9 (September 1903): 307.

32. Bourgault-Ducoudray, *Conférence sur la modalité dans la musique grecque*, 12.

33. For example, in the index of the 1905 issues of the *Revue musicale*, a section with this name included *chansons populaires* from Armenia, Spain, the Arab countries, Guatemala, and Morocco, as well as sacred Brahman dances and harmonized "Oriental melodies."

34. Madame Albert Roussel gave this sketchbook to Marc Pincherle on 7 April 1951, and in 1978 its owner André Peeters (founder and editor of the *Cahiers Albert Roussel*) allowed me to consult it. Besides Indian melodies, the sketches include three tunes described as "Thai," "Cambodge," and "Annadhapura." The diary Roussel kept from 6 October through 13 November 1909 is published in Roussel, *Lettres et écrits*, 178–202.

Daniel Kawka has written a long analysis of the notebook Roussel kept on a previous journal to Africa, the Middle East, and the Antilles in 1889–1890. See his *Un Marin Compositeur Albert Roussel 'Le Carnet de bord,' (1889–1890)* (Saint-Etienne: Ed.

du C.I.E.R.E.C., 1987) and his "Le Carnet de bord d'Albert Roussel" in Kelkel, *Roussel: Musique et esthétique*, 45–61.

35. C. R. Day explained that Europeans at the time rarely had a chance to hear "the good or classical music" of India: "What is usually played for them consists . . . of modern ditties, sung by ill-instructed, screaming, dancing women at crowded native durbars, marriages, and other ceremonials" (*Music and Musical Instruments of Southern India*, 58). In this chapter, I maintain the distinction between classical and folk music not to imply that the boundaries were clear nor that folk and popular musics did not share many of the complexities of classical music—on October 31, 1988 in New Dehli, Vijay Verma pointed out to me that the "border between professional folk and classical music is quite thin." Rather, it is because composers and musicologists thought in these terms at the time.

36. A. H. Fox-Strangways, *The Music of Hindostan* (Oxford: Clarendon Press, 1914).

37. A Muslim or Hindu religious ascetic. From the Arabic "faqir," meaning poor. In his *Tribes and Castes of the Central Provinces of India*, vol. 3 (London: Macmillan, 1916), R. V. Russell compares the fakirs of India to the monks of the Oriental church, who "were alike persuaded that in total abstraction of the faculties of the mind and body, the pure spirit may ascend to the enjoyment and vision of the Deity." As religious mendicants and devotees of Siva, they believe "in the power of man over nature by means of austerities and the occult influences of the will" (243–45). In volume 2, Russell explains that "the principal religious exercise of the fakirs is known as Zikr, and consists in the continual repetition of the names of God by various methods, it being supposed that they can draw the name from different parts of the body. The exercise is so exhausting that they frequently faint under it" (537–39).

38. Tiersot, *Notes d'ethnologie*, 66.

39. Roussel, *Lettres et écrits*, 38.

40. Arthur Hoérée, "Lettres de Vincent d'Indy à Roussel," *Cahiers Albert Roussel* 1 (1978): 46.

41. Roussel, *Lettres et écrits*, 42.

42. Arthur Hoérée, *Albert Roussel* (Paris: Rieder, 1938), 37.

43. Said, *Orientalism*, 179.

44. Among his other activities as a critic, Calvocoressi lectured at the Schola and was the editor-in-chief of their biweekly publication, *Les Tablettes de la Schola*, which detailed the concerts and other events at the school. He also wrote about Russian music and was an active member of Ravel's circle, the Apaches.

45. I am grateful to Dr. Prem Lata Sharma, Professor Emeritus of Benares Hindu University in Benares (Varanasi), Lalta Parsad, and Jay Parkash for their help in identifying this tune.

46. I had the opportunity to hear such music sung by a group of devotees at a temple in front of the train station in Benares. The "jai-lan" music goes on continuously until 4 A.M. every night, without a pause even between different singers.

47. In his monumental study of Orientalism in music, "Constructing the Oriental 'Other': Saint-Saëns' *Samson et Dalila*," *Cambridge Opera Journal* 3, no. 3 (1991), Ralph Locke describes "Orientalist stereotypes of Middle Eastern males as smug, single-minded, intolerant, power-mad despots and fanatics, impulsive and prone to violence" (280).

48. See the text as analyzed in Kawka, *Un Marin Compositeur* and "Le Carnet de bord d'Albert Roussel."

49. Roussel, *Lettres et écrits*, 85.

50. Roussel cited in Marc Pincherle, *Albert Roussel* (Geneva: René Kister, 1957), 53, 54.

51. Calvocoressi, *Musicians' Gallery*, 61.

52. In my article "Stravinsky and the Apaches," *Musical Times* (June 1982), I discuss this group and suggest that Delage was perhaps Stravinsky's closest friend in Paris before World War I. In a letter of 9 August 1905, Ravel mentions that the brother-in-law of an Apache, Bénédictus, was appointed to a judiciary position in Pondichéry, India. *Maurice Ravel: Lettres, écrits, entretiens,* ed. Arbie Orenstein (Paris: Flammarion, 1989), 78. Around the same time, Ravel too hoped for a government assignment ("mission") in the East, possibly India.

53. See Ravel's letter of 16 January 1909 to Koechlin in Orenstein, *Ravel: Lettres, écrits, entretiens,* 101–2. The work is missing and was possibly destroyed.

54. Ibid., 128.

55. A close friend of Delage's, the composer/conductor Manuel Rosenthal, provided this information to me in an interview in Paris in spring 1977. In his *Ravel: Souvenirs de Manuel Rosenthal,* ed. Marcel Marnat (Paris: Fayard, 1995), he notes that Delage's father sold this business to an Englishman who paid royalties to Delage for years (164).

56. Maurice Delage, "Lettre de l'Inde," from Kandy, 4 March 1912, *Revue musicale S.I.M.* (15 June 1912): 72–74. Except where noted, quotations in the following paragraphs come from this essay.

57. The text of Delage's radio program, "Une Géographie musicale," broadcast on Channel A on 25 April 1948, is currently in the Bibliothèque Nationale, Paris, Rés. Vmc. Ms. 46.

58. In his *Histoire de la musique* (Paris: Colin, 1913), Jules Combarieu rehearses the standard view of counterpoint as the "cradle of harmony and the principle of all modern art" (350) and thus the essence of Western music, an idea shared with many Scholists.

59. In his "The Soldier and the Exotic," Parakilas points out that musical performance can signify cultural resistance in India. In *Lakmé,* for example, the bell song is "a political act in the Hindus' struggle for cultural survival" (50).

60. See Chris Bongie, *Exotic Memories: Literature, Colonialism, and the Fin de Siècle* (Stanford, Calif.: Stanford University Press, 1991), 107–18.

61. The violin became popular in southern India around the time of the first Tanjore Palace Band and has remained so ever since. By the late 1880s, according to *Hindu Music and the Gayan Samaj: The Gayan Dnyan Prakesh (March 1882)* (Bombay: Bombay Gazette Steam Press, 1887), "The European violin had made great encroachment on popular favor"(27–28).

62. The use of the harmonium has been a subject of much debate, and was so particularly around the time that Delage visited the country. See my "Reinterpreting Indian Music," 145, n. 14.

63. If this writer is representative, their anxiety at the time seems to have been focused more on homogeneity within the country than on growing too close to the West, for he continues, "But all must admit that every race and nationality in India

has an individuality which it should strive to preserve at the same time that it aspires to a closer political union with the rest of India. . . . A non-descript and amorphous cosmopolitanism which would destroy the identity and eliminate the peculiar racial characteristics of the Bengalis, Hindustanis, Punjabs, Gujaratis, and Marathis and fuse them into an incongruous whole seems equally Utopian and unwise." *Modern Review* (February 1912): 220–25.

64. In his *Musings of a Musician* (Bombay: Wilco Publishing House, n.d. [apparently after 1977]), 55, R. R. Ayyanyar makes this point.

65. In his "The Rise of Ethnomusicology" (53), Bor points out that probably the first description of the vīnā in Western sources was in Mersenne's *Harmonie universelle* (1636–37). It is possible that Delage knew the vīnā from the Musée du Conservatoire in Paris. In his *Notes d'ethnologie,* Tiersot discusses one as part of the collection there (78).

66. Day, in his *Music and Musical Instruments of Southern India,* was also impressed by similar techniques of vīnā-playing, notably the peculiar tuning of the instrument, the staccato sounds achieved, and the striking of the instrument by the left hand on vīnās in the north and by the right hand on the somewhat different ones in the south (110).

67. In his "Une Géographie musicale," Delage describes a singer, dressed as a tiger, who performed "*vocalises* produced by a staccato at the back of the throat with a whole lemon in his mouth." S. A. K. Durga and V. A. K. Ranga Rao explained to me that in the "Puli attam," a tiger's dance, performers even today place lemon wedges in each cheek so that their mouths won't get dry while they make purring/growling noises for hours.

68. As Hardgrave and Slawek point out in their "Instruments and Music Culture in 18th-Century India," early nineteenth-century writers on Indian music observed that the high castes were prohibited from playing wind instruments but often sang and accompanied themselves on this instrument, "a favorite amongst the better classes" (4). This was equally true at the end of the century, notably in the Gayan Samaj, schools formed in Madras and Poorna in the 1870s "to give European residents an idea of the excellence of Hindu music." (In "The Rise of Ethnomusicology," Bor points out, futhermore, that "these institutions played an important role in the emancipation of classical Indian music" [63].) In this context, according to *Hindu Music and the Gayan Samaj,* the "best musician plays all but wind instruments," which were not considered appropriate for Brahmins; "wind instruments and stringed instruments are, of course, never played together" (21–28). In *The Music and Musical Instruments of Southern India,* Day echoes these observations; however, he points out that Brahmins can play a flute if blown with their nostrils (103).

69. Ibid., 110.

70. Recordings were introduced in India just after the turn of the century. As Pekka Gronow reports in "The Record Industry Comes to the Orient," *Ethnomusicology* 25, no. 2 (1981): 251, the Gramophone Company's representative Fred Gaisberg first recorded there in 1901. The first factories opened in Calcutta in 1908. See also Peter Manuel, "Popular Music in India 1901–1986," *Popular Music* 7, no. 2 (May 1988): 157–76.

In his 1948 radio program, Delage listed and described the eight recordings he played, ranging from rhythmic improvisations on the simple iron bars, called Khattali, accompanying a wedding procession (Odeon 96.541) and the oboe-like Nadaswaram played in the temples of Ellora (Odeon 96.453) to the complex singing of Kishori Lal (Gramo 12.533) and Coimbatore Thayi (Gramo 5–013022). These were among those he collected in India in 1912. According to my sources in India, most were extremely rare. Unfortunately Delage's collection has apparently been lost.

What and who were recorded in the first decade has been a subject of debate. In her "Recording Technology, the Record Industry, and Ethnomusicological Scholarship," in *Ethnomusicology and Modern Music History,* ed. Stephen Blum, Philip Bohlman, and Daniel Neuman (Urbana: University of Illinois Press, 1991), Kay Kaufman Shelemay has found that many of these early recording efforts focused on indigenous folk music (281), whereas Delage's collection included classical music. On 15 October 1988 in New Dehli, Vijay Verma offered me a possible explanation: anyone with a patron or money, he posited, could make recordings, and consequently popular singers, not necessarily the best ones, tended to make the most recordings. Moreover, many musicians refused to work within the three-to-four minute limits of the early 78-rpm disks or to have their voices heard by "just anyone."

71. Robert Craft, ed., *Stravinsky: Selected Correspondence,* vol. 1 (New York: Knopf, 1982), 24.

72. Ibid., 33.

73. A surbahār is a bass sitar with unmovable frets and a wider range. A north Indian *ālāp* is a slow exposition without a fixed pulse. I am indebted to Vijay Verma for pointing out the *rāg jaunpuri* in the cello part and to the staff of the Music Department of B.H.U. for help in locating two Khan recordings, both Gramo G.C. 17364, the source of the "Lahore" opening, and Gramo G.C. 17365. Michael Kinnear kindly provided me with the probable date of these recordings. There is a 1994 reissue of this by EMI called *Chairman's Choice: Great Gharanas: Imdadkhani* (CD CMC 1 82507–08).

74. When Khan shifts his melody to another string to move higher in pitch and weaves a duet between two strings, Delage gives the melodic line to the viola which then enters into a duet with the cello. The subtlety of this instrumentation very much captures that of its model.

75. Delage was perhaps the first French composer to use such a technique for solo singing. However, one finds this technique in choral singing in other Orientalist works such as Delibes's *Lakmé,* Pierné's *Izyel,* Florent Schmitt's *Danse des devadasis* (1900–1908), and Lili Boulanger's *Vieille Prière bouddhique* (1917).

76. Gramo G.C. 8–13793. I am grateful to S. A. K. Durga for suggesting I consult the collection of V. A. K. Ranga Rao, and to Mr. Rao for allowing me to peruse his collection on the morning of Diwali in fall 1988.

77. Delage, "Une Géographie musicale." She is among those whom R. R. Ayyangar heard and included in his list of famous women singers before 1930, published in his *Musings of a Musician,* 40. Those interested in the *devadasis* of Tamilnadu should consult Saskia C. Kersenboom-Story's *Nityasumangali: Devadasi Tradition in South India* (Dehli et al.: Motilal Banarsidass, 1987). I am grateful to Rita Ganguli and T. Sankaran for help in this research. When Delage met Thayi, Sankaran surmises, she must have been at Mahabalipurnam for a festival. No one seems to know to which temple she was attached.

78. A. Danielou's *A Catalogue of Recorded Classical and Traditional Indian Music*

(Archives of Recorded Music, 1952), 160–62, is a very incomplete listing of her recordings, which are extremely rare.

79. In *The Ragas of Northern India* (London: Barrie and Rockliff, 1968), A. Danielou notes that the system tonic used by most singers was often B flat (23–24).

80. In his *Orientalism,* Said writes: "French pilgrims . . . ruminated about places that were principally *in their minds.* . . . Theirs was the Orient of memories, suggestive ruins, forgotten secrets, hidden correspondences, and an almost virtuosic style of being . . . " (169–70).

81. "Wagner et nos musiciens," *Grande revue* (10 April 1909): 562–63.

82. J. Marnold in *Mercure de France* (16 August 1912), 863; cited in Christian Goubault's "Les Premières Oeuvres de Roussel" in Kelkel, *Albert Roussel: Musique et esthétique,* 24.

83. A. Sériyx, "À propos des 'Evocations,'" *Revue musicale S.I.M.* (May 1913): 65–66; cited in Goubault, ibid., 25.

84. Jean-Aubry, *La Musique d'aujourd'hui* (Paris: Perrin, 1916), 135–36.

85. Hoérée, *Roussel,* 39.

86. A. Mariotte, *Le Courrier musical* (1 November 1919), cited in Goubault, "Les Premières Oeuvres," 26.

87. Roussel began this Indian-inspired work in December 1913 but it was not premiered until 1923. *Padmâvatî* has an Indian subject, the story of Padmini at Tchitor, based a novel written in 1856 that Roussel and his collaborator Louis Laloy found in the Bibliothèque des Langues Orientales in Paris (see Arthur Hoérée, "Lettres d'Albert Roussel à Louis Laloy," *Cahiers Albert Roussel* 2 [1979]: 73–74). Given what he says in his diary and their absence in his sketchbook and *Evocations,* one can surmise that the numerous ragas Roussel used in *Padmâvatî* he learned after his return to Paris.

88. Edward Said, *Culture and Imperialism* (New York: Knopf, 1993), xxi.

89. I am using the term *capital* here in the sense of cultural capital as coined by Pierre Bourdieu in *La Distinction: Critique sociale du jugement* (Paris: Minuit, 1979).

90. Said, *Culture and Imperialism,* xxvi.

91. The first of these is dedicated to Delage.

92. Interview with the author, 1977.

93. Delage used similar material in an orchestral work, *Les Batisseurs de ponts* (The bridge-builders), conceived as a pantomime for the Ballets Russes; the third movement of *Contrerimes* (1927–1932); the Vocalise-Étude (1929); and "Themmangu," from *Chants de la Jungle* (Songs of the Jungle, 1914–1934).

Bartók, the Gypsies, and Hybridity in Music

Julie Brown

I. INTRODUCTION

To talk about Hungarian modernist composer Béla Bartók is almost inevitably to talk about ethnicity and race. Considered a great of twentieth-century music, Bartók succeeded in the 1920s in creating a musical language that mediated between the increasingly polarized Schoenberg and Stravinsky camps—twelve-note atonalism on the one hand, neoclassicism on the other. Most notably, however, he forged a recognizably Hungarian modernist voice. The basic story of his quest for this voice is well known. Around 1906, influenced by nineteenth-century *völkisch* nationalism, though more directly by the celebration of folk culture at Hungary's 1896 millennial commemoration of a thousand years of Magyar presence in the Carpathian Basin, Bartók became, with Zoltán Kodály, a pioneering collector and student of folksong. His initial aim was to expand the available repertory of *magyar nóta* (Hungarian tunes, often by amateur composers of the middle classes, transmitted as folk songs), but this grew into one of identifying an "authentic" Hungarian source music, an ur-Hungarian folksong which he hoped might enrich his own efforts to create a distinctively Hungarian modernist art music. (His main compositional influences at this time were Strauss, Debussy, and Liszt.) His Magyar nationalism may later have undergone significant revision, and the emphases he placed on individual activities may have shifted over the years. He concerned himself, for instance, with an increasingly wide range of ethnic musics, not only from provinces within Hungary, and clearly took increasing pleasure in ethnographic study for its own sake. But his foundational project was undoubtedly nationalist.

One of Bartók's major achievements as folklorist was his "discovery" of peasant song, something quite different from the folk music with which urban Hungarians were familiar. In his scholarly essays he represented peasant music as the authentic Hungarian folk source and hence the proper basis for a national art music, but in doing so famously positioned himself against widely held perceptions that Gypsy music—that is to say, the music played by urban Hungarian Gypsy musicians—occupied this position.[1] Yet as Judit Frigyesi has persuasively argued, the concept of Nationhood for which (up to about 1903) Gypsy music was widely perceived to be the true voice, was upheld at the turn of the century by conservative forces.[2] Nationhood was defined by them to the exclusion of the peasants: Frigyesi notes that until the turn of the century "the equation of the nobility with the Hungarian nation and the ranking of the middle nobility as the *populus* or 'core of the Hungarians' was a deeply rooted historical belief. . . . The gentry played the role that the peasant had played in the romantic notion of 'folk.' "[3] The gentry classes held power in Hungary and made claims for the true Magyar spirit, courtesy of historical narratives of conquest over the Hungarian land and its native people. Peasant music was excluded from cultural self-definition. Gypsy music, on the other hand, had long played a central part in gentry lifestyle; it was "effectively the property of the 'gentleman.' "[4] By the late nineteenth century it comprised mainly eighteenth- and nineteenth-century songs, often composed by dilettante gentry musicians, and had come to be an integral part of the conservatives' construction of nationhood. The "weeping-rejoicing" mode of Gypsy performance was the authentic voice of Hungarian pathos.[5]

Frigyesi, like Bence Szabolcsi before her, reads Bartók's critique of Gypsy music as part of a modernist reaction to this conservative position, as much an aversion to a romantically sentimental performance style as an attempt to find a nonfake nationalism.[6] Yet these readings gloss over an important aspect of Bartók's work which German musicologist Heinrich Möller highlighted as early as 1932. Within the context of an acrimonious exchange with Bartók, sparked off by the composer's negative review of his anthology of Hungarian folk songs, Möller pointed out that while Bartók had clearly discovered an important new source in peasant songs, his conception of Hungarian folk music was based on a norm/deviancy model. Möller implied that Bartók's project fit into a broader discourse of cultural degeneracy allied with theories of social Darwinism and ideals of racial purity. He noted that "Gypsy music" was on the deviant side, and that for Bartók it comprised

> second-rate folk songs and degenerate phenomena, because foreign (German, Gypsy) influences can be detected in them and they cannot be pressed into the pattern of the peasant stanzaic structures. . . . It seems to be hardly unbiased, as Bartók does [*sic*], to consider the variations the melodies undergo during this transforming process as "disfigurations" in one sense and purification or national stylization in the other.[7]

Möller denied such "mystic belief" that a creative "national spirit" can be found in peasant song. He agreed instead with Wilhelm Scherer's definition of folk song: "There is no other criterion of the folk song but wide propagation and general popularity."[8]

By focusing in 1932 on Bartókian tropes of "disfiguration" and "degeneracy" on the one hand, and "purification or national stylization" on the other, Möller may have somewhat misrepresented Bartók's most recent thoughts on the subject. But Bartók did likewise when he baldly denied having excluded Hungarian popular art music (a.k.a. Gypsy music) from the category of genuine Hungarian folk music as Möller claimed he did: Bartók's denial, while strictly true, hides the fact that he had only recently shifted position on the subject. Yet even allowing for the selectivity of the polemic's claim and counterclaim, Möller touches here on an important aspect of Bartók's folkloristic project as a whole: the embeddedness of Bartók's work in discourses (characteristic of his time) of cultural formation steeped in race. I mean by this that Bartók's writings about folk and even art music use discourses of race analogically, and this long before he admitted doing so in an essay of 1942 entitled "Race Purity in Music." ("I apply the word racial here to the music itself, and not to the individuals creating, preserving or performing the music.")[9] To contemplate Bartók's scholarly output from this perspective is to add another layer of complexity to Judit Frigyesi's account.

My purpose here is to examine this aspect of Bartók's work more closely, and particularly to consider how issues of cultural hybridity appear in his scholarly output. (Unfortunately, space prevents me from comprehensively considering the implications this might have for his own modernist art music.) By historicizing his representation of Gypsy music, I seek to show that repressive politics of othering were not the sole domain of conservative forces within Hungarian nationalism.[10] I do so mindful of some of the traps of practicing racial discourse analysis. Not only is it easy to replicate that very discourse in the analytical act, but unravelling the threads of what was a highly dispersed racial trope in cultural discourses of the prewar period is far from straightforward.

One of the difficulties, it seems almost trite to point out, is that although racialist thinking is rooted in nineteenth-century nationalism and the social Darwinism frequently associated with it, as the twentieth century progressed it came to be freighted with ever more alarming potential. When widespread racial stereotyping and prejudice was replaced in the 1930s by a politicized racial hatred seeking practical social "solutions," something of a watershed in racialist discourse occurred. Many people reevaluated their positions.

It is with a mind to such shifts that I read Bartók's prose constructions of Hungarian music as operating in an ongoing dialogue with these wider cultural shifts. The Gypsy and the conceptual construct of the hybrid provide for us the clearest windows from which to catch a glimpse of the broader racialist context of Bartók's work, even if both ultimately emerge as signs of confusion or indeterminacy. As figures, they subtly mutate within a web of cultural values as Bartók conceived and then reconceived what an "authentic" Hungarian music might, and even should, be.

II. BARTÓK AND THE GYPSIES: 1906–1920

Bartók's ethnomusicological activities are so well documented that only a brief overview is necessary.[11] He originally set out hoping to find peasants who could provide him with additional *magyar nóta* to add to the repertory of national songs, but after hearing "genuine" peasant songs in mid-1904 on a trip to Transylvania (now in Romania) he wrote to his sister in December 1904 outlining his plan to collect the finest of these melodies and "to raise them, adding the best possible piano accompaniments, to the level of art song." In 1905 he teamed up with Zoltán Kodály, who was writing a doctorate on Hungarian folksong for the University of Budapest, and together they set about the systematic collection of folk songs by phonograph. From his first major field trip Bartók's intention was to compile a scientifically precise collection of Hungarian folk songs. An element of proselytizing was initially involved—the two hoped that their 1906 publication of twenty settings (ten each) would serve to popularize what they considered to be "genuine" Hungarian folk songs—but Bartók was also driven by a hope that these materials might become part of his own compositional tool box.

Most of Bartók's fieldwork was carried out between 1906 and 1918. He spent the summer of 1907 in Transylvania, collected Slovak songs from 1906, Romanian from 1909, Ruthenian and some Bulgarian and Serbian songs from 1912. He also went to considerable lengths in 1913 to arrange a field trip outside the province of Eastern European neighbors—to Biskra in North Africa, where he collected two hundred Arabic melodies. After World War I, when the Austro-Hungarian Empire collapsed and many of his collection sites became part of other nation states, Bartók wound down his field work. His only other field trip was to Turkey in 1936.

To perform a discourse analysis of Bartók's scholarship is to discover a catalogue of discursive features standard in any nineteenth-century book on natural history or race: the related concerns of ethnic origins and cultural hybridity,[12] a maintenance of careful distinctions between high and low culture, the ideological construction of Orientalism,[13] the enlightenment figure of the noble savage, and Darwinian theories of evolutionary cultural development: degeneration on the one hand, and replenishment or "healing" of the cultural stock on the other.

What emerges quite strongly from the writings is Bartók's tendency to maintain a distinction between a "good" hybrid, or a healthy and authentic hybrid music language, and a "bad" or potentially degenerative hybrid. At first, the potentially good hybrid was the sought-after fusion of his own art music with folk sources; the bad hybrid was Gypsy music. As Möller noted, when Bartók wrote down his ethnographic findings on "authentic" peasant musics, he frequently held up Gypsy music as a type of negative image. Indeed, his earliest writings portray the Gypsy as a type of blot on the Hungarian musical landscape—an attitude that went beyond simple aesthetic aversion. His association of Gypsies with the conservative forces of nationalism via the gentry classes is not apparent at this early stage. Bartók's first major paper arising out of his folksong collecting dates from 1911. Written after five years in the field, "On Hungarian Music" is effectively a position paper, portraying the Gypsy as the slightly threatening Oriental "other." Bartók speaks critically of the "Oriental fantasy" and "melodic distortions" to which true Hungarian peasant music is subjected by that "immigrant nation," the Gypsy.[14] Their status as the supposed embodiment of Hungarian music is erroneous. Bartók's essential message—that what Hungarians think of as Hungarian music, Gypsy music, is not authentic—was already widely acknowledged: as professional musicians, Gypsies appropriated, performed and disseminated all sorts of music—popular, folk, and light art music. Bartók's contribution was to gloss this knowledge with negative critique, saying that Gypsies mar this music "by their Orientalist fantasy."[15] He charges such music with inauthenticity, initially according to the trope of the alien-among-us, feared, contaminating influence. At the same time, he promotes peasant music as a purer musical expression of his country. Charges of perversion and contamination are explicit in an essay on Romanian music dating from 1914: "Gypsies pervert melodies, change their rhythm to 'Gypsy' rhythm, introduce among the people melodies heard in other regions and in the country seats of the gentry—in other words, they contaminate the style of genuine folk music."[16] In short, he sees Gypsies as agents of illegitimate musical dissemination, and also as creators of music from an illegitimate fusion of styles.

I will consider below ways in which this representation subsequently changed; however, it is worth focusing on Bartók's ethnographic point of departure at some length, since the premises established remained largely in place in his later years, even if he refashioned and redirected them. In these early writings Bartók marshals to his cause some familiar Orientalist tropes. That he should characterize the music Gypsies played in Hungary according to such tropes is not surprising. Gypsies fell within the orbit of Orientalist representation. They were popularly thought to have entered Eastern Europe in the Middle Ages from Egypt,[17] a country which was one of the central nineteenth-century sources of Orientalist fantasy, and from whose name the English word "Gypsy" (like the Greek *gyphtos* and the Spanish *gitano*) is derived. Anthropology may remain far from united on the question of Gypsy origins even now, but it is clear that in the late nineteenth and early twentieth centuries Gypsies were, along with Jews, the "'Orientals' at home."[18] In her study of Bizet's *Carmen,* Susan McClary describes how Gypsies were frequently represented through Orientalist tropes as figures of otherness, dark, exotic and slightly threatening in the European context. Jews were similarly represented. As figures of racial otherness, McClary notes, the two were considered virtually interchangeable.[19]

It is not hard to imagine how Bartók, as an inheritor of the Western cultural tradition living within the Austro-Hungarian Empire (since the Compromise of 1867 a dual monarchy), should come to perpetuate these tropes; but as a Hungarian nationalist, he was even more susceptible to them. Gypsies were less culturally other in Hungary than in wider Europe. Musically and even culturally speaking, Gypsies were at the very center of Hungarian national identity: even if, as David Crowe points out, for centuries Hungarian Gypsies had been subjected to varying degrees of discrimination and prejudice, musically they were widely considered to embody the national spirit.[20] By the end of the nineteenth century, music-making for money in Hungary was almost entirely associated with Gypsies; they played for the nobility, but also in restaurants for the "fallen nobility," the gentry.[21]

When Bartók writes of the "perversion" of melodies by Gypsies, their marring of folk song by "Orientalist fantasy," he is essentially referring to a performance style. Applied to Hungarian music, the term "Gypsy music" refers to a repertory that is performed in a highly characteristic way by urban Gypsies but is composed by others, not usually Gypsies.[22] The repertory of songs draws from a number of traditions: popular art songs of the nineteenth century mostly composed by amateur musicians of the gentry class, popular dance repertoire (especially the *csardas*), and the *verbunkos* (for ornamental figures). The last, a dance form used in the eighteenth century as part of a method of enlisting recruits into the imperial army, reached the status of a national style at the hands of a small number of virtuoso Gypsy violinists in the early nineteenth century, and entered the nineteenth-century high art music repertory, notably through Brahms and Liszt, as the essential Hungarian voice.[23] Urban Gypsies brought to this varied repertory a characteristic performance mode, a series of formulae which apply to harmonization, figurative elements, and cadences. Almost any tune can be turned into Gypsy music if improvised on, using some of these formulae. *Style hongrois,* on the other hand, was a style, or "topic," of (Western) art music generally associated with Austro-German composers of the late eighteenth and nineteenth centuries. In the eighteenth century it drew predominantly on the *verbunkos,* with its characteristic dotted semiquavers in duple time, but also a shared range of effects with the related exoticism of Turkish music: repeated "stamping" chords, tonic drones, double mordents, pizzicato, double stops on string instruments. In the late nineteenth century, *style hongrois* drew more and more on Gypsy music-making, especially in works by Brahms and Liszt.

Odd though it seems that *style hongrois* should remain an exoticism of the Austro-German art music tradition in the late nineteenth century, in view of the fact that Hungary had long been part of the most powerful empire in Europe, and since 1867 had enjoyed equal status (theoretically at least) with its complementary half, the "exotic" status of *style hongrois* may reflect something of the political (im)balance of power that operated within the empire up to this time.

Bartók's Orientalist troping suggests an extra layer to his cultural anxiety as modern nationalist. The fact that his national music was intimately associated with a people discursively constructed as Oriental was likely to have sat with Bartók's initial nationalistic project as uncomfortably as the fact that it was an inherent part of the lifestyle of the ruling conservative elite. For although Bartók *was* a nationalist, chauvinistically so in the early years— initially his nationalism found expression in avowals of a fundamental Hungarian superiority and came with negative Jewish stereotyping[24]— he was also very much a West-looking modernist. The binarism of an advanced West standing in opposition to a backward Orient was a crucial tenet of late-nineteenth-century Orientalism. Yet for Bartók the Orient was not an exotic other, a realm of sensuality and mystery to be mastered and represented, an other experienced as simulacrum rather than genuinely felt and experienced. For him it was the most powerful force in Hungarian musical culture, as conceived not only inside but also outside Hungary.

As a West-looking modernist, Bartók took essentially the same position as *Nyugat* (The West), a literary journal at the heart of cultural nationalism in early twentieth-century Budapest. *Nyugat* published plays by archnationalist Endre Ady, some of which were eventually set by Bartók as operas, ballets, and pantomimes, but it also promoted both a fierce nationalism and what André Karátson describes as a "scandalous Westernism."[25] As Karátson and others have pointed out, because in Hungary the notion of the East-West trajectory was complicated, Hungarian nationalism was somewhat paradoxical. For instance, *Nyugat* combated Hungarian conservatism in the name of the West, yet did so even though since the middle ages that very conservatism had been formed precisely on the West. And even though Hungary shared the most powerful empire in Europe, the journal published articles by Hungarian intellectuals about the barrenness and backwardness of Budapest and Hungary. In the first decade of the century at least, Westernism equated with modernism, which equated with the positive and good.

Understood as Orientalist, Gypsy music was backward, the antithesis of the aspired-to modernism. But entwined with this understanding of the Orient as inherently backward were theories of cultural intermixture drawing on the "science" of race. In wider European culture in this period, racial and evolutionary thought served as new, scientific proofs legitimating long established prejudices against Jews and Gypsies. Count Gobineau's *Essai sur l'inégalité des races humaines* (1853–5) developed the idea that there were "higher" and "lower" races (Aryan and Nordic races were the higher), and linked this to the decline and fall of civilizations: if white people have created all history, then degeneration through the mixture of higher and lower races might explain the decline of civilization.[26] The distinction between higher and lower races was developed by Cesare Lombroso's influential *L'uomo delinquente* (1876), in which he attributes to their supposed lower racial origin the depraved and criminal activities allegedly typical of Gypsies and Jews. Lombroso took a divided view of Gypsies, regarding their undeniable musical gifts as simply "a new proof of the genius that, mixed with atavism, is to be found in the criminal."[27] To read Bartók's representation of Gypsy music within this context is to understand the "contaminating" Oriental influence as contributing through inauspicious hybridization to a degeneration of Hungarian musical "stock" along Darwinian lines.

There is by now a growing literature exploring ways in which a similar racialist discourse found cultural expression with the birth of modernism in Vienna.[28] I have argued, for instance, that Schoenberg's symbolic construction of his step into atonality around 1909 relied heavily on a Wagnerian ideology of cultural regeneration.[29] Increasingly anti-Semitic and pan-German, Vienna was of course Budapest's twin capital city within the dual monarchy. It is hard to imagine Bartók not being familiar, like Schoenberg, with Wagner's theories of German national cultural identity, including their anti-Semitic and frankly racialist side. He was certainly familiar with Liszt's book *Des Bohémiens et de leur musique en Hongrie* (On Gypsies and Their Music in Hungary), published in 1859, nine years after Wagner's infamous pamphlet "Das Judentum in der Musik."[30] Like Bartók, Liszt had drawn on Orientalist tropes to characterize Gypsy music. However, there was a crucial difference between his and Bartók's later representations. For Liszt, Gypsy music was a wholly positive thing. In his book, he wrongly attributed most Hungarian music (*Magyar notá* and more recently composed popular songs circulated by Gypsy bands) to the Gypsies. Moreover, Liszt included in his study considerable material on Jews for the purpose of drawing distinctions between their music and that of Gypsies, evidently mindful that Jews and Gypsies were virtually interchangeable as racial others in Europe.[31] It may even be that he was prompted by Wagner's notorious pamphlet to clarify and defend the status of Gypsy music precisely because of this figurative interchangeability.[32] Liszt's association with Wagner in the 1850s is well-known.[33] Liszt broadly replicated Wagner's negative critique of Jews, yet gave an extremely glowing, if somewhat idiosyncratic, account of Gypsy music. Yet it was against the grain that he claimed for Gypsies a musical role more than that of mere guardian of Hungarian national music—as the storm of protest that greeted his book attested.[34] Several of Wagner's charges against Jews seem significant here. For whereas Wagner alleged that Jews always speak the language of the country they are in as a foreigner, that it is inherently impossible to write "true poetry" in a foreign language, and that Jews engage in "reflected," not "instinctive," expression,[35] Liszt claimed that Gypsies are genuine creators of an authentically Hungarian music. It is as if Liszt adopts this idiosyncratic and possibly even knowingly erroneous position about Gypsies in order to prevent them from being tarred with the same brush. Liszt is known to have enormously admired and closely identified with the virtuosity of Gypsies as performers and improvisers. In this light, it seems all the more pointed that Bartók's own early writings about Gypsy music should "correct" Liszt on these two fundamental points: by and large, Gypsies did *not* invent their own songs (a philological, though within Hungary hardly necessary, clarification); and they *should* be considered to be agents of cultural degeneration (an ideological judgment).

Before going on to sketch ways in which Bartók's account of Gypsy music changed over the course of the ensuing two decades, I should consider some of the conceptual structures that contributed to his representation. For his account of Gypsy music was conceived as part of a larger ethnographic project in which a slightly different brand of "internal Orientalism" operated.

III. BARTÓK AND THE GYPSIES: 1920–1940S

As a group outside normal definitions of the nation, peasants occupied a position in Hungary as internal "ethnic" other.[36] Like the Oriental other, their little-known music was something Bartók perceived to require Western attention. His obsessive documentation of folk musics in Hungary and wider Eastern Europe mimics the Orientalist's desire to possess the Orient by "knowing" it in exhaustive documentary detail; it was something to be analyzed and to have its connections and influences traced by an educated, urban, and West-looking Hungarian. I admit that here there is a sense in which I am "creating" Bartók's project as internally Orientalist in order to constitute an object for analysis and resistance. However, such an analysis is the more convincing when you bear in mind the markedly different attitude that Bartók took toward folk music—"their" music, as against his own art music. While he placed a premium on coming to a close understanding of folk and peasant music, he was extremely tight-lipped about his own compositional processes and intentions, betraying little on the subject over the entire course of his career. "Their" music could, perhaps even should, have its secrets probed; his was permitted to retain its mystery.[37]

If Bartók understood Gypsy music to be a source of "contamination" and "degeneration" of the Hungarian musical stock, he took peasant music conversely to be a source of replenishment and healing. He presented peasant music as the functional inverse of Gypsy music. There is even a sense in which peasant music emerges from Bartók's painstakingly "scientific" accounts as essentially a type of genetic material, all the more so when one considers that peasant music was not greeted at the time as being intrinsically interesting in Western musical terms (Möller describes it as involving "clumsy melodies devoid of all charm"). This "scientific" conception of peasant song had a figurative equivalent: the notion that it was Hungarian music's noble savage. For in many ways Bartók attributed to peasant song and its supposedly primitive and natural characteristics the sorts of fetishistic qualities that Hayden White has associated with the trope of the noble savage: extravagant trust or reverence, and some sort of magical transforming power.[38] In 1924, Bartók wrote that what characterizes peasant music is a special "natural force whose operation is unconscious."[39] Earlier, in 1920, he spoke of its "throbbing life" and "folk spirit," and in 1921 of its "transforming power."[40] Even if such fantasies of magical power amount only to hyperbole, they remain strangely, almost apotropaically, logical given that in his portrayal of the peasant Bartók had to match, or neutralize, his negative image of Gypsy music.

Underpinning Bartók's broad appropriation of Orientalist representation is the concept of the hybrid. As Robert Young has pointed out, from the 1840s onwards discussion of hybridity was a regular feature of books on natural history or race, including the writings of Herder and other theorists of culture.[41] Herder may be best known for theorizing culture as something nationally specific, connected to soil and geography, but he is also notable for grounding his *Outlines of a Philosophy of the History of Man* (1784–91) in an argument which takes the principal law of history to be one of difference and diversity. Thus, despite his primary association with notions of national cultural authenticity, Herder recognized that culture is always hybrid, dependent on interaction for its creation and definition.[42] He was a relativist, questioning the Enlightenment ethos of civilization and progress: culture was no longer fundamentally associated with civilization or cultivation, but rather with natural values. Young argues that for those who read him in the nineteenth century, Herder's notion of "culture" formed the basis for an attack on what was seen as "the mechanical, over-industrialised, over-rationalised, materialistic character of nineteenth-century civilization."[43] Yet despite this relativism, Herder also retained—somewhat paradoxically—Enlightenment ideas of the progress of civilization. At the same time that he produced a critique of universal histories as a linear process, he maintained that German *Kultur* represented the most advanced creative civilization. He subscribed, in other words, to a view of cultural formation that was paradoxically both isolationist and diffusionist. Later writers, especially Count Gobineau, appropriated aspects of this paradoxical theory accommodating mid-century ethnology and the new science of race. They fashioned newer versions of elitist cultural theory involving clear hierarchies between Western and primitive culture, between high and low within Western culture itself, and eventually, with the addition of late nineteenth-century social Darwinism, between cultures deemed degenerate through inauspicious racial intermixture and those considered of a higher evolutionary order through "favorable" intermixture.

Not only Bartók's initial conception of Gypsy music but his entire folk music project is consistent with these nineteenth-century discussions of cultural formation. From his earliest writings, he was aware of a process of hybridization in connection with Gypsy music; however, he later became aware that searches for the origins of folk and peasant music are made in vain; hybridization happens throughout history through all manner of cultural confrontation. But I have not yet reached that point. My brush strokes have so far been broad, covering Bartók's earliest prose writings. They have not taken into account the evolution of his thought. I now return to sketch in something of the evolution of his ideas after these initial imaginings of incremental cultural degeneration.

In 1920 Bartók still used some Orientalist jargon in connection with the music played by Gypsies, referring to its "exotic melodies" and its "remnants of an Asiatic musical culture."[44] By this stage he had drawn his (trademark) distinction between Hungarian peasant music and Hungarian "national melodies"—the latter referring to those disseminated by Gypsies. He is far less concerned with pointing out the potential of these national melodies to pervert (though he doesn't hesitate to call them vulgar, something true Hungarian peasant music is not) than he is with underlining the obscurity of their origin and the complexity of their nexus of influence. In this, he echoes a slightly different strand of Orientalist thought, one that conceives of the East as an eccentric, aberrant, and unfathomable phenomenon. By contrast, he is confident he has unraveled the origins of Hungarian peasant music. He particularly asserts that older melodies are specifically Magyar products.[45]

After 1920, Bartók starts to take his Gypsy critique in a new direction, gradually redirecting his interest away from questions of relative ethnolinguistic purity to that of the mode and place of cultural production: rural versus urban. In other words, his critique shifts from an explicitly ethnic, ostensibly racialist one to an economic one. As a group, however, Gypsies continue to do badly. Here, the connection between Gypsy music and gentry lifestyle stressed by Judit Frigyesi begins to emerge. In 1921 Bartók attributes their prominent role as musicians to their greed, a greed which led them gradually to replace what originally was a musically empowered peasantry. He goes further. The reason Gypsy melodies found their way back to the peasants was because peasants fell for the noble manners the Gypsies picked up from their gentry masters—presumably meaning that they easily fell for fake authority, an odd line of argument for someone who consistently portrays peasants as children of nature, instinct, and cultural "authenticity."[46]

Although Bartók maintained his original *judgment* here (namely, that peasant music possessed a certain purity compared to Gypsy music's impurity), his rhetoric has shifted from one of contamination as a result of undesirable ethnic confrontation—Gypsies marring authentic folk song by Orientalist fantasy and so forth—toward one of natural beauty versus commercial vulgarity. This critique enabled Bartók to continue to exclude Gypsy music from the "good" side of the cultural equation, even as his concept of Hungary's essential ethnic pluralism and hybridity developed. (He had by now studied the peasant music of a number of the ethnic groups within and neighboring Hungary.) Gypsies had now come to represent a kind of insidious reflection of the ruling class, a group situated somewhere between the gentry and the peasantry, which acted in a similar way to colonial aggressors. In their current domination of the music profession, Gypsies had greedily seized what belonged to the peasants and exploited it for commercial gain, even (illegitimately) inspiring peasants to adopt elements of Gypsy music themselves.[47] The move here from a (pseudo)scientific to a cultural account of race was remarkably smooth.

The Hungarian Folk Song, Bartók's monograph of 1924, is notable for offering very similar accounts of the sources of peasant music and of Gypsy music. Bartók acknowledges that even peasant music can draw on tunes from another class and from urban culture. But: "As to the question of the origin of the [peasant] tunes . . . our definition waives it aside as non-essential." What characterizes peasant (as opposed to Gypsy) music is a special "natural force whose operation is unconscious." Even though peasants have an imitative tendency, they also strive to preserve old traditions; they are able to exert a special transformational power over any borrowed elements.[48]

By 1931 something seems to have triggered a significant reorientation. Socialist politics of a sort are now more explicitly a part of Bartók's self-definition. He also begins to portray the Gypsy in a new and sympathetic way. In his essay "Gypsy Music or Hungarian Music?" he shifts from regarding Gypsy musicians as their own agencies of greed to considering them as a type of pawn in the world of gentry social pretension. They only play this (bad) music because Hungarian gentlemen find it beneath their dignity to play it for themselves: the Hungarian gentleman may compose it, but it is "traditionally unbecoming to his social status to perform it 'for money'—only Gypsies are supposed to do that."[49] In another essay of the same year he defines authentic folk music as produced by those people also engaged in producing prime requisites and materials. He now also deems it best to stop speaking of Gypsies as a people or single ethnic group and to replace the "confusing" terminology "Gypsy music" with "Hungarian popular art music" (clearly a much less confusing term!). Unfortunately the alternative Bartók elaborates involves their division into two equally neat groups on the basis of the familiar urban-rural binary divide: there are rural Gypsies, who are more like peasants, and there are urban Gypsies, who play in restaurants.

This urban-rural account of culture stems ultimately from the French Enlightenment. But in the late nineteenth and early twentieth centuries, it was essentially another representational turn in the pervasive discourse of cultural decline. One theoretical solution to assumptions of cultural degeneration through adverse intermixture came via racialist thinking: while inauspicious hybridization leads to decline, "healthy" hybridization leads to cultural strengthening. An overlapping solution was based on theories of authenticity. This latter involved the invention of imaginary categories like the illiterate folk or peasants, supposedly untouched by modern civilization or transformation, whose "natural" culture stands in contrast to anything implicated in urban life and affected by commercial interests.[50] The two solutions are distinct, yet they overlap insofar as the basis of healthy hybridization was supposedly untouched, natural culture. The other "authentic" sphere was "high" culture, similarly supposed to be unsullied by commercial concerns. "Culture" in this sense did not extend to any form of popular or commercial culture, but reflected the original "cultish," "venerational" associations of the term.[51] Bartók's discomfort with music implicated in the urban-commercial sphere reflects this strand of nineteenth-century thought. Yet even he was prepared to relativize such a view if a larger issue—a national issue—was at stake. For instance, in 1931 he decided that compared with the even greater cultural threat of American popular music, Gypsy music was relatively acceptable. With a new ethnic other to fear, Bartók found himself able to celebrate Gypsy music for being at least in some way Hungarian. He hoped that in the face of "the onslaught of the jazz and salon orchestras," which he called "foreign trash," Gypsy music would hold its own as a specifically Hungarian form of popular music.[52] In other words, Bartók's revaluation of Gypsy music's cultural position here reflects a pragmatic incremental expansion of what he considers Self as much as it does a reconsideration of a politics of fear and exclusion; the demonized other is simply redefined and "owned." As with wider fears of Americanization, for Bartók American popular culture becomes the new other.

By 1933, Bartók's redefinition both of the social character of urban Gypsies and their music (and their opposite, the rural peasant) is seemingly complete. He asserts that "ancient peasant music . . . is undoubtedly a remnant of the old, common cultural values of the entire Hungarian nation (and not, therefore, of the peasant class only)."[53] Bartók has therefore ceded on the final point. Not only is the Gypsy no longer a single demonized ethnic category, but the very idea of peasant purity is itself questioned. Moreover, by speaking of ancient peasant music as a remnant of the cultural values of the entire Hungarian nation and not only of the peasant class, he gestures in 1934 toward an even more inclusive hybrid:

> The most pleasing thing of all would be if each country, each region, each county, even each village, could produce something of its own, original and

unique. But this is impossible, for people—whether they speak the same language or not—come into contact with one another, influence one another—It is these interactions that we, as research workers, must endeavour to unravel with the utmost impartiality.[54]

This model of migrations and colonizations of peoples, and associated emigration of melodies, is repeated in two essays of the early 1940s, "Race Purity in Music" (1942) and "Diversity of Material Yielded Up in Profusion in European Melting Pot" (1943).[55] At this time, when the race issue was at the front of the European political stage, Bartók self-consciously played with racialist discourse in order to strike a blow on behalf of the *anti*racialists. He declared that "'racial impurity' . . . is definitely beneficial. . . . A complete separation from foreign influences means stagnation: well assimilated foreign impulses offer possibilities of enrichment."[56]

IV. UNDERSTANDING BARTÓK'S SHIFT IN RHETORIC

Since it was not philological discoveries that drove the two major changes in Bartók's construction of Gypsy music (the "scientific" evidence was in place as early as 1920), we might speculate as to what did. Bartók's association with the short-lived Communist government of Béla Kun (March–July 1919)—he acted as the musical adviser—and his close association with György Lukács must have contributed to the shift of position in 1921. The Gypsies' playing for money in cafés and restaurants cannot have sat comfortably with either world view, nor could their association with a fallen aristocracy or petit bourgeois class. In 1931 there are several possible influences: Bartók's participation in July that year in a League of Nations summit on artistic and ethical matters;[57] his exchange with Heinrich Möller, whose brief but pointed analysis of Bartók's representation of Gypsies alluded to the racialist dimension; and the increasingly vocal ultra-Nationalist fascist parties in central Europe, including Hungary itself. In 1931, Prime Minister Bethlen resigned and was replaced by fascist Gyula Gömbös. Significant therefore that Bartók now acknowledged that the people called Gypsies do not collapse into a neat racial group. It may be that this critical move reflects a consciousness of certain parallels between his original conception of the Gypsies and the now extreme racist rhetoric in neighboring Germany. At the precise moment when questions of racial supremacy were becoming cultural policy in Germany, when organized acts of oppression had already begun to take place there, and when work emerged from musicologists such as Ernst Bücken and Richard Eichenauer that was complicit with the Nazi regime and its cultural policy,[58] and only a little before the 1935 Nuremberg Laws that treated both Gypsies and Jews as "alien races," Bartók leaves us with a very different view of Gypsy music. He still dislikes it aesthetically. But he now considers it to be, if anything, a cultural product of the Gypsies' social oppression.

Bartók remained committed to a national Hungarian character even after he had come to an understanding of the complex processes of cultural hybridization that occur over millennia. Both nationalism and cultural intermixture are celebrated in his oft-quoted and -discussed letter referring humanistically, but in stark contradiction to his earlier thinking, to a "brotherhood of peoples." The letter, which describes his own compositions as a reflection of this political idea, dates from 1931 and was addressed to Octavian Beu, who was writing an essay about Bartók's works of a Romanian character:

> My creative work, just because it arises from 3 sources (Hungarian, Romanian, Slovakian), might be regarded as the embodiment of the very concept of integration so much emphasized in Hungary today. . . . My own idea, however— of which I have been fully conscious since I found myself as a composer—is the brotherhood of peoples, brotherhood in spite of all wars and conflicts. I try—to the best of my ability—to serve this idea in my music; therefore I don't reject any influence, be it Slovakian, Romanian, Arabic or from any other source. The source must only be clean, fresh and healthy![59]

Bartók's comments acknowledge Hungary's undeniable ethnic hybridity, a character which remained significant even after the collapse of the Austro-Hungarian Empire following World War I, and the subsequent Treaty of Trianon's drastic redrawing of Hungary's borders. Only 32 percent of the territory and 41 percent of the people remained of the former Kingdom of Hungary; Romania and Slovakia had even become separate countries, the latter part of Czechoslovakia.[60] Bartók himself embodied something of his country's hybridity, having a Southern Slav paternal grandmother and a German mother, and having been born in what is now part of Romania. In this letter, of course, he casts his net even wider, permitting elements into his music from any "clean" source.

Frigyesi argues that nationalism and subscription to a "brotherhood of nations" are incompatible and represent two distinct ideological positions.[61] However, Malcolm Gillies reminds us that in the continuation of the above passage, Bartók continues to project a plainly nationalistic ideal on top of the universally humanist one. He envisaged an integration of what either were (in the case of Arab music) or by this stage had become (in the case of Slovakian and Romanian music) foreign ethnic elements within a Hungarian-dominated style.[62] He was not advocating a freewheeling pluralism, or internationalism, for his own music. Rather, Bartók argued that because "character and milieu must somehow harmonize with each other" his "style— notwithstanding its various sources—has a Hungarian character."[63] In other words, his model of Hungarian culture, even at this *least* chauvinistic stage of his thinking on the subject, echoed Herder's isolationist-diffusionist model of German culture. In 1942 Bartók held that in the case of folk music, "more or less ancient styles are generally well preserved" despite the enriching processes of intermixture and melodic migration.[64]

But how is it possible to support such a notion? How is it possible to deem intermixture and hybridization necessary aspects of cultural formation, and yet at the same time remain committed to the notion of an immutable national spirit? To follow the diffusionist/hybridization position to its logical conclusion is, surely, to acknowledge that the eventual consequence might be a complete flattening of difference.

Bartók's solution to the paradox comes through recourse to a brand of metaphysics—that is, the "magical" aspect of the noble savage fetish. He writes about this clearly in his monograph, *The Hungarian Folk Song*, in connection with the intermixture of peasant musics: "borrowed elements undergo a certain transformation, so long as they do not constitute mere sporadic outcrops but take firm root among the peasant class, spread, and endure."[65] He states it very clearly in 1942: "The trend toward transformation of foreign melodies prevents the internationalization of the music of these peoples."[66] Thus, even though new melodies inevitably come into contact with various peasant musics, he argues that the "home" music is capable of transforming the "new" music into its own type.

Bartók speaks about a similar transforming power in connection with art music's borrowings from folk music. Contemporary art music needs the "spirit" of authentic folk music, that metaphysical aspect embracing the supposedly spontaneous expression of the physical and spiritual life of the folk: its "throbbing life." Art music, he argues, has indeed begun to be imbued with it. Nineteenth-century composers used popular folk music as an exoticism, but twentieth-century composers such as Ravel, Debussy, Stravinsky, and Kodály (and, we are invited to add, Bartók himself) have imbued their music with the true "spirit" of folk music.[67] Never specified in technical terms, the notion of spirit exists mainly at the level of a special positive aura of the natural that can be transferred from peasant music to art music by a genius.[68] At this level, his idea is part of a *völkisch* formulation firmly rooted in nineteenth-century thought. It is as if we are invited to draw a parallel between the "transforming" folk spirit and the genius of art music composers who draw on folk music; we are invited to consider Bartók's compositional activities as a high art equivalent of the (imagined) musical activities of the peasants he idealized.[69]

However, Bartók acknowledges elsewhere that there is a third type of musical domination: that exercised by state authorities over cultural activities within their jurisdiction. With the rise of cultural fascism in central Europe, such forms of control were a contemporary issue. Domination of this kind seems to have been in Bartók's mind in 1931 when he wrote about good and bad penetration. Describing the effect of various influences on Slovak music in very positive terms, as factors that contribute to its "exceptional melodic riches," Bartók seeks to distinguish in an essay on Slovak peasant music between institutionalized and gradually occurring influence:

> It would be fallacious to believe that this influence [i.e., certain Hungarian influences on Slovak peasant music] is created in an artificial manner, such as by the aid of schools or authorities as an act of oppression on the part of Hungary. In the first place the Hungarian upper classes which wielded power are acquainted neither with the older nor the newer Hungarian folk music, and, therefore, are unable to exercise even the slightest propaganda on its behalf. . . . For the refiguration of native art and music is absolutely impossible when approached in an artificial manner. The procedure of penetration was a thoroughly natural and spontaneous one.[70]

Interestingly, in May that year Bartók wrote on behalf of the Hungarian section of the ISCM (International Society for Contemporary Music) to the President of the ISCM, defending Toscanini's and art's right to autonomy from aggressive interference from outside authorities.[71] Toscanini's antifascism, his refusal to open performances at La Scala with the Fascist hymn, had become well known; on May 14 he was pummeled by thugs outside Bologna's Teatro Comunale, and back in Milan had his passport confiscated and his house put under surveillance by the authorities. This was also the year before Bartók attended an extraordinary international congress in Egypt, an event that bears witness to the fact that in the early twentieth century neither attempts at cultural domination by government authority nor genetically purposeful crossbreeding were the sole domain of Western art music. The congress of 1932 was an overt attempt on the part of the Egyptian government to apply the "sciences" of "positive" evolution to Arab music.[72] Convened by the King himself and overseen by the Egyptian government, the Cairo congress's express aim was to draw on the knowledge of Western scientific scholars "in order to discuss all that was required to make the music civilized, and to teach it and rebuild it on acknowledged scientific principles."[73] In other words, the Egyptian authorities sought help in bringing about the positive evolution of Arab music through favorable racial and cultural intermixture. Blunt as the Egyptians' statement of belief in Western cultural superiority was, mechanical as their proposed solution was, and perverse as it all seems now and must have seemed to many of the delegates, the proposition driving the congress was nonetheless a logical response to Western Orientalist portrayals of non-Western cultures via tropes of primitivism, degeneracy, and cultural inferiority. It was also conceptually quite similar to Bartók's own project, even as the terms of that project stood in 1931.[74] Social Darwinism was clearly not the exclusive domain of the West.

Yet while Bartók betrays in the essay on Slovak music a consciousness of the rising tide of fascism and the cultural oppression that went with it, he is keen to absolve Hungary from charges of deliberate cultural oppression. Hungarian cultural penetration was different, he seems to be arguing. Bartók's national self-interest is plain. But he was clearly floundering by this stage in the face of a mass of data about processes of folk music hybridization on the one hand and a conviction that art and non-art music operate in completely separate spheres on the other, together with a need to refine and even redefine political positions in tune with world events, all the while remaining at core a committed Hungarian nationalist. Bartók does not discuss fully how these various types of hybridization differ from each other. However, the sphere of high culture seems to have been a priori authentic, and the metaphysics of composer genius capable of any transformation. And so, despite his years of empirical ethnographic work, Bartók still resorts to the nineteenth-century discourse of the ineffable to describe almost every aspect of his understanding of cultural hybridization: to solve the isolationist-diffusionist paradox (foreign melodies are subject to transformation), to account for his conviction that such appropriations are good for art music generally (folk music's "throbbing life" and its transforming power are good), and to justify his claim that his and his contemporaries' appropriations are better than those of earlier composers (the analogous transforming power of genius).

What Bartók failed to recognize in his critique of Gypsy music was the network of connections and associations which meant not only that Gypsy music was, as Frigyesi points out, "the common ground between the 'rich' and the 'poor'"—the wealthy nobility and the gentry, or *populus*—but that stylistically it was at the "crossroads of folk, popular, and high art."[75] Gypsy music crossed class and cultural groupings, all the while remaining, through the *verbunkos,* intimately associated with received notions of Hungarianness. While in many ways identifiable with an urban gentry lifestyle, its stylistic inclusiveness could nonetheless be read, contra Bartók, as a particularly auspicious hybrid construction, a point of symbolic resolution to Hungary's years of political and social struggle. But in the end, Bartók was a cultural elitist. He disliked what he characterized as the romantically sentimental Gypsy flourishes, and felt, in stark contrast to Liszt, that Gypsies did not possess the creative genius that high art composers and (noble savage) peasants did (or might).

It seems almost redundant to invoke Robert Young's thesis that theories of race were, because of their concern with racial intermixture and therefore hybridization, covert theories of desire.[76] Nor Homi Bhabha's psychoanalytic gloss on Edward Said, that Orientalist knowledge is not always instrumental, that colonialism worked as much according to protocols of fantasy and desire.[77] Bartók wore all of this on his sleeve. His ethnographic activities and resulting constructions of folk and Gypsy music were clearly associated with his own desire to create, through hybridization with (the desired) "natural" or "fresh" folk sources, a new Hungarian art music. But creating and defining a new modernist Hungarian musical language involved pinning down, in order to have power over, the core of its former identity: urban Gypsy music. Bartók's obsession with terminological clarity in this respect—"Gypsy music," "Hungarian folk-style art music,"[78] "Hungarian popular art music"[79]—betrays this concern with national self-definition. As Seamus Deane has pointed out, "the naming or renaming of a place, the naming or renaming of a race, a region, a person is, like all acts of primordial nomination, an act of possession."[80] In view of Gypsy music's investment "with enormous emotional and political energy" in the name of conservative Magyar nationalism,[81] Deane's continuation is telling: "That for which there is no all-embracing name cannot be comprehensively possessed. Instead of possession, we have various modes of sectarian appropriation."[82] Bartók's obsessive renaming bears witness to his need to possess Gypsy music in order to discount it in the name of progressive modern Hungarian nationalism. And if we have to expand our conception of "progress" and "modernism" in the social domain in the early twentieth century, and to accept that it frequently relied on Darwinian theories of evolution, such acceptance can only lead to a more rounded picture of the birth of musical modernism. Narratives of Bartók as the heroic, enlightened progressive struggling against conservative forces whose less enlightened path somehow connected them, in contrast to Bartók, to the political fascism of the 1930s and 1940s, need greater nuance.[83] The hybrid and its contrasting agents, the Gypsy and the peasant, figures on which Bartók's evolutionary account of cultural and musical formation relied, ultimately emerge from writings spanning a fraught period in history as signs of confusion and anxiety.

It is beyond the scope of the present essay to consider ways in which references to Gypsy music, music based on the *verbunkos* type, changed in Bartók's own compositions. I shall simply note that having abandoned the *verbunkos* style around 1905, after the *Kossuth* symphonic poem (1903) and the Rhapsody op. 1 (1904), Bartók began to use it again in 1928. Although this came two or three years before the spate of essays in which he comprehensively reconstructed Gypsy music (and followed quickly upon Kodály's own return to *verbunkos*), there is a suggestive broad parallel between this stylistic return and his change in representation of Gypsy music. Perhaps more significantly, his Concerto for Orchestra of 1942, recently characterized as "historically embedded in world crisis . . . a lament for man's inhumanity to man," brings Bartók's life's work full circle, as David Cooper notes, through its inclusion of Gypsy, *verbunkos,* and peasant elements in the mature Bartókian style.[84]

NOTES

1. As will become clear in the following discussion, the very category "Gypsy music" is contested. However, to avoid needless complexity, unless otherwise specified

I will continue to use the expression "Gypsy music" to refer to music associated with Gypsies in urban Hungary.

2. Judit Frigyesi, "Béla Bartók and the Concept of Nation and Volk in Modern Hungary," *Musical Quarterly* 78, no. 2 (1994): 255–87. Frigyesi has provided a summary of this article in her subsequent book—*Béla Bartók and Turn-of-the-Century Budapest* (Berkeley: University of California Press, 1998)—but unless otherwise indicated, all subsequent references to Frigyesi are to the more detailed article.

3. Ibid., 263.

4. Ibid., 270.

5. Ibid., 267–274.

6. Bence Szabolcsi, *A Concise History of Hungarian Music,* trans. Sára Karig (London: Barrie and Rockliff, 1964), 79–88. Compare Frigyesi, 271.

7. "The Bartók-Möller Polemical Interchange," *Béla Bartók Studies in Ethnomusicology* (hereafter *BBSE*), selected and edited by Benjamin Suchoff (Lincoln: University of Nebraska Press, 1997), 153–54.

8. Quoted by Möller without source, in *BBSE,* 154.

9. *Béla Bartók Essays* (hereafter *BBE*), ed. Benjamin Suchoff (Lincoln: University of Nebraska Press, 1976), 29–32.

10. Compare Frigyesi, 278.

11. See for instance Sándor Kóvacs, "The Ethnomusicologist," in *The Bartók Companion,* ed. Malcolm Gillies (London: Faber, 1993), 51–63.

12. See Robert J. C. Young, *Colonial Desire: Hybridity in Theory, Culture and Race* (New York: Routledge, 1995).

13. Edward Said, *Orientalism* (London: Routledge & Kegan Paul, 1978; London: Penguin, 1985).

14. *BBE,* 301.

15. Ibid.

16. *BBE,* 198. I use the spelling "Gypsies" throughout, replacing alternative quoted spellings if necessary.

17. Angus Fraser, *The Gypsies* (Oxford: Blackwell, 1992), 10–32.

18. Susan McClary, *George Bizet: Carmen* (Cambridge: Cambridge University Press, 1992), 34.

19. Ibid., 29–43.

20. Gypsies suffered especially badly in the Romanian principalities of Wallachia and Moldavia, which had treated Gypsies as slaves until their emancipation in 1864. See David Crowe, "The Gypsies in Hungary" and "The Gypsy Historical Experience in Romania," in *The Gypsies of Eastern Europe,* ed. David Crowe and John Kolsti (Armonk, N.Y.: M. E. Sharpe, 1991), 117–31, 61–79.

21. Frigyesi, 267.

22. For a comprehensive account of Gypsy music, see Bálint Sárosi, *Gypsy Music,* trans. Fred Macnicol (Budapest: Corvina, 1978).

23. Jonathan Bellman, *The Style Hongrois in the Music of Western Europe* (Boston: Northeastern University Press, 1993).

24. See Malcolm Gillies, "Bartók and His Music in the 1990s," in *The Bartók Companion,* esp. 10–11; Leon Bostein, "Out of Hungary: Bartók, Modernism, and the Cultural Politics of Twentieth-Century Music," in *Bartók and His World,* ed. Peter Laki (Princeton: Princeton University Press, 1995), esp. 16–18; and Frigyesi, esp. 256. Ex-

pressions of cultural superiority may be found in *Béla Bartók Letters* (hereafter *BBL*), collected, selected, edited and annotated by János Demény, trans. Péter Balabán and István Karkas, translation revised by Elisabeth West and Colin Mason (London: Faber, 1971), 50; and *BBE*, 201–3.

25. André Karátson, "Paradoxes in Hungarian Adepts of Symbolism and Decadence at the Beginning of the Twentieth Century," in *Decadence and Innovation: Austro-Hungarian Life and Art at the Turn of the Twentieth Century*, ed. Robert B. Pynsent (London: Weidenfeld and Nicolson, 1989), 66–81.

26. Young, *Colonial Desire*, 100.

27. Quoted in Fraser, *The Gypsies*, 249.

28. See, for instance, Jacques Le Rider, *Modernity and Crises of Identity: Culture and Society in Fin-de-Siècle Vienna*, trans. Rosemary Morris (Cambridge, England: Polity Press, 1993).

29. Julie Brown, "Schoenberg's Early Wagnerisms: Atonality and the Redemption of Ahasuerus," *Cambridge Opera Journal* 6, no. 1 (1994): 51–80. See also Julie Brown, *Re-reading Schoenberg* (Cambridge, England: Cambridge University Press, forthcoming).

30. *BBE*, 206.

31. "Christian society always distinguished too little between the Jew and the Gypsy in theory and too much in practice." Franz Liszt, *The Gypsy in Music*, vol. 2, trans. Edwin Evans (1859; London: William Reeves, 1924), 243.

32. It is important to note that while in the original 1859 edition Liszt included a section on the "Israelites," Princess Carolyne von Sayn-Wittgenstein intercepted the proofs of a later edition (published in 1881) and vastly increased the proportion of the text devoted to Jews. Liszt nonetheless stood by the finished text against all criticism. See Alan Walker, *Franz Liszt: The Weimar Years 1848–1861* (London: Faber, 1989), 380–90.

33. Liszt provided refuge when Wagner was on the run from the Dresden authorities after his involvement in the failed uprising of 1849, and was arguably the most important force in ensuring that Wagner's music became more widely known. Paul Merrick reports that in 1851, when Wagner published his inflammatory essay "Das Judentum in der Musik," Liszt immediately suspected it as being from Wagner's hand. Yet, as Merrick also points out, the two parted company when it came to solutions: Wagner's retreat from religion and increasing recourse to Schopenhauerian pessimism at this stage differed considerably from Liszt's religious faith and spiritual optimism; he reported particularly loathing Schopenhauer. See letter from Adelheid von Schorn quoted in Merrick, *Revolution and Religion in the Music of Liszt* (Cambridge: Cambridge University Press, 1987), 43.

34. Walker, *Franz Liszt*, 385–88.

35. Wagner, "Judaism in Music," *Wagner* 9 (1988): 20–33.

36. As Judit Frigyesi notes, 275.

37. A trip that Bartók made to the Biskra region of Algeria in June 1913 in order to collect Arab music also falls within an Orientalist framework. The usual account given for the trip is that Bartók had detected in the Romanian *hora lunga*—"a certain kind of highly ornamented, orientally coloured and improvisation-like melody" (*BBE*, 11)—an echo of Arab music he had heard while on a concert tour in Tangier and wished to trace the connection (*BBSE*, xii–xiii). Yet, considering how

central Gypsy music was to Hungarian musical and cultural identity at the time, and how prominent the Orientalist troping was in Bartók's (and Liszt's earlier) accounts of Gypsy music, this documented interest might have coincided with an equal desire to collect and analyze music from somewhere "genuinely" Oriental: Arab lands rather than Hungary and Eastern Europe. For a full account of the trip, see Márta Ziegler, "Bartóks Reise nach Biskra," *Documenta Bartókiana*, vol. 2, ed. Denijs Dille (Mainz, 1965).

38. Hayden White, *Tropics of Discourse: Essays in Cultural Criticism* (Baltimore: Johns Hopkins University Press, 1978), 192.

39. Béla Bartók, *The Hungarian Folk Song*, ed. Benjamin Suchoff, trans. M. D. Calvo-coressi, with annotations by Zoltán Kodály (1924; Albany: State University of New York Press, 1981), 3.

40. *BBE*, 318, 317, 321.

41. Young, *Colonial Desire*, 11.

42. Ibid., 36–43.

43. Ibid., 42.

44. *BBE*, 304–5.

45. *BBE*, 305.

46. *BBE*, 70.

47. *BBE*, 70.

48. Bartók, *Hungarian Folk Song*, 1–3.

49. *BBE*, 206.

50. In *The Hungarian Folk Song*, 3, Bartók writes of peasant music as "the outcome of changes wrought by a natural force whose operation is unconscious; it is impulsively created by a community of men who have had no schooling; it is as much a natural product as are the various forms of animal and vegetable life."

51. See Raymond Williams, *Culture and Society: Coleridge to Orwell* (1958; London: Hogarth Williams, 1993), xiii–xx.

52. *BBE*, 207.

53. *BBE*, 71.

54. *BBL*, 230.

55. *BBE*, 29–32, 33–34.

56. *BBE*, 31.

57. For Bartók's description of the League of Nations event, see *BBL*, 211–16.

58. Pamela M. Potter, "Musicology under Hitler: New Sources in Context," *Journal of the American Musicological Society* 49, no. 1 (1996): 70–113.

59. *BBL*, 201.

60. I take these figures from Iván T. Berend and György Ránki, "The Horthy Regime," in *A History of Hungary*, ed. Ervin Pamlényi (Budapest: Corvina Press, 1973), 461. In 1910, as part of the Dual Monarchy, its crown lands (including Croatia-Slavonia) comprised (in descending proportion of population share) Magyars (48%), Romanians, Germans, Slovaks, Croats, Serbs and Ruthenians (László Makkai, "The Origins of the Hungarian People and State," in ibid., 15–27).

61. Frigyesi, 256.

62. Malcolm Gillies, "Bartók and His Music in the 1990s," in *The Bartók Companion*, 12.

63. *BBL*, 201.

64. *BBE,* 30.

65. *The Hungarian Folk Song,* 2.

66. *BBE,* 30.

67. *BBE,* 324.

68. *BBE,* 317, 323. I have to disagree with Judit Frigyesi's reading of the same passage. She reads the following passage as indicating that for Bartók the "spirit" of folk music was its expression of "the totality of lived experience" (in *Béla Bartók and Turn-of-the-Century Budapest,* 120): "The melodies of a written or printed collection are in essence dead materials. It is true though—provided they are reliable—that they acquaint one with the melodies, yet one absolutely cannot penetrate into the real, throbbing life of this music by means of them. In order to really feel the vitality of this music, one must, so to speak, have lived it—and this is only possible when one comes to know it through direct contact with the peasants. . . . " All he seems to be saying here is that in order to get a sense of the "throbbing life" he identifies, it is important to hear the music played in its original setting, not mediated through transcription.

69. Conversely, elsewhere we are invited to consider peasant music through the vocabulary of classical art music: Bartók describes it as being near aesthetic perfection on account of its perfect miniature forms and general concision, valorized modernist traits. He also argues that the melodies lend themselves to either tonal or totally chromatic harmony, though about eight years later he would modify that claim (*BBE,* 322–24). In 1928 he even claims that folk melodies are a type of archaism similar to archaic art forms, as if to argue that their use was completely up to date at that time (i.e., neoclassical). In these ways we are invited to consider fundamental features of folk music as being completely adequate to, even especially appropriate to, contemporary approaches to art music.

70. *BBE,* 135.

71. On this incident, see Joseph Horowitz, *Understanding Toscanini: How He Became an American Culture-God and Helped Create a New Audience for Old Music* (New York: Knopf, 1987); reprinted as *Understanding Toscanini: A Social History of American Concert Life* (Berkeley: University of California Press, 1994), 116ff.

72. Ali Jihad Racy, "Historical Worldviews of Early Ethnomusicologists: An East-West Encounter in Cairo, 1932," in *Ethnomusicology and Modern Music History* (Urbana: University of Illinois Press, 1991), ed. Stephen Blum et al., 68–91.

73. From an official document, quoted in Racy, 69.

74. Bartók joined the Recording (Sub)Committee where he took a characteristically Western view of the matter. Consistent with his own internally Orientalist position in relation to East European folk music, he exhorted his hosts to collect on disc as much music as possible, but only those melodies devoid of any traces of Western music. It would be interesting to know how he would have responded if asked to advise on the way forward for contemporary Arab music. Would he have similarly drawn a distinction between "theirs" and "ours"? Would he have advised them to avoid Western influences, even though he freely borrowed from the East?

75. Frigyesi, 267.

76. Young, *Colonial Desire.*

77. Homi K. Bhabha, *The Location of Culture* (London: Routledge, 1994).

78. *BBE,* 71.

79. *BBE*, 206.

80. Introduction to Terry Eagleton, Frederic Jameson, and Edward Said, eds., *Nationalism, Colonialism, and Literature* (Minneapolis: University of Minnesota Press, 1990), 18.

81. Frigyesi, 270.

82. In *Nationalism, Colonialism, and Literature*, ed. Eagleton et al., 18.

83. Even Frigyesi implies this: "This passionate defense of Gypsy music illustrates how desperately the conservative circles wanted to preserve the illusion of an all-encompassing, original national style. More and more, this style became the symbol of the powerful Hungarian race that was going to defeat the symbol of the minorities, the Jews, the socialists, and all those of the bourgeoisie who desired change. We need not be reminded where this politics led" (278).

84. David Cooper, *Bartók: Concerto for Orchestra* (Cambridge: Cambridge University Press, 1996), 21.

Modernism, Deception, and Musical Others: Los Angeles circa 1940

Peter Franklin

I do not attach so much importance to being a musical bogy-man as to being a natural continuer of properly understood, good old tradition!
ARNOLD SCHOENBERG TO WERNER REINHART, 1923

In a short essay on the nature and implications of postmodernity, Jean-François Lyotard neatly labels the opposing axes between which the development of high-culture modernism has often been charted as an ethical, implicitly political project. Artists who aspire to be progressive and "authentic" must "question the rules . . . as learnt and received from their predecessors": "They soon find that such rules are so many methods of deception, seduction and reassurance which make it impossible to be 'truthful.'"[1] To agree with those rules, Lyotard suggests, has been to affirm the way things are and embark upon an evasively therapeutic career in "mass conformism." The nonconformists' path of progressive modernism is noble but comfortless; those artists who persistently question the rules "are destined to lack credibility in the eyes of devoted adherents of reality and identity, to find themselves without a guaranteed audience."[2]

The more elaborate version of this model developed by Theodor Adorno, in his writings on music and aesthetics, drew upon complicatedly mediated historical attitudes. As an instrument, theory is itself, of course, historical, selecting and foregrounding evidence in a manner that may ideologically reinscribe what it seeks to explain. Opposition to traditional or academic norms does appear to have linked an extensive body of fin-de-siècle European artists and their heirs: the more aggressively politicized avant-gardistes of the 1920s and beyond. The use of this model as a historical tool is now, however, deeply problematic. Criticizing oversimplified interpretations of the history of European and American modernism, postmodernism has sought to restore the complicating nuances of difference within fields of cultural activity that Adorno, for example, often treated as unitary—such as popular entertainment. Also crucial to a significant strand of such analysis has been an examination of the grounds and implications of what Andreas Huyssen has labelled the "Great Divide" between modernism and mass culture.[3] Huyssen provocatively interpreted the latter as the discursively compromising "other" of modernism, rather in the way that modernism itself had typically been positioned as an opposing alternative to traditional cultural assumptions about art. The purpose of highlighting such discursive strategies is to understand more about the concerns of those who use them and, as a consequence, reconsider their historical narratives.

My specific aim here is to bring these two projects together in an exploration of how we might extend the critique of the dominant narrative of modernism still further into the territory of twentieth-century music, particularly that of two of its canonic representatives: Igor Stravinsky and Arnold Schoenberg. Their ideas and creative practice were elaborately marked by the network of contradictions that ensnared an unlikely and disparate group of composers who, late in their lives, in the 1930s and 1940s, found themselves living in close proximity in Los Angeles. They were émigrés, uprooted from their native environments, who had been brought together by the upheavals of European and Russian politics. All suffered the experience of finding themselves outsiders in a foreign land for which they had varying degrees of respect. All perceived themselves as representatives of a "high" artistic culture in whose techniques and values they had been trained. Their relations with tradition, modernism, and mass entertainment nevertheless prove sufficiently confused to undermine standard accounts of the historical triumph of modern music. In the Los Angeles mirror-hall of otherness, where most were foreign, few "at home," the search for both cultural authority and authentic modes of opposition proves instructively confusing. Dogmatic preconceptions rear up like distorted monsters before shrinking humorously into midgets; heroes wobble, while the mocked grow touching in contemplation of their own strangeness.

PRELIMINARY REFLECTIONS: RACHMANINOV AND STRAVINSKY

In 1939, while still in Europe, although long an exile from his native Russia, Sergei Rachmaninov had responded to a request from an American journal that he contribute to a symposium on modern music. Two years before he was finally to settle in Beverly Hills, Rachmaninov's letter was a cry from the heart. As a composer whom history seemed to have left behind, his personal sense of artistic otherness reflected the literal alienation of a man whose homeland had become a lost and inaccessible place:

> I feel like a ghost in a world grown alien. I cannot cast out the old way of writing, and I cannot acquire the new. I have made intense effort to feel the mu-

sical manner of today, but it will not come to me. . . . Even with the disaster of living through what has befallen the Russia where I spent my happiest years, yet I always feel that my own music[,] and my reactions to all music, remained spiritually the same, unendingly obedient in trying to create beauty. . . . [4]

This is not to be confused with immanent, intramusical evidence of alienation of the kind sought by Adorno, who located in art a suprapersonal "truthcontent," reflecting rifts within society. It is simply a document of the personal *experience* of alienation, both geographical and cultural. It has been taken to be indicative of an anti-modernist position that the works reinforced. Adorno, indeed, unequivocally positioned Rachmaninov the composer as a representative of "old" cultural values in their most commodified and debased form.[5]

American reviews of the few late compositions that he managed to complete between his gruelling recital-tours as a virtuoso pianist opposed each other on ostensibly predictable grounds. Conservative critics reacted either with warmth or a rueful sense of déjà vu. Progressive critics were more likely to respond with anger to what they regarded as manifestations of sterility and irrelevance. Only Rachmaninov's celebrity as a pianist, they implied, gained attention for works that were pale reflections of long-ago favorites like the Prelude in C-sharp Minor (1892) or the Second Piano Concerto (1901). The notoriously progressive music critics of New York dealt characteristically with the first performance there of his last work, the Symphonic Dances, early in 1941. Louis Biancolli's review in the *New York World Telegram* seems to have been representative in its description of the work as "long and derivative," its occasionally weird effects suggesting to him a "rendezvous of ghosts": "Of course Mr Rachmaninoff does what he wants with the orchestra. His arsenal of effects is large and can send shivers quivering down the length and breadth of the string section. But the work sounds like a rehash of old tricks. . . . "[6]

Should we take this, along with Rachmaninov's own sense of being a "ghost in a world grown alien," as evidence that in America, at least, the modernist narrative is historically accurate, that its project had succeeded? Had old-style tonal music, with its latent realist tendency to programmatic representation, nothing more to say in a world where the art had demonstrably "progressed"? The tension that exists in Adorno's later writing on music—between his consistent approach to Schoenberg as exemplifying the dialectical challenge of dissonant "new music," and his similarly admiring treatment of Mahler—resounds in this question.[7] Much depends upon Biancolli's dogmatic belief in allusion-rejecting "originality." To question such a belief might be to find in his review material for a more complex reading of the Symphonic Dances. Could not their allusions and rhetorically stressed, "haunted" character be interpreted as integral to their meaning? Additional problems about pleasure clearly emerge in Biancolli's references to Rachmaninov's "arsenal of effects" and "old tricks." These barely conceal an antipopulist feeling that often emerged in American treatment of Rachmaninov's later works. Writing about the widely successful 1934 Rhapsody on a Theme of Paganini, Robert Simon, at the height of the Great Depression, made the following ironic point in his review of an early performance of the work under Bruno Walter: "The Rhapsody isn't philosophical, significant, or even artistic. It's something for audiences, and what our orchestras need at the moment is more music for audiences. More music for audiences means more audiences for music, and with sage apothegm, I conclude another salute to Mr. Rachmaninoff."[8]

The persistence of the discourse of artistic idealism in the land of Disney and popcorn was fully internalized by Rachmaninov, whose authentic artistic alienation was posthumously compromised by the film industry's frequent reliance on his style. Conservative and popular clearly meant "bad"; the dubious implications of his wide appeal were thus confirmed by the practice of a culture that seemed curiously at odds with itself. By comparison, his younger countryman, Igor Stravinsky, was much more judicious about establishing an alliance with matters of philosophy, significance, and art; he *had* mastered the new way of writing music and the discourse that supported it. As one of the most famous living representatives of "modern music," Stravinsky valued his image as a diametrically opposite kind of composer to Rachmaninov. The two became personally acquainted for the first time in Beverly Hills in 1942. Moved to fellow-feeling by the progress of the war in Europe, it was Rachmaninov who instigated their encounter, although the internalized sense of artistic inferiority to which I have referred almost overwhelmed his initiative:

> I'm eager to meet someone whose family, like mine, is living over there, and with whom I could discuss ways to send money and other things. As I know how much Igor Fyodorovich has always disliked my compositions, even though he respects me as a pianist, and must know my attitude to modern music, I'm not sure whether I could invite him and his wife to my house—which I'd love to do—because I don't know how he would receive my invitation.[9]

Rachmaninov's assessment of Stravinsky's attitude toward him seems to have been more or less correct, but the invitation was accepted and subsequently returned.[10]

In the Los Angeles hall of mirrors, however, Stravinsky's position as an official *grand maître* of modern music also gave rise to a critical and contradictory image of his artistic personality and significance. The hostile gazer in this case was again Theodor Adorno, himself a Los Angeles immigrant, whose 1948 *Philosophy of New Music* contained what is still the most consistently negative critique of Stravinsky in the literature. Whatever the larger problems of his theoretical analysis of the modernist project, Adorno's role as a protagonist in the cross-reflecting discourses of the European émigrés in the 1940s remains a provocatively interesting one. An adviser to Thomas

Mann, who read *Philosophy of New Music* in manuscript during the gestation of Mann's "musical" novel *Doctor Faustus* (1947), Adorno was a theoretical supporter of the scornfully mistrustful Schoenberg, and had once admired Stravinsky. His devastating reexamination of Stravinsky in *Philosophy of New Music* nevertheless positioned the Russian unequivocally as Schoenberg's other. Neoclassicism in music became, for Adorno, a reflection of authoritarian politics.[11] From this perspective, Stravinsky's celebrated belief in music's incapacity to "express" anything[12] started to look like a strikingly compromised version of traditional idealism.

Rather than insuring the purity of his music, Stravinsky, Adorno suggested, had become committed to wholesale evasion. Stylistically divorced from the subject, Stravinsky's music was "absolute" in direct proportion to its evasiveness: "Compositional spontaneity itself is overwhelmed by the prohibition placed upon pathos in expression: the subject, which is no longer permitted to state anything about itself, thus actually ceases to engage in 'production' and must content itself with the hollow echo of objective musical language, which is no longer its own."[13] Certain aspects of Stravinsky's life and professed beliefs appear to reinforce Adorno's suggestions about his music. His aristocratically refined obsession with orderliness, his opposition to the Russian Revolution and ardent support of Mussolini (to whom he announced in 1935 that he felt "like a fascist myself")[14]—all this must confuse either the image of Stravinsky as a leading modernist or the theoretical definition of modernism being employed. The Symphony in Three Movements (1945) presents a useful case-study of the problems involved. It even posed some for Adorno, who found in it an almost Beethovenian authenticity ("cleansed of antiquated elements") but considered the "contrived void of its elements" to be typically insufficient: a site where degenerating music could only suggest what it failed to achieve.[15]

It is certainly an interesting work. Stravinsky's comments on the symphony imply, with strategic diffidence, that it was (in Robert Craft's phrase) "marked by the impression of world events":

> It both does and does not "express my feelings" about them, but I prefer to say only that, without participation of what I think of as my will, they excited my musical imagination. And the events that thus activated me were not general, or ideological, but specific: each episode in the Symphony is linked in my imagination with a concrete impression, very often cinematographic in origin, of the war.
>
> The third movement actually contains the genesis of a war plot, though I recognized it as such only after completing the composition. The beginning of the movement is partly, and in some—to me wholly inexplicable—way, a musical reaction to the newsreels and documentaries that I had seen of goose-stepping soldiers. The square march beat, the brass band instrumentation, the grotesque *crescendo* in the tuba, these are all related to those repellant pictures. . . .

> But enough of this. In spite of what I have said, the Symphony is not programmatic. Composers combine notes. That is all.[16]

What are we to make of this confusing statement? Without it we might have taken the Symphony's finale as a characteristic example of Stravinsky in muscular, energetic mode, as it pounds its way to a final, abstractly bracing tonic-dominant chord of D-flat major. To learn that goose-stepping soldiers, grotesquerie, and "repellant pictures" were involved leads us to wonder about the mentioned "plot"; his claim that the fugue marked the "rise of the Allies" appears to stress the contradictory otherness of what had preceded it.[17] Elsewhere Stravinsky also explained that the second movement had begun life as an embryonic film-score composed, at Franz Werfel's encouragement, for the vision-scene in the screen version of the latter's best-selling, conservative 1941 novel *The Song of Bernadette*.[18] The idea of seeing Jennifer Jones at the grotto of Massabielle in the central section of the Andante (from one bar before cue 124) is as tempting as speculation about the consequent meaning of the *faux-naïf*, rather pastoral folksiness of the outer sections.

Stravinsky's music is richly interesting when it admits to being representationally concrete, but Hollywood understandably chose Alfred Newman to score *The Song of Bernadette* in 1943. Stravinsky's fundamental lack of sympathy with entertainment cinema was confirmed by his sour response to the Disney Studios' use of *Le Sacre du Printemps* for the dinosaur sequence in *Fantasia* (1941). He believed that silent-era Chaplin films alone represented "Hollywood, in its brief age of art."[19] He also, on one occasion, came close to turning on its head Adorno's image of him as the other of the alienated and authentic Schoenberg by hearing the latter's first Chamber Symphony as an eclectic montage of other composers' styles and satirically associating its original scoring with the sound of silent-era cinema orchestras:

> I admire the *Kammersymphonie*, but am not attracted by the sound of the solo strings—they remind me of the economy-sized movie-theatre orchestras of the 1920s. . . . At times the *Kammersymphonie* sounds to me like a joint creation of Wagner, Mahler, Brahms and Strauss, as though one of these composers had written the upper line, one the bass etc.[20]

Film repeatedly surfaces in discourse about musical values in this period. It was, of course, a pervasively influential new medium, but it seems to have awakened a special kind of fear that readily turned to anger in the laboriously shored-up institution of Great Music.

SCHOENBERG'S REWARDING PAIN

Musicologists' concern with identifiable "techniques" traditionally favored comparisons between composers in this period on purely stylistic grounds. Labels such as "expressionism," "serialism," "neoclassicism," or "postromanticism" have accounted for certain objective features of musical works, which may be arranged taxonomically. More critically constructed categories of modernism are imperfectly (if at all) accommodated in that style-discriminating discourse. The problems posed by objectively defined "modernist" composers in this period and context are nowhere more sharply focused than in the case of Arnold Schoenberg, who took up residence in Brentwood Park, Los Angeles, in 1937.

He commanded nothing like the celebrity of Stravinsky in America. Those who knew his name, or even some of his works, would have been unlikely to regard him as anything other than an extreme, cerebral modernist whose music, apart from the relatively well-known *Verklärte Nacht,* was notoriously "difficult to listen to." An image of unpleasurable dissonance, occasionally associated with the imperfectly comprehended serial or "twelve-tone" system of composition, was as close as popular awareness got to Schoenberg. This, of course, appears to validate Adorno's rigorously searching theoretical vindication and critique of him that formed the major part of *Philosophy of New Music.* Presenting Schoenberg, at his most progressive, as Stravinsky's dialectical other, Adorno discursively pushed Stravinsky back toward the mass-entertainment ethos that he despised. That move is clarified by Adorno's broad categorization of what Schoenberg's music philosophically opposed—a decaying Western civilization which was being systematically infected by the manipulative false consciousness of the "culture industry":

> Advanced music has no recourse but to insist upon its own ossification without concession to that would-be humanitarianism which it sees through, in all its attractive and alluring guises, as the mask of inhumanity. Its truth appears guaranteed more by its denial of any meaning in organized society, of which it will have no part—accomplished by its own organized vacuity—than by any capability of positive meaning within itself. Under the present circumstances it is restricted to definitive negation.[21]

Schoenberg was as scornful in his response to *Philosophy of New Music*[22] as he was angry at Thomas Mann's appropriation of the twelve-tone system in *Doctor Faustus.* While he occasionally appeared in the 1940s to confirm Adorno's interpretation of his position and significance, the manner in which he did so was paradoxical, to say the least. For example, his short essay "A Self-Analysis," which first appeared in English in 1949, began with the following disarming acceptance of his own musical otherness: "If people speak of me, they at once connect me with horror, with atonality, and with composition with twelve tones."[23]

That sense of otherness had been expressed still more strikingly in Schoenberg's 1947 letter of thanks to the National Association of Arts and Letters, which had awarded him a thousand-dollar prize for "outstanding achievement." Explaining his own perception of the artistic course he had followed, he likened his earliest innovatory works to an "ocean of boiling water" into which he had fallen. He found no assistance but sensed that many would have wished to see him sink: "It might have been to get rid of this night-mare, this unharmonious torture, of these unintelligible ideas, of this methodical madness. . . . "[24]

The tone of that sentence is of course ironic, but it demonstrates a remarkable awareness of the primary associative images that were available to a lay audience for his nontonal music: images of physical and mental pain, experienced and inflicted, and of insanity. Still more remarkable is the extent to which such imagery was actually reinforced by the subject matter of many of his texted or dramatic works. These prove to have been far from "organized vacuity" in Adorno's meaning-rejecting sense—a fact of which Adorno was clearly aware in the case of "Expressionist"-era works like *Erwartung* and *Pierrot Lunaire,* whose dramatic narratives he appropriately defined as revelations of the subconscious. Works composed in the 1940s in fact extended the repertoire of images of otherness with which his music might be linked. The op. 44 Prelude for chorus and orchestra of 1945 formed part of a curious biblical project. Nathanial Shilkret, a popular song writer and light-music director, had conceived the idea of putting the Bible onto records with musical accompaniment. The Genesis section was the only one completed, with background music from a number of "leading composers" of the day, including Stravinsky ("Babel"). Schoenberg elected to provide the prelude: a musical image of Chaos as a serially organized structure with a double-fugue at its center.[25] A similar conjunction of Schoenberg's "progressive" style with images of alienating pain and chaos is found in the 1947 melodrama *A Survivor from Warsaw,* which seems at times to position the orchestral "accompaniment" to the speaker and chorus as if it were a representation of the horror which the protagonist endures. Equally striking was the "inner program" of the purely instrumental String Trio of 1946, written in the hospital in the aftermath of a serious illness during which Schoenberg's heart had briefly stopped. The work appears to have been linked with the condition and its treatment, not least with the bodily intrusions of the doctors. Schoenberg told Hanns Eisler that certain chords represented injections, and was still more forthcoming in conversation with Thomas Mann:

> He told me about the new trio he had just completed, and about the experiences he had secretly woven into the composition—experiences of which the work was a kind of fruit. He had, he said, represented his illness and medical treatment in the music including even the male nurses and other oddities of American hospitals. The work was extremely difficult to play, he said, in fact almost impossible, or at least only for three players of virtuoso rank; but, on the other hand, the music was very rewarding because of its extraordinary tonal effects. I worked the association of "impossible but rewarding" into the chapter [of *Doctor Faustus*] on Leverkühn's chamber music.[26]

These indications of direct representational intent in Schoenberg are especially interesting. They clearly contrast with the more orthodox idealist disclaimers of Stravinsky, who flirted with representational imagery only to assure us, in the end, of music's naively innocent autonomy ("Composers combine notes. That is all"). This perversely reinforces Adorno's dichotomous interpretation of the two composers' relationship within modernism. Stravinsky is more eloquently in command of the "official" ideology of bourgeois music; Schoenberg appears to unmask its ideological nature by revealing that his own music was indeed representing all the things with which an uninformed popular audience might have associated it. This he does, however, in a private, covert way that emphatically links him with the late nineteenth-century Austrian and German modernists, particularly Mahler. Tensions in Mahler's relations with tradition were often mediated by public ambivalence about expressive representation in the debate for and against "program-music." Note the term "secretly" that Mann attributed to Schoenberg above. My earlier use of the Mahlerian term "inner program" is vindicated by this indication that the claim of nonrepresentational autonomy in that tradition was often no more than a convenient veil drawn over the truthful but embarrassing or even transgressive implications of music.[27]

Schoenberg admired Mahler, having had a somewhat disputatious personal relationship with him in his youth. Both Mahler and Strauss (initially supportive of Schoenberg) were "moderns" before the First World War in a manner that was often deemed threatening to the bourgeois values they in fact supported and articulated. Other features of Schoenberg's later aesthetic philosophy tend to emphasize the links between him and the classical tradition, whose technical principles he taught indefatigably at UCLA until his retirement in 1944. Dika Newlin's diaries, recording her experiences in Schoenberg's classes from 1939 and later as a private pupil, amply confirm other testimonies to his characterful, charismatic, and yet ruthless insistence upon his students' mastery of the tonal procedures of the masters (Bach, Mozart, Beethoven, Schubert, Brahms). Only then might they venture to use more "advanced" techniques. His refusal on one occasion even to discuss the tonal implications of the fourths chord seems to have been typical.[28] As a teacher Schoenberg appeared altogether in line with the dominant Western construction of music as a higher art whose mastery was a penitential pilgrimage, accompanied by self-denial and frequent scourgings: a pilgrimage through the established canon designed not least to separate the sheep from the goats on elitist grounds (as Schoenberg resonantly put it in 1947):

No violinist would play, even occasionally, with the wrong intonation to please lower musical tastes, no tight-rope walker would take steps in the wrong direction only for pleasure or personal appeal . . . and in the same manner, no artist, no poet, no philosopher and no musician would degenerate into vulgarity in order to comply with a slogan such as "Art for All." Because if it is art it is not for all, and if it is for all it is not art. . . . There is only "l'art pour l'art," art for the sake of art alone.[29]

Was the boiling ocean of Schoenberg's modernist quest an extreme practical interpretation of official bourgeois musical idealism that ended up, rather as with Rachmaninov, tortuously representing its own otherness in an alien world? At the same time, did not the bitterness of Schoenberg's objections to Mann's appropriation of his "intellectual property" in *Doctor Faustus* emphasize the extent to which he relied on the image of the Great European Composer as a heroic subject, storing up his achievements in the course of a life designed for biographical celebration?[30] The gap between discursive constructions of Schoenberg's compositional practice — particularly Adorno's—and his actual aesthetic and political views challenges conventional theories about modernism even more than in the case of Stravinsky. Schoenberg seems to emerge, with all his contradictions, precisely as the culminatory figure of the old Western Great Tradition that he often claimed himself to be—trying to hold on to its culturally dissipated authority in ways that had as much to do with power as with rebellion or subversion. Attempts to resolve the contradictions of his nature via the decontextualizing discourses of psychoanalysis or visionary spirituality are strategically unconvincing.[31]

Schoenberg's secret representational intentions unmask the deception of the mystically revealed and yet unrepresentable truth upon which his unfinished opera *Moses und Aron* had turned. Adorno has been accused of misrepresenting the actual programmatic intentions and world view of Gustav Mahler,[32] but oddly not those of Schoenberg, whose disarming admission of 1950 seems to address more than a McCarthyite threat to himself and his family: " . . . before I was twenty-five, I had already discovered the difference between me and a labourer. I then found out that I was *bourgeois* and turned away from all political contacts."[33] Adorno should have been in a position to see that pre–First World War "opposition" to the bourgeois tradition often expressed itself in ways which were wholly bourgeois, their romantic notion of mystical inspiration linking the unfettered artist with some higher realm of subjectively mediated truth. His understanding of Schoenbergian expressionism nevertheless seems implicitly reliant upon documents like the idealistic letter the composer wrote to the painter Wassily Kandinsky in 1911. Here the aristocratic Walther von Stolzing of Wagner's *Meistersinger,* rather than any anarchic agitator, seems to hover before his inner eye: "Every formal procedure which aspires to traditional effects is not completely free from conscious motivation. But art belongs to the *unconscious!* One must express *oneself!* Express oneself *directly!* Not one's taste, or one's upbringing, or one's intelligence, knowledge or skill. Not all these *acquired* characteristics, but that which is *inborn, instinctive.*"[34]

To celebrate Schoenberg's "fracturedness" as the measure of his status as a modernist, of his music as critique, is to miss the power and significance of his own belief that his music was in fact as exemplary in its organic unity and logical order as music of the Great Tradition was always supposed to be, and no less secretly representational. In 1949 he protested his case in the following peculiar manner:

> . . . a satisfactory number of first-class musicians . . . were able to recognize that logic, order and organization will be greatly promoted by application of the method of composing with twelve tones.
>
> Even under Hitler, twelve-tone music was not suppressed, as I have learned. On the contrary it was compared to the idea of "Der Fuehrer" by the German composer, Paul von Klenau. . . . [35]

Schoenberg's unlikely achievement was not to salvage some newly autonomous music from the chaos of subjective representation so much as to demonstrate the resilience of bourgeois ideology as encoded in official European music-aesthetic theory. But in the Emerald City tradition was also a movie set that was never quite as it tried to appear. Behind the monstrous image of Dorothy's wizard lurked a vulnerably human figure. In a 1947 letter to the conductor Hans Rosbaud, Schoenberg, the bogy-man of European modernism, made the following touching announcement: " . . . there is nothing I long for more intensely (if for anything) than to be taken for a better sort of Tchaikovsky—for heaven's sake: a bit better, but really that's all. Or if anything more, then that people should know my tunes and whistle them."[36]

The alienation expressed here is, once again, not at all of the Adornian kind. It is that of an artist who had realized that the values which he had sought to articulate and by which he believed his own development to have been validated were no longer the dominant currency in this other culture. He had painfully rediscovered himself as just another foreign composer without an audience. History nevertheless fails to record his response to the society hostess who, one glittering night at Ira Gershwin's, approached him with the no doubt innocent and well-intentioned invitation: "Give us a tune, Arnold."[37] That, it appears, was what part of him had wanted to do all along; that was why his expressionist works were such authentic manifestations of (self-imposed) pain—its rationale an extreme form of subjective individualism that was rooted in the culture it appeared resolutely to oppose.

For someone who almost regretfully succeeded where Schoenberg self-destructively failed, we might finally turn to another Viennese-Jewish émigré, a composer who by all standard criteria would have to be regarded as the Rachmaninov to Schoenberg's Stravinsky. This was Erich Wolfgang Korngold.

KORNGOLD'S PLEASURE, AND DECEPTION

Korngold's name was less likely to be encountered in serious musical circles than that of Rachmaninov, or even of an admired American aspirant to seriousness like George Gershwin (with whom Schoenberg played tennis). The reasons were historical. While not a representative of patronizable popular culture in quite the accepted sense, Korngold had long been an admirer of Richard Strauss and Puccini; his own late-romantic style was clearly influenced by them. He had begun his career as a child-prodigy composer in pre–First World War Vienna, earning the approval of Mahler, lessons from Schoenberg's friend Alexander Zemlinsky, and the fascinated adoration of audiences, who were astounded by such works as his ballet-pantomime *Der Schneemann* (The Snowman), performed at the Vienna Court Opera when he was thirteen years old. The young Korngold then went on to commit the unpardonable sin of maintaining the momentum of his early successes by becoming one of the most popular of living German composers after Richard Strauss. Frequent performances of his chamber, operatic, and orchestral works often exasperated the Schoenberg circle, whose wrath must have been further inflamed when the *Neues Wiener Tagblatt* ran a 1930 poll of its readers on how they ranked prominent Austrians in various walks of life. Of the composers cited, Richard Strauss (who was in fact Bavarian) came first, Korngold second, and Schoenberg third.[38] Korngold had the further misfortune to be the son of one of Vienna's leading music critics: the conservative, antimodernist successor to Hanslick on the *Neue Freie Presse*, Dr. Julius Korngold. The younger Korngold's crimes against higher artistic ideals, let alone those of serious-minded modernists, were further compounded by the fact that he succeeded where both Schoenberg (who made ridiculous financial demands) and Stravinsky inevitably failed: he became a successful film-music composer. His tunes were sufficiently whistleable for them to become major selling features of some of the Warner Brothers movie hits of the 1930s and early 1940s.

He had started in 1934 by extending and arranging Mendelssohn's music for Max Reinhardt's film *A Midsummer Night's Dream;*[39] in that role he was just one of the many Europeans drafted in to add "tone," a touch of "class" to Hollywood's lucrative popular productions. Soon he had been drawn into scoring action-adventures. He resisted and protested his ideals, as any self-respecting European composer could be expected to do; but he was good at his job, although he affected to despise it. In 1938 the German annexation of Austria sealed his fate and forced him to remain in Hollywood to score another hated "action-picture," whose commission he had initially declined:

The Adventures of Robin Hood, with Errol Flynn and Olivia de Haviland.[40] That won him an Academy Award. Settled in Beverly Hills, Korngold and his wife, Luzi, applied themselves to helping family and friends to leave Austria. His children were brought to safety, then his parents. Julius Korngold thus virtually became a neighbor of his old adversary, Schoenberg, while the name of his more amiable son began to appear in the pages of Thomas Mann's diary, as it would figure later in Alma Mahler-Werfel's record of her years in Los Angeles.[41] The Korngolds even found themselves socializing with Schoenberg and his family.

In her biography of her husband, Luzi Korngold observes that she did not know what Schoenberg thought of her husband's compositions.[42] Erich, who admired Schoenberg but found his music alien and unsympathetic,[43] could readily have suggested what he *should* have thought. Korngold's perception of his own Hollywood scores was that they were indeed "not serious," that they were simply a way of earning money until the war ended. Only then, he said, could he conceive of composing "for himself" once more. The power of the inherited, linked discourses of European high art and modernism is demonstrated in his shared sense of precisely the kind of alienation that Rachmaninov came to feel. It had impressed itself upon Korngold even before his first Hollywood trip in 1934. His father had chronicled his son's growing depression in an idiosyncratic journal (it is essentially a biography of him):

> He had already been touched by both open and covert opposition of the kind that the Third Reich sought to establish within music. Against his inclination and commitment, the former prodigy of unusual modernity had become associated with developments in respected, older music; at least he had not turned into some finicky "new music" man, groping his way into chaos. The result: ostracism by the closing ranks of the partisan coteries of artists, performers, and critics. "Why write operas, why compose in such times?"—these expressions of resignation, coming from one usually so cheerful and creatively unconstrained, affected me painfully.[44]

What Korngold became involved in during the period of this disillusionment was a form of popular music; he had made almost a new career for himself as an arranger and reviser of "golden era" Viennese operettas. He had, in other words, stepped back even further than Richard Strauss after *Elektra* from the challenge of so-called "advanced" music. His links with the world of popular culture, later specifically with the emergent world of cinematic mass entertainment, were to grow ever stronger.

As a film composer Korngold took the final step into a kind of music that represented the converse of all that European Great Music, traditional or modernist, was supposed to be, from the perspective of an Adorno, a Schoenberg, or even a Stravinsky. Film music was the antithesis of the idealized art of both the traditionalists and the modernists, and their journalistic and academic supporters. It was a commodity produced to commission, often at great speed. Demanding the converse of heroic individualism, it required the composer to lose most of his autonomy by becoming part of a production-team in which his cherished control and status as author were eroded by sound producers, staff orchestrators, and directors. Furthermore, it dealt openly in representation, drawing upon a rich, often suspect repertoire of nineteenth-century operatic and programmatic musical signification in scores whose form was blurred and confused by the fade-out, whose expressive subject-position slipped manipulatively between the multiple specificity of individual characters and metanarrative generalization. The "badness" and institutionalized otherness of such music were so ingrained as valuations that it came to be ignored by virtually all of the histories of twentieth-century music (along with most of the music of popular culture, of course).

Korngold was himself disparaging about his elaborate, voluble scores for historical action pictures. Their extension of the techniques of the already marginalized European world of protocinematic popular opera and operetta is nevertheless interesting. *Captain Blood, Anthony Adverse, The Adventures of Robin Hood, The Private Lives of Elizabeth and Essex* could all be analyzed as spoken grand operas, with love scenes, arias, choruses, processions, and even orchestral interludes. Sometimes the music will be unbroken for periods of twenty minutes or more; it heralds, frames and adds luster to the whole product as well as referentially shadowing, sometimes projecting or anticipating its events and moods. Still more interesting things happen in his generally less well-known, melodramatic, at times almost expressionistic scores for *King's Row* (1942), the remake of *Between Two Worlds* (1944), and *Deception,* for which Korngold wrote his last original score in 1946—the year of Schoenberg's String Trio, the year in which Mann finished *Doctor Faustus* and the war in Europe ended. Its title appropriately signals its particular relevance to my present theme.

Deception is a love-triangle melodrama which also belongs to the genre of "artist-movies" or "musician-movies," which seems to have reflected a rather complex Hollywood wartime policy of idealizing while ostensibly democratizing conventional European high culture and its values. The complexity derives from the fact that those values were becoming globally somewhat foreign to a general public whose tastes were both manipulated and represented by Hollywood in narratives about artistic pleasure and aspirations. Classical music, great literature, European languages and accents coalesced into an image of a privileged realm that was attainable only by the gifted few ("artists, people like us," as Bette Davis puts it in *Deception*).[45] At the same time that realm was growing temporally as well as geographically more distant, out of practical reach or detailed comprehension. Madame von Eln in *King's Row* represents an emblematically foreign figure in small-town America, speaking in French to her young charge, the piano-playing and intellectually gifted

Parris. Moved by the eventually disclosed news of Madame von Eln's fatal cancer, Colonel Skeffington muses aloud: "When she passes, how much passes with her—a whole way of life: a way of gentleness and honor and dignity. These things are going . . . and they may never come back to this world." In *King's Row*, "these things" seem unequivocally associated with European high culture, ancestral wealth, and aristocratic manners.

This popular idealization of European culture is partly undermined by its association with the past, with something that is dying. That association permitted alternative, more critical resonances and implications to fill the spaces where "higher" artistic strategizing was often precluded by brutal deadlines. In *Deception* the tension between conventional aesthetic ideology and its more distanced critical reflection is of particular interest in that all three main characters are musicians of European origin. At the start of the film two lovers, presented as having been uprooted and separated by the war, are reunited in a New York concert hall. Bette Davis's Christine had arrived first, hoping to be followed by cellist Karel Novak (Paul Henreid); only at the end of the war, however, had he arrived to try to reestablish his career in America and to find Christine. A poster has led her to the hall, where she arrives as he is playing the finale of Haydn's D-major Cello Concerto.

Korngold, himself an Austrian émigré, provided a remarkable score for the film, in which long stretches of diegetic classical music (Haydn, Schubert, Beethoven) threaten almost to usurp his "background" music, although a composition of his own subsequently plays a special part in that process. A clear distinction is nevertheless maintained between the realm of the classics and Korngold's characteristic late-romantic sound and style. The dialectic of their respective otherness is emphasized no less than is that between the world of the classical concert, at the beginning, and that of the city outside: Davis and Henreid exit the hall into an almost Ivesian montage of cab whistles, a Salvation-Army band, and traffic noise. Such contrasts and oppositions are explored by the film in a kind of aural subtext to its revelations about "artistic" behavior.

At first there is the title music, featuring a typically post-Straussian skyrocket of a theme that leaps improvisationally heavenwards as the word "Deception" fills the screen. The theme rapidly sinks into a protracted, dark-hued cadence, brooded over by a tolling bell as the titles give way to a long shot of a rainswept street and what looks like the façade of a church. Bette Davis climbs up the steps (it is a temple of art) and the background music is replaced by a plush silence, defined by the distant sound of classical concert music. Her susceptibility to it is ostensibly stressed in the first close-up. The camera finds her shadowed face high at the back of the hall; is it personal or purely aesthetic emotion that has brought tears to her eyes as she gazes longingly, sadly down at the platform? A huge pipe-organ rears up there, visually explaining the solemnity of the musicians.

Authentic classical music is presented as social and serious. In contrast, the "background" music is interpreted ever more deliberately as the deceptive, sentimentally oceanic image of a gendered subjectivity. This is a woman's music; it emanates from Christine and seems to engulf Karel as she strives to dispel his jealous doubts and assure him that they are truly united in love. This music seems to be constructed as "woman" in the bad old patriarchal sense that has been unmasked by Susan McClary; music that is dangerous and threatening in its siren-promise of perfect bliss. The musical plot is further thickened, however, by the cause of Christine's deception: the haughty "great composer," Alexander Hollenius (played in fine style by Claude Rains). He had adopted aspiring pianist Christine as his protégée and mistress. She plays, in fact, just once in the film (the *Appassionata,* at the party after her marriage to Karel), but Hollenius interrupts by breaking a wine glass in his jealously tense and angry hand. She covers for him by suggesting, deceptively as ever, that his sensitivity to music is to blame. She had become the muse to his creations (of course), the most recent of which, a cello concerto, he uses as a counter in the game of threatened revelation that he plays with Christine and her new husband, from whom she strives to conceal the truth of her former relationship with its composer.

Korngold's complicity with the ever more ambivalent positioning of his "own" music in the film is complicated by the fact that he published the one-movement Hollenius piece as his op. 37 Cello Concerto in C major. Denied any semiotically revealing links with the main thematic and motivic material of the rest of the score, it is a work whose closed form frames rich, postromantic lyricism within stretches of purposefully energetic contrapuntal passagework that are closer to Hindemith than to Rachmaninov. While in musical terms the Concerto thus seems judiciously autonomous, that very autonomy is interpreted within the film in such a way as to problematize Korngold's employment of the work in his doomed postwar attempt to reestablish his career as a "serious" concert composer. In *Deception* the Concerto is revealingly positioned not only as a man's music, but also as the music of a very particular kind of man, who is marked by all the popular signifiers of "high art" that the film subjects to historicizing critique. Hollenius, Christine tells Karel, is "rich, immensely rich, like a king!" When we see him at home, it is in a sumptuously furnished studio, looking like Wagner's drawing room at Wahnfried—silk dressing-gown, potted palms, rich drapery, and "art" everywhere. The imperialist implications of his aristocratic decadence are stressed by the presence of an oriental servant; a Siamese cat purrs in the great man's lap. "Sooner or later," he tells Christine after her wedding, "you'll realize that nothing really matters but music—and me." Aesthetic idealism seems conclusively unmasked as an instrument of patriarchal domination.

The point is further stressed by Hollenius's use of the Concerto in his dealings with Karel Novak, who becomes vulnerable to attacks and put-downs of a particularly effective kind when rehearsing and performing the piece under Hollenius's masterful baton. Furthermore, when we first see Hollenius playing it on the piano in his studio, where he is surprised by Christine's unannounced arrival, it appears unequivocally and expressionistically linked to his anger and sense of betrayal. He plays its ending as if he meant to kill.

There is something slightly corny and compromised about the dialectic thus set up between the great male composer—whose concerto is, of course, played brilliantly by Karel at the end—and his desired other in Christine, whose nondiegetic "inner" music is consistently presented as self-indulgent, its deceptiveness of a fundamentally honest and thus self-consciously authentic type. The film's dénouement nevertheless focuses the implied subtext. Visiting Hollenius on her way to the Concerto performance that he is to conduct (Karel had gone on earlier), Christine fails to win from him the assurance that he is not planning to tell all after the concert. She shoots him and leaves the gun near the body to make it look like suicide. Feminized mass culture finally puts paid to patriarchal European high culture, but might well have to pay the price. Her distraught revelation in Karel's dressing-room after the concert seems to prepare us for an arrest-of-the-fallen-woman scene, until Karel (another cliché looms: the man corrupted by the femme fatale) wonders if they might yet escape the clutches of the law and maintain the deception that Hollenius died by his own hand. For a moment, Bette Davis's look, as a well-wisher greets their hurried departure with "You must be the happiest woman in the world!" threatens to sunder her from her recurring, now more purposefully cadencing music, first heard in the titles. It also, however, begins to sound more defiant than deceptive, almost transgressively aware of the responsibility it has assumed. While completing the score, Korngold might justifiably have felt a sense of common purpose with Rachmaninov as his pen turned momentarily into a gun in a feminine-looking hand, the hovering images of Schoenberg and Stravinsky merging before him into one that bore a curious likeness to Claude Rains.

A FINAL REFLECTION

The familiar historical narrative of the advance of modernism has often assumed the character of an imperial or colonial history: strategically marginalizing and diminishing different or dissenting voices as those of the conquered and the outmoded. The uprooted European artists and intellectuals of 1940s Los Angeles blamed that city, and Hollywood in particular, for a destructive levelling and blurring of distinctions.[46] The fear behind the blame was that the traditional social function and ideology of high art, of which avant-garde modernism was really an integral part, was threatened by the resultant clarification of the oppositions of power and gender which had defined its discourse. *Deception*'s part in that clarification is summed up in an emblematic moment when Bette Davis actually encounters and seems momentarily to question her own image in a mirror before setting out to shoot a composer. No less questioningly might a critical, postmodernist musicology confront the institutionalized history of Twentieth-Century Music. Wary of ideological snares, its authors long remained cautious about politically committed composers of the Left like Kurt Weill and Hanns Eisler, whose own experiences of American exile form a different, if related, story to the one sketched here. Meanwhile, anxiously deployed strategies of marginalizing scorn and self-critical apologetics generated a complex discursive accompaniment to the unmasking of high art in and as the popular culture it had long feared and despised. The trading of constructions of modernism between Stravinsky and Schoenberg against Rachmaninov and Korngold marked a significant stage in the decline and transformation of European music's "good old tradition" as part of it slipped out of the downtown concert hall and into the local cinema.

NOTES

1. Jean-François Lyotard, *The Postmodern Explained to Children: Correspondence 1982–1985* (London: Turnaround, 1992), 15.

2. Ibid., 16.

3. See Andreas Huyssen, *After the Great Divide: Modernism, Mass Culture and Postmodernism* (London: Macmillan, 1988).

4. Sergei Bertensson and Jay Leyda, *Sergei Rachmaninoff: A Lifetime in Music* (New York: New York University Press, 1956), 351. I have adopted "Rachmaninov" as the most widely used transliteration; formerly current spellings of his name have been retained in quotations.

5. Rachmaninov's Prelude in C-sharp Minor is treated in scorching style in Theodor Adorno, *Quasi una Fantasia: Essays on Modern Music,* trans. Rodney Livingstone (London: Verso, 1992), 38–40.

6. Quoted in Bertensson and Leyda, *Rachmaninoff,* 363–64.

7. See Max Paddison, *Adorno's Aesthetics of Music* (Cambridge: Cambridge University Press, 1993), 263–64, 269ff.

8. Bertensson and Leyda, *Rachmaninoff,* 309.

9. Ibid., 374.

10. See *Stravinsky in Conversation with Robert Craft* (London: Pelican Books, 1962), "Conversations with Igor Stravinsky," 55–56.

11. Theodor Adorno, *Philosophy of Modern Music* (a strict translation of the German title would be "Philosophy of *New* Music"), trans. Anne G. Mitchell and Wesley V. Bloomster (London: Sheed and Ward, 1973), 209.

12. The clearest formulation of that position had appeared in Stravinsky's *Chronique de ma vie* in 1936, reprinted as *An Autobiography* (London: Calder and Boyars Ltd., 1975), 53 ("I consider that music is, by its very nature, powerless to *express* anything at all. . . . ").

13. Adorno, *Philosophy of Modern Music,* 181–82.

14. See Harvey Sachs, *Music in Fascist Italy* (London: Weidenfeld and Nicolson, 1987), 168.

15. Adorno, *Philosophy of Modern Music,* 211.

16. See Igor Stravinsky and Robert Craft, *Dialogues* (London: Faber, 1982), 50–52.

17. Ibid., 51.

18. See Igor Stravinsky and Robert Craft, *Expositions and Developments* (London: Faber, 1981), 77.

19. For Stravinsky's response to *Fantasia,* see ibid., 145–46; the comment about Chaplin films appears in Igor Stravinsky and Robert Craft, *Memories and Commentaries* (London: Faber, 1981), 109.

20. See Stravinsky and Craft, *Dialogues,* 106n2. Stravinsky's own analysis of the difference between him and Schoenberg is set out there on 107–8.

21. Adorno, *Philosophy of Modern Music,* 20.

22. See H. H. Stuckenschmidt, *Arnold Schoenberg: His Life, World and Work,* trans. Humphrey Searle (London: John Calder, 1977), 508.

23. In *Style and Idea: Selected Writings of Arnold Schoenberg,* ed. Leonard Stein (London: Faber, 1975), 76.

24. See Stuckenschmidt, *Arnold Schoenberg,* 545–46. The text of what was in fact a recorded message, played in his absence, also appears, slightly differently arranged on the page, in *Arnold Schoenberg Letters,* 245–46.

25. I refer here particularly to Eric Salzman's note "Prelude to the Genesis Suite" in the leaflet accompanying the 1965 CBS recording under Robert Craft: *The Music of Arnold Schoenberg,* vol. 2 (BRG/SBRG 72268).

26. Thomas Mann, *The Genesis of a Novel,* trans. Richard and Clara Winston (London: Secker and Warburg, 1961), 172. The English translation, by H. T. Lowe-Porter, of *Doctor Faustus* (chapter 43) renders the phrase as "impossible but refreshing" in the section on Leverkühn's Trio. The comment to Eisler about the injection chords is recorded in Stuckenschmidt, *Arnold Schoenberg,* 479.

27. Precisely relevant here is Schoenberg's revelation in 1940 that his First String Quartet (op. 7) had a "very definite—but private!" program; see Dika Newlin, *Schoenberg Remembered: Diaries and Recollections (1938–76)* (New York: Pendragon Press, 1980), 193.

28. Ibid., 96.

29. *Style and Idea,* 123–24.

30. On the Schoenberg-Mann controversy about *Doctor Faustus,* see Thomas Mann, *The Genesis of a Novel,* 32–33; the "Author's Note" appended to all editions of the novel (where the twelve-tone system is acknowledged to be "the intellectual property . . . of Arnold Schoenberg"); *Arnold Schoenberg Letters,* 255; Stuckenschmidt, *Arnold Schoenberg,* 491–92.

31. I say this notwithstanding the interesting arguments developed in Alexander Ringer, *Arnold Schoenberg: The Composer as Jew* (Oxford: Clarendon Press, 1990). The specific tendency to "explain" Schoenberg psychoanalytically, or in terms of his Jewish background, seems to have been followed by Ringer, Reinhold Brinkman, and others at the 1991 Los Angeles conference "Constructive Dissonance: Arnold Schoenberg and Transformations of Twentieth-Century Culture—Vienna, Berlin and Los Angeles." See Charlotte M. Cross's report in *Current Musicology* 54 (1993): 88–93.

32. See Constantin Floros: "Zur Wirkungsgeschichte Gustav Mahlers" in *Fragment of Completion? Proceeedings of the Mahler X Symposium*, Utrecht 1986, ed. Paul Op de Coul (The Hague: Universitaire Pers Rotterdam, 1991), 188.

33. *Style and Idea*, 505.

34. Jelena Hahl-Koch, ed., *Arnold Schoenberg/Wassily Kandinsky: Letters, Pictures and Documents*, trans. John C. Crawford (London: Faber, 1984), 23. Emphasis in original.

35. Egbert M. Ennulat, *Arnold Schoenberg Correspondence* (London: The Scarecrow Press Inc., 1991), 260–61. See also *Style and Idea*, 249–50 ("Is it Fair?" 1947). An earlier (1931) assertion of the specific "Germanness" of his own music appears there on 173.

36. *Arnold Schoenberg Letters*, 243.

37. John Russell Taylor, *Strangers in Paradise: The Hollywood Émigrés 1933–1950* (London: Faber, 1983), 210.

38. Brendan Carroll, *The Last Prodigy: A Biography of Erich Wolfgang Korngold* (Portland, Oregon: Amadeus Press, 1997), 211. See also Hans Moldenhauer, *Anton Webern — A Chronicle of His Life and Works* (London: Gollancz, 1978), 140.

39. *A Midsummer Night's Dream*, directed by Max Reinhardt and William Dieterle (Warner Brothers, 1935).

40. Korngold's initial letter to Hal Wallis, declining the commission, appears in Rudy Behlmer, *Inside Warner Bros (1935–1951)* (London: Weidenfeld and Nicolson, 1986), 52–53.

41. See Alma Mahler-Werfel, *And the Bridge Is Love: Memories of a Lifetime* (London: Hutchinson, 1959), 258, 277.

42. See Luzi Korngold, *Erich Wolfgang Korngold* (Vienna: Elisabeth Lafite/Österreichischer Bundesverlag, 1967), 71.

43. Ibid.

44. Julius Korngold, *Die Korngolds in Wien: Die Musikkritiker und das Wunderkind* (Zürich: M & T Verlag, 1991), 363.

45. All quotations from films are transcribed by the author.

46. See Mike Davis, *City of Quartz: Excavating the Future in Los Angeles* (London: Vintage, 1992), 18.

Experimental Oriental:
New Music and Other Others

John Corbett

In this essay I will seek to explicate some aspects of the underlying paradigm that frames and makes sensible the use of non-Western elements in Western art music of recent vintage. Specifically, we should wonder: How does Orientalism function in the experimental tradition? And what different forms does it take within that compositional world? Though we should not avoid the fact that there can, indeed, be a sinister side to the practice, it seems relevant to try to fully think through these issues before lumping all such borrowings together, bundling them up and tossing them overboard. Even if such dismissal or dressing-down *were* desirable, on the overdetermined cruise ship that transnational culture has now become, utopian separatism just is not feasible. Indeed, as we shall see, certain of the Orientalist appropriations have long ago been reappropriated by non-Western agents and put back to use in varied ways. The move to disentangle "authentic" ethnic music from its hybridized new-music forms can be seen as a reassertion of the peculiar Western power to define (and preserve) "pure" expressions of cultural ethnicity as opposed to their "tainted" counterparts. Better, it seems, to describe the underlying epistemic framework which provides a context for American and European classical music's overwhelming turn to the music of "other" cultures.

To elaborate the Orientalist tradition in new music in any comprehensive way would require a book of its own. What I aim to do here is simply lay out some overarching ideas and a sampling of pivotal figures and their work, primarily—though not exclusively—through the lens of the American experimental tradition and its polyglot offspring.

I. EXPERIMENT (OCCIDENT)

Though its exact genealogy is open to debate, American experimental composition first acquired escape velocity from the dominant European model in the work of Charles Ives. A widespread syncretic historical phenomenon stretching from coast to coast, post-Ivesian American experimental composition has, in its eighty-year history, incorporated people from vastly divergent backgrounds—its ranks typically swell to include Carl Ruggles, Edgard Varése, Charles Seeger, Henry Cowell, Harry Partch, Ruth Crawford, Henry Brant, Conlon Nancarrow, Lou Harrison, Morton Feldman, Earle Brown, and Christian Wolff. Later branches include the minimalists (Steve Reich, La Monte Young, Philip Glass, Terry Riley, Tony Conrad); electronic, tape and computer conceptualists like Alvin Lucier, Gordon Mumma, and David Behrman; and text-based performance artists like Charles Amirkhanian, Laurie Anderson and Robert Ashley.[1] But one composer's name is never left out: John Cage.[2]

Cage became a spokesman for experimental music, a role preceded (and inspired) by the publication of Cowell's important treatise *New Musical Resources,* written in the teens but unpublished until 1930.[3] Starting in the late 1930s, during a period in which Cage was beginning to utilize percussion and electronics as a way of introducing nonmusical elements into his compositions (the work that led to his development and refinement of Cowell's notion of prepared piano), he began to actively theorize his brand of experimentalism. "Centers of experimental music must be established," he insisted in a lecture in 1937. "In these centers, the new materials, oscillators, turntables, generators, means for amplifying small sounds, film phonographs, etc., available for use. Composers at work using twentieth-century means for making music."[4] Cage's father, it has often been noted, was an inventor.

The many forms that American experimental composition has taken between that time and today have been well chronicled elsewhere.[5] The point here is to indicate how the notion of experimentation rhetorically carries into the process of musical composition a connotation of science—of laboratory experimentation, as in Cage's proposed "centers"—and to indicate how that rhetorical turn functions to disavow any political or ideological dimension that the work might yield. There have, of course, been notable postwar composers who were both committed experimentalists and politically active, some (like Cornelius Cardew, Frederic Rzewski, and Luigi Nono) explicitly intertwining the two. But even apart from any of its specific incarnations (a few of which we will examine later), the basic association of experimentation with composing potentially configures music-making as a clean slate, without the ideological baggage of European tradition to weigh it down. This break is clearly one of the distinguishing marks of American experimental and avant-garde composition: music is suddenly about looking for new forms, processes, and materials. And it is also about the conducting of experiments without predicting or manipulating the results. Reflecting Cage's well-known desire to rid himself of ego and style, the experiment functions to impart the same ideological blankness, the same un-

partisan pretense, and, ultimately, the same universal scientificity as experimental methodology does in the realm of hard science. Where an older
model of scientific inquiry as the apex of control and rationality was the discursive formation in which serialism was elaborated, experimentalism takes
the image of science as inquiry and looks forward to new paradigms of fuzzy
logics, chaos theory, probability and chance.[6] In her essay "Chance Operations: Cagean Paradox and Contemporary Science," N. Katherine Hayles describes this as "the entanglement of causal determinism with an open and
unpredictable future."[7]

It is important to recall the basic assumption behind the idea of experimental method: namely, that the outcome of the experiment is always undetermined. The hypothesis can never assume its results, but must await their
appearance; experimental results then help prove or disprove the hypothesis (or, in other cases when they expose design flaws in the experimental
framework, they may help redesign the experiment), but they are (at least
ideally) inert, open-ended, and potentially subversive of the desired outcome.
By definition, experimental data must be able to behave in a way not predicted by the hypothesis. Thus, the experiment is conceived as an excellent
setting for exploration and discovery, a perfect opportunity for an encounter with the new, the unforeseen, and the unfamiliar.

II. CONCEPT

In a certain wing of experimental music the concerns of the composer shift
from conventional ones of tone, dynamic, rhythm, harmony, form and timbre to more strictly experimental ones, such as process, method, procedure,
tools, framework, and even context.

Cage examined the possibilities of musical composition as process very
thoroughly, especially in his many aleatory, indeterminate, or chance-pro-
cedures pieces, which he began composing in the 1950s. He initially did this
work with the help of the ancient Chinese oracle *I Ching* (or *Book of Changes*),
to which he was introduced in its first English publication in 1951 by like-
minded composer Christian Wolff. Cage later utilized many other devices,
from Hans Arp–like random collage methods to the use of computers to
aid in the decision-making process of composition. Cage forecast the waning importance of preordained structure in works like his *Sonatas and Interludes* (which he wrote with the compositional device of flipping coins), a
presence only felt as a part of the overarching compositional process. "The
structure . . . determined the beginning and ending of the compositional
process," he explained at Darmstadt in 1958, discussing *Sonatas and Interludes*. "But this process, had it in the end brought about a division of parts
the time-lengths of which were proportional to the original series of numbers, would have been extraordinary. And the presence of the mind as a rul-

ing factor, even by such an extraordinary eventuality, would not have been established. For what happened came about only through the tossing of coins."[8] By eliminating the governing principle of structure and supplanting taste with process, Cage sought explicitly to divorce composing from "the mind as a ruling factor," and thereby liberate sounds from their social and political connotations.

Subsidiary Trope: Terra Incognita

In close conjunction with the rhetoric of experimentation, we find an associated set of tropes clustered around the idea of exploration and discovery. The experimenter (and much has been made of the fact that Cage's father actually *was* an inventor) is also a rugged cartographer of new lands or navigator of unknown waters, a sonic De Soto or musical Magellan. In this discursive regime, the composer is configured as an explorer looking for terra incognita. This notion of discovery or exploration helps undergird the idea that the composer is engaging in a value-free, experimental endeavor, even as it allows us to suggest the colonialist impulse submerged in its rhetoric. It is assumed that the discoverer-composer, out on the open seas of aural possibility, surely will bring back ideas and practices from distant lands, perhaps ones that can enhance the quality of Western musical life. Musical experimentation becomes metaphorical microcolonialism. To be a cultured mid- to late-twentieth-century Westerner, then, means to appreciate the spoils of such musical exploration, to be a healthy relativist. As Lou Harrison puts it:

> Along with Henry Cowell I deem it necessary to know well at least one musical tradition other than the one into which one is born. This second acquisition ought to be "equivalent." If Haydn is known, then an equivalent court music should be studied and learned: Javanese Gadon for example, or Chinese or Japanese or Korean court or chamber music. It will not do to extend from Beethoven sonatas to Bluegrass banjo; the social and intellectual contents are largely incommensurate.[9]

In Harrison's statement one can detect both the globalizing undertone that informs most contemporary "world music" projects and a peculiar stratification that mandates a transcultural link between musics of similar hierarchical status and social provenance. Listeners should explore, chart new territory, but make sure not to stray from music of the same caste; breaking down cultural barriers may be a good idea, but leave class lines alone.

II. EXPERIMENT (ORIENT)

An interest in non-Western, nonclassical materials was not introduced into American experimental composition through Cage's work with the *I Ching*, however. Indeed, Cowell had written long before of the potential utility of nondiatonic, microtonal scales: "Successful experiments, and the well-known practice of Oriental music, show that these tones are not beyond the capacity of the human ear. . . . Sliding tones, based on ever-changing values of pitch instead of steady pitches, are sometimes used in music. Such tones are very frequently used in primitive music, and often in Oriental music. . . . "[10] Cowell also suggested that the stiff, unyielding rhythms characteristic of Western music might benefit from the nuances of alien input: "Not only do nearly all Oriental and primitive peoples use such shades of rhythm, but also our own virtuosi, who instead of playing the notes just as written, often add subtle deviations of their own." The proximity of "primitive" and "Oriental" is telling here. Indeed, it should be noted that Cowell is sometimes grouped with Leo Ornstein and George Antheil, who were arguably the musical equivalents of Picasso in their overt use of primitivism.[11] Ornstein (composer of "Danse Sauvage") and Antheil (composer of "Sonata Sauvage") both professed interest in what they saw as a rawness and brutality of "primitive" cultures and sought to translate that aspect into a productively shocking effect in the West, just as Picasso had in his works influenced by African masks and sculptures.

Johannes Fabian has unpacked the way that cultural anthropology tends to position its object at a temporal distance from itself, even when the people in question are contemporaneous with the inquirer. Fabian locates this in the context of a capitalist, colonialist-imperialist expansionism in which "*geopolitics* has its ideological foundation in *chronopolitics*": "Anthropology emerged and established itself as an allochronic discourse; it is a science of other men in another Time. It is a discourse whose referent has been removed from the present of the speaking/writing subject."[12] Already, right at the outset of the proverbial golden years of American experimentalism, a familiar nineteenth-century form of Orientalism helps guide an overriding interest in non-Western musics: "Oriental" music is linked, at least by persistent proximity, with the "primitive," and both are looked to for their rejuvenative powers in a period of mounting dissatisfaction with conventional Western musical civilization. The Oriental is first distanced from the West (to suggest its difference), then embraced as a potent import—it is, in Edward Said's terms, Oriental*ized:* "Primitiveness therefore inhered in the Orient, *was* the Orient, an idea to which anyone dealing with or writing about the Orient had to return, as if to a touchstone outlasting time or experience."[13] What various "traditional" musics bring to the Western classical scene is a sort of shock of the ancient—they are seen as having values that were lost over the course of European art music history, or perhaps were never there in the first place. It is important, then, that these traditions be configured as old—perhaps primitive—so that they can whisper their secrets in the ear of the Western composer. Of course, this means that those traditional musics must not change, and never have. As Said suggests: "The very possibility of development, transformation, human movement—in the deepest sense of the word—is denied the Orient and the Oriental. As a known and ultimately an immobilized or unproductive quality, they come to be identified with a bad sort of eternality: hence, when the Orient is being approved, such phrases as 'the wisdom of the East.'"[14] In addition to positioning the Orient as this sort of timeless knowledge, another way Orientalist discourse functions, according to Said, is by empowering the Westerner to typify, generalize, and subsequently represent what is Oriental: "In a quite constant way, Orientalism depends for its strategy on this flexible *positional* superiority, which puts the Westerner in a whole series of possible relationships with the Orient without ever losing him the upper hand."[15] Within Orientalism the Oriental object can never represent itself, but is essentialized and represented as a combined projection of Western desires and anxieties and a reassertion of Western control. American experimentalists have consistently defined the Oriental as a generalized set of potential "new musical resources." Cowell, for instance, only barely distinguishes *which* Oriental musical practice or practices he is referencing (in *New Musical Resources* his most specific citations are of Javanese and Siamese music, ancient Greek music, and Hawaiian music),[16] and he never specifies whether he means classical or court musics (of which there are many, centuries old, and hardly "primitive"), popular musics, or traditional folk musics. Note the difference from Harrison's dictate that people should know more than one music culture; though curiously stratified and clearly elitist, Harrison is very specific about which kind of music—art/court, folk/popular—is "equivalent," hence calling for a more detailed and less blanketlike understanding of other musics and an admission that there are art music traditions other than the Western classical lineage. Like Harrison's, Cowell's encounter with non-Western music was facilitated by the fact that he lived on the West Coast, and in San Francisco as a young person he spent much time studying various musical traditions, especially Chinese and Japanese vocal technique, Indonesian gamelan and Indian classical music.[17] By referring to these musics in a generalized way, Cowell retains his positional superiority, defining and then appropriating elements that help him dislocate conventional European harmony and rhythm.

Nevertheless, in comparison with the bald exoticism of Antheil and Ornstein, Cowell's early work—especially the remarkable body of solo piano music he composed in the 1910s and 1920s—remains particularly interesting and valuable in its oblique use of non-Western musics, the way that it tends to treat them as inspiration and catalyst rather than as exotic, "savage" incendiary devices to be thrown at polite concert conventions. One can, for instance, hear certain aspects of koto music in his celebrated development of clusters and other dense voicings; and it is easy in retrospect to see his instructions to perform directly on the strings of the piano with fingers or foreign implements—abstracting the major icon of Western art music and turning it into an *objet retrouvé*—as relating to Asian string traditions for instruments performed similarly, such as the chin and kayagum. As pianist Chris Burn, a Cowell specialist, explains: "He often transferred playing techniques from other stringed instruments. These include strumming, plucking, scraping and stopping the strings, the latter to produce muted tones and a wide variety of harmonics."[18] Cowell's distance from the primitivist camp is reflected in the titles of these pieces, which all relate to the mythology of the Celtic isles, his father's ancestry. In these formative and important pieces, rather than reference Asian musics, Cowell develops his own music out of them, developing new instrumental techniques and approaching the piano (and, consequently, certain entrenched aspects of Western harmony) anew. According to this model, non-Western musics provide a mirror that allows Western music to reconsider itself. In his piano repertoire, at least, Cowell resisted the lure of superficial exoticism. Composer, instrument-inventor, and resolute outsider Harry Partch also fits this description. In the arsenal of new musical tools he created—thoroughly theorized in his book *The Genesis of a Music*—Partch too took inspiration from non-Western musics he heard as a young person in California and developed his own music from them, building his own tools where Cowell looked for a new one already waiting in the piano. Further, Partch was profoundly struck by Chinese and Japanese theatrical traditions, and he took pains to discuss his work as ritual and drama, rather than autonomous concert music.

Early on, Cage discussed the inherent possibilities of percussion and improvisation directly in relation to Asian and African American music. In 1937 he wrote: "Methods of writing percussion music have as their goal the rhythmic structure of a composition. As soon as these methods are crystallized into one or several widely accepted methods, the means will exist for group improvisations of unwritten but culturally important music. This has already taken place in Oriental cultures and in hot jazz."[19] This pair of musical archetypes provides Cage with a springboard for decades of consideration, specifically by embracing certain aspects of the "Oriental" and eventually rejecting the expressive, narrative orientation of jazz.[20]

While teaching at Cornish School in Seattle, Washington, in the late 1930s, Cage was first introduced to the teachings of Zen Buddhism, and Cage's budding interest in Zen was further stimulated by his encounter with Zen proselytizer and philosopher Daisetz T. Suzuki at a lecture at Columbia University in 1945. Cage studied with Suzuki and actively read various philosophical texts (not by any means limited to Zen); his noted favorites included the gospel of Sri Ramakrishna and Aldous Huxley's *The Perennial Philosophy*. In his work with words—both written and spoken—and in lectures and explanations of his working methods, Cage consistently referred to the writings of non-Western philosophers; some of his best-known writings on boredom, aesthetics, and politics are as much steeped in Zen and Indian philosophy as in Thoreau and Duchamp. He attributed his important reconsideration of the role of silence in musical composition to Hindu and Buddhist concepts. "My concern toward the irrational," Cage remarked in 1967, "and my belief that it is important to us in our lives, is akin to the use of the koan in Zen Buddhism. That is to say, we are so accustomed and so safe in the use of our observation of relationships and our rational faculties that in Buddhism it was long known that we needed to leap out of that, and the discipline by which they made that leap take place was by asking a question that could not be answered rationally."[21]

III. CONCEPTUAL ORIENTALISM VS. CONTEMPORARY CHINOISERIE

It would be false to assume that all forms of cultural appropriation are alike. In the case of experimental music, we can trace two basic, very different kinds of work that directly relate to and emanate from the encounter with non-Western cultures. As we have seen, these two lines may well have been closely related in their infancy—Cage's interest in percussion music and Cowell's initial development of techniques for prepared piano were both derived from a sheer delight in the new timbres and textures of various kinds of Asian, Indonesian, and African musics. And some of Cage's early keyboard music clearly exploits the possibilities of turning the piano into a one-man gamelan. But where Cowell later went on to exploit other musics for their exotic appeal, as we shall see, Cage saw the use of non-Western music and philosophy as a potential strategy for the disruption of the Western preoccupation with harmony, structure and intentionality.

Through his increasing use of Zen (rather than simple exotic musical material), Cage developed a substantially altered version of Orientalism, an Orientalism based not on the acquisition of new sonic objects but concerned with posing unanswerable or indefinite musical questions. The image of the musical koan—an unsolvable riddle or paradox used in Buddhism to derail rationality—became Cage's badge of honor, and he himself became, for many new-art followers and makers alike, a pop-Zen icon. He was known for telling Buddhist jokes, parables, and anecdotes, as well as translating into musical composition the ideas of triviality, paradox, contempt for absolute meaning, and respect for sound-as-sound. Indeed, some significant degree of Cage's lasting public image is inextricably bound up in what he referred to (usually in the aggregate, rather than specifically) as "Oriental philosophy," and he was seen by many as being a major figurehead for non-Western thought in America. The way that soprano saxophonist Steve Lacy characterizes late 1950s New York bohemia, for instance, says much about that close link: "Zen was in the air, everybody was reading Cage. . . . "[22] Cage's preoccupation with the irrational led him to conceive of strict systems in which he could produce random events or chance occurrences. But if we have already configured him as a prime conceptualist in contemporary music, it is necessary to see that move in relation to a persistent Orientalist orientation.

Ryoanji

Cage's conceptual Orientalism does not start by trying to import an alien idea into his work or graft an exotic element onto it, nor does it base itself around a non-Western system or sound. It is not about semblance, not about "sounding" non-Western. Instead, Cage creates the conditions for certain events to happen, the concept for which may be roughly based, for instance, in an Asian source. The resulting music, however, may have little or nothing aesthetically to do with the originary system—indeed, Cage was usually at pains to avoid such stylistic or idiomatic markers. In his 1983 composition *Ryoanji*, for example, he used the visual image of the Japanese stone garden as the starting point for the piece. He prepared paper with two rectangular areas, then in the first traced parts of the perimeter of stones (placed using chance procedures), indicating glissandi in relatively conventional graphic notation (sliding between bottom=low and top=high). This created a series of solos, each followed by a silence of unspecified length. In the other rectangle, Cage composed the accompaniment, guided by the image of the raked sand that sits under stones in a garden; this suggested to him that he should utilize five unison parts distributed randomly (but systematically) on the page.

While referring in its title and working process to Japanese culture, the resulting piece *Ryoanji* (of which Cage made versions for oboe, trombone, flute, voice, and bass-and-voice, all accompanied by percussion) does not resemble anything specifically Japanese at all. The instrumentation is primarily standard-issue Western classical (save the percussion part, which, in dedicatee Michael Pugliese's performances, included a rock, pod rattle, small log, and drum), and the superimposition of the two pieces—each conceived as a solo, but played simultaneously—creates something that is conceptually and processually indebted to a non-Western inspiration. This is an oblique form of Orientalism, not the direct incorporative or syncretic form to which the West is more accustomed. But it is still Orientalist. Cage's use of systems—superimposed sets of rule-based parameters for the construction of works—qualifies him as one of the most genuinely experimental composers of American experimentalism. He designed concepts and executed them without knowing for certain what the outcome would be. (At times, like many scientists, he even admitted to cheating to get the results he desired.) But we have already seen how that cloak of ideological blankness, grounded in the scientific connotation of experimentation, does not evade the underlying value system that produces it. In other words, while Cage's conceptual work may not *seem* Orientalist, in the final analysis the ends never totally escape the means.

Persian Set

If Cage's conceptual Orientalism stirred others into concept-based work—
his progeny ranging from Fluxus composers like George Brecht and Nam
June Paik to a long laundry list of academic Cageans—another lineage of
Orientalist work continued unabated. That more generic type of Orientalism might be best titled "contemporary chinoiserie,"[23] in homage to the decorative tradition it most closely resembles. In this case, it is specifically the
exotic sounds, textures, instruments, voices and shapes of non-Western music that are appropriated for use in a new-music context. These can be seen
as vibing up the senile classical music scene, adding thrilling new grist to
the moribund old elitist mill. But they also continue a tried and true tradition, well established in the nineteenth century, of exotic Orientalist musical
decoration.

Consider, for example, Cowell's composition *Persian Set*. Written in 1957,
while Cowell and his wife were visiting Tehran, Iran, during a world tour
funded by the Rockefeller Foundation, *Persian Set* is a far cry from the systematic experimental work of Cage. Cowell characterized it as "a simple record
of musical contagion,"[24] and it has the air of an idiomatic study of the basics
of Iranian music. Obviously indebted to late romanticism, it also sounds reminiscent of Copland's Americana (Cowell, too, was composing Americana
such as *American Melting Pot* and *Old American Country Set* as early as the late
1930s), and it is not too distant in feel from something like Rimsky-Korsakov's
Scheherazade or Ravel's *Bolero*. Like both those widely recorded, popularized
pieces, *Persian Set* has an air of pastichery and world-music kitsch about it. It
borders more on easy listening music's global exotics—extremely popular
in the mid-1950s, along with tiki lounges and widespread chop suey—than
on Cowell's earlier promise of an armada of startling new musical resources.
(It is interesting to note that a popular easy listening duo of that period, Fer-
rante & Teicher, specialized in using prepared pianos in many of their explicitly exoticist, pseudo-Polynesian pieces.) In 1958, Cage pointedly wrote:
"Cowell's present interests in the various traditions, Oriental and early
American, are not experimental but eclectic."[25]

Conceptual Orientalism and contemporary chinoiserie—most of the relevant experimental and new-music movements since World War II, when they
have explicitly used non-Western elements in their construction, have had
their feet planted in one of these two camps. The lineage of composers creating pure chinoiserie is quite strong, and certainly includes Alan Hovhaness,
whose work Brian Morton eloquently sums up as combining "semi-mystical
'Eastern' hokum with Orthodox and Western church music, and routine
'classical' form . . . a hefty warning of the superficiality and bland eclecticism

that lies in wait even for more adventurous experimenters and that seems a particular pitfall of West Coast culture."[26] Colin McPhee's compositions, such as his best known 1936 piece "Tabuh-tabuhan," stretch the definition of "influence" by being perilously close to the actual *sound* of Balinese gamelan music. He studied the Indonesian court music very closely and wrote the ethnomusicological classic *Music in Bali* while living there from 1931–39. This raises the problem of the ethical dimension of its authorship.[27] Though on paper he may have required more specific knowledge of musical traditions than Cowell, Lou Harrison too created works more notable for the craft of their panglobal exotic referentiality—using Indonesian scales and orchestras consisting of both Western and non-Western instruments in rather forced, lushly arranged East-West cultural grafts—than for their intellectual innovation. Unlike Cowell, Partch, and Cage, who were stimulated by non-Western musics to come up with something conceptually and/or sonically original, Hovhaness, McPhee, and Harrison tended to pay homage with the sincerest form of flattery—cheap imitation. The political blank slate of experimentality gave them license to imitate at will, to continue the venerable tradition of, in Said's words, "domestications of the exotic."[28]

To be sure, some composers have used a combination of conceptual and decorative Orientalism. The minimalists, for instance, adopted both sounds *and* ideas from extraneous sources, allowing them to both resemble classical Indian (in the case of drones and modalism) or West African music (in the case of cyclical polymeter) and, at the same time, to use sounds and systems derived from those traditions as tools with which to interrogate and dislocate conventional Western musical reality.

IV. STRUCTURALIST MINIMALIST

I am not interested in improvisation or in sounding exotic.[29]
STEVE REICH, 1969

Fifty years after Cowell had formally suggested the turn to other cultural traditions in experimental music, the impulse was still strongly felt by American composers, particularly those wishing to find a different path from both the European serialist and postserialist line and the Cagean conceptual line. For Steve Reich, Cage's compositional use of chance process had been impossible to detect, and Reich instead wanted a process that was audible as it was being performed or played back. In 1970, after spending five months studying Ewe music with master drummer Gideon Alorworye in Ghana, Reich wrote *Drumming,* his landmark piece. Though he'd already been exploring phase-relation pieces in which a musical process of changing rhythmic relations between repeating figures clearly occurs, this work launched his career and cemented his reputation as one of the foremost minimalist figures. Two years later, he spent a summer studying Balinese gamelan with I Nyoman Sumandhi. Fellow minimalist Philip Glass was similarly influenced by North Indian classical music through studies with tabla player Alla Rakha in the late 1960s, and Terry Riley had even earlier been using looping and phasing rhythms. Their music, too, attempted to use complexities of cyclical time to undermine composerly practice and moreover to rethink the conventions of Western musical *structure*. Outspoken in his desire not to sound like the musics he was learning about, Reich posed the problem of absorbing influences: "What can a composer do with this knowledge?" His answer was specifically to suggest that a Western composer should study non-Western structures, allowing them to influence rather than seeking to imitate them. "This brings about the interesting situation of the non-Western influence being there in the thinking, but not in the sound," he concluded.[30] Thus, while he initially thought of writing *Drumming* for African instruments, he decided against this so as not to be too literal. While he was clearly inspired by his transcriptions of African music and study of Indonesian musics, Reich attempted to utilize what he learned as a way of challenging the formal and structural components of Western classical music, particularly its moribund sense of how to deal with pulsed time. "What was it about Steve Reich's 'Drumming' that brought the audience to its feet at the Museum of Modern Art on December 3?" asked composer/writer Tom Johnson in an early column for the *Village Voice* in 1971. "Was it the pleasure of seeing African and European elements so thoroughly fused— almost as though we really did live in one world?"[31] Utopian syncretism is probably not what Reich had in mind, but the opacity of the process and the reliance on rhythmic structures kept *Drumming* and subsequent phase-pieces from being distant enough from their source inspirations to obscure the connection.

V. MATERIALIST MINIMALIST

Reich was equally vocal in his disdain for the other wing of minimalism, which he characterized as "this search for acoustic effect today where one repeats say piano tones over and over again until one can hear the third, fifth, seventh, ninth or a higher partial."[32] Various performers working collaboratively in New York in the early 1960s, including La Monte Young, Marian Zazeela, Angus MacLise, John Cale, and Tony Conrad, began examining not the underlying structure of non-Western music but the very stuff of its being, its acoustical material in physical sound. "Our music is, like Indian music, droningly monotonal," wrote Conrad in 1966, "not even being built on a scale at all but out of a single chord or cluster of more or less tonically related partials."[33] Again, this music was not so much imitative of as inspired by non-Western music; it was, indeed, much more bare and single-minded than any

Indian classical music. But the other source of inspiration was domestic: Conrad reports that he and many others were profoundly troubled by Cage's revelation that sounds could be considered music, and he suggests that this caused a serious crisis in composition.

> Of course the modernist interpretation was that Cage was shifting the emphasis in composition toward the strategies rather than the materials of the traditional music composer. But for us, for me, I chose to take the more radical lesson to heart, which was boiled down into a one-word composition by Dennis Johnson: "LISTEN!" Listening as an active way of entering into the sound was an answer to the challenge of being a composer and being invested in music. The way in which musical listening comes apart into rhythm and into melody and into pitch and timbre is something that we wanted to reduce to one instant, and indeed, then, listening at that instant produced the interaction among pitches and rhythms and timbres and melodies, all within the inner fabric of the sound which we could understand by knowing more and more about harmonic structures and exploring different harmonic structures and seeing the kinds of things that happen. So we began to develop different relationships between notes than anyone had worked with before.[34]

Deeply reflecting on the possibilities of single tones played on violins and violas (amplified to allow greater access to upper partials), picking the static sounds apart in the mind's ear—the influence was in the thinking, but not in the sound. Like Cowell, Conrad and company used non-Western music as a catalyst to develop and discover new musical materials from their existing instrumental means.

VI. "FAKE TRIBES":
FIRST WORLD + THIRD WORLD = FOURTH WORLD

In 1980, after Glass and Reich had already solidified their international reputations as the leading minimalist composers, trumpeter Jon Hassell released a record in conjunction with Brian Eno called *Fourth World Vol. 1: Possible Musics*. Hassell, who had performed drone-based pieces with La Monte Young's reformed mid-1970s Theater of Eternal Music and had also played on an influential version of Riley's seminal *In C,* had already issued *Earthquake Island* and *Vernal Equinox* on the Tomato label (which had also released important records by Cage and was the fortunate home of Glass's popular breakthrough *Einstein on the Beach*). These records anticipated much of the world-jazz fusion of the ensuing period, with bubbling electric bass (obviously influenced by the electric period of Miles Davis) and exotic percussion, but the "possible musics" Hassell was aiming at were somewhat more complex, at least in theory. They dealt with a fantasy of new hybrid transculturation, an imaginary musical universe in which existing social and political boundaries—individuals, nations, and what Hassell specifically calls "tribes"—are overlaid with "a new, non-physical communications-derived geography—tribes of like-minded thinkers."[35] The Fourth World.

Hassell's verbal theorization, taken both from materials issued at that time and retrospective comments, defines the Fourth World as a sort of phantom topography of alternative possibilities, a distinctly utopian interzone where all cultures mingle freely and without anxiety over authenticity or propriety. In this definition, the fourth world might refer to something beyond the contemporary "three," just as one speaks of a sixth sense.

Of course, this concept tends to veil any power politics inherent in such a program, to bury the intricate hegemonic relations between dominant Western musical ideology and local music cultures worldwide. The notion that such fantasy blendings are desirable is taken as a given, and while Hassell insists that the message of the Fourth World is "that things shouldn't be diluted" and that the "balance between the native identity and the global identity via various electronic extensions is not one that can be dictated or necessarily predicted," his proposed merge-world of latent possibilities clearly points in the other direction to a place where new Western technologies and the wisdom of "other cultures, small cultures" are fused. In this respect, Hassell's music continues to be fusion; taking bits of non-Western music, particularly in the form of Indian and African percussion, and grafting them onto Western structures. On Hassell's *Dream Theory in Malaya* ("Fourth World Vol. 2") and Eno and David Byrne's *My Life in the Bush of Ghosts,* both from 1981, the producers go so far as to sample their non-Western elements; the material is less integrated than it is literally quoted. All these projects use an exotic-sounding, echoey mix, a long standing trope of sonic Orientalism, usually linked to a "mysteries of the East" mentality. Reverb is also the trademark of Hassell's electronically treated trumpet, as heard on "Houses in Motion" on Talking Heads' *Remain in Light,* for example. Exotic new-age primitivist funk fusion: Hassell performs a little addition—the music on *Possible Musics* and *Dream Theory in Malaya* is, figuratively, the simple sum of First and Third World musics. And while it is unquestionably seductive music, at least from a Western perspective, it relies on a familiar Orientalist form of seduction, preferring the slinky, superficial, exotic, ethereal artifacts of various non-Western musics over their deeper structural implications and different, clunkier, less overdeterminedly otherworldly-sounding aspects. The distinct spirit of Fourth World lives on in many of the more recent transcultural productions undertaken by Bill Laswell, among others.

What seems especially suggestive in Hassell's Fourth World musical concept is the overt idea of fantasizing, of creating what he calls a "*faux* tribe."[36] In one of the "swollen appendices" to his book *A Year with Swollen Appendices,* Eno takes this one step further, documenting a role-playing game he'd come up with in which musicians were given a new identity with instructions for musical behavior; the specific futuristic identities he created included music played in "the Afro-Chinese ghetto in Osaka," in a (presumably Brooklyn-based) "Neo-M-Base improvising collective," by "a Soul-Arab band in a North-African role-sex club," by a "New Afrotech" band in a suburb of Lagos, by "NAFTA's leading Force Funk band," and by "a leading recordist at Ground Zero studios in Hiroshima, the largest studio in the Matsui media empire." Eno describes a related game, "Notes on the Vernacular Music of the Acrux Region," as "an attempt to imagine a new musical culture, and to invent roles for musicians within it."[37]

Recall that one of the primary sites in Said's initial analysis of Orientalism is the Western *imagination*,[38] and that one of the main activities of academic Orientalists was to invent a consistent image of the Orient. Furthermore, Said explains that the sheer number of Orientalists grew after the end of the eighteenth century "because by then the reaches of imaginative and actual geography had shrunk, because the Oriental-European relationship was determined by an unstoppable European expansion in search of markets, resources, and colonies, and finally, because Orientalism had accomplished its self-metamorphosis from a scholarly discourse to an imperial institution."[39] To what degree is the Fourth World a mere extension of this imperialist mapping of a fantasy space of otherness into the electronic telecommunications era? The Orient was, for Orientalists, in part invented to explain and facilitate exchange—albeit exchange with no pretense of parity—between colonial powers and their distant territories. How then does Hassell's fantasy of a new geography differ from this paradigm? In truth, very little.

Writer and musician David Toop's book *Ocean of Sound* turns to Hassell's Fourth World frequently in its exploration of the history and nature of ambient and related musics. Over the course of his "personal nomadic drift," Toop takes one pass at Said, but instead of grappling with *Orientalism*'s critical edge, he dismisses the work as "a comprehensive demolition job on the West's obsessive appropriation of the East," and performs a quick sleight-of-hand with a quotation by putting a positive spin on the idea of "unsettling influences" offered by non-Western music, citing Debussy's always-mentioned ur-encounter with Vietnamese and Javanese music as a "catalyst for his break from the powerful influence of Wagner."[40] But Toop's sentiments lie much more with the new ethnography of James Clifford and George Marcus, the performance studies fieldwork of Victor Turner and Richard Schechner, and the legacy of surreal anthropology—all of them overwhelmingly optimistic about the politics of cross-cultural inquiry—than with the post-Foucauldian institutional discourse critique of someone like Said. One can see why, quite plainly: where the latter seeks to understand the power dynamic in Orientalism, it seems to me that Toop prefers to uncritically experience and enjoy the effects of that power dynamic. If that were not the case, the ramifications of Said's "demolition job" for the study (and championing) of ambient and

Fourth World productions would clearly need to be spelled out and dealt with. Like Hassell and Eno's *Possible Musics, Ocean of Sound* is historically and aesthetically seductive, but its politics remain deeply impacted.

VII. OCCIDENTALISM OR ASIAN NEO-ORIENTALISM?

We are in a very subtle artistic world where there can be no direct relationships, no Western rationality, no look-what-I-made. Only coincidence.

TOM JOHNSON, DESCRIBING A 1979 PERFORMANCE
BY TAKEHISA KOSUGI AND AKIO SUZUKI

Starting in the 1950s, initially through the work of Japanese composer Toru Takemitsu, Western classical music was faced with a refracted version of the Oriental-experimental tradition. Into the 1960s, Takemitsu wrote pieces that utilized Japanese classical court instruments—biwa, shakuhachi, and, in the case of *In an Autumn Garden,* an entire gagaku ensemble—as well as composing a large number of works using the conventional Western orchestral instrumentarium.[41] Though Takemitsu was the best known, a wave of new-music composers soon hit the scene from various Asian points of origin, all of them studying and most settling in the West. The godfather of Japanese composition, Toshiro Mayuzumi (born in 1929, one year before Takemitsu) composed his rather Western-sounding "Mandala Symphony" (1960) as a "Japanese Buddhist view of the omnipotent universe," while Somei Satoh, a composer nearly twenty years younger than Mayuzumi, also uses romantic and late-romantic Western elements, as well as material closely verging on chinoiserie. Other noteworthy figures from three generations of Asian composers working in the European and American vanguard include Kazuo Fukushima, Akio Yashifo, Toshi Ichiyanagi, Yuji Takahashi from Japan, Franco-Vietnamese composer Nguyen-Thien Dao, and Chou Wen-Chung from China.[42] Like Takemitsu, young Chinese composer Ge Gan-ru has composed orchestral scores that include parts for instruments from China and, more tellingly, for Japanese koto—hence, a trans-Asian string aesthetic allows for cultural borrowing not only *from* but *between* these traditions.

What is particularly interesting about many of these composers is that when their work considers "the Oriental," it tends to do so as it is found in Cage and his lineage (or, alternately, using a European vanguard vocabulary) as much as it does in Asian traditions closer to home. Paul Griffiths succinctly nails Takemitsu's Asian neo-Orientalism when he writes: "If Takemitsu's delight in evanescent, apparently unwilled sonorities seems on the surface to be a Japanese trait, on further reflection it may be found to link him at least as much with Feldman, while his orchestral writing draws much more from Debussy and Boulez than from indigenous traditions."[43] Several Korean composers are important exceptions. Isang Yun, who settled in Germany in 1971 after decades of political persecution, integrates Asian elements drawn from his experience of listening to Korean court, particularly flute, music (hear, for instance, the extraordinary clarinet pieces "Piri" and "Riul") while reportedly remaining "suspicious of Cage's 'oriental' indeterminacy."[44] Nam June Paik was born in Seoul and educated in Japan, and became a key member of the Fluxus (non)movement in the 1960s. An active composer who later stopped composing music, Paik took the Cage line in a much more extreme direction, writing Fluxus-oriented conceptual works. A younger figure, Younghi Pagh-Paan was also born in Seoul; she studied in Germany and now divides her time between Germany and Italy. In her extremely rich, modernist music, Pagh-Paan seems to put Western instrumentation and aspects of postserialist techniques into direct contact with a distinctly Korean aesthetic, without resorting to pastiche or cultural grafting.

Chinese-born composer Tan Dun, since 1986 a resident of New York City, is an excellent contemporary example of the new wave of Asian neo-Orientalist. Take, for example, his 1992 composition *Circle with Four Trios, Conductor and Audience:* in an overtly Cagean move, he scored the piece with a part for the audience to participate by means of improvised "twittering, gossiping, and shouting." And accompanying the recorded version, the liner booklet includes the following statement from Cage himself: "What is very little heard in European or Western music is the presence of sound as the voice of nature. So that we are led to hear in our music human beings talking only to themselves. It is clear in the music of Tan Dun that sounds are central to the nature in which we live but to which we have too long not listened. Tan Dun's music is one we need as the east and the west come together as our one home."[45] Positioned by Cage as a champion of "the presence of sound as the voice of nature," Tan Dun's work is made to fit snugly into the "wisdom of the East" variety of Orientalist discourse. Thus, it is interesting to consider how his work (as well as the work of other Asian, Asian-American, and Asian-European composers) is used to confirm and uphold contemporary forms of Orientalism, legitimizing the prevalent "East meets West" mentality. A stronger form of Orientalism is perhaps permitted by means of identity politics: the work is placed beyond analysis or critique by being created by a genuine Oriental composer. What otherwise inaccessible truth is Tan Dun's neo-Orientalist vision offering the Western listener? As Gayatri Spivak puts it: "When the cardcarrying listeners, the hegemonic people, the dominant people, talk about listening to someone 'speaking as' something or other, I think *there* one encounters a problem. When *they* want to hear an Indian speaking as an Indian, a Third World woman speaking as a Third World woman, they cover over the fact of the ignorance that they are allowed to possess, into a kind of homogenization."[46] Where the notion of an Oriental "voice of nature" might seem an overstated Western stereotype, when articulated through the work of a one-time Chinese farmworker "raised in a rural area filled with magic, ritual and shamanism,"[47] it is suddenly endowed with the irrefutable aura of ethnic authenticity. And as such it no doubt speaks more forcefully to cardcarrying, hegemonic, dominant folks.

Tan Dun scored his 1994 composition *Ghost Opera* for string quartet and pipa, with water, stones, paper and metal—the later elements comprised of bowed gongs and stones, water bowls, metal cymbas, a paper whistle, and a large paper installation. The piece interweaves a Chinese folk song and a Bach prelude, as well as text and live sound-effects created on the objects and instruments. "When *Ghost Opera* debuted in Beijing," Tan Dun reported, "there were more than 1500 people. They knew the folk song and they recognized the ancient tradition, but they did not know that a string quartet could play stones along with Bach, and play paper, gongs, water and voice."[48] Here, the neo-Orientalist composer turns the usual paradigm on its head, taking Cage-like nature sounds "back" to China, where they're greeted as exotic items much the way the pipa and folk melody function in a Western setting.

This anecdote points out the dominance of Western classical norms—"proper" materials for a string quartet to use, namely their violins, viola and cello—in the art-music of Revolutionary China (where the avant-garde and experimentalism were roundly denounced as decadent) at the same time as it slyly mocks the supposed Asianness of Tan Dun's elemental objects: returned to their (mythic) cultural point of origin, the stones, paper, and metal are not even recognized as musical. The deep complexity of neo-Orientalist strategies is revealed: an Asian composer in the West uses techniques devised by a Western composer inspired by Asian philosophy—the work is played for an Asian audience which hears it as an artifact of the bizarre West. Orientalism is reflected back-and-forth like a musicultural *mise-en-abyme*.

Fragments of imperialist (exporting Western musical values through conservatory education) and colonialist (importing non-Western musical materials for use in Western art-music settings) ideologies are both found here, but the music of the Asian neo-Orientalists, at its best and most provocative, manages to subtly subvert them both.[49]

VIII. THE CLASSIC GUIDE TO STRATEGY: ORIENTALISM AND IMPROVISED MUSIC

Where the connotation of scientific method in experimental composition, in part, allowed Cage and others to ignore the political consequences of their Orientalism, various modes of music-making in the experimental diaspora have had to grapple with similar ideological and pragmatic dilemmas.[50] For example, we find the perpetuation of some of the same Orientalist tropes—exploration, discovery, terra incognita, Eastern wisdom—within the world of freely improvised music and its associated compositional fields. Guitarist

Derek Bailey frames the issue in terms of disposition toward the instrument, and he finds what might be termed a naïve or *art brut* attitude among players with what he calls an "anti-instrumental" strategy:

> Instruments very much in favour with this school are, naturally enough, those which are ethnic in origin or, at least, in appearance. These meet the requirement that the instrument should have a fixed, very limited capability and that very little instrumental skill is needed to play it. The idea is, I think, that because of limited opportunities for technical virtuosity, a more direct expressiveness is possible. Some of these players have shown a great interest in the practices and rituals of ethnic music and particularly what is taken to be primitive uses of the voice. So, in performance, grunts, howls, screams, groans, Tibetan humming, Tunisian chanting, Maori chirping and Mozambique stuttering are combined with the African thumb piano, Chinese temple blocks, Ghanian soft trumpet, Trinidadian steel drum, Scottish soft bagpipe, Australian bull-roarer, Ukrainian stone flute and the Canton one-legged monster to provide an aural event about as far removed from the directness and dignity of ethnic music as a thermo-nuclear explosion is from a fart.[51]

At the time that Bailey originally composed this unforgiving and incisive paragraph, he was implicitly engaging in a polemic with other British improvisers like David Toop[52] and Paul Burwell, both of whom (separately and together in their group Rain on the Face) used a huge array of "ethnic" instruments and techniques; Burwell created performances called "whirled music" out of multiple players whipping drones on bull-roarers. Clive Bell is perhaps the epitome of this intercultural lineage, performing on a host of different, usually non-Western instruments including Thai flute, shakuhachi, and Laotian mouth organ (khene). The difference with Bell is that, contrary to Bailey's statement, his interest in these (quite difficult) instruments does not seem to come from a desire to skirt instrumental virtuosity; Bell is, indeed, a virtuoso shakuhachi player.

While some of the eclectic exoticism of that era is perhaps gone from improvised and other forms of creative music today, there is undoubtedly a persistent strain of Orientalism bubbling under in certain places. John Zorn, for instance, has consistently returned to Asian music (reportedly fascinated by Japan since childhood, he first visited in 1985 and now spends some portion of the year living there) both as a supporter of indigenous Asian creative musics—releasing records by, performing together with and otherwise promoting the work of different composers, sound-artists and improvisers—and at the same time incorporating fragments of different kinds of Asian music and speech into pastiche pieces such as "Forbidden Fruit" and "Godard."[53] Zorn's deployment of Asian women's voices in these two collages suggests a complex sense of irony. At once, the whispery, exoticized voice can serve the traditional eroticizing-othering function in which gender doubles the intensity of a given non-Western voice's exoticism; on the other hand, Zorn arguably

pushes that stereotype past itself, mocking it, revealing it as a constructed image and reveling in the kitschiness of such antiquated Orientalism. Of course,
such ironic instances have the advantage of both embodying and disavowing
the stereotype they seem to poke fun at, hence allowing both the pleasure of
highly eroticized/exoticized Asian women's voices—in the case of "Forbidden Fruit," which is expressly *about* a Japanese woman's voice (that of Ohta
Hiromi), an explicitly passionate embrace, replete with sighs and coos—and
providing the safety of simultaneous ironic distanciation.

Zorn's relationship to Japan is multifaceted, as is evident from a statement
that was included in the liner notes to his important 1987 record *Spillane:*

> The Japanese often borrow and mirror other people's cultures, that's what's
> so great about the place. They make a crazy mix out of it all. Of course, as a
> foreigner one can have a very strong sense of being outside their world—there's
> a certain kind of understanding that I'll never quite get. But then again, I was
> always an outsider here in America. I mean, when I was growing up in Queens,
> with long hair, wearing weird clothes, looking like a hippie, people called me
> all kinds of bizarre names. . . . I perform with Japanese musicians when I'm
> there. I write a lot, wander around, searching for rare Japanese pop singles,
> go to the movies, old book and poster stores, eat incredible food, and look at
> girls—the same stuff I do here. . . . It's a stimulating change in perspective, not
> only with regard to the music scene, but also with regard to who I am as a per-
> son, how I fit into American culture, what I am in Japanese culture.

One of the major struggles that the "new ethnographers" of anthropology in the post-poststructuralist period like Steve Tyler, James Clifford, and
George Marcus have had to face is the way that looking at other cultures has
traditionally been a process of the West examining itself in the mirror. That
same dilemma—going to Japan to learn about one's own personality and
identity—is epitomized in Zorn's statement, his identification with the om-
nivorous eclecticism of contemporary Japanese culture and the perspective
that being there provides him on himself. Perhaps that introspection is part
of what has led him to pursue the investigation of his own Jewish heritage
so assiduously in recent years. Some of the complexity of Zorn's relationship
with Asian culture was foregrounded a few years ago when Zorn was taken
to task by some Asian-American organizations for his use of images of violence against Asian women on record covers on his label, Avant. Zorn
officially apologized for hurting anyone's feelings, though in fact the images
in question were almost exclusively made *by* Asian artists, which further com-
plicates the equation.[54]

There is unquestionably an ongoing presence of Orientalist discourse in
contemporary music, and as a problematic it remains complex, recursive,
and impacted, as one can see in Zorn's example. Consider the following line,
a parenthetical (but telling) remark lifted from a press-release for Japanese
bassist Kato Hideki's 1996 record of improvisations *Hope & Despair:* "Japan-

ese musicians are justifiably acclaimed for their ability to see music from a very different perspective."[55] The exact angles and lines of sight (or hearing) of that "different perspective" (the same terms Zorn used to describe his love of Japan) continue to be left as an undefined, reductive, and implicit stereotype, and at the same time the overarching idea of difference continues to be romanticized, essentialized, and implemented in the attempt to enliven Western musics, be they classical, experimental, creative, or improvised. Meanwhile, the political dimension of that implied difference continues to go largely unexamined.

If such a forced reading, taken from the casual pen of a PR writer, seems just *too* forced, too tenuous, then think about the following explanation of the name of New Albion Records, a California-based company with a strong connection to the minimalist tradition: "As Sir Francis Drake, noted explorer and pirate, discovered California for the Elizabethan world, New Albion discovers new musical territories for the modern world. Then as now there are savages, pagans, exotic flora and fauna."[56] Perhaps the context for such Orientalizing rhetoric has changed, but the rhetoric itself stays remarkably consistent: exoticism and savagery, exploration and discovery, the conquest of fresh aural geography. In the ears of new Western musics, the other continues to be effectively other.

NOTES

1. This chapter deals primarily with the American experimental tradition, to the exclusion of the contemporaneous European avant-garde tradition, though an analysis of the way that non-Western music is represented and instrumentalized in the work of Olivier Messiaen, Karlheinz Stockhausen, Mauricio Kagel, and Pierre Boulez is a necessary complement to this work.

2. Many well-known American composers, such as Aaron Copland, Elliott Carter, Samuel Barber, Virgil Thomson, and Roger Sessions, are normally categorized outside the experimental camp, for various reasons—Carter, for instance, comes more directly out of a European avant-garde lineage, while Copland is perhaps best thought of as an American neoromantic. Wilfrid Mellers argues vigorously for the inclusion of the more obscure composer Charles Griffes among his experimentalists; see Mellers, *Music in a New Found Land: Themes and Developments in the History of American Music* (1965; reprint, London: Faber and Faber, 1987), 145–48.

3. Henry Cowell, *New Musical Resources* (1930; reprint, Cambridge: Cambridge University Press, 1996). Cage studied with Cowell at the New School for Social Research in New York in 1934, and he cited *New Musical Resources* and Mexican composer Carlos Chavez's *Toward a New Music* as especially influential to him.

4. Cage, "The Future of Music: Credo," in *Silence* (1973; reprint, Middletown, Conn.: Wesleyan University Press, 1983), 6.

5. David Nicholls, *American Experimental Music 1890–1940* (Cambridge: Cambridge University Press, 1990); Alan Rich, *American Pioneers: Ives to Cage and Beyond* (London: Phaidon, 1995); Paul Griffiths, *Modern Music: The Avant-Garde Since 1945*

(New York: George Braziller, 1981); Michael Nyman, *Experimental Music: Cage and Beyond* (New York: Schirmer, 1974); Thomas B. Holmes, *Electronic and Experimental Music: History, Instruments, Technique, Performers, Recordings* (New York: Charles Scribner's Sons, 1985).

6. Fruitful comparison between Iannis Xenakis's stochastic (probability-based) compositions, based on calculation, and Cage's chance-operations, based on some degree of lack of calculation, provides an interesting insight into the status of science in European and American experimental traditions.

7. N. Katherine Hayles, "Chance Operations: Cagean Paradox and Contemporary Science," in *John Cage: Composed in America*, ed. Marjorie Perloff and Charles Junkerman (Chicago: University of Chicago Press, 1994), 240.

8. Cage, "Composition as Process," in *Silence*, 21–22.

9. Lou Harrison, "Cloverleaf: A Little Narrative with Several 'Off-Ramps,'" in *Companion to Contemporary Musical Thought*, vol. 1, ed. John Paynter, Tim Howell, Richard Orton, and Peter Seymour (London: Routledge, 1992), 255.

10. Cowell, *New Musical Resources*, 18–19. Note Cowell's use of an explicitly scientific notion of "successful experiments."

11. Hear Antheil's "Sonata Sauvage" and Ornstein's "Wild Men's Dance" performed by pianist Steffen Schleiermacher on *The Bad Boys!* (hat ART CD 6144, 1994).

12. Johannes Fabian, *Time and the Other: How Anthropology Makes Its Object* (New York: Columbia University Press, 1983), 144, 143. See also Marianna Torgovnick, *Gone Primitive: Savage Intellects, Modern Lives* (Chicago: University of Chicago Press, 1990), and Patricia Leighten, "The White Peril and *L'Art negre*: Picasso, Primitivism, and Anticolonialism," *The Art Bulletin* 72, no. 4 (December 1990): 609–30.

13. Edward W. Said, *Orientalism* (New York: Vintage Books, 1979), 231.

14. Ibid., 208.

15. Ibid., 6–9.

16. See pages xiv, 12, and 21, respectively.

17. Rich, *American Pioneers*, 113–16. The "Pacific Rim" influence on American experimentalism via Cowell, Partch, and Harrison, as well as other West Coasters like Cage (born and raised in Los Angeles) and Terry Riley, is often discussed in historical accounts. See Nicholls, *American Experimental Music*, 220.

18. Chris Burn, liner notes to *A Henry Cowell Concert* (Acta 7, 1993).

19. Cage, "The Future of Music: Credo," in *Silence*, 5.

20. See George E. Lewis, "Improvised Music after 1950: Afrological and Eurological Perspectives," *Black Music Research Journal* 16, no. 1 (1996): 91–107. Cage did compose "Jazz Study" in 1942, a piece that went unperformed until 1992; however, his opinion changed drastically later, and in 1982 he said: "When I listen to jazz, I don't find it as interesting as people tell me it is." (Quoted in *Conversing With Cage*, ed. Richard Kostelanetz [New York: Limelight Editions, 1988], 225.)

21. *Conversing with Cage*, 267.

22. Personal interview with Steve Lacy, Berlin, October 1996.

23. Steve Reich suggests the term "chinoiserie" in "Writings about Music," in *Breaking the Sound Barrier*, ed. Gregory Battcock (New York: E. P. Dutton, 1981), 163.

24. Quoted by Dana Paul Perna in liner text to Henry Cowell, *Persian Set* (Koch International Classics 3–7220–2 H1, 1993).

25. Cage, "History of Experimental Music in the United States," in *Silence*, 72.

26. Brian Morton, *The Blackwell Guide to Recorded Contemporary Music* (Oxford: Blackwell Publishers, 1996), 163.

27. For a much more rewarding example of the encounter between American music and gamelan, seek out the work of pianist and composer Anthony Davis, particularly his record *Episteme* (Gramavision, 1981).

28. Said, *Orientalism*, 60.

29. Steve Reich, "Writings about Music," 153.

30. Ibid., 163.

31. Tom Johnson, *The Voice of New Music* (Eindhoven, Netherlands: Het Apollohuis, 1989), 26.

32. Quoted in Edward Strickland, *Minimalism Origins* (Bloomington: Indiana University Press, 1993), 189.

33. Reprinted in the liner text to Tony Conrad, *Outside the Dream Syndicate* (Table of the Elements 3, 1993).

34. Personal interview with Tony Conrad, 1995.

35. Quoted in David Toop, *Ocean of Sound* (London: Serpent's Tail, 1995), 168.

36. Ibid., 123.

37. Brian Eno, *A Year with Swollen Appendices* (London: Faber and Faber, 1996), 382–89.

38. Said, *Orientalism*, 4.

39. Ibid., 95.

40. Toop, *Ocean of Sound*, 21.

41. Brian Morton astutely notes of Takemitsu's best-known composition, *November Steps*, which uses both *shakuhachi* and *satsumabiwa*, "There is no doubt that the popularity of *November Steps* is due in part to a taste for musical exotica." Morton, *The Blackwell Guide*, 194.

42. In 1958, the American CRI label produced the first LP of compositions by Chou Wen-Chung. Hear also two recent CDs on CRI, one featuring work by Chinese composer Chen Yi (now living in the States), *Sparkle* (CRI, 1999); and a collection of Chinese and Chinese-American composers including Ge Gan-Ru, Kawai Shiu, Luo Jing Jing, James Fei, Jason Kao Hwang, Byron Au Yong, Fred Ho, Chen Yuanlin, Ying Zhang and Jin Xiang, *China Exchange* (CRI, 1999).

43. Griffiths, *Modern Music*, 198.

44. Morton, *The Blackwell Guide*, 318.

45. Epigram in liner text to Tan Dun, *Snow in June* (CRI CD 655, 1993).

46. Gayatri Chakravorty Spivak, *The Post-Colonial Critic* (New York: Routledge, 1990), 60.

47. Mary Lou Humphrey, liner text to *Snow in June*.

48. Tan Dun, in liner notes to *Ghost Opera* (Nonesuch 79445, 1997).

49. It falls outside the scope of this chapter, but the work of a new generation of Asian-American jazz musicians offers a very interesting, aesthetically and ideologically complex version of the neo-Orientalist approach, one that is deeply critical of stereotypes but doesn't avoid the problem by shying away from using traditional musical elements but instead incorporates them into the context of jazz and improvised music. See Corbett, "Form Follows Faction? Ethnicity and Creative Music," in *New Histories*, Lia Gangitano and Steven Nelson, eds. (Boston: Institute of Contemporary Art, 1996), 46–51. The important development of the kind of post-industrial music

known globally as "Japanese noise" also deserves mention in this context; Japan has the reputation, among fans of aggressive, overdriven sound, of producing such music's most extreme and violent practitioners, including Hanatarash, Masonna, Merzbow and numerous others. These were presaged, in Europe, by the so-called "kamakazi jazz" musicians clustered around the Yosuke Yamashita Trio, as well as guitarist Yosuke "Jojo" Takayanagi. An investigation of the valences of such violence—both within Japanese listening contexts and in the various Western contexts in which such images are most actively promulgated—is long overdue.

50. The heading for this section is taken from John Zorn's two volumes of solo reed music, which in turn take their title from Miyamoto Musashi's *A Book of Five Rings.*

51. Derek Bailey, *Improvisation: Its Nature and Practice in Music* (New York: Da Capo, 1992), 102.

52. This is the same David Toop who authored *Ocean of Sound;* he still makes records, but no longer specifically identifies himself as a free improviser.

53. "Forbidden Fruit" on John Zorn, *Spillane* (Elektra/Nonesuch 9 79172, 1987); "Godard" on The Godard Fans, *Godard: Ça Vous Chante?* (Nato 634, 1985).

54. As well as being an extremely active advocate for Asian musicians, Zorn has strongly supported Japanese visual artists, frequently using their work on record covers. Japanese-born drummer Ikue Mori designs releases for Zorn's Tzadik label.

55. Roger Richards, director of Extreme Records, press release for Kato Hideki, *Hope & Despair* (Extreme XCD 036, 1996).

56. From a promotional survey postcard distributed in New Albion CDs in 1998.

Composing the Cantorate: Westernizing Europe's Other Within

Philip V. Bohlman

VORSPIEL—COMPOSING THE SYNAGOGUE

"The Jews here have received permission from the emperor to build a large temple, which is just about finished, and now they would like to have a new musical work from you, with chorus, for which they would pay very generously. Rothschild is a part of this. In many ways it would be a good idea for you to take this on."
JOHANN VAN BEETHOVEN TO HIS BROTHER, 1825

When turning to Beethoven to compose a grand new work for the dedication of the Viennese Stadttempel (city temple), the Jewish community of Vienna maintained a practice instituted in the urban centers of Europe during the Baroque: a new musical composition should be created to open the space that would come to embody the community itself. Beethoven was not the first non-Jew to be commissioned for a dedicatory composition, but, at the height of his career and as the most famous composer of his day, Beethoven was surely a symbolically loaded choice. It was a choice that would mark a radical transformation of the Jewish community in the capital of the Austro-Hungarian Empire, opening the community to the world beyond the synagogue walls. The result of this transformation would be the possibility of full participation in the public sphere of nineteenth-century Central European society. In Beethoven's conversation books we witness that he accepted the commission, and that he had already reviewed the libretto for what was called both an oratorio and a cantata.[1] There is no other evidence for this work, either in the records of the Jewish community or in surviving conversations from Beethoven's last years.[2]

The dedication of the Vienna Stadttempel[3] took place in 1826, and it quickly became the home for one of the greatest cantors of the nineteenth century, Salomon Sulzer (1804–1890). Sulzer made his career as a composer, indeed as a composer who achieved enormous fame during his lifetime. He took to center stage in Vienna at precisely that moment Beethoven was to have given his musical blessing to that stage, but in fact the symbolic rite of passage that might have happened did not: the Stadttempel composition was among those Beethoven did not or could not complete in the years of declining health before his death. Had the Stadttempel been dedicated, say, five or ten years later, it is doubtful that the Jewish community would have commissioned Beethoven, whose fame, had he lived so long, would not have diminished. Surely the community would have turned to its own cantor to compose the spaces of its synagogue, to symbolize to the world its presence in Vienna. In those few years, the space of the synagogue had changed to a remarkable degree; the world of the cantor as a composer and musician in the service of the Jewish community and the city of which it was a part had changed even more. The music of Europe's Jews was undergoing a radical transformation at the hands of the cantor, who had begun to compose music for the public spaces they, for centuries among Europe's "others," had never before occupied. In this essay I explore the dilemma confronted by these others as they crossed the threshold into those spaces.

IMAGINING WESTERN MUSIC'S OTHERS

Europe is unimaginable without its others. Its sense of selfness, of Europeanness, has historically exerted itself through its imagination of others and, more tragically, through its attempts to control and occasionally to destroy otherness. Western music, too, has no ontology without imagining otherness. West of whom, of what? In willing Western music into existence, Europeans and other Westerners have admitted music's complicity in the larger historical endeavors that have sought to proffer Europe power and control. Jesuit colonizers in seventeenth- and eighteenth-century South America were no less obsessed with music's powers to control the other than Nazi ideologues attempting to reconfigure and recolonize the spaces within Europe's twentieth-century boundaries. If these uses of music to imagine and control others characterize different historical moments and different assertions of European selfness, they are nevertheless still related by the degree to which their obsessiveness is inseparable from European history and the history of Europeanness. I take both the relatedness and distinctiveness of these different uses of music to imagine otherness as fundamental to the argument in this essay. In order to invest itself with the power to control and maintain its external domination and its internal order, Europe has consistently employed music to imagine its selfness.

Europe has been obsessed with musical others. To some degree, one might argue that Europe defines its selfness by creating cultural objects outside of the history and progress that it wishes to claim solely for itself.[4] It is, in part, because of music's special capacity to represent something exotic that it has so frequently provided a symbolic system to convey the exotic and the other. Music acts as a powerful form of "mystic speech," necessary, as Michel de Certeau has observed, for the construction of otherness.[5] This held no less in the imagination of street songs as Renaissance *cantus firmi* than in Baroque opera or in twentieth-century cinema. Music both frames and mystifies, controls and yet evokes a sense of uncontrollability. Music magnifies otherness as it makes speech even more mystical. This is one of the reasons that European explorers and colonizers reported their mystification when encountering the ceremony, ritual, and song of the other.[6] It is one of the reasons that Rousseau thought of national difference in song as a quality of speech,[7] and that Wagner disparaged the impact of Jewishness on music as a distortion, that is mystification, of speech.[8]

Western music's others are not simply "out there," ontologically immanent at the edges of a known musical world. Western music—or rather, those who claim Western music to represent their selfness—makes its others. Johannes Fabian's charge that "anthropology makes its objects" resonates for this volume and the different ways in which Europe has made its musical others.[9] Issues of identity are central, not least because the artifice of creating others demands reconceptualizing time, acts of distancing, and the recognition of conditions that make the other's everyday world completely different from the observer's. Western music, too, makes its objects from others in many ways, each resulting from complex processes of distancing.

In this essay I suggest that Western music's others form into two larger categories, external and internal others, that is those within Europe and those outside its borders. The most familiar others are those who fulfill the conditions of being outside Europe. Historically, the first external others were those who did not fit within the polity of the Holy Roman Empire, in other words, non-Christians. In the Middle Ages, these external others should reside beyond the borders of Europe, and when they did not at various times—in the Crusades, during fourteenth-century Jewish pogroms in the Rhineland,[10] the incursion of the Ottoman Empire—steps were taken to push them back beyond the borders. The Age of Discovery demanded a new means of constructing external others, which European explorers and colonizers achieved by inscribing an insurmountable distance through the accounts of their encounters with the other.[11] External others were "primitive" and exotic, so distant that they posed no threat to Europe, which preferred instead to privilege the power of its selfness through the expansion of its borders. The Westernness of music assumed a more tangible and bounded quality as the conquest and colonization of the Age of Discovery proceeded apace.[12]

Europe's internal others also began to assume a more distinctive and threatening shape at this same historical moment in the sixteenth century. At base, the fundamental characteristics of internal otherness were sets of cultural traits that were mystical, or beyond the religious and intellectual understanding of those in power. The mixture of music and magic, for example, created the conditions of otherness, investing music with a power that the Church could not control, if indeed music's capacity to possess such power was not also fundamental to the Church's own uses of music.[13] Beginning in the sixteenth century and continuing through the seventeenth and early eighteenth centuries, religious otherness increasingly became sharpened as an internal, rather than external, presence in Europe. Sephardic Jews, driven from the Iberian Peninsula, settled in communities along Europe's littoral— Italy, Bosnia, Greece, the Ottoman Empire, England, and the Netherlands— and together with the large Ashkenazic communities of Eastern Europe, they bounded Europe. Pietistic and resistant Protestant sects emerged in Central Europe, the Amish, Mennonites, and Hutterites the best known among them. Facing persecution, however, the pietistic sects migrated, both eastward to Europe's boundaries with Asia and westward to the colonies of the New World. The European response to these internal others was generally to force them into exile, to force them into the position of external others, nevertheless increasingly defined by their position vis-à-vis Europeanness. Additional European responses tolerated intra-other coexistence and cultural exchange — for example, when Sephardic Jews in the Habsburg Empire managed financial and political negotiations with the Ottoman Empire.[14]

When Europe began to reprocess the world it encountered during the Age of Discovery and to reconfigure its others, the first stirrings of modernity began to take place. Otherness gradually began to cross the boundaries separating it from European society, and various forms of cultural mixing ensued. By no means can one speak of cultural integration, but rather of an exoticization of the surface of European society, as composers selectively chose melodies and images to evoke otherness (e.g., in eighteenth-century *alla turca* movements or nineteenth-century appropriations from so-called Gypsy scales). The crossing of boundaries was first fully sanctioned during the Enlightenment, as the other became increasingly necessary in the genres of literature and music which formed the vanguard of the European belles lettres, for example the novel and opera.

The growing presence of print culture in the urban working class, too, created new exchanges between art music and what would only be called "folk song" at the end of the eighteenth century. The imagination of folk song itself, following on the heels of Herder's coinage of the term in 1779, took the form of a site onto which Europeanness and internal otherness were juxtaposed.[15] By the early twentieth century, German folk-song scholar John Meier had reformulated the relation between Western art music and its internal other to a status of mutual dependency, with folk songs actually "art songs in the mouths of the folk."[16] With Europe's empires—both internal and external—decaying, its imagination of otherness was to assume new forms, with sharpened boundaries and new fears about the possibility that these others would become indistinguishable from self.[17] One response to the possible dissolution of otherness frames the historical narrative of Jewish cantors as composers at the core of this essay.

ENCOUNTERING THE OTHER WITHIN

Western music's others have not all been imagined in the same ways. The other within and the other without are quite different, and that difference is essential to understanding how Europe has constructed otherness to define—and defend—its selfness. Fundamental to these different forms of otherness are the ways in which they configure Europe's sense of its own geographic and historical spaces. The other without exists at the "rim of the world," and the great distance between that other and the self generated for Europeans in the Age of Discovery a sense of awe and wonder.[18] Encountering and gazing upon the other at a distance, even when enclosed in museums or inscribed as something mysterious in a travel book or a recording of world music today, is necessary as a means of retaining the awe and wonder. The self is thrown into sharper focus and historically redefined with rubrics such as "civilization."

The other within exists within the space also occupied by the self, thereby creating a situation of competition rather than awe. Competition for cultural resources and public attention is immediate, which in turn may lead to a sense of being threatened by the other. Rather than the wonder of distance, the other within generates a nervousness of proximity, even competition. The polity of constructing the self in communities may depend on politics of marginalization, placing the other at the outskirts of a town or locating it in socioeconomic conditions outside the acceptable norms for the self.[19] These gestures of civilizing the self do not eliminate competition, but they postpone it until future pressures on communal spaces again become too great.

We can, therefore, view European history—and music history—as a dialectical conflict between selfness and otherness. A challenge to Europe's spaces results from this conflict and from the different ways in which otherness intrudes upon those spaces. Modern European history is legible, it follows, as a competition for spaces, and urbanizing Central Europe, which figures in the historical narrative of this essay, encountered this competition in increasingly complex forms as its peripheries were reined in during the nineteenth and twentieth centuries. Music marks and narrates this competition in Central Europe in many ways. The broadside sellers and street hawkers who performed popular music on the streets of Central Europe made the encounter with the other impossible to avoid, and indeed it is in the texts of these popular songs from the eighteenth and nineteenth century that we encounter the other within entering the public sphere of Central Europe. At the end of the twentieth century, this competition is no less pressing, and it is again in the public spaces—on the streets of Central Europe—that street musicians symbolically perform the dialectic between new selves and others that will form the basis for a New Europe.[20]

In this essay my primary focus falls on Vienna, the center of an empire that was decaying throughout the nineteenth century until it politically ceased to exist as an empire in 1918 with defeat in World War I. The others in the Habsburg Empire were in the east, in Hungary, Romania, and the Slavic-speaking lands. It was in the east, moreover, that the largest communities of Jews lived, some of them imagined, if not incorporated, fully into the culture of empire, for example in cities such as Czernowitz (Tschervowzy) and Lemberg (Lviv). The music of these Jewish communities was also symbolically eastern: Yiddish secular music and *mizraḥi* (lit. "eastern," meaning connected to the east where Jerusalem was located).[21] As Jewish communities underwent emancipation, the confrontation with the east took new forms: synagogues, for example, were built in Moorish style, with minarets and arabesque on their external surfaces, though with new internal spaces for the performance of liturgical music; outside, the synagogue became more Oriental and Orientalized, while inside Jewish ritual and musical life became more occidental and Westernized. Jewish music became a vehicle for transforming the private and public spaces of an empire in transition. The questions that Jewish music help us articulate, then, are whether Austria's internal otherness could be contained by (1) a shrinking empire and (2) the more tangible presence of ethnic groups from the periphery and other manifestations of difference.

This essay examines what happened to one type of Jewish musician, the cantor, entering the public spaces of the shrinking Habsburg Empire. If it is the transformation of spaces within Europe that creates the encounter between self and the other within, the capacity to enter the public sphere of modern Europe was a necessary step in making it possible for musicians who created and performed Jewish music to enter Western music, itself a sphere of selfness. Cantors changed the nature of the spaces that musically defined the Jewish community and then became an extension from the community into the non-Jewish world.

I am also concerned in this essay with the effect of the cantor on the demystification of the other's speech, that is of the musical speech understood to characterize Jews. The use of German, the absorption of tonal harmony to give voice through new polyphonic textures to the entire Jewish community, and the performance of new compositions in public, where the musical language was experienced without wonder and accepted by many Austrians as belonging to the world of the self—all these were major transformations of the musical speech of European Jews. The demystification of Jewish musical speech symbolizes the changing confrontation between self and other, a confrontation whose future chapters would assume the shape of even greater

tragedy: the Holocaust. Understanding the role of music in that history, however, requires that we imagine the public spaces created by the musical specialists of the Jewish community, the cantors, who, as they studied "their art"
in music academies and concertized outside the synagogue, were intensely
aware of their growing proximity to European musical selfness in the century
that led up to the Holocaust.

THE CANTOR'S WORLD

In the nineteenth century the cantor's world became that of the stage. The
stage empowered the cantor to transform both the sacred spaces of the synagogue and the public spaces outside the synagogue. It was, indeed, from the
stage that the cantor was able to enact the transformation that was so crucial
to the changing status of otherness in the Jewish community. Historically, the
stage upon which the cantor performed changed in the way it permitted the
musical specialists of the community to mediate identity, an identity ascribed
by different representations of Jewishness through music. I refer to this part
of the cantor's world as a stage not to suggest a metaphor, but rather quite
intentionally, because the raised pulpit of the synagogue from which the cantor sings has the Hebrew name *bima*. In theatrical usage, the *bima* is quite literally a stage, as we witness in the name of the Israeli national theater, *Habima,*
"the stage." The cantor's stage also functioned as a catalyst because of the identity of professionalism that it ascribed to the cantor himself. From the stage,
the cantor could shape his own profession, serving the community, but also
providing consumable goods, for which he could expect financial compensation. The increasing value of those goods during the nineteenth and early
twentieth centuries went hand in hand with the capacity of the cantor to identify himself as a professional, as a composer of the cantorate.

Already in the early Middle Ages, the position of the cantor in Jewish life
was one of the most important professions embedded in the polity of the
community. In community records, as well as in rabbinical discussions concerning the nature of Jewish polity, the cantor was first identifiable as the
hazzan, the Hebrew word that today exclusively identifies the cantor. Prior
to the Modern Era, however, the *hazzan* was responsible for diverse activities
in the community, ranging from the religious education of young males to
the general maintenance of the synagogue.[22] Among these early *hazzanim,*
some also had musical duties, but these were in no sense aesthetically sepa-
rable from community life. The *hazzan* was in reality more a figure whose
professionalism was defined by service to the community, witnessed by the
later use of the terms *Diener* ("one who serves") or *Tempeldiener* ("one serving in the temple") in Yiddish and German, both of which terms evoke an
intentional sense of functionality.

The specific professional connection of the *hazzan* to music first developed during the Modern Era—that is, after the Reformation, when European Jews gradually began to acquire rights to participate in social and financial activities outside the Jewish community. Still prior to the Enlightenment, the figure of the cantor, often with this Latin form, appears in the official records of Jewish communities, such as those from Burgenland, the rural border region between the Austrian and Hungarian parts of the Habsburg Empire.[23] We encounter these particular cantors in the archive of Sopron, Hungary, the administrative center for Burgenland, because they paid taxes, signalling a turn in the degree of their professionalization. During the Enlightenment the position of the cantor increased significantly. It was also during the Enlightenment that the cantor began to assume a central role in the musical life of emigrant communities, particularly those in North America. Mark Slobin has observed that the figure of the cantor appears far more often in American synagogue records from the period than does the figure of the rabbi, a fact Slobin interprets as representing the role played by the cantor in building new Jewish communities around synagogues in the New World.[24] During the early nineteenth century the Central European cantor also acquired a more dominant public presence than that of the rabbi, and by the end of the century this public presence developed to such extreme popularity that those with great voices or those particularly active as singers outside the community, for example in opera, had achieved the status of stars.

The changing world of the cantor unfolded as a set of local variants, depending on the extent of local transformations. In Vienna the financial position of the cantor improved substantially throughout the nineteenth century. At the beginning of the century it was impossible for a Jewish artist or musician to earn money in any sort of public capacity. With the passage in 1817 of an Edict of Tolerance, Jews gradually won the possibility of holding so-called "free professions," though these were subjected to taxation. Finally, in 1848, Vienna officially removed the heavy tax burden placed on Jews earning money outside the Jewish community, and Jews could hold positions in the public sphere without special burden.[25] As this liberalization of Austrian law came into being, so too did structural transformations within the Jewish community itself, especially the creation of "central" institutions for all Jews in Vienna, such as the Israelitische Kultusgemeinde. Professions in the Jewish community—among them that of cantor—were given the status of *Beamten,* or civil servants. It was precisely during this period that Salomon Sulzer's career spread well beyond the Jewish community and his status as one of Vienna's leading musical figures was assured. At the same time, other musical positions in the synagogue underwent processes of professionalization, for example when members of the chorus also earned a living as musicians outside the synagogue and the life of the Jewish community. During the second half of the nineteenth century, synagogues throughout Vienna, as well as elsewhere in Central Europe, instituted the position of cantor, consolidating the musical undertakings incumbent upon the holder of that position.[26] By the turn of the century, even Vienna's Sephardic community, whose musical practices and repertories had previously borne no resemblance to that of the Ashkenazic community coalesced around the Stadttempel, had engaged conservatory-trained cantors, Isaac Alteras and Isidor Löwit, whose musical activities transformed the liturgy of the community.[27] In the broadest sense possible, by the end of the nineteenth century a musician in the service of the synagogue acquired the possibility of earning his or her living as a professional musician in Vienna, as well as in other Central European urban centers with growing Jewish populations.

THE PUBLIC SPHERE: THE EXCHANGE
BETWEEN JEWISHNESS AND WESTERNNESS

The nineteenth century was a moment of transformation for the Central European synagogue. Throughout the century many new synagogues were built, but just as significantly the new structures led to an intersection between sacred and public realms.[28] For the first time, men and women mixed in the liberal synagogue, which meant, moreover, that musical voices mixed, not only male and female voices within the polyphonic texture of the new choral liturgy, but also the voices of musical instruments (e.g., the organ) and of musical specialists, who throughout the nineteenth century appeared in growing numbers on the transformed synagogue *bima*. Because the new musical voices within the synagogue drew attention to major issues of religious conflict, they also became the focus of new questions about the nature of the public sphere within the Jewish community.[29] What was, then, the music of the synagogue, and how was it distinguished from other types of Jewish music outside the synagogue?[30]

The newly composed choral music for the synagogue, its new form of mystical speech, served as a symbol for the structural transformation of the Jewish community itself. For the first time the sanctuary was truly a public space. Prior to the nineteenth century such a structural transformation would not only have been unthinkable but also entirely improbable, for the partition between the sanctuary, representing the Jewish world, and the secular or public realm of the non-Jewish world was absolute. Already in the 1820s and 1830s the boundaries around the sacred space of the synagogue were becoming permeable, with movement across them into the European public sphere frequent.[31]

Among those who most often enjoyed the new permeability of these boundaries were cantors, Salomon Sulzer not least among them in Vienna.[32] The public activities of cantors should not exactly be understood as secular, but rather as politicized through participation in a Viennese public sphere that had begun to tolerate a Jewish presence. In the case of Sulzer, who was active as a composer during the liberal politics that followed upon the heels of the Biedermeier Era in the nineteenth century, we witness a clear example of just how extensively Jewish, public, and political musics could enter into a new mix. At the height of his career Sulzer set many texts that stressed an open nationalism, particularly during the revolutionary year of 1848.[33] Sulzer's musical fame, it follows, was transformed through his activities in the public sphere. He sang not only from a stage bounded by the symbols of the sacred Jewish world, but from the public stage of Viennese society. At the end of his life, Sulzer even appeared in depictions and publications as if he were performing on a public stage where Jewish and non-Jewish symbols are symbolically juxtaposed.[34]

By no means was the transformation of the music in the synagogue an isolated phenomenon; rather, it was symptomatic of a fundamental transformation in the life—and musical life—of the Jewish community. The sweeping cultural change within Jewish musical life reflects the historical processes observed by Jürgen Habermas in his studies of the public sphere, which plot an unfolding of European social activities from the Enlightenment until the present, with private domains persistently giving way to an omnipresent public sphere.[35] Habermas further portrays the unfolding public sphere as a space in which cultural practices are "popular" in the broadest sense—that is, accessible to the public as a whole. Prior to the historical transformation of the Jewish community one would not have been able properly to speak of a musical life that was popular in this sense because music took place in the family or within the *kehillah* (Hebrew, "community").[36] Popular and public musical practices became possible only in conjunction with the historical transformation.

In Vienna, the transformation made other cultural developments possible, notably the integration of Jews from the eastern parts of the Habsburg Monarchy, who were settling in growing numbers in the imperial capital. These new immigrants brought other musical traditions with them. The responses to these new traditions varied, ranging from acceptance as the true Jewish folk tradition to parody, but they spread through the Jewish public sphere nonetheless. In so doing, they provided the complex basis for new forms of popular Jewish music-making.

The cantor became popular at the same time he became a public figure. In the early nineteenth century, the selection of cantors still lay in the hands of synagogue committees, whose members determined which traits—religious, social, and musical—they regarded as essential for their candidates. The 1825 letter from Isak Noa Mannheimer to Salomon Sulzer survives, affording the chance to understand the role the Vienna community wished Sulzer to fulfill. The "representatives of the tolerated Israelites in Vienna" expected their *ḥazzan* to comport himself with "moral and religious reservation," but then to possess the following traits:

1. A powerful, sonorous, studied voice;
2. Musical insight and polish, which would enable him at times to lend a hand in the organization of the choir; and
3. Grammatical knowledge of the Hebrew language.[37]

As a list of priorities, it is clear that these traits emphasize the role of the singer, but situate that role in a public position within the life of the synagogue. In 1825, there is no evidence that the Vienna community was interested in a cantor who would creatively contribute to the liturgy or to any process of reform. Thirty years later, in 1855, when the officially reorganized polity of the Viennese Jewish, the Kultusgemeinde ("religious community"), advertised the position for the new synagogue in the rapidly growing Jewish neighborhood of the second district, the Leopoldstadt, a very different set of criteria or priorities for the cantor of the synagogue was advertised in Vienna's major Jewish newspaper, *Allgemeine Zeitung des Judenthums:*

1. Fundamental knowledge of the Hebrew language and liturgy;
2. The education necessary for comprehending and interpreting the Hebrew language and liturgy;
3. Musical training, not only in voice but also in choral-conducting, and in certain musical skills, for example, composing necessary melodies;
4. The skills necessary to teach religion in the school; and
5. An unassailable character, which demonstrates itself fully in the cantor's lifestyle and public profile.[38]

By the mid–nineteenth century, the cantor had become an entirely different figure, indeed a public figure. Major cantorial positions were already being advertised in the print media, especially newspapers in the major urban communities, and cantorial traditions were associated with individuals rather than with places or *kehillot*, and by extension the local liturgical traditions and religious customs, or *minhagim*, of those places. The Viennese Rite composed by Salomon Sulzer, for example, was disseminated throughout Eastern Europe by Sulzer's students, who came to Vienna to study with Sulzer and then returned to Budapest (Meir Friedmann), Breslau (Moritz Deutsch), Odessa (Osias Abraß), or Königsberg (Eduard Birnbaum).[39] The public transformation of the cantor took place on numerous levels, which, in turn, reflected the numerous levels on which the Jewish community itself was undergoing public transformation. The soloist of the early nineteenth century was the choral director of midcentury; the singer prized for his bel-canto tenor became the baritone valued for effecting a blend of sound within the music of the congregation; the ability to improvise, marked "Polish" in most contemporaneous commentaries, was supplanted by a highly intelligent vocal training (*Stimmausbildung*), marked "German" by those same commentaries;[40] the cantor who reproduced tradition as a singer gave way to the cantor who created tradition as a composer. The cantor had found his way into the limelight of publicity, and the stage was set for the creation of a new popularity.

One of the most important conditions for the complex new popular music was language. Each stream of immigration from a different part of the monarchy brought with it different dialects, Ashkenazic and Sephardic, which in turn were distinct from the other dialects found in Vienna. Dialect differences often appear in popular songs, marking not only the variety of characters and ethnic types, but also social and class distinctions. In Viennese Jewish broadside, dialect distinctions also lend themselves to representation in different melody types, with Eastern European melodies far more embellished—I might argue "mystical"—than those of economically and musically assimilated Viennese Jews.[41]

Speech and language played a further role in the historical transformation of Jewish music, not least because of the partial supplanting of Hebrew with German in the synagogue. The linguistic transformation of the synagogue took place only slowly, and in orthodox synagogues one cannot properly speak of a disappearance of Hebrew; in fact, within the larger community, the proper use of language increasingly became a source of strife, thereby creating rifts and factions, but also problematizing the nature of community itself.[42] For the musical life of the larger Jewish community this linguistic strife had two immediate results: first, the creation of new repertories to accommodate different languages, and second, the emergence of new forms of musical specialization. The polyphony of synagogal music itself became a metonym for the many voices now constituting the Jewish community.

The proliferation of Jewish dialects of German and of different dialects of Yiddish in Vienna had a profound impact on the city's popular culture. Although the initial transformation of Vienna's public sphere predated the massive immigration of Jews in the nineteenth century, there can be little doubt that Jewish culture, in the process of becoming Viennese culture, was primarily responsible for spurring on the transformation by the turn of the century. The *Wienerisch* (Viennese dialect) that contributed to the formation of the genre known as *Wienerlied* bears direct witness to the specific influences of Jewish dialects.[43] The linguistic-musical overlap provided the basis for parody and double entendre, for example in the Jewish cabaret traditions that moved from the outer areas of the empire to the outer districts of Vienna in the mid–nineteenth century, and then into the First District in about 1890. It was in the public sphere that such linguistic exchange necessarily took place, with popular forms of music-making serving as an increasingly important site for the dissemination of a new urban and urbane Jewish presence in the popular culture of the monarchy during its final decades.

GENRES AND FORMS OF POPULARITY

In order to transform Jewish music the cantorate first needed to establish the groundwork for a new popularity, a term I use here to represent aspects of both text and context. The music itself had to embody recognizably popular traits, in its melodies, in its forms, and in its capacity to connect the listener's experiences to those of other musics. The performance of liturgical music, moreover, radically recontextualized music within the synagogue, making it resemble the music inside the synagogue and yet represent the much larger world outside. The mixed chorus, for example, symbolized a cross-section of society, and its members increasingly performed not as religious specialists but as musical specialists. Performance, one might argue, replaced worship, or at least expanded it; the practices of ritual, it follows, increasingly came to resemble the concert, with its concomitant distance and distinction from those listening, who were both worshipers and audience.

The spread of Jewish music into the public sphere of Vienna and the Habsburg Empire would not have been possible without a growing dependency on print culture, the publication and sale of printed music. The publication of Jewish music took place in three different forms, which require quite different ways of understanding the nature of Jewish music. The first was the professional world of the cantor. Cantor/composers created journals and presses to disseminate the music they themselves composed for their own services. *Die liturgische Zeitschrift zur Veredelung des Synagogengesangs mit Berücksichtigung des ganzen Synagogenwesens* ("The Liturgical Journal for the Edification of Synagogue Song, with Concern for Its Relation to the Entire Life of the Synagogue"), published between 1848 and 1862, was one of the first journals to publish new works for use by cantors. Each issue included new compositions, new liturgical combinations and experiments, and theoretical discussions faced by the cantor in his daily or weekly practices. At mid-century, such publications seldom circulated outside the professional world of cantors themselves, but they nonetheless contributed substantially to the definition of that world. Surviving issues are generally those from the private libraries of cantors, and these bear witness to considerable use as performance scores.[44] Later in the nineteenth century, however, cantor's journals broadened their appeal. The most important cantorial journal in the Habsburg Empire, the *Österreichisch-ungarische Cantoren-Zeitung* ("The Austro-Hungarian Cantor's Newspaper"), was founded in 1881 and appeared every ten days, advertising itself as the "Central Organ for the Interests of Cantors and Religious Officials [Ger.: *Cultusbeamten*]" in its subtitle. The *Cantor's Newspaper* publicly reported liturgical developments not only throughout the empire but throughout the world, including in synagogues in North and South America.

A second form of popularity developed when some cantors sought to use print media to create standard repertories, for local and regional use, but also for performance within new liturgical canons. Salomon Sulzer's *Schir Zion*,[45] the first and most famous of these new anthologies, also demonstrates the ways in which such volumes connected the professional world of the cantor to a popular world beyond the synagogue, and even beyond the Jewish community (see figure 6.1).

A liturgical anthology such as *Schir Zion* consisted of numerous possibilities for different liturgical works. A cantor would use the anthology to mix and match, of course within the appropriate religious guidelines or for the appropriate holidays. The subtitle of the anthology refers to it as "A Cycle of Religious Songs for Use in the Worship Service of the Israelites," but comparison of the contents makes it clear that "cycle" has both sacred and secular meanings, sacred because of the annual cycle of Torah readings and recitations, but secular because 37 of the total 150 songs were by non-Jewish composers, including a posthumous choral setting of the Ninety-second Psalm, "Tov le-chodos," by Franz Schubert.[46] Each anthology contained numerous compositional styles, thus allowing the cantor the freedom to adapt its contents to the tastes of his own congregation. Through dissemination and adaptation an anthology might form a distinctive canon, which in turn depended on the degree of popularity. The Sulzer *Schir Zion* became the core of a canon known as the *Wiener Ritus*, "the Viennese Rite." This entirely composed and composite rite functioned within the Habsburg Monarchy like other symbols of Vienna, namely as a center of power, to be accepted, rejected, or modified. A cantor did not need to employ the rite, but it was impossible to ignore its impact on Jewish music and its presence within the monarchy, disseminated through a genealogy of cantors and the journals they collectively read.[47]

Print culture also formed the basis for a third form of Jewish popular song, the broadside. Prior to the mid–nineteenth century Jewish themes appeared in broadsides almost entirely as anti-Semitic parodies. By the late decades of the century, however, Jewish broadsides began to appear, indicating that composer, publisher, and consumer were Jews. Some of these broadsides had religious contents, common also for published popular songs, which historically had often relied on moralistic narratives. At an opposite extreme, there were new songs in which intraethnic satires provided the narratives, usually demanding that the consumer be aware of the subtleties between different dialects spoken by Jews in the large cities.[48]

At first glance these new genres of popularizing Jewish music may seem unrelated, but they derived from and were integrated into what Friedrich Kittler has called "discourse networks."[49] Cantors did not compose Jewish broadsides, nor to my knowledge do they appear in the narratives of these popular songs. Broadside hawkers, likewise, did not rely on public knowledge of the tunes in cantorial anthologies. Still, all these genres relied on the same modes of production, reproduction, and dissemination in order to create a popular music culture. Composers, whether Viennese cantors or tunesmiths, created a music that was identifiably Jewish, but in its creation of a Jewish identity took variation and changeability for granted. Though dependent on print culture, the musical genres of the nineteenth-century

Figure 6.1 Cover of the 1905 edition of Salomon Sulzer's *Schir Zion*

Jewish discourse network were never independent of oral tradition, which was necessary for the transformations of musical style and repertory to occur. Each form of musical print medium undergirded new possibilities for what it could mean to be Jewish in the new public spheres—Jewish and non-Jewish—of nineteenth-century Central Europe.

THE *ḤAZZANUT* AS DISCURSIVE SPACE

With more publishing resources at their disposal, Central European cantors re-created their own selfness through their compositions, which increasingly came to represent the *ḥazzanut*. In Hebrew, the *ḥazzanut* literally bears the sense of "that created by cantors," though it is usually glossed in English as "the cantorate," meaning the larger group of musical specialists comprising all or most cantors. In this essay I wish to suggest that both meanings are present in the *ḥazzanut* created by Central European cantors. On one hand, the anthologies of new works composed for the synagogue were described as components of the *ḥazzanut*, whereas on the other these works served to reproduce the cantorate itself, the collectivity of individuals who created the compositions. In twentieth-century European usage, volumes of transcriptions and composition were published simply as the *ḥazzanut* for a particular community, tradition, or region.[50] The published *ḥazzanut* may embody the genealogy of cantors serving a community, each cantor contributing to the continuation of musical life. The rhetoric of the *ḥazzanut* is one of passing the tradition on from cantor to cantor, each cantor therefore creating the musical life of the community through the living out of his professional service.

As Central European cantors compiled their compositions within the space of a text itself, those compositions contained within that text increasingly became a metaphor for the *ḥazzanut*. The spaces of the composed musical text, therefore, became discursive spaces, metonyms for the life of the Jewish community as the other within.[51] The text of the *ḥazzanut* therefore represented the changing public role of the cantor when, in published form, it circulated in the public sphere. It represented the shrinking Austro-Hungarian Empire through its reconfiguration of different communities, for example as the "Viennese Rite" that could be purchased in Budapest or Prague and performed in the synagogues of those cities. It represented the emancipation of the Jewish community, for the *ḥazzanut* provided a text from which all members of the community, as well as non-Jews outside the community, could select compositions and perform them in any context.

The *ḥazzanut* represented a discursive space in which the separate metaphorical domains of space and speech came together—were in fact inseparable from each other. Historically, the *ḥazzanut* plots a history of the European Jewish community, composed by the cantorate. That history began with the composition of new works to dedicate the new synagogues, with their reconfigured space for musical sound. Cantors gathered compositions from diverse sources to represent the liberal attitudes of these synagogues. In his first attempts to gather materials for an early version of *Schir Zion,* for example, Salomon Sulzer solicited a composition from Franz Schubert on the text "Lecha Dodi," a song welcoming the Sabbath, but received instead a choral setting of the Ninety-second Psalm.[52]

The *hazzanut* also took shape through the compositions and liturgical settings circulated among cantors themselves, for example those in cantorial journals such as the *Liturgische Zeitschrift* and the *Österreichisch-ungarische Cantoren-Zeitung.* When a cantor had composed a sufficient body of work to serve the liturgy of his synagogue during the course of the daily and weekly services and of the holidays, these were generally gathered and published as a sort of "monument," a spatial metaphor appropriate to an age in which monuments symbolized cultural achievement. Sulzer's *Schir Zion* was one of the first examples of a composed cantorial monument. Louis Lewandowsky's *Kol Rinnah u' T'fillah* monumentalized the Reform Movement in Berlin in similar fashion.[53]

During the first decades of the twentieth century the Latvian-German cantor A. Z. Idelsohn, conducting research with support from the Austrian Academy of Sciences, transformed the *hazzanut* into a basic tool for modern Jewish music historiography, basing the ten volumes of his *Hebräisch-orientalischer Melodienschatz* on the repertories created by cantors, whether through oral tradition in Jerusalem or the printed liturgies of European cantors.[54] The *hazzanut* was not just a musical lens for viewing music history; it had become the tool with which to perform and then write Jewish history. Composing the cantorate had metaphorically and literally become the means of inscribing a history of European others.

The discursive space of the cantorate entered its final phase as the history of European Jewry was impelled toward the Holocaust. Many cantor-composers in the early decades of the twentieth century emigrated, especially to North America,[55] while others consolidated their local traditions as pressures from the outside became more restrictive. The public sphere that contained both Jewish and non-Jewish sectors eventually collapsed into a Jewish sector alone, stripped to a large degree of its public character, but even more intense because of the world of music it provided for the Jewish community—for example, in the restrictive *Jüdischer Kulturbund* imposed by the Nazi government in Germany beginning in 1933. Even in the late 1930s, many Central European cantor-composers turned to the World Centre for Jewish Music in Palestine as a potential discursive space for the *hazzanut* in mandatory Palestine. Despite their efforts, few secured exit permits from Germany and Austria, and still fewer gained entrance visas for the British Mandate in Palestine.[56] After 1938, the public spheres that shaped the discursive spaces of the *hazzanut* ceased to exist as new forms of dealing with Central Europe's others within were implemented.

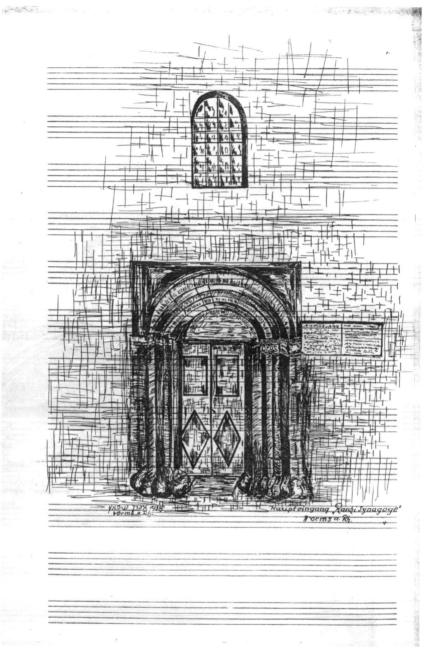

אדות שער שראל
Worms a. Rh.

Haupteingang "Raschi Synagoge"
Worms a. Rh.

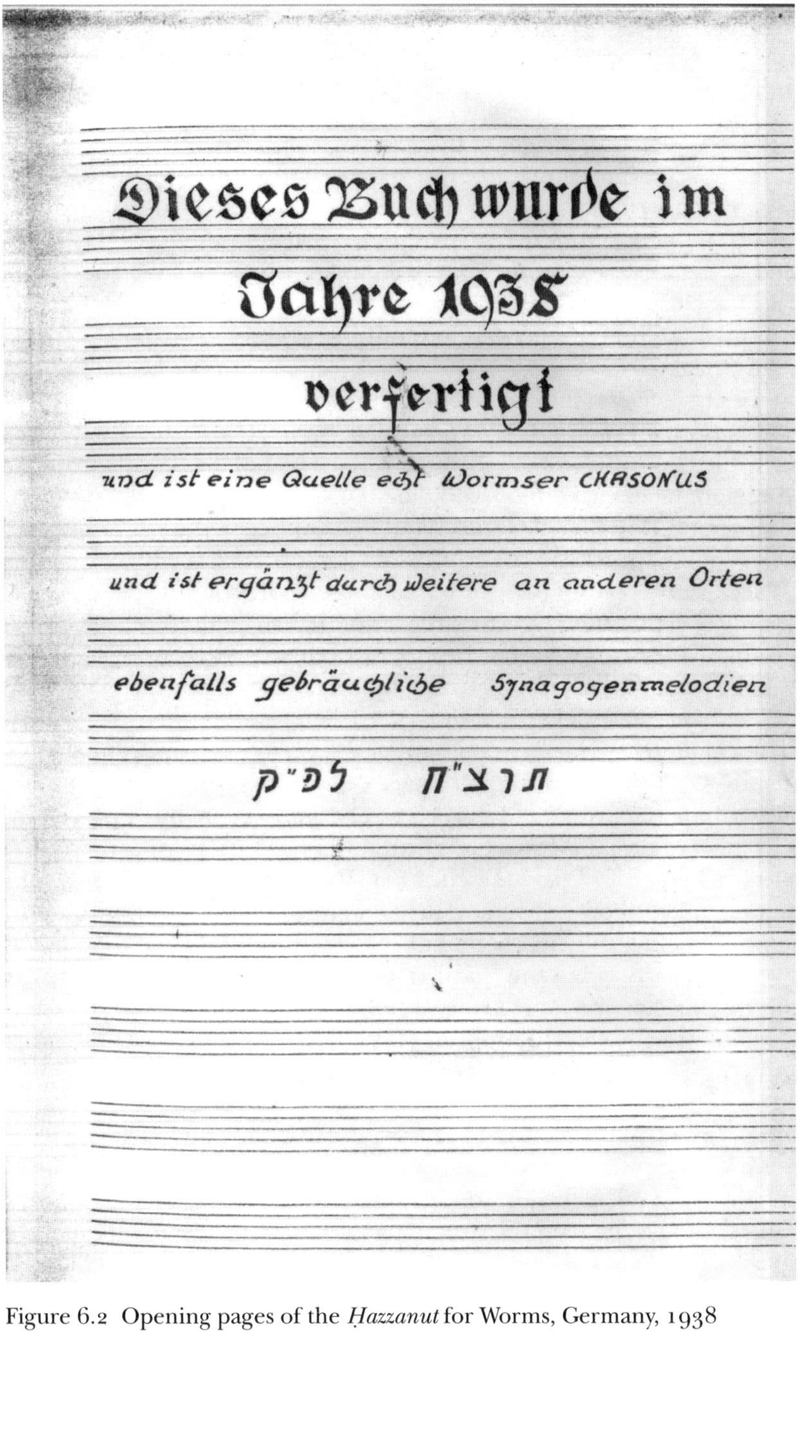
Dieses Buch wurde im
Jahre 1938
verfertigt
und ist eine Quelle echt Wormser CHASONUS
und ist ergänzt durch weitere an anderen Orten
ebenfalls gebräuchliche Synagogenmelodien
תרצ"ח לפ"ק

Figure 6.2 Opening pages of the *Ḥazzanut* for Worms, Germany, 1938

NACHSPIEL/ENDSPIEL—EXIT INTO THE WORMS ḤAZZANUT

I close this essay with images of the *ḥazzanut* compiled in Worms, one of the most important centers of European Jewish culture, in 1938, as passage along the path to the Holocaust had become irreversible. The opening pages of the Worms *ḥazzanut* (figure 6.2) depict the entrance to the Raschi Synagogue faced by the title page in the hand of an unknown compiler.[57] These images evoke the closure of history, the completeness of the *ḥazzanut* itself, reduced to the juxtaposition of spaces entirely within the Jewish community. The door of the synagogue is seen from the outside; situated at the beginning of the manuscript, it invites the user to enter from the world outside. The title given to this *ḥazzanut* ("This Book Was Finished in the Year 1938") also bears witness to the closure it symbolized, indeed to the year of the Kristallnacht, when the synagogue depicted here would be burned to the ground. The subtitle, moreover, observes that the book is the "true source of the Worms *ḥazzanut*," albeit a source embellished by "useful synagogue melodies from other places."

This *ḥazzanut* bolstered its internal contents by consolidating tradition, gleaning meaningful songs from the larger Jewish community of Germany. The 1938 Worms *ḥazzanut* had become a discursive space for survival. It embodied a local musical tradition that would fail to survive the Holocaust. A final act of creativity, executed by a cantor informed by the past century of transformation in the Jewish community, the Worms *ḥazzanut* retreated from the public sphere into the sacred space of the synagogue.

Inscribing the history of Europe's internal others has often proved to be an ironic and desperate project. For the Central European cantors, whose collective biography I have sketched in this essay, the discursive space of the *ḥazzanut* failed to provide a safe surrogate for the public spaces into which the Jewish community was seemingly entering with fewer restrictions. The history inscribed within the *ḥazzanut* functioned in a radically different, entirely unexpected way: it was one of the final representations of space and speech to which Central European Jews could retreat as their history disintegrated in the 1930s and ended in annihilation in the 1940s.

The *ḥazzanut*, as a discursive space, has not entirely disappeared from Europe at the end of the twentieth century, and to some extent it has not ceased inscribing the history of the New Europe's internal otherness, though perhaps the irony of its historical narrativity is even greater. Today, one encounters the *ḥazzanut* on the street, sold as tapes by cassette vendors in Budapest or Prague, or filling "Judaica" or "Yiddish" bins in record stores in Vienna and Berlin. Cantorial compositions appear on the programs of revival concerts, attempts to reconstruct the traces of the past. Groups claiming to be traditional Jewish folk ensembles, or *klezmer* bands, bandy about the names of cantors between pieces during a performance, as if to claim some authority from these revered musicians of the past. Surviving communities, many of them rebuilt after World War II, have endeavored to publish volumes of *hazzanut*, representing the past and connecting them to a possible future.[58] In these ways the *hazzanut* depends on the public sphere, indeed the spaces in which the New Europe struggles to determine a new selfness. This new selfness is as dependent on the imagination of others as it was prior to World War II. The competition for public spaces increases as new and old internal others—Turkish guest workers, Roma and Sinti, refugees from Southeastern Europe, to name just the most obvious—compete for public recognition and the rights that should accrue to them as residents of Europe. In much of Europe, however, Jewish communities do not compete for these spaces. Composing the cantorate, accordingly, has ceased. The otherness the cantorate sought to transform has, as yet, found no new place in the various "Europes" constructed after World War II. If the song of the cantor again fills the public spaces of the New Europe, it is as mystical speech, the music from some other time and place.

NOTES

Research for this essay initially took place in Central Europe during 1990–91, and I should like to thank the National Endowment for the Humanities and the Alexander von Humboldt Foundation for their generous support of that research, with a Summer Stipend and Forschungsstipendium, respectively. During 1995–96 I conducted further, intensive research in Vienna when serving as Fulbright Guest Professor at the University of Vienna. I should like to thank the Council for International Exchange of Scholars for that teaching opportunity, which allowed me to offer three courses on Jewish music. To my Vienna students, who ceaselessly stimulated my thinking, I owe a special debt of thanks.

1. K. H. Köhler and G. Herre, eds., *Ludwig van Beethovens Konversationshefte*, vol. 7 (Leipzig, 1978), 132. The epigraph is to be found on page 43b of Beethoven's conversation book from 22 January to early February 1825; cited in ibid., 130.

2. Speculations about possible sketches for this work or appearances of themes (e.g., from the "Kol Nidre") appear in Hanoch Avenary, *Kantor Salomon Sulzer und seine Zeit: Eine Dokumentation* (Sigmaringen: Jan Thorbecke Verlag, 1985).

3. The term *Stadttempel* literally means "city temple," both nominal components signalling a recognition of a more sweeping presence of the synagogue in the public sphere of Vienna. The Stadttempel consolidated the polity of the Vienna Jewish community, eventually becoming the center of the Israelitische Kultusgemeinde (IKG), which increasingly oversaw the public affairs of the Jewish community (e.g., the financial affairs or maintenance of cemeteries). Diversity by no means disappeared in the Jewish community—Orthodox and Sephardic communities, at least for several decades, retained their independence—but the consolidation of authority through the Stadttempel and its location in the First District dramatically resituated the Jewish community onto Vienna's modern cityscape.

4. The claim that the other calibrates its world outside of time, which is to say, outside of history and therefore without civilization, has been essential not only to

colonial officials but to ethnographers who rely on difference to enforce their own disciplinary being. For examinations of this phenomenon from the perspectives of anthropology, cultural history, and literary theory, see Johannes Fabian, *Time and the Other: How Anthropology Creates Its Object* (New York: Columbia University Press, 1983); Eric Wolf, *Europe and the People without History* (Berkeley: University of California Press, 1982); and Stephen Greenblatt, *Marvelous Possessions: The Wonder of the New World* (Chicago: University of Chicago Press, 1991).

5. Michel de Certeau, "L'Énonciation mystique," in *Recherches de science religieuse* 64, no. 2 (1976): 183–215.

6. See, e.g., the numerous accounts of this sort in Jean de Léry, *History of a Voyage to the Land of Brazil, Otherwise Called America,* trans. Janet Whatley (Berkeley: University of California Press, 1990), 141–44 and passim. See also Greenblatt, *Marvelous Possessions,* 14–19; Philip V. Bohlman, "Missionaries, Magical Muses, and Magnificent Menageries," in *The World of Music* 33, no. 3 (1988): 5–27; and idem, "Representation and Cultural Critique in the History of Ethnomusicology," in Bruno Nettl and Philip V. Bohlman, eds., *Comparative Musicology and Anthropology of Music: Essays on the History of Ethnomusicology* (Chicago: University of Chicago Press, 1991), 131–51.

7. Especially in Jean-Jacques Rousseau, *Dictionnaire de la musique* (Paris: Chez la veuve Duchesne, 1768). Not well known because of false attribution to Marin Mersenne is the fact that Rousseau included transcriptions of melodies by Jean de Léry in the *Dictionnaire;* see Timothy J. Cooley, "Casting Shadows in the Field," in *Shadows in the Field: New Perspectives for Fieldwork in Ethnomusicology,* ed. Gregory F. Barz and Timothy J. Cooley (New York: Oxford University Press, 1997), 6–7.

8. See Richard Wagner, *Das Judentum in der Musik* (Leipzig: J. J. Weber, 1869; orig. 1850). Passages such as the following serve as relentless attacks on the mystic—and alien—nature of Jewish speech and music; quoted in Sander L. Gilman, *Inscribing the Other* (Lincoln: University of Nebraska Press, 1991), 104–5: "By far more weighty, nay, of quite decisive weight for our inquiry, is the effect the Jew produces on us through his *speech;* and this is the essential point at which to sound the Jewish influence upon music. The Jew speaks the language of the nation in whose midst he dwells from generation to generation, but he speaks it always as an alien. . . . Our whole European art and civilization, however, have remained to the Jew a foreign tongue; for, just as he has taken no part in the evolution of one, so has he taken none in that of the other."

9. Fabian, *Time and the Other.*

10. Not coincidentally the political heartland of the Holy Roman Empire.

11. Tzvetan Todorov emphasizes the role of writing and the reproduction of images of the other in the New World in *The Conquest of America: The Question of the Other,* trans. Richard Howard (New York: Harper & Row, 1984).

12. One form of boundedness in the colonial context is evident in the ways that European genres—for example, *villancico* in Catholic Latin America or hymnody in African missions—were understood to be suitable for indigenous musics. The essentialization of melody in Baroque homophonic textures was coeval with the musical transformation of the other's speech and melodies during the Early Modern Era.

13. For the otherness embedded in music's complex presence in magic see Gary Tomlinson, *Music in Renaissance Magic: Toward a Historiography of Others* (Chicago: Uni-

versity of Chicago Press, 1993). To a large extent it was music itself, as a form of mystical speech separate from human speech, that was magical. Attempts to reform compositional practices in the Counter-Reformation (e.g., the Tridentine reforms) held most forcefully that music should not obscure, that is overwhelm, the text.

14. See Ruth Burstyn, "Die Geschichte der türkisch-spaniolischen Juden im Habsburgerreich," in Peter Bettelheim and Michael Ley, eds., *Ist jetzt hier die "wahre" Heimat? Ostjüdische Einwanderung nach Wien* (Vienna: Picus, 1993), 17–66. The practice of representing Jewish and Roma folk musicians together, even in jazz and cabaret traditions, is a modern trace of this persistent trope of creating internal others.

15. See Johann Gottfried Herder, *"Stimmen der Völker in Liedern"* and *Volkslieder,* 2 vols. (1778–79; reprint, Stuttgart: Reclam, 1975). Herder's fascination with folk song accompanied his pursuit of the origins of language. Folk song and early forms of language intersected as profound cases of mystical speech.

16. See John Meier, *Kunstlieder im Volksmunde: Materialien und Untersuchungen* (Halle: M. Niemeyer, 1906), the classic articulation of this theory, which has influenced German folk-song scholarship throughout the twentieth century.

17. In many national ethnographic traditions in Europe, the other within has been both created and erased by deliberate quarrels about the possibilities of naming them and according them social and political status. For discussions of the problem of nomenclature see the essays in Ursula Hemetek, ed., *Echo der Vielfalt/Echoes of Diversity: Traditionelle Musik von Minderheiten/ethnischen Gruppen* (Vienna: Böhlau Verlag, 1996), especially Hemetek, "Einführung," 11–16; Alica Elscheková and Oskár Elschek, "Theorie und Praxis der Erforschung der traditionellen Musik von Minderheiten," 17–30; and Max Peter Baumann, "'Listening to the Voices of Indigenous Peoples . . .': On Traditional Music as Policy in Intercultural Encounters," 31–39.

18. Greenblatt, *Marvelous Possessions,* 13–14.

19. Jewish communities in Europe formed along the outskirts of villages and cities for these reasons. Roma and Sinti (Gypsies), in particular, have been the victims of socioeconomic distancing, not least because their own propensity to relocate and move communities has made control through physical marginalization more difficult.

20. For a study of street music in the new Germany, see Philip V. Bohlman, "Music, History, and the Foreign in the New Germany," in *Modernism/Modernity* 1, no. 1 (1994): 121–52.

21. For the role of the East in the otherness Jews represented for Europe, particularly through the discourse of music in the long history of the Diaspora, see Philip V. Bohlman, "La riscoperta del Mediterraneo nella musica ebraica: Il discorso dell' 'altro' nell' etnomusicologia dell' Europa," in *Antropologia della musica e culture mediterranee,* ed. Tullia Magrini (Bologna: Società editrice il Mulino, 1993), 107–24. See also Daniel Boyarin, *Storm from Paradise: The Politics of Jewish Memory* (Minneapolis: University of Minnesota Press, 1993).

22. For a history of the professional structure of the Jewish community, see Daniel J. Elazar and Stuart A. Cohen, *The Jewish Polity: Jewish Political Organization from Biblical Times to the Present* (Bloomington: Indiana University Press, 1985). The professional designation, *hazzan,* appears throughout this historical survey, always occupying a position of central importance in community life.

23. I examined these records in the Municipal Archive of Sopron, Hungary (Tax Records, 1734). For studies of the cantor in rural villages in Central Europe see Wal-

ter Salmen, "... *denn die Fiedel macht das Fest"*: *Jüdische Musikanten und Tänzer vom 13. bis 20. Jahrhundert* (Innsbruck: Edition Helbing, 1991), and Philip V. Bohlman, "Musical Life in the Central European Village," in *Modern Jews and Their Musical Agendas*, ed. Ezra Mendelsohn, special edition of *Studies in Contemporary Jewry*, vol. 9 (New York: Oxford University Press, 1993): 17–39.

24. Mark Slobin, *Chosen Voices: The Story of the American Cantorate* (Urbana: University of Illinois Press, 1989), 29–50.

25. Documents in Avenary, *Kantor Salomon Sulzer*, 72–75, provide a detailed record of the improvement in the financial status of Vienna's Jewish musicians.

26. The classic study of the German, particularly North German and northern European, liturgical and musical transformation is Ismar Elbogen, *Jewish Liturgy: A Comprehensive History*, trans. Raymond P. Scheindlin (1913; Philadelphia and New York: Jewish Publication Society and Jewish Theological Society of America, 1993). For a more extensive look at the cantorate in Berlin and Budapest, the latter in the twentieth century, see Philip V. Bohlman, "The Worlds of the European Jewish Cantorate: A Century in the History of a Minority's Non-Minority Music," in Ursula Hemetek, ed., *Echo der Vielfalt / Echoes of Diversity* (Vienna: Böhlau Verlag, 1996), 49–63.

27. Alteras immigrated to Vienna from Sarajevo, thus strengthening musical connections with that center of Sephardic Judaism in the Austro-Hungarian Empire. Löwit enjoyed a particularly public career and fulfilled the duties of his office until 1938. See Burstyn, "Die Geschichte der türkisch-spaniolischen Juden," 44–48.

28. For contrasting perspectives on the Viennese Stadttempel, the city's central synagogue, as a symbol of religious, social, and musical transformation during the nineteenth century, see the chronicle of its rebuilding after World War II: Israelitische Kultusgemeinde, ed., *Die Wiener Stadttempel: Die Wiener Juden* (Vienna: J & V Edition, 1988).

29. We witness the importance of these debates in articles such as the one devoted to the "struggle over the organ," which appears in the major dictionary of Jewish culture in German-speaking countries, *Jüdisches Lexikon*. See Joseph Max and Cäsar Seligmann, "Orgelstreit," in *Jüdisches Lexikon* (Berlin: Jüdischer Verlag, 1930), columns 601–4.

30. One emic response to this question is Elbogen, *Jewish Liturgy*.

31. Ibid., 297–333.

32. The publicness of Sulzer's life appears frequently in the documents on his life in Avenary, *Kantor Salomon Sulzer*.

33. Texts to such songs (e.g., the "Nationalgarde-Lied," based on the poem by Max Emanuel Stern) appear in Avenary, *Kantor Salomon Sulzer*, 107–12. It is notable that Johann Strauss, Franz von Suppé, and other operetta composers later wrote songs on the same themes, the "national guard" and the defense of the monarchy. My point here is that it is not essential whether such compositions were for public entertainment or not, but rather that they evoked the same public and national arena as compositions by the most distinguished cantor in Vienna.

34. See, e.g., the engraving across from page 241 in Avenary, *Kantor Salomon Sulzer*. I discuss the interrelatedness of sacred and secular "stages" for music in the Viennese Jewish community in Philip V. Bohlman, "Auf der Bima—Auf der Bühne: Zur Emanzipation der jüdischen Popularmusik im Wien der Jahrhundertwende," in *Vergleichend-systematische Musikwissenschaft: Beiträge zu Methode und Problematik der systema-*

tischen, ethnologischen und historischen Musikwissenschaft, ed. Elisabeth Th. Hilscher and Theophil Antonicek (Tutzing, Germany: Hans Schneider, 1994), 417–49.

35. Jürgen Habermas, *The Structural Transformation of the Public Sphere: An Inquiry into a Category of Bourgeois Society,* trans. Thomas Burger (1962; Cambridge, Mass.: MIT Press, 1989).

36. In Hebrew usage, *kehillah* represents the community as a social unit, as well as a religio-cultural unit. Musical life in one *kehillah,* then, differs from that in other *kehillot* on the basis of this cultural boundedness.

37. In Avenary, *Kantor Salomon Sulzer,* 34; cf. Thomas Dombrowski, "Der 'Sulzerkantor'—Ein Phänomen seiner Epoche," in *Salomon Sulzer—Kantor, Komponist, Reformer,* ed. Bernhard Purin (Bregenz, Austria: Land Vorarlberg, 1991), 75.

38. *Allgemeine Zeitung des Judenthums,* ed. Ludwig Philippson, vol. 19 (1855), 263; see also Dombrowski, "Der 'Sulzerkantor,'" 76.

39. Birnbaum was one of the most distinguished of all cantor-composers, and the liturgical repertories he created for Königsberg/Kaliningrad among the most modern in sound.

40. For a discussion of "Polish singing" see Joseph Singer, "Polnisch-Singen in der modernen Synagoge," *Sammlung kantoral-wissenschaftlicher Aufsätze,* ed. Aron Friedmann (Berlin: C. Boas, 1922), 191.

41. Reproduced examples of such broadsides appear in Philip V. Bohlman, "Die Volksmusik und die Verstädterung der deutsch-jüdischen Gemeinde in den Jahrzehnten vor dem Zweiten Weltkrieg," in *Jahrbuch für Volksliedforschung* 34 (1989): 25–40.

42. See Elbogen, *Jewish Liturgy,* 308–19.

43. Viennese dialect includes many Hebrew words, which it absorbed through contact with Yiddish. Nouns in both Yiddish and Viennese assume endearing or small forms through the same shift, namely the addition of the suffix "-l" and an umlaut to the vowel in the final syllable. These similarities result from the fact that Yiddish and Viennese have long existed in the same speech area. See Albrecht Etz, "Zur Mundart im Wienerlied," *Jahrbuch des österreichischen Volksliedwerkes* 18 (1969): 47–60.

44. This is the case, for example, with the issues in special collections of the library at the University of Augsburg, which I have examined. Performance annotations in the owners' hands cover the pages of printed music, clearly indicating the special needs and modifications for different services and holidays.

45. The first edition appeared in 1840, published privately by Sulzer himself. *Schir Zion* appeared in subsequent editions, the best known of which was edited and expanded by his son, Joseph Sulzer (Leipzig: M. W. Kaufmann, 1905).

46. Walter Pass, "Der Liedkomponist und Liedinterpret Salomon Sulzer," in *Salomon Sulzer,* ed. Purin, 54–56.

47. While undertaking fieldwork in Hungary during the early 1990s I found that, during interviews, Hungarian cantors defined their own stylistic characteristics primarily as they conformed to or differed from those in the Viennese Rite. Such alignments were as much historical and ideological as they were musical.

48. I discuss the different themes and publishers of Jewish broadsides in considerable detail in "Die Volksmusik und die Verstädterung der deutsch-jüdischen Gemeinde," op. cit.

49. Friedrich A. Kittler, *Discourse Networks 1800/1900,* trans. Michael Metteer with Chris Cullens (Stanford, Calif.: Stanford University Press, 1990). According to Kit-

tler, a discourse network (German, *Aufschreibesystem,* a system for taking up and writing out) forms through the connections that develop as different media transform the meaning of communicative practices. The typewriter and the telephone transform the social functions of speech; new technologies enable new musical instruments to transform the nature of what music is. Through diverse forms of publishing music, it follows, Jewish music itself underwent radical transformation and assumed new and different identities.

50. See, e.g., A. Z. Idelsohn, *Die traditionellen Gesänge der süddeutschen Juden,* vol. 7 of *Hebräisch-orientalischer Melodienschatz* (Leipzig: Friedrich Hofmeister, 1932), and Hans Bloemendal, *Amsterdams Chazzanoet: Synagogale muziek van de Ashkenazische Gemeente,* 2 vols. (Buren, The Netherlands: Frits Knuf, 1990). Slobin, *Chosen Voices,* does not observe this distinction for the *ḥazzanut* in North America, where the cantorate is the profession and professional organization of cantors.

51. I use the concept of "discursive space" in ways similar to Edward W. Said's concept of "narrative space" in *Culture and Imperialism* (New York: Knopf, 1993), 62–80: that is, as a designation of a narrative representation of historical conditions impinging on the actors in the text. Whereas Said examines the presence of external empire, especially the British Empire, in nineteenth-century novels, I am concerned here with the presence of empire—the internal empire of Austria and Hungary—in the public musical activities of Jews living and migrating within that empire.

52. For a discussion of the composers approached by Sulzer, see Avenary, *Kantor Salomon Sulzer,* and Pass, "Der Liedkomponist."

53. Louis Lewandowsky, *Kol Rinnah u' T'fillah* (Berlin: Bote und Bock, 1871). See also Bohlman, "The Worlds of the European Jewish Cantorate," 52–55.

54. A. Z. Idelsohn, *Hebräisch-orientalischer Melodienschatz,* 10 vols. (Berlin [et al.]: Benjamin Harz [et al.], 1914–32).

55. This was the case with the cantor described by Mark Slobin as "the most famous cantorial superstar," Yosele Rosenblatt (1880–1933), who nonetheless composed paeans in various genres to the Austrian Emperor, Franz Josef I, during his sojourn in Vienna prior to World War I; Slobin, *Chosen Voices,* 21.

56. For a documentary history of the World Centre for Jewish Music, including English translations of letters from many cantors to that organization, see Philip V. Bohlman, *The World Centre for Jewish Music in Palestine: Jewish Musical Life on the Eve of World War II* (Oxford: Clarendon Press, 1992).

57. The anonymity of this manuscript, located in the Municipal Archive of Worms, makes it impossible to know if the hand was that of the cantor of the Raschi Synagogue or not. The choice, order, and preparation of the pieces in this *ḥazzanut,* however, make it clear that the compiler knew *ḥazzanut* well and certainly had studied many aspects of the cantorate. The transliterated text underlay, for example, was clearly executed by a professional.

58. This is the explicit goal of the compilers of Bloemendal, *Amsterdams Chazzanoet.*

East, West, and Arabesk

Martin Stokes

A long-standing theme in Orientalism's postcolonial critique has been "the East's" participation in its own representation.[1] The issue evokes an unstable and potentially infinite regress. East looks at West looking at East; servant looks at master/mistress looking at servant; distinctive shapes and patterns fade into the murky green darkness that one glimpses peering into the gap between mirrors facing one another. Its theoretical interest for postcolonial scholarship derives, at first, from the attention it draws to semiotic implosion, the ultimate fate of all binary oppositions, and the subversion and eventual collapse of the forms of coercion and domination in which they participate.[2] But the echoing reverberations of East and West on Europe's southeastern fringe draw attention to other matters. Who and what is involved in deciding where (and when) Europe and its programmatic modernity begin and end? Who is included and who excluded? How are we to comprehend the turbulent dynamics of sentiment and violence that these acts of definition have generated over the last three decades? What genuinely democratic options remain for those who find themselves on the wrong side of them? Colonial categories of representation of self and other, dismantled and reassembled, expropriated and indigenized, continue to haunt these kind of questions.[3]

This chapter presents an account of a Turkish popular musical genre known as *arabesk*. Arabesk has provided a particularly important space in which people in Turkey have considered, and continue to consider, their place in the world. They do so with reference to an underdeveloped internal Orient, the site of complex fantasies and fears on the part of the Turkish republican intelligentsia, and, currently, a ongoing war between the Turkish military and the predominantly Kurdish population of the area. Drawing on a long-standing ethnomusicological concern with matters of representation,[4] the chapter explores arabesk's imbrication with the tropes and rhetorical figures of western Orientalism, the dynamic irresolution of Turkey's "arabesk debate" (as it is sometimes described in Turkey), and the multiplicity of positions which musicians and the intelligentsia in Turkey construct for themselves around arabesk's "East."

Orientalism and nineteenth-century symphonicism, together with its academic musicology, are closely intertwined, as a great deal of recent writing has shown.[5] Wagner's music and writing, and the subsequent Aryanization of music history in Germany in the 1920s and 1930s,[6] were particularly conspicuous aspects of a construction of a Teutonic Europe in which European Muslims and Jews were represented as parasitic outsiders (see Bohlman's chapter in this volume). The aesthetic project of the Wagnerian music drama engaged the other in a particularly tight and ambivalent embrace, nowhere more so, perhaps, than in *Tristan*. In this, to put the issue in Adorno and Horkheimer's stark but revealingly problematic terms, the forces connecting mimetic representation to the "*ratio*" of racial erasure and the Holocaust are all too striking.[7]

There are other ways of understanding this picture, though, and other histories than those which inexorably lead to (and from) Wagner. The Turkophilia which gripped Vienna in the late eighteenth century[8] and the taste for musical exotica in late eighteenth- and early nineteenth-century England were driven by a process of what one might describe as domestication,[9] but the exotic also generated complex and often radical currents of speculative musical thinking. The scramble for territorial influence by Bourbon and Habsburg dynasties in seventeenth-century Europe was partly promoted through struggles for cultural innovation, which generated an intense interest in the music of the Ottoman near east in the court of Louis XIV. His minister, Colbert, sent Petis de la Croix to study languages and music in the Levant, and his observations in turn allowed Charles Perrault (a Fellow of the Academie Française) to put the case for a new kind of vocal declamation, sensitive to the meaning and affect of words, by reference to Turkish musical practice.[10]

In this way, largely imagined musics of the East have provided the justification and raw materials for significant processes of innovation in Western art music, and these have taken varied and distinct trajectories from the Enlightenment period on (followed in the modern period by such disparate figures as Messaien, Cage, and Reich; see Corbett's chapter in this volume).[11] Orientalisms are many and varied. In a recent and important essay on David, Bizet, Saint-Saëns, Goldmark, and others, Ralph Locke reminds us that Orientalism can cut in a variety of directions, and that works "about" the Middle East were not only or simply about empire, but complex and often radical explorations of sexual politics, individual psychology, urbanism, and modernity.[12]

Locke's account, however, leaves us firmly in the world of a representing "us" and a represented oriental "other." "They" remain outside the framework altogether: silent, marginalized, and ultimately irrelevant to questions of analytical significance. The critique of Orientalism thus has a way of reproducing the very voicelessness that the critique itself diagnoses and problematizes. These same others themselves engage with, reproduce, and manipulate colonial representations, diverting them toward more localized struggles for power, accommodation, or resistance, nuancing and adding to them in ways which owe little (while remaining in certain respects connected) to their original configurations. These are important to understand, especially as they come to bear, with increasing cultural insistence, on the Euro-American metropolis.[13]

The point is twofold. Firstly, colonial representations have a trajectory in (post)colonized society which require understanding in their own locale, with attention to their local specificities. And secondly, these too have to be understood (and critiqued) in local and plural terms. As Paul Rabinow puts it, "A basic move against either economic or philosophic hegemony is to diversify centers of resistance: avoid the error of reverse essentializing; occidentalism is not a remedy for orientalism."[14]

Whether effective in Rabinow's terms or not, techniques for resisting these processes in the contemporary Middle East consist both of Occidentalisms, the self-conscious embracing of an "Easternness" predicated on a unitary Western other (notable particularly in the case of religion), or equally self-conscious hybridizations, which challenge the claims of state-appointed guardians of a unitary national culture. Indeed, the state in the Middle East has relinquished a great deal of its meaning-making powers to multinational industry. This is a direct consequence of the systematic, IMF-instigated liberalization programs spearheaded by Özal in Turkey and Sadat in Egypt, and the proliferation of information technologies which render transnational information and images, in the Middle East and elsewhere, impossible (or extremely difficult) to censor and control.

This fact places musicians and their audiences in a complex position, and introduces the problem of the specificity of musical modes of representation. On one hand the raw materials (sounds, techniques, instruments, technologies) with which hybrid forms can be constructed circulate with an extrovert and energetic freedom which continues to excite, startle, and invigorate musicians and their audiences in Turkey; on the other, the embracing of transnational forms locates musicians and listeners in the structures of an emerging multinational capitalism, necessitating the purchase of expensive (foreign-manufactured) instruments, sound recording and playback equipment, and increasingly expensive cassettes and CDs. The contradictory effect of collapsing state cultural control and expanding global cultural economies has followed a similar trajectory in many Balkan, Middle Eastern, and Asian situations.[15] Under these conditions, we should not be surprised that debates about the state's role as guardian of public culture and the forms and imagery of popular musics, films, and literatures have much in common across the Middle East today.

Music both reflects and shapes these conditions in a particularly direct way. The nonverbal, gestural quality of music offers, to quote Born, "little resistance to discursive invasion."[16] At the same time, musical performance is multitextual, embracing all manner of contradiction (between, for example, a lyric, a musical phrase, and a tone of voice).[17] Musical performance, while peculiarly open to discursive invasion, is also therefore open to discursive debate: its meanings can never be fixed conclusively in spoken language, and the "same" music can thus be appropriated by different groups for quite different reasons. While this allows veiled criticisms to be expressed when open criticism is impossible, it also allows dominant groups in turn to interpret musics in ways that suit their interests, to promote these interpretations with the resources available to them, and to exclude those which oppose their interests.

This means that lines of domination and resistance are particularly hard to define in relation to Middle Eastern popular musics, least of all in terms of a dominant West and a subaltern East. Instead, they should be seen as discursive fields in which emerging constellations of interests and groups define themselves through representations in and of popular culture. These representations have involved outright condemnation, but also, and more recently, the attempt to control and co-opt. This historical movement, from discursive exclusion to discursive inclusion, is firmly linked to the collapse of the state project, the emergence of a new intellectual elite which looks beyond Turkey, and the response of the old elites to emerging cultural priorities. The fact that the clearest and most resonant symbols of this shift have been located in a form of music is far from insignificant.

ARABESK

In Turkey, arabesk formulates a distinct set of problems concerning order, disorder, West, and East. Through lyrics, cassette covers, films, *fotoroman* (photo-novels with speech-bubbles, serialized in the popular press) and now video clips, it represents a world of decay and despair, in which signifiers of disorder are linked directly to signifiers of a subversive, internal Orient. It would be easy to interpret this material in terms of a dominant Western Turkey extending its hegemony over a subaltern Eastern Turkey. This would, however, be to take the representations of arabesk at face value, and ignore the ways in which they are used, manipulated, inflected, and ironized. There is, to paraphrase Rabinow, more to social experience and meaning than the formal dimensions of representation.[18] Bearing this in mind, I intend to discuss the ways in which this music has been criticized and more recently co-opted by the state and by Turkish intellectuals and to identify the ways in which arabesk has been constructed in a competing discursive field. I will be focusing on a few of the increasing number of texts on the subject of arabesk (in particular those by Yılmaz Öztuna, Ertan Eğribel, Nazife Güngör, Murat Belge, Meral Özbek, Nilufer Göle, Nedim Karakayalı) in order to draw out more general themes.

Firstly, what is arabesk? No single, all-embracing definition is possible, since arabesk is, and means, a lot of different things. Turkish definitions and explanations can roughly be divided into two basic categories: those in which the idea of Arab-influenced hybridity are significant (a position taken by intellectual commentators) and those in which it is not (a position taken mainly by musicians and fans). Intellectual commentators see arabesk in sociological or historical terms. Arabesk is, for them, the more or less disastrous consequence of certain processes of modernization and urbanization, in which state-led attempts to forget a Muslim and Arab past in pursuit of a secular and Western destiny ran aground. By contrast, for most fans, the "Arabness" of the music is not its most significant feature. To generalize, for fans, the singers are ordinary suffering human beings like them, who share, as outsiders from the Turkish provinces, uncertain destinies on the fringes of the big cities. Arabesk, for fans, is about love, separation, manipulation, betrayal, and hopeless dreams of glamour, wealth, and escape.

Musicians see it in somewhat technical terms. The application of the term "arabesk" itself is credited to Orhan Gencebay's 1969 recording *Bir teselli ver*, although he has publicly and repeatedly disavowed the term. While the elements of a shared Middle Eastern musical culture might be described by arabesk musicians as "of Arab origin," more often than not, musicians tend to stress either a musical synthesis that has to be seen in local (Turkish) terms, or a much more cosmopolitan syncretism. Apparently contradictory comments by Orhan Gencebay will illustrate both points. In an interview in 1981,[19] Gencebay claimed that arabesk was *olduğu gibi Türk Müziği* ("Turkish music through and through"), combining art and rural genres in a way that reflects most provincial Turks' musical experience but is nonetheless anathema to the state's reformed musical styles (see below). In other interviews, however, Gencebay repeatedly evokes *68 ruhu* ("the spirit of '68") and the student movements of the 1960s in western Europe,[20] aligning arabesk with a somewhat romantic reading of Western rock. In an interview with Meral Özbek in 1987 he claims as his influences, alongside various Turkish mentors (in particular Abdullah Bayşuğ, Adnan Varveren and Ahmet Sezgin), the revived *gazel* style of Abdullah Yüce, Bach and Elvis.[21] The unlikely presence of Johann Sebastian Bach in Gencebay's list of influences reflects his early training with a Crimean refugee, Emin Tarakcı, in his native Samsun, a man who had received his musical education in the Soviet system. Gencebay is at pains to present a cosmopolitan and intellectual face when discussing the origins of his eclectic music.[22]

When pressed by Özbek to define what exactly it is that makes arabesk arabesk, Gencebay focuses on the use of a large violin chorus, brought back to Turkey by musicians working in the nascent Egyptian musical film industry (especially Haydar Tatlıyay in the 1920s) and appropriated by the singer Sedat Sayın in the 1960s. The reluctance to identify "Arab influence" among well known singers is partly a response to criticisms of arabesk by nationalists (and consequent exclusion from state radio and television), but it arises also from the fact that, whatever arabesk's supposed origins, it is today performed by singers and musicians with a highly cosmopolitan musical awareness. While many arabesk singers, such as Ibrahim Tatlıses, undoubtedly seek to imitate Arab singing styles (prolonging nasal tones on consonants, exaggerating—in relation to spoken Istanbul Turkish—their glottal and guttural qualities, and emphasizing a certain hoarseness), and this imitation is undoubtedly a major component of a "burning" (yanık) aesthetic in Turkish music,[23] others have quite different ideas. Mustafa Keser, for example attempts to imitate the "cotton-like softness" (pamuk gibi yumuşaklığı) of Frank Sinatra and Nat King Cole. The same is true of arabesk instrumentalists. Bağlama players are equally fascinated by electric guitars and sitars, darbuka players by Egyptian, Indian, and Latin popular music rhythm styles.

It follows that it is difficult to define arabesk in terms of style, and that people often disagree as to whether a particular singer is an arabesk singer or something else. The singers don't necessarily provide any help. The odium attached to arabesk by the state and intellectual commentators is such that most singers market themselves without reference to arabesk, preferring other definitions: halk (folk), sanat (art), or, when pressed into a corner, fantezi or taverna. Fantezi generally means a style of popular song with particular emphasis on extended and often virtuosic instrumental passages, while taverna refers to what is essentially a way of performing arabesk on an electric keyboard (usually an Arab-scale Roland or Yamaha synthesizer) plus a rhythm box modified to play Turkish rhythms. Particularly in the 1980s, a period that witnessed an explosion of clubs and bars in outlying districts in Istanbul, the taverna style was an attractive proposition for club owners in that they only had one or possibly two people to pay. Taverna's popularity was eclipsed by new forms of popular music which emerged in the mid-1990s, but arabesk is still described and marketed in many places as fantezi.

What distinguishes this broad area of musical practice from other genres is its emphasis on the human voice: bands provide a predominantly monophonic accompaniment for a single voice. Its singers are generally identified with the predominantly Kurdish southeast of Turkey and with the squattertown peripheries of large cities in the west, where many migrants from this region settle. Arabesk has in recent years shared the popular cultural stage with a significant number of guitar-based forms, notably Türkce sözlü hafif müziği ("Turkish language light music"), Türk popu[24] ("Turkish pop") and *özgün*[25] ("Original"). The latter is a form of protest rock, heavily modeled on *nueva canción* (a guitar-based Chilean genre, drawing on Andean musical forms and closely associated with left protest), that foregrounds overtly politicized lyrics, often adapted from leftist poets such as Nazım Hikmet. While the guitar has introduced distinct and new ways of composing a song, and groups rather than soloists are often involved, the production values of the music industry have become so attuned to arabesk over the last ten years that these different styles leave the recording studio sounding very much like arabesk in key ways. Certainly in 1990 Fatih Kısaparmak's cassettes had precisely those elements which many people identified to me as arabesk: a violin chorus, a means of vocal production focusing on the throat (and the ornamentation that goes with that) rather than the chest (as in the case of earlier *özgün* singers, such as Ahmet Kaya), and lyric themes that were not so much specifically political as sentimental (*aciz*) or pained (*acılı*). The generation of pop singers that emerged in the mid-1990s (in particular Mirkelam, Kayahan, Izel, Volkan Konak) are also the products of a music industry that still thinks and operates in terms of arabesk production. The leftist-Kemalist intelligentsia are keen to label contemporary pop as a kind of speeded-up arabesk, identifying the roots of both in the aggressive liberalism of recent decades.[26] The notion of *popbesk*, which explicitly links the two, has gained some currency as a result.

CRITIQUE

Definitions, critiques, and histories of arabesk are intertwined, and are often clearly and explicitly politicized. It will be clear from the above that musical practice itself provides plenty of room for maneuver. On the right, or rather those sections of the right that have moved against Ataturkian secularism over the last decade, arabesk has its origins in the degeneration of the art music tradition. In this scenario, art music stands as a useful metaphor of the Ottoman cultural legacy that has been squandered during seventy years of secularist republicanism. Yılmaz Öztuna's recent history of Turkish music provides a good example.[27] In this account, arabesk is represented as the inevitable result of the popularization of the art music (*sanat müziği*) genre, the influence of Egyptian film, and the heavy-handed attempts by modernist reformers in the early decades of the Republic to invent and then propagate a music which symbolically turned its back on the Ottoman past and celebrated instead an Anatolian rural "culture" (*hars*). With the conservatories that propagated art music closed down and art music banned (albeit briefly) from the radio airwaves, art music went into decline. Öztuna implies that Turks were inevitably going to identify with this music, since it was the only one that provided any cultural continuity with the past. The problem was that it had by now been subverted by Egyptian film music and lost any claim to intellectual legitimacy: the result was a lack of rules, a lack of compositional skills, and an unruly emphasis on vocal skills and large, hybrid orchestras.[28]

Öztuna identifies and interprets a number of issues which are undoubtedly extremely significant in the emergence of arabesk. First, the Ottoman urban music tradition now thought of as art music or sometimes as palace music (*saray müziği*) always had one foot in the palace and another in urban popular practice. "Elite" music has circulated widely outside of court circles. Following the Tanzımat reforms and the penetration of European trade in the Ottoman domains in the 1860s, a minority (Christian and Jewish) bourgeoisie emerged which constituted a new market for musicians, one with different demands and tastes, which can be identified in the new song forms of Hacı Arif Bey at the end of the nineteenth century. Subsequently this new market was mediated and molded by a relatively extensive music publishing industry and, later, a recording industry.[29] From the turn of the century until the 1930s and the coming of cinema, an emerging Muslim bourgeoisie in Istanbul sought its musical and erotic pleasures in an area known as Dileklerarası (arcades),[30] which rivaled the largely Christian-dominated district of Beyoğlu. Here a syncretic music-hall genre called *kanto* flourished, attracting many of the best musical talents of the time, such as Sadettin Kaynak, Yesari Asım Ersoy, and Refik Fersan, as well as Armenian and Greek women performing bawdy music hall routines and Greek male dancers called *köçek*. It was at this moment, according to commentators operating from the elitist platform, that the art music genre was finally and irreversibly emptied into the popular morass, and thereby lost any claim to cultural legitimacy. By the 1950s many of the remaining classical forms had what we now might identify as mass appeal and mass distribution: the *gazel* (a free rhythm vocal genre) in particular was popularized through the recordings of Abdullah Yüce and Hafız Burhan Sesyılmaz in the 1950s.

The second issue raised by Öztuna is that Egyptian film music, particularly that of Mohammed Abdelwahhab, was of incalculable significance, introducing new ideas and practices into the Turkish popular domain. American musicals were no less significant, to start with—*The Jazz Singer* was shown in Istanbul in 1929—but the supply of American musicals dried up during the Depression years and World War II.[31] Egyptian musicals filled the gap: Abdelwahhab's *Dumua' hubb* (The Tears of Love) was shown in Istanbul in November 1938, but precipitated a ban on foreign-language films. This ban backfired disastrously, since it unintentionally initiated a large industry entirely dedicated to the plundering of Egyptian films and singers. Film directors such as Vedat Örfi Bengü and composers such as Sadettin Kaynak and later Suat Sayın worked in Arab countries (particularly Egypt), bringing back techniques and ideas which were widely imitated.[32] The best composers and singers of the day were involved. Munir Nureddin Selçuk produced and sang in one of the most famous imitations of *Dumua' hubb* in 1939 (*Allahin cenneti,* with Muhsin Ertugrul). Singers such as Hafız Nuri Sesigüzel based their fame in the 1950s on Turkish translations of Egyptian songs. Vedat Yıdırımboğa was famous for his versions of the songs of Umm Kulthum (who was by this time a household name throughout the Middle East), and Zeki Müren made his name with a version of Farid al-Attrache's *Zennübe.*[33] This exuberant appropriation of Arab popular music continues unabated today.[34]

Thirdly, Öztuna is undoubtedly correct in problematizing the long history of state intervention in Turkish music, whether one agrees with his reasons for doing so or not. From the early 1930s, republican ideologues set out to systematically eradicate all traces of what could be defined as Ottoman and Arab. Ottoman music was banned from the radio airwaves from 1934–36 (although why the ban was reversed is unclear). The Darülelhan, the classical music conservatory, was replaced by a conservatory propagating Western classical music and training a symphony orchestra. When radio was nationalized in 1937, attention turned to the production of a "folk" music purged of its supposed urban, Ottoman, and foreign influences. Teams of researchers and archivists began to document a rural Anatolian music with the help of European folklorists such as Bela Bartók. It was not until 1948, with the formation of Muzaffer Sarısözen's famous Yurttan Sesler Korosu ("Voices from the Homeland Chorus"), that such a new folk music was "reinvented" on the basis of what had been collected. A new state conservatory was founded in 1976 to propagate this music: its members still rail against arabesk in their official publications. Seen with the most dispassionate eye in the world, it is impossible not to conclude that the state's musical policies failed to engage with the musical tastes of urbanites or peasants: by the 1940s the habit of tuning radio sets to Egyptian radio was well entrenched.[35]

The left critique of arabesk, which is perhaps most clearly stated in Eğribel and Güngör's books, inflects these facts in a different way, although, inasmuch as they are thoroughly dismissive of arabesk, their critique has much in common with that of Öztuna. It is organized around the assertion that while the state was correct in attempting to construct an egalitarian, secular, and Anatolian culture in music as in everything else, it did so in a heavy-handed and misconceived way. The response of the Turkish peasant was to muddle through, culturally, politically, and economically, as well as possible under difficult circumstances, and in spite of poor leadership. This has until recently allowed the left to praise the popular creativity involved in arabesk but to dismiss it as a cultural "solution." The left critique focuses heavily, for this reason, on the *gecekondu*—semilegal squatter towns that began to appear on the fringes of Turkish cities in the late 1940s in response to urban industrialization and rural modernization programs. The Turkish state has had an ambiguous relation with the *gecekondu*. On the one hand, they brought a market and a labor force to the new industrial areas of Istanbul (and now to the Marmara region), and (as sociologists pointed out in the 1960s and

1970s)[36] introduced the rural peasant to modern urban gesellschaft existence in a semirural but nonetheless well-ordered, well-built environment.
On the other hand, the squatter settlements imposed an intolerable strain
on urban infrastructures and were quickly identified by subsequent sociologists (such as Eğribel) as both the symbol and practice of urban disorder
and unacceptably laissez-faire development policies. In this literature, arabesk
is strongly associated with the *gecekondu* and its semiurban proletariat.[37] This
identification was fixed in the 1980s through the concept of arabesk as *dolmuş*
(shared taxi) music: like the *dolmuş*, arabesk connects the rural, the semirural, and the urban, the periphery and the center, and like the *dolmuş*,
arabesk possesses a kind of meandering vitality that seems to go simultaneously everywhere and nowhere—a perfect symbol of rapid but directionless
and alienating social mobility. Ultimately, for Eğribel and Güngör, using the
language of Frankfurt School Marxism, arabesk encodes and transmits a
process of alienation and leads to passive despair. For them, the leitmotif of
arabesk is *kader* (fate).

Critics on the left have necessarily been particularly attentive to the material bases of arabesk production. Arabesk came into existence in 1969, at
a time when 45 rpm singles were still relatively new in Turkey. As cultural
theorists have pointed out at least since Enzensburger, changes in technologies of cultural production have initially resulted in a radical diversi-
fication of the "ownership" of culture.[38] Arabesk can be seen as the initial
product of the emergence of the 45, and in the mid-1970s of the cassette,
which was particularly significant in the establishment of an indigenous music industry, much of it operating outside of state control. Today in Unka-
panı, the center of the music industry, there are 120 firms producing, according to Özbek, forty to fifty million cassettes a year. Güngör, Eğribel, and
Özbek point to the introduction of *teleks* cassette duplication machines in
the mid-1970s and their contribution to cassette piracy, on which, they imply, arabesk has thrived. For Güngör and Eğribel this is a cause for despair,
constituting yet more evidence of the state's inability to intervene in and control public culture.[39]

Critique of arabesk is not restricted to academic prose. Books, despite
the intense liberalization of the late 1980s and 1990s, are relatively expensive and troublesome objects;[40] while a wide range of musical knowledge
and knowledge about music draws on academic texts, it is by no means restricted to them. Discussions of arabesk draw on a wide range of oral lore,
located in jokes, jokebooks, comics, popular journalism, and cinema, whose
principal focus is the city, especially its entertainment spots and their
denizens. Arabesk is identified with *gazino* bars, restaurant/bars providing
musical and other entertainment, many of which, in Istanbul, are situated
in well-known beauty spots, usually with a view of the sea, the islands, or the
city's bridges. The perception of these bars in written discussions of arabesk

is generally negative. Güngör, for example, relates the development of a *gazino* subculture to the period of political and economic liberalism in the 1950s under prime minister Adnan Menderes. Nouveau riche provincials (*anadolu eşrafları*) who profited from these policies could appropriate pre-existing *meyhane* (bar) culture in the traditional and predominantly Christian pleasure areas of Istanbul, to celebrate their economic success and reflect on their past.[41] Arabesk, which deals in sharp juxtapositions of the traditional, rural, provincial life and modern urbanism, was a convenient symbol of this. Entrepreneurs such as Orhan Gencebay were undoubtedly extremely quick to fill this niche. Academic commentators see the *gazino* as a place of furtive, kitsch pleasures; musicians too refer to the *gazino* somewhat dismissively as the *piyasa* (market), a world in which they are obliged but not particularly happy to live. It is only recently that the role of the *gazino* today in patterns of urban pleasure has been evaluated in more positive terms, in line with the process of intellectual co-option discussed later. Nilufer Göle, a prominent feminist critic, points to the *gazino* (with its music and dance) as a place in which the fundamental contradictions of cultural existence (between men and women, rural and urban, west and east) are explored. In a memorable phrase, she describes it as "a place where men and women belly dance to a *piyanist-şantör* under disco lights in order to work out their urbanite fantasies and Alaturka proclivities. . . ."[42]

The *gazino* is firmly linked in popular discourse to a distinct personality type. The association of arabesk with semiurbanized rural types throwing their weight around in the city is now focused on the remarkable personality of Ibrahim Tatlises—a man of extensive wealth (often included in celebratory lists of payers of Turkish high taxes) but, in the opinion of arabesk critics, of oafish and provincial bad manners. The terms *maganda, kırro,* and sometimes *kabadayı* are used today by critics to describe this "arabesk-type." The term *kabadayı* is a double edged one. Formerly it was a label attached to neighborhood men of honor, who protected the neighborhood and took on significant political roles in times of radical change and uncertainty.[43] Today it refers to self-styled tough guys. The protagonists of brawls in traditional and *gecekondu* quarters of cities are referred to in highbrow newspapers as *kabadayıları,* and such types are widely ridiculed in popular literature and comics. The first real comic *kabadayı* that I have come across was Kadri the gorilla in *Fırt*'s "Tarzan" strip. *Fırt* was one of the most popular and quietly critical Turkish comics to emerge after the 1980 military coup, and its concern with the *kabadayı/maganda* has been taken up in more recent and more overtly critical comics, such as *Leman. Kabadayı* is, however, a term widely appropriated by young male fans of arabesk. For them, the term indicates not just a meticulous concern for male honor and the violence needed to define and protect it, but a minute attention to nuances of speech and accent, dress, the tilt of a cigarette in the mouth. Intellectual

Example 7.1 Orhan Gencebay, opening vocal
line from "Dünya dönüyor." Adapted from Gencebay's notation, published in *Müzik magazin*
(1988): 20.

opponents are quick to associate matters of musical style (*tavır*) with social "type," and link both to Özal's brash, "Eastern" style of political rhetoric.

The complex effects of this highly public critique of arabesk are worth mentioning briefly. Particularly as a foreign researcher, one cannot talk to an arabesk musician without getting sucked into discussions about its value, and whether or not the state and the intelligentsia are right in condemning it. Shortly after one period of particularly intense public debate in 1990, the arabesk star Gökhan Güney addressed a large crowd in one of his public (*halk*) concerts in Gülhane Park in Istanbul. Arabesk, he claimed, is not what they say it is. In fact, he said, arabesk has "everything in it: joy, happiness. . . ." (*Arabeskte her şey var: neşe, sevinç. . . .*) Critique, he implies, relies upon misrepresentation, and proponents of arabesk need to go about representing themselves in a different way. The criticism of fatalism (*kadercilik*) that is often applied to arabesk is a case in point. For liberal-left critics such as Eğribel, fatalism is anathema to the republican spirit, justifying passivity and evidencing a failure to take command of one's own destiny. It also implies a mystification of antagonistic class relations, which in turn reduces the possibility of effective class-based resistance.

Fate is indeed a recurrent theme in many arabesk songs, but in many the concept of fatalism is examined from different critical angles. A useful example is the song "Dünya dönüyor," from Orhan Gencebay's 1987 cassette *Cennet gözlüm*.[44] In an interview with *Müzik magazin* he states explicitly that the song questions fatalism, and promotes the idea that one has to pick oneself up after misfortune and get on with life:

> I'll put it like this: as far as I can see, people love one another, and get together. So far, so good, but after they split up, they render the world unlivable for themselves [*dünyayı kendilerine yaşanmaz haline getiriyorlar*]. As far as I'm concerned, this is very wrong, because life goes on. In the light of these considerations I wrote and composed *Dünya dönüyor*. I mean, I wanted to stress that people should not let themselves go [*kendisini bırakmamasını vurgulamak istedim*]. I think it is a bit difficult, but it turned out to be a nice piece.[45]

Example 7.2 Orhan Gencebay, from "Dünya dönüyor."
Adapted from Gencebay's notation, published in *Müzik magazin* (1988): 20.

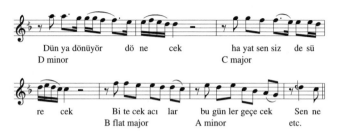

The song text puts the point in straightforward terms, while the music appears to tell a slightly more complex story. It is significant in this context that even self-styled *Orhancis* ("Orhan-followers") find his spoken and poetic utterances banal in the extreme, determining the true value of Gencebay's arabesk to lie in the music. There is a self-conscious complexity to the music (as the quote above indicates), which is a significant aspect of the way in which Orhan is compared favorably, by his fans, to others. A key component of this complexity is the eclecticism of the music: references to rock, salsa, Latin, Egyptian film musics, flamenco, and Western European and Turkish classical genres follow one another thick and fast. "Dünya dönüyor" is, in these terms, undoubtedly a complex song. Within the general exploration of melodic construction and instrumental technique that characterizes Orhan Gencebay's arabesk, the broad organization of the song follows classical *şarkı* form, differing mainly in its extended instrumental introduction. It shares with most other arabesk the principal organizing features of alternating blocks of sound and melodic material, often in a question-and-answer manner. Here this constructive process appears to be particularly closely related to the textual message. The *zemin* and *zaman* sections, before the higher *meyan* section, present two clearly differentiated themes. One (see example 7.1) is an ascending sequence in a modality (Saba *makamı*) characteristic of Turkish folk music.[46] The other (example 7.2), immediately following, is a descending sequence, underpinned by a chordal harmony and in a tonality which bears some relation to the descending Kürdilihicazkar/ Phrygian tonality identified by Manuel as the bedrock of "Mediterranean harmony."[47] The first accompanies the apparently fatalistic lyric "Say what you will" (i.e., "You can't change anything"). The second accompanies the statement that "the world will turn and carry on turning, life will go on without you, and the pain and these miserable days will come to an end" (i.e., "It doesn't matter anyway"). The instrumentation of these themes in the introductory instrumental passage makes a similarly stark contrast. The first is played on a solo *ney*, a sound intensely associated with popular urban Islamic mysticism, while the second is played on the Western trumpet, a sound with military connotations.

The lyrics and the musical phrases construct, it would appear, a clear binary structure, opposing resignation with optimistic resilience, the *ney* with the trumpet, the Eastern makam system with the Western harmonic system, the quarter-flattened "saba" D with its subsequent effacement in passages of chordal harmony. However, unlike more explicitly representational modal systems, the *makam* system does not specify moods and affects. Turkish musicians feel that one *makam* can represent not one but a range of moods and emotions. The composer himself, presented with a situation in which the binary logic of West and East seems to operate with particular clarity, refuses to be drawn out on the point.[48] The appearance of a binary East/West logic dominates the structure of the song, but the composer refuses to reduce the meaning of the song to this simplistic binarism. On the contrary; each term seems to deconstruct its other. This indicates in the clearest possible terms that musicians and those who interpret their music live in a more complicated world than arabesk commentators suppose: Arabesk cannot be reduced to one set of ideas, or one East-West dichotomy. If anything, "Dünya dönüyor" represents, at least to Gencebay, an ironization of these categories, a refusal to validate them, a desire to show that life is too rich and complicated to be squeezed into these limited representational systems, that resilience and fatalism are connected, not opposed.

In the first instance, what arabesk "represents" depends upon the distinct ideological/critical position taken by those who respond to it (collectively or individually). In the second, the creators of the music are quite clear about the fact that they see their music as questioning and commenting upon dilemmas and cultural problems, and reflecting a multiplicity of viewpoints, even if they are (verbally) unclear about how these ideas are represented in the musical text.

CO-OPTION

Özal's ANAP party took the initiative in co-opting arabesk in the mid-1980s with a move which was entirely consonant with his promotion of a laissez faire economy and the dismantling of the state's patrimonial role in civil society. The managers of the Turkish state in the 1980s sought a more proactive role in the Middle East, which necessitated public symbolic statements stressing the Ottoman past and the significance of the Ottoman state as a European Muslim power. Istanbul, under its ANAP mayor, Bedrettin Dalan, increasingly became a powerful symbol of a golden era. Dalan's planning schemes were focused heavily on restoring the mosques and other Ottoman monuments in the old city, and he broke with traditions decisively by naming new public constructions after Ottoman sultans and not Ataturk. The public emergence of Islam, which was perceived to accompany this process, horrified the secularist left. For the left, arabesk was yet more worrying evidence of this new "hegemony of the periphery."[49] The Özal period was often referred to by Özal's detractors as one of *arabesk politikası,* indicating a certain populist cynicism, cultural confusion, and a deliberate turning away from the principles of Ataturk's secular republic on matters relating to religion. The term also aptly described a new form of political populism in which the co-option of arabesk, along with conspicuous involvement in Istanbul's major football clubs, played a significant role. A ministerial aide spoke of the need to reverse the Turkish Radio and Television ban on arabesk in an article published in *Cumhuriyet* on 12 October 1988.[50] This was followed by a music congress in Istanbul in February 1989 (accompanied by much publicity, and later a weighty publication from the Ministry of Education) at which the possibility of a new arabesk was aired. This arabesk was to lack the element which most offended its critics: its pessimism, sentimentality, and *acı* (pain). The "painless arabesk" was duly launched with all seriousness by an aging arabesk star, Hakki Bulut, and light music composer Esin Engin. This quite clever attempt to simultaneously promote cultural liberalism and to reform in the name of the state failed—since it attempted to remove precisely the element which makes it significant for its fans, its *acı.* For their part, TRT programmers dug in their heels and remained resolute in their hostility to arabesk, although their attempts to stem the tide were soon overtaken by the wave of satellite channels operating outside of the Turkish Radio and Television's cultural guidelines. Arabesk stars, notably Emrah, Orhan Gencebay, Bülent Ersoy, and Ibrahim Tatlises, were courted by ANAP politicians; Emrah and Ibrahim were engaged to perform at ANAP rallies, and their songs were used to promote pro-ANAP slogans.

This co-option was a matter of substantial dismay to critics of the left. The response of writers such as Belge, Özbek, Göle, and Karakayalı to this move, writing in "popular" intellectual journals such as *Istanbul, Birikim,* and *Toplum ve Bilim,* amounts to a strategy of counterrepresentation to challenge the center-right's cultural hegemony from within.[51] There is a nostalgia involved in this project. The potentially oppositional qualities of arabesk have now been subverted by the fact that arabesk appears to many to have been absorbed into the establishment, and the public presence of arabesk stars, and even the music they sing, seems to have changed to accommodate this fact. Quite independent of the "painless arabesk" movement, the lugubrious and solitary melancholy of Müslüm Gürses appears to have been "replaced" by the up-tempo, cheerful arabesk of Ibrahim Tatlises and Emrah, with cassettes that even include brief spoken dialogues between the singer and a woman.

Meral Özbek's remarkable book, *Popüler kültür ve Orhan Gencebay arabeski* (Popular Culture and Orhan Gencebay's arabesk)[52] is very much a product of this particular moment. What makes this book unusual is the fact that Özbek is one of the first commentators to take the singers and their songs seriously enough to actually engage in dialogue with them, even though the candidate for this treatment is the one star who has remained somewhat aloof from current developments (never, for example, appearing in public concerts) and has consequently attained a moderate degree of respect among Turkey's intelligentsia. The critical apparatus of Frankfurt School Marxism, in which mass culture (*kitle kültürü*) is seen as false consciousness and diversion, is replaced by that of the British New Left, who were also dismayed, from the 1950s on, by the failure of the left to take popular culture seriously enough as a means by which and through which progressive social transformations might be effected. The extensive use of the Gramscian theories of Raymond Williams and Stuart Hall allows Özbek to see arabesk not as a message which purely and simply speaks the unmediated experience of a particular class, but as a cultural field in which the power struggles of everyday life are played out. Its messages will inevitably be contradictory, since it is a field of simultaneous resistance and coercion (*hem direnme hem de bir boyun eğme alanıdır*).[53] The contradictions it gives voice to are not those between traditional and modern, rural or urban, but between capitalist rationality and a more progressive *paylaşımcı rasyonalite* ("rationality of sharing").[54]

After setting out her theoretical premises in detail, Özbek anxiously combs through Orhan Gencebay's life story, songs, and films for evidence that the themes of emotion, love, and fate are metaphors for, or rather vehicles of, popular cultural utopian thinking. When it comes to the crunch, in the extensive interviews at the end, Gencebay himself refuses to acknowledge the faintest possibility of this: Özbek at one point invites him to talk about the film *Batsın bu dünya*, which, he agrees, contains his most "oppositional" (*muhalefet*) song, and has a story which presents in unusually forceful terms the traditional plot concerns of the virtuous poor man pitted against the corrupt rich man. However, in the final analysis, Gencebay argues, it is a film not about class or power but sensitivity (*hassasiyet*) and love (*aşk*).[55]

This exchange illustrates some of the complex dynamics of the discursive invasion of musical sounds mentioned above, located as they are within a distinctly new kind of engagement of star and cultural commentator. Two quite independent and apparently incompatible discursive frameworks have been constructed around the musical text. For Gencebay, *Batsın bu dünya* is about *hassasiyet* and love, for Özbek it is about *muhalefet* and resistance. It would be quite erroneous to privilege authorial intention here; in the absence of a systematically verbalized theory of musical affect available to musicians, the verbal elaboration of authorial intention is never going to constitute anything more than another discursive invasion of the music. Gencebay's interviews, indeed, draw heavily on the "official view," although recasting it in more positive terms. For Gencebay, there is such a thing as arabesk, which does have a demoralizing effect on the Turkish people; there is a popular music which imitates Arab music; there is a music of the *gecekondu* and the *dolmuş;* it's just that what he does has nothing to do with it. Özbek also, although in quite different ways, draws upon and recasts the same critique. As with many Gramscian intellectuals who are currently attempting to rethink popular culture, she sees arabesk in dichotomous and interventionist terms framed around somewhat sharply defined questions: political acceptance or rejection? artistic success or failure? So while these two discursive invasions of the musical text are in many ways irreconcilable, in others they reproduce many of the features of the more general critical discourse.

In this more general discourse, both critique and co-option of have been driven by a kind of reverse essentialism. Critics initially saw arabesk as a kind of unacceptable Orient lurking on the peripheries of a Turkey whose modernity and Westernity were inseparable aspects of the state's self-definition. The Özal government sought to reintegrate arabesk into cultural and political life as an aspect of an East that had been excluded by an over-powerful and undemocratic state apparatus. Arabesk music and arabesk musicians have consequently been woven into the endlessly elaborated and contradictory themes of Middle Eastern modernity by those who appropriate it: West versus East, the need to shed the past versus the need to remember; the imperative of adaptation and change versus the dangers of imitation. As Rabinow suggests, reverse essentialism does not transcend the basic dichotomies posed by essentialism, and the dominant means of representing arabesk leave most of its basic terms in place.

This chapter has attempted to illustrate some of the more critical counterdiscourses in arabesk thinking, represented in particular by the voices of articulate musicians such as Gencebay reflecting on his own music and writers such as Özbek identifying a plurality and hybridity at the heart of the music—approaches which transcend some of the sterile representational binarisms that, at first sight, arabesk appears to encode. These more questioning and, in some sense, less conclusive representations emerge in a space shaped by the music's rich and often dissonant multitextuality, and the play of power that has taken place between the Turkish state, the intelligentsia, the musicians, and the music industry. This is a music which has never merely "spoken for itself."

NOTES

This chapter has greatly benefited from readings in various forms at the Department of Sociology, University College Cork, the School of Music, The Queen's University of Belfast, the Middle East Centre, St. Anthony's College, Oxford, and discussions with Meral Özbek and Orhan Gencebay.

1. Edward Said's *Orientalism* (New York: Pantheon Books, 1978) has by now generated an enormous secondary literature of its own. James Clifford and George Marcus's *Writing Culture: The Politics and Poetics of Ethnography* (Berkeley: University of California Press, 1986) focused an already well-established sense of unease on the part

of anthropologists that ethnographic practice constructed Others in ways that were far from neutral, and James Clifford's writing continues to generate heat. That Others become embroiled in colonial and postcolonial representational regimes has been an important aspect of the discussion. What anthropologists might do to extricate themselves and their ethnographic Others from the problematic consequences of this involvement is far less clear. For one of many recent critiques of anthropology's "representational turn," see Allison James, Jenny Hockey and Andrew Dawson, eds., *After Writing Culture: Epistemology and Praxis in Contemporary Anthropology* (London: Routledge, 1997).

2. See Homi Bhabha, "Signs Taken for Wonders: Questions of Ambivalence and Authority under a Tree outside Delhi, May 1817," in Henry Louis Gates Jr., *Race, Writing and Difference* (Chicago: University of Chicago Press, 1985), 100–125.

3. There is a large literature which addresses these questions from an ethnographic point of view, but Michael Herzfeld's work has been particularly significant. See his *Cultural Intimacy: Social Poetics in the Nation-State* (New York: Routledge, 1997) for a recent discussion.

4. See in particular Bruno Nettl and Philip V. Bohlman, eds., *Comparative Musicology and Anthropology of Music: Essays in the History of Ethnomusicology* (Chicago: University of Chicago Press, 1991), and Stephen Blum, Philip V. Bohlman, and Daniel Neuman, eds., *Ethnomusicology and Modern Music History* (Urbana: University of Illinois Press, 1993). On practices of ethnographic "othering" in ethnomusicology, see Thomas Turino, "Structure, Context and Strategy in Musical Ethnography," *Ethnomusicology* 34, no. 3 (1990): 399–412, and L. Grenier and J. Guilbault, "'Authority' Revisited: The 'Other' in Anthropology and Popular Music Studies," *Ethnomusicology* 34, no. 3 (1990): 381–97.

5. The critique of musicological transcendentalism has, of course, been a major project over the last two decades. See Janet Wolff, "Foreword: The Ideology of Autonomous Art," in *Music and Society*, ed. Richard Leppert and Susan McClary (Cambridge: Cambridge University Press, 1987), 1–12, for an influential contribution. See Jonathan Bellman, ed., *The Exotic in Western Music* (Boston: Northeastern University Press, 1998) for a recent collection addressing exoticism.

6. See Philip V. Bohlman, "La riscoperta del Mediterraneo nella musica ebraica: Il discorso dell' 'altro' nell' etnomusicologia dell' Europa," in *Antropologia della musica e culture mediterranee,* ed. Tullia Magrini (Venice: Levi Foundation, 1992).

7. Theodor Adorno and Max Horkheimer, *Dialektik der Aufklärung* (1944; Frankfurt: Fischer, 1980). I draw on Seyla Benhabib's discussion and critique in her *Critique, Norm and Utopia: A Study of the Foundations of Critical Theory* (New York: Columbia University Press, 1986); see especially 165–223. This notion of mimesis draws heavily on Freudian psychoanalysis, revisiting the Oedipus myth; mimetic representation is universalized and taken out of the historical process in its entirety. Figured as a primordial aspect of the human psyche, representation is placed beyond historical comprehension, and beyond political engagement.

8. See Karl Signell's discussion of late eighteenth-century Viennese Orientalism in "Mozart and the Mehter," *Turkish Music Quarterly* 1, no. 1 (1988): 9–15. Mozart's *Ballet turc* in *Lucio Silla,* his A major piano sonata (K. 331), the violin concerto in A (K. 219), and *Entführung aus dem Serail* were not based on any direct experience of Turkish music but on a distinctly Viennese genre of musical Orientalism. The subject

of women trapped in the harem was the focus of particular contemporary fascination. Gluck's *Pilgrime von Mekka* of 1764 was an influential model of "Turkish music."

9. Notation and the addition of a figured bass provided the means by which this music could literally be brought into domestic space and sociability. See for example Edward Jones's 1804 transcription of "Lyric Airs, consisting of Specimins of Greek, Albanian, Wallachian, Turkish, Arabian, Persian, Chinese, and Moorish National Songs and Melodies," reprinted in *Turkish Music Quarterly* 5, no. 4 (1992): 20–29. As Ian Woodfield points out, this fascination was exported to the colonies themselves. The transcription of Indian music for keyboard performance was much in vogue among the colonial elite of late eighteenth-century Lucknow. Woodfield, "Collecting Indian Songs in Late 18th-Century Lucknow: Problems of Transcription," *British Journal of Ethnomusicology* 3 (1994): 73–88.)

10. Perrault's "Parallel" of 1697 is translated by Robert Martin in *Turkish Music Quarterly* 4, no. 1 (1991): 10–11.

11. Even in the Enlightenment period, it was not only the music of the East which fulfilled this role, but that of the "New World." See Philip V. Bohlman, "Representation and Cultural Critique in the History of Ethnomusicology," in *Comparative Musicology and Anthropology of Music*, ed. Nettl and Bohlman, 131–51.

12. Ralph P. Locke, "Cutthroats and Casbah Dancers, Muezzins and Timeless Sands: Musical Images of the Middle East," in *The Exotic in Western Music*, ed. Bellman.

13. See in particular Joan Gross, David McMurray, and Ted Swedenburg, "Arab Noise and Ramadan Nights: Rai, Rap, and Franco-Maghrebi Identity," *Diaspora* 3, no. 1 (1997): 3–39.

14. Paul Rabinow, "Representations Are Social Facts: Modernity and Postmodernity in Anthropology," in *Writing Culture*, ed. Clifford and Marcus, 241.

15. See Peter Manuel, *Cassette Culture: Popular Music and Technology in North India* (Chicago: University of Chicago Press, 1990); Lila Abu-Lughod, "Bedouins, Cassettes and Technologies of Public Culture," in *Middle East Report and Information Project* 19, no. 4 (1989): 7–12; and Timothy Rice, *May It Fill Your Soul: Experiencing Bulgarian Music* (Chicago: University of Chicago Press, 1994).

16. Georgina Born, *Rationalizing Culture: IRCAM, Boulez, and the Institutionalization of the Musical Avant-Garde* (Berkeley: University of California Press, 1995), 20.

17. A locus classicus in the discussion of this kind of contradictory multitextuality in musical performance is Barbara Bradby and Brian Torode, "Pity Peggy Sue," *Popular Music* 4 (1984): 183–205.

18. Rabinow, "Representations Are Social Facts," 257.

19. Orhan Gencebay, "Soyleyişi," *Türkiye Yazıları* 54 (1981).

20. Orhan Gencebay, "Benim Müziğim Kurallara Isyandır," *Boom* 2, no. 4 (1990): 34–35.

21. Meral Özbek, *Popüler kültür ve Orhan Gencebay arabeski* (Istanbul: Iletisim, 1991), 182.

22. His 1993 CD *Yalnız değilsin* contains, among other things, a mock Baroque overture. The particular feature imitated involves a rhythmic semiquaver violin motif repeated over a descending walking bass figure. This gives way to a brief elektrosaz solo and then a reprise of the main figure, which reaches a climax with a loud gong crash. The whole is broadly speaking in the Turkish mode Nihavent, and the piece is called Nihavent Üvertürü.

23. For a full discussion, see Martin Stokes, *The Arabesk Debate: Music and Musicians in Modern Turkey* (Oxford: Clarendon, 1992), 134–38.

24. Key exponents in the 1980s include Sezen Aksu, Aşkın Nur Yengi, Ajda Pekkan, and Levent Yüksel, and in the 1990s, Kayahan, Mirkelam, Tarkan, Rafet El Roman.

25. The main names associated with this already dated genre are Ahmet Kaya, Fatih Kısaparmak, and the groups Grup Yorum and Yeni Türkü (the latter a translation of *nueva canción*, meaning "new [folk] song.")

26. Can Kozanoğlu, *Pop cağı ateşi* (Istanbul: Iletişim, 1995).

27. Yilmaz Öztuna, *Türk musikisi: Teknik ve tarihi* (Istanbul: Türk Petrol Vakfı Lale Mecmuası Neşriyatı, 1987).

28. Ibid., 48–49.

29. Dominated by HMV, Odeon, Pathe and Columbia. The first Turkish recording company (Şençalar) came into existence in 1962 (Özbek, *Popüler kültür,* 123). The first music publication was that of Haci Emin Efendi, of the Imperial Music School (Mızıka-i Hümayun) in 1876, rapidly followed by commercial publishers such as Artin, Baba Tahir, and Samli Selim, and foreign publishers such as Comendinger and Karl and Alfred Kopp, in the wake of piano exports to the Ottoman empire (Bülent Alaner, *Osmanlı imparatorluğu'ndan günümuze belgelerle müzik yayıncılığı* [Ankara: Anadol, 1986]).

30. This area stood in today's Şehzadebaşı Caddesi, running between Beyazit and Fatih in what is known as the Old City. Music halls here included the Hilal, Milli, Ferah, Narşit, and Dümbüllü. All were eventually converted to cinemas in the 1930s, a number of which still exist.

31. G. Scognamillo, *Türk sinema tarihi, 1895–1959* (Istanbul: Metis, 1987).

32. Özbek, *Populer kültür,* 153.

33. Nazife Güngör, *Arabesk: Sosyokültürel acıdan arabesk müzik* (Ankara: Bilgi, 1990), 56.

34. A recent example being Neşe Karaböçek's 1993 cassette *Yam yam,* which was circulating widely in south Turkey in both its original Egyptian version and in Karabocek's (unacknowledged) version of it.

35. By 1935 there were already over eight thousand radio sets in Turkey. Güngör, *Arabesk,* 55.

36. See in particular Kemal Karpat, *The Gecekondu: Rural Migration and Urbanisation* (Cambridge: Cambridge University Press, 1976).

37. See especially Taner Senyapılı's *Müzik ansiklopedesi* (Ankara: Uzay, 1985).

38. For a more recent elaboration of this argument, see Chris Cutler, "Technology, Politics and Contemporary Music: Necessity and Choice in Musical Forms," in *Popular Music 4: Producers and Audiences* (Cambridge: Cambridge University Press, 1984), 279–300.

39. Güngör, *Arabesk,* 31; Ertan Egribel, *Niçin arabesk değil?* (Istanbul: Surec, 1984), 21–23.

40. Books have little value as "shelf furniture" in middle-class households in Turkish cities: books and music notation often seemed to me to be tucked away in chests, or in back rooms, to be produced to substantiate an issue of discussion and then hidden away again. One of my music teachers burned his entire library on the day of the 1980 military coup. Although he later regretted doing this, it does indicate a more pragmatic concern underpinning the need to keep books tidied away.

41. Güngör, *Arabesk,* 60.

42. Nilufer Göle, "Istanbul'un Intikami," *Istanbul* 3 (1993): 36–39.

43. Philip Khoury, "Abu Ali al-Kilawi: A Damascus Qabaday," in *Struggle and Survival in the Modern Middle East,* ed. E. Burke III (London: I. B. Tauris, 1993), 179–90.

44. A lengthier transcription and analysis of this song can be found in Martin Stokes, *The Arabesk Debate: Music and Musicians in Modern Turkey* (Oxford: Clarendon, 1992), 181–92.

45. Orhan Gencebay, interview, *Müzik magazin* (1988): 20.

46. Adapted from Gencebay's own notation, published in *Müzik magazin* (1988): 20. The B-flat sign in the first example indicates a four-comma flat (approx. 4/9 tone) and the D-flat sign indicates a one-comma flat (approx. 1/9 tone, although in practice this is played as a slightly bigger interval, in conformity to Arab art music practice). One crotchet = 116, and the notation is transposed up a minor seventh (plus an octave) from the recorded version. The chords are my own addition.

47. Peter Manuel, "Modal Harmony in Andalusian, Eastern European, and Turkish Syncretic Musics" *Yearbook for Traditional Music* 21 (1989): 70–95.

48. Interview with the author, 4 August 1995.

49. I am indebted to Bahattin Akşit of the Middle East Technical University, Ankara, for this comment.

50. It was difficult to establish what the TRT "ban" actually consisted of, and how it was worded, if indeed it was worded at all. The 1948 law prohibiting the public broadcasting and performance of "foreign" music lay in the background, selectively mobilized according to changing political circumstances. For programmers in the folk and art music sections of the TRT, it would go without saying that "foreign" included arabesk.

51. Belge's article "Toplumsal degisme ve 'Arabesk,'" *Birikim* 17 (1990): 16–23, and Karakayali's "Orhan Gencebay projesi," in *Toplum ve Bilim* 67 (1995): 136–56, are good examples.

52. Op. cit.

53. Ibid., 27.

54. Ibid., 54.

55. Ibid., 220–22.

Scoring the Indian:
Music in the Liberal Western

Claudia Gorbman

The resistance of both filmgoers and film critics to acknowledging the powerful role of music in feature films leads us to associate music with the film's unconscious. As we follow a movie's narrative in the perceptual foreground, music inhabits the shadows of our attention, inflecting our reception of screen events by means of a musical language that has been elaborated over many decades. Film music is also the hypnotist that lulls us into a hyperreceptive state, in order that we receive and identify with the movie's fantasy. If it normally avoids being attended to on a fully conscious level, it resurfaces in the form of a multimillion-dollar industry in soundtrack albums, which, as it were, bring the movie experience back. Film music is like the medium of a dream, forgotten in the waking state; but this medium is itself not neutral. It embodies and disseminates meaning, all the more powerful in not actively being noticed.

This essay examines the musical representation of Indians in westerns. The western owes its enduring popularity to its staging of elemental struggles on the mythic frontier of proto-America, and the Indian plays a key role in representing the cultural "other." The nature of this otherness has changed in tune with social and political history. The Indian served in the 1930s and 1940s as an obstacle to the fulfillment of manifest destiny. In the 1950s and beyond, the Indian continued to be a symbolic repository of American fears, guilts, and preoccupations—few of which concerned actual Native American history or politics. What role does music have in determining the spectator's reception of the other, or better yet, how does music inflect the nature and degree of the Indian's otherness?

ANTECEDENTS: MUSICAL STEREOTYPES AND THE "INDIANISTS"

The western's pervasiveness in literature, drama, painting, film, and other media testifies to its significance in America's ongoing mythic self-definition.[1]

Set in a particular historical period—roughly 1865 to 1900—it embodies a defining moment in America's psychosocial evolution. These years embrace the aftermath of the Civil War, the American Industrial Revolution and the building of the railroads, the ongoing establishment of markets and routes for westward expansion, the apogee of the Indian Wars in the west, and the reservation movement.

The movie western centers on the white male hero in some aspect of the process of pushing ever westward the borderline between civilization and wilderness. Among the hero's adversaries are nature, outlaws, and Indians. In Hollywood, the genre has not treated the many Native American tribes as peoples with their own histories. Indians in the classical western are ahistorical, functioning dramatically in most cases as an "all-purpose enemy ready at the drop of a tomahawk to spring from the rocks and attack wagon trains, cavalry patrols and isolated pioneer settlements."[2] They exist in relation to the narrative structure, not to American history—although, like daytime residue that finds its way into dreams, a good number of Indian characters and events have historical antecedents.

In the classical pre–World War II western, the film score represented Indians by means of a small inventory of stable and unambiguous musical conventions. Accompanying the onscreen Indian savage one usually hears a "tom-tom" rhythmic drumming figure of equal beats, the first of every four beats being accented. This percussive figure is typically heard either played by actual drums or as a repeated bass note or pair of notes in perfect fifths, played in the low strings. Additionally, a modal melody might play above the tom-tom rhythm, sometimes monophonically, sometimes in parallel fourths, often with a falling third (e.g., F-D) concluding a melodic phrase. A more "threatening" variant of the melody line consists of a two-note motif, the initial note being brief and strongly accented, followed by a longer note a second or third lower. Examples of these patterns abound in popular culture, from movies to recorded songs to television commercials.[3]

The Indian-on-the-warpath motif accounts for most Indian music before 1950, but not all. Just as the feminine other in Hollywood cinema appears as a binary set—as either the madonna/wife (accompanied by violins) or the vamp/whore (introduced by a sultry jazz saxophone or clarinet)—Hollywood Indians are manifested either as bloodthirsty marauders or romanticized noble savages. The latter type appears less frequently in the prewar sound western, but his literary antecedents can be found in James Fenimore Cooper and Henry Wadsworth Longfellow.[4] He is the natural man, the emblem of the lost Eden. The film-musical stereotype of the romantic Indian deletes the tom-tom rhythm, typically featuring a modal melody played legato by a flute or strings, accompanied by sweet, pastoral harmonies.[5]

Where did these musical stereotypes come from? Part of the answer is that they descend from a Euro-American all-purpose shorthand for representing primitive or exotic peoples. Musical representation of Turks, Chinese, Scots, and generic peasants since the late eighteenth century have tended toward pentatonicism, rhythmic repetitiveness, and open fourths or fifths. Reviewing these devices in concert music of the nineteenth century, the musicologist Michael Pisani locates a "ready-made toolbox of exotica" for composers undertaking Indian topics for the stage. As of the late nineteenth century, this toolbox included sustained fifths, a "Gypsy-Turk" thumping 2/4 rhythm, the "folk" sound of gapped scales, the suggestion of pentatonicism or modality, and a three-note descending motif, usually as two sixteenths and an eighth note (short-short-long).[6] Pisani finds an example of the stereotypical features as early as 1859 in Robert Stoepel's dramatic symphony *Hiawatha*. Pisani argues that the clichés emerge mostly on the popular stage throughout the nineteenth century. This development was most probably inflected by actual exposure to American Indian song (through ethnographic recordings and Wild West shows) to sound a bit more Indian and a bit less all-purpose exotic. Virtually all the ephemeral music for popular stage entertainments is lost, but it is the clichés developed for these entertainments that make their way into silent movie music collections for movie-house accompanists, such as the Sam Fox volumes of the 1910s and the encyclopedia of Erno Rapee (1924).

The ethnographers' transcriptions (and, later, field recordings) of actual songs of American Indian tribes beginning in the 1880s thus seem to have had a less direct bearing on the evolution of the popular stereotypes. The authentic melodies were, however, appropriated by certain art composers in the period 1890–1920.[7] A digression into these art-song adaptations will prove illuminating. In the context of romantic composers' fascination with the exotic, the music of the Negro and American Indian offered a new source of inspiration as these composers consciously strove to develop an American school of composition. This movement was inspired in part by Antonin Dvořák, who, during his stay in the U.S. from 1892 to 1895, famously declared that such indigenous music could provide "all that is needed for a great and noble school of music."[8]

At the vanguard of the Indianist movement was Arthur Farwell (1872–1951), who published a collection of "American Indian Melodies" for piano in 1901. He adapted ten tribal songs from transcriptions by Harvard ethnologist Alice C. Fletcher.[9] Farwell set these melodies in a nineteenth-century harmonic idiom, thus fashioning more or less conventional salon pieces out of vocal monody from an entirely alien culture.[10] He states in his introduction that his arrangements were engendered by the spirit of the occasion on which they would be sung in their native cultural context. Farwell thus gains a new cachet of the exotic:

> I realized that if the musical imagination could be fired by a consideration of
> the particular legend pertaining to a song, it will give rise to a combination

of harmonies . . . vitally connected with the song's essence, its spiritual significance. . . . Miss Fletcher has also met with a question with which the present writer is often confronted,—namely, is not the musical value of these results due entirely to the harmonic treatment, and not at all to the melodies themselves? An unqualified, almost an impatient "No," is the only response to this question. The harmonic color-scheme is purely the outcome of the melody and its specific religious significance, and is merely an aid to its more complete expression. . . . The final result is the consequence of a trained intellect seizing upon, and expressing in a mode comprehensible to its kind, a feeling already developed in a race whose mode of expression is more primitive, or perhaps merely different.[11]

A century later, the reader of Farwell's comments may find the musical appropriation and his remarks to be a rather bald example of imperialism. As progressive an impulse as this was, does it not have as its end result the self-consciously liberal, high-art equivalent of the tom-tom stereotype that prevailed in popular culture around the same time? Farwell's early songs, as well as those of others in the movement, are sentimental arrangements.[12] Their faithfulness to the Indian melody in the top voice produces little variation from turn-of-the-century convention, aside from shifts in time signature and an often repetitious-sounding upper melody. "The song's essence, its spiritual significance," leading to its "more complete expression," is determined through Farwell's Euro-American sensibility.

But looking beyond the inadvertent cultural imperialism, we recognize here an issue central to any cross-cultural understanding, which we might call the issue of translation or mediation. In what respects can a listener "understand" the musical language of an alien culture without some form of mediation, whether this be the listener's education or a translation in the broadest sense? How can an Osage or Apache chant "mean" to a Euro-American listener? Musicologist Richard Crawford discusses the dialectical tension between authenticity and accessibility: something is always lost in even the most faithful transporting of music from one culture into another, in each stage of presenting original music to a mass audience.[13] To what degree can we consider the transcriptions of the Plains songs, then their harmonizations, faithful? Farwell's final sentence above clearly if self-servingly indicates the problem of bringing such alien music to white America "in a mode comprehensible to its kind."

In all probability, then, the tom-tom and modal stereotype arose in tandem with the Indian conflicts of the nineteenth century and entered popular culture primarily through melodrama, fairs and Wild West shows, and other forms of popular theater. Presumably when the Indian became a stock character on the stage, stock Indian music developed accordingly. Certainly as far as the cinema is concerned, stock Indian music had come into full bloom by the 1910s.[14] Hugo Riesenfeld's incidental music for *The Covered*

Wagon (1923), which was widely imitated in subsequent silent westerns, includes the tom-tom rhythmic pattern and modal melodic figures to accompany appearances of Indians; Riesenfeld's score itself borrowed liberally from clichés circulating in his day.

THE CLASSICAL WESTERN

The coming of sound may actually have pared down and consolidated the already limited range of representations of Indians. For the most part, the Indian in 1930s westerns was a threat, and the music playing behind him was de rigueur stereotypical. The score of John Ford's *Stagecoach* (1939, by the team of Richard Hageman, John Liepold, W. Franke Harling, and Leo Shuken) is a locus classicus of "Indian music" in the pre–World War II sound western, demonstrating how such music functioned as an efficient narrative cue. The main title music includes a few bars of Indian music: the tom-tom motif in the form of fifths in the low strings; and the two-note motif in French horns, joined by trumpets, with a brief section of the treble voices moving in parallel fourths (example 8.1, theme A).

Barely two minutes into the story, soldiers at a cavalry post learn that the telegraph line to Lordsburg has been cut. The villain responsible, and the last word that got through before the line went dead? "Geronimo!" and the Indian theme plays behind the utterance of his name. Much later, during a rest stop on the stagecoach's odyssey from Tonto to Lordsburg, the Ringo Kid (John Wayne) looks off toward the hills. The camera has no need to pan to the smoke he sees on the horizon: we hear a modal melody in parallel fourths, and a pedal point in the lower register (example 8.1, theme B). And so it goes with each reference to the Indians, until the stagecoach is seen from a high angle wending its way through Monument Valley. A sudden pan finally reveals the Apaches on horseback, spying on the stagecoach from a cliff above—accompanied by a fortissimo line of trumpets in parallel fourths, a drum thundering the requisite beat, and trombones (playing the two-note motif) in dialogue with the trumpets (example 8.1, theme C). Wordless throughout the film, and virtually invisible until the climactic chase sequence on the plain, the Indians serve as the faceless antagonist, often signaled by music alone.

Bear in mind that the Indian musical clichés are sonic signs, useful bearers of meaning in the system of classical Hollywood film music, whose overriding drive is to convey narrative and emotive meanings with hyperexplicit clarity. Were the Indian music to stray from the well-established conventions, it would not be doing its job. Both narratively and musically, the Indians are reduced to ciphers, bits of local color, narrative functions. The paucity of musical language for designating the "redskins" stands in direct contrast to

Example 8.1 "Indian music" from the score of *Stagecoach* (1939)

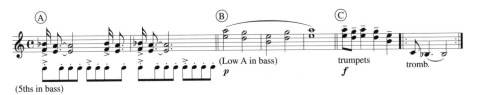

the variety of musical expression for the hero and other individualized characters in their movement through the story.

POSTWAR WESTERNS: THE 1950S AND 1960S

The postwar era ushered in a sea change for the western. Its hero became a man of reflection as well as action. Older, more battered and worn, he was not so certain of "civilized" America's moral superiority and divine right. Like Hollywood's film noir hero, the western hero suffered an identity crisis, his confidence disintegrating and his masculinity in question. The western hero's faltering machismo becomes identified with political uncertainty, with the increasingly questionable prerogative of Manifest Destiny.[15]

As part and parcel of the new psychological and politically relativist tendencies of the period, the liberal western took on the project of humanizing the Indian. *Broken Arrow* (1950) and others of its kind served as catharses for national guilt, portraying Indians as proud, intelligent, misunderstood and oppressed. Many a western would henceforth emphasize Indian culture and traditions—although these in fact remained the creation of screenwriters' imaginations, and all tribes, with a few exceptions, were treated as one, with minor individuations in each screenplay. (Almost all Indian speaking parts were played by whites; Native Americans from various tribes were hired to play members of a given tribe in a particular film. Despite efforts toward "authenticity," the Hollywood Indian remained largely generic.)

It would be simplistic to mark 1950 as the magic moment of the Indian's transformation in the western; there were sympathetic Indian characters before and many unidimensionally evil Indians after. What is new around 1950—and what prompted one French critic to call this year "the 1789 of the western"[16]—is the sheer number of films whose project it was to rehabilitate the Indian to the point of fundamentally altering the prevailing mythology. The liberal western discovers the Indians' humanity; their aggression is revealed as a defense against encroachment on their lands, and against the cruelty and ignorance of white settlers and soldiers. It need hardly be said that this rehabilitation of the Indian partakes in "the usual

American fascination with its own exercise of power and, in the aftermath, its own grief, anger and remorse."[17] The true subject of the liberal western is rarely the Indian, but the white hero as reflected in the Indian's otherness. The Indian remains a foil for the hero's negotiation of his historical/cultural identity.

Broken Arrow, A Man Called Horse (1970), and Dances with Wolves (1990) are films about a hero who slowly befriends a tribe considered by the whites to be savagely hostile. Each hero learns the ways of the tribe; each falls in love with an Indian woman and marries her. The Indians emerge as people with honor, and white society is revealed in its boorish, destructive ignorance; the hero finds himself in a tragic position between the two cultures. Broken Arrow is a manifestation of postwar antiracism. It is also a product of its time in its political optimism: its revisionist history-making depicts fair treaties being drawn up between the U.S. government and the Native Americans as equals. A Man Called Horse was released at the height of the U.S.'s military involvement in Vietnam and Cambodia; the Indian community it depicts stands metaphorically for both Southeast Asia and a hippie fantasy counterculture— organic, natural, spiritual, psychedelic, and free of the constraints of conventional society.[18] Dances with Wolves, for its part, responds to 1980s cultural debates on postfeminism, multiculturalism, and environmentalism. The truly civilized society here belongs to the Sioux; white society is shown to be decadent, mad, and brutal.

To return to 1950s westerns: their Indians variously represent actual Indians (in the new spirit of historical revisionism), Communists (in the context of the McCarthy era), and African Americans.[19] On this latter point, Thomas Cripps traces the depiction of blacks in postwar American cinema and shows that the touchy subject of race emerged in disguised form. Since so many African Americans had fought in the armed forces overseas, political pressure came to bear on the studios to move beyond the degrading stereotypes for black characters. A number of postwar films began to portray black characters and racial problems with new depth, in a cycle of message movies that included Pinky (1949), Intruder in the Dust (1949), and No Way Out (1950). But race relations could be treated with even more frankness once safely couched in the guise of a western. So movies from Broken Arrow and Devil's Doorway (1950) to Flaming Star (1960) explored in a remarkably candid way the virulent hatreds of white society.[20]

Delmer Daves's Broken Arrow is emblematic of the new meanings overdetermining the Indian. Tom Jeffords (James Stewart) comes upon an injured young Apache in the wilds. Instead of killing him, he realizes that "Apaches have mothers who cry over them too" and nurses him to health. "Tired of all the killing," Jeffords learns Chiricahua Apache ways and succeeds in befriending the Apache chief Cochise (Jeff Chandler), as well as marrying an Apache girl, Sunseeahray (Debra Paget). He serves as an intermediary between Cochise and General Howard, whose mandate is to establish peace in Arizona. Racist whites raid the Apaches, killing Jeffords's pregnant wife in the process and threatening the fragile truce. But Cochise exercises even greater conciliatory restraint than the sacrificial liberal Jeffords, and resolves to keep the peace: "As I bear the murder of my people, so you will bear the murder of your wife."

The success of *Broken Arrow* spawned many socially conscious westerns in the 1950s which rewrote history in terms of peaceful coexistence and reconciliation, and which seriously probed racism in dominant white society.[21]

POSTWAR WESTERN MUSIC: 1950S AND 1960S

Once the narrative roles of Indians began to diversify, what happened to the musical score? Logically we might expect that the simple labeling function of the classical "Indian motif" would no longer suffice. But in the 1950s liberal western at least, musical representations evolved slowly at best.

Hugo Friedhofer's score for *Broken Arrow* is typical in remaining well within the established traditions of Hollywood Indian music. The principal motif for Cochise and his tribe undergoes wholly conventional treatment, and the music for Jeffords's romance with his Indian beloved, in its flute-and-strings modal sweetness, is also in keeping with the pastoral side of the Hollywood Indian. The greatest departure from prewar western scores arises from the story's very emphasis on the Indians. Since the narrative dwells at some length on action in the Apache village, the score is called on to elaborate upon characters, moods, and action with greater variation than the classical western score demands.

Broken Arrow: Apache Theme

The main title theme is predictably modal. When the story begins, we hear it almost immediately, as Jeffords comes upon the injured brave (example 8.2). In the course of the film this theme comes to be associated with the Apaches. As Jeffords nears the entrance to Cochise's stronghold for the first time, the dramatic tension is expressed in the form of a slow tom-tom beat played forte by the tympani, as horns play a repetitive motif in tritones. Finally, as he rides over the pass to discover the Indian village below, the main title motif is announced in full force, now accompanied by the customary tom-tom figure, up to tempo, on tympani. The theme is also heard when Cochise tells Jeffords that Sunseeahray's parents will not consent to his marrying their daughter. Here the theme conveys the stern Apache law, in effect representing the absolute racial/ethnic boundary and the futility of Jeffords's desire. Until, that is, Cochise admits he's only kidding, the parents have accepted, and the music playfully segues into something lighter. At the climactic

Example 8.2 Apache theme from *Broken Arrow* (1950)

peace conference bringing Cochise and the other Apache leaders together with Jeffords and General Howard, we hear the Apache motif: fifths in the bass, the melody played by the brasses in fourths, and more dissonances in a particularly serious and grave arrangement.

Diegetic Indian Music

Jeffords makes his pitch to Cochise about allowing the U.S. mail riders to travel through Apache territory in peace. When they have finished their business, Cochise invites him to stay overnight in the village, where a ceremony happens to be in progress. This scene has been described by Anne Dhu McLucas as the film's "big musical surprise,"[22] for what we see and hear are the actual music and dance of the Mountain Spirit from the girls' puberty ceremony of the White Mountain Apache. It is a surprise because Hollywood cinema as a rule does not worry about authenticity—one chanting voice with drums is just as good as another.

In truth, seeing Indians singing and dancing in a western has the same effect as seeing Indians speaking their language. Such sights show the Indian as the impenetrable other. Their language and music bestow their aura, give them the stamp of authenticity. Sometimes a knowledgeable character— a white old-timer, a half-breed, or an Indian leader—will translate into "American" what is said or sung. *Broken Arrow* adopts the conceit that when we hear the Indians speak English, we are to understand that they are speaking Chiricahua. Some movies after the 1960s provide subtitles as Indians speak. But the singing—whether really that of the tribe depicted or not—is most often unmediated for the white listener.

Recall that Farwell's idealizing harmonizations of Indian tribal songs are in part an attempt to make the songs intelligible to Euro-American listeners. It is curious that such a strategy did not occur to Friedhofer, or indeed to any Hollywood composers at the time. There must have existed a desire to preserve the diegetic music as sound effects, rather than a language to be understood, and simultaneously to retain the clichés of orchestral "Indian music" on the other hand: both strategies keep the Indians alien.

To return to *Broken Arrow*, then: the system of authentic diegetic tribal songs and orchestral modal-and-tom-tom music preserves the basic self/other dichotomy. Someone made a considerable effort to represent Apache culture with a modicum of fidelity. All the same, when it comes to cueing in the filmgoer on an important dramatic development such as the surge of feeling between Jeffords and Sunseeahray when they first meet, just after the colorful ceremony scene, orchestral background music quickly takes over, featuring a celeste as well as the requisite romantic strings.

The Romance Theme

A musical theme is assigned to the romance between Jeffords and Sunseeahray. This features a modal flute melody accompanied by simple harmonies in the strings; in later iterations, flute, oboe, or violins carry the melody (example 8.3, theme A). Curiously, after their nuptial night, a viola dripping with sentiment plays a different, nonmodal (and non-"Indian") melody as Jeffords promises he'll never leave her for his own people (example 8.3, theme B).

Has their marriage canceled out Sunseeahray's otherness? Although the film shows Jeffords now living among the Apache, the music suggests that ethnically the union of white and Indian is white. The music, verbal language, and use of Caucasian actors encodes the hybrid sexual union as being assimilated not to Indian but to white culture—signifying encompassment of the other by the (white) self.

The second, romantic melody is the theme upon which the film ends. Sunseeahray has been killed in the white men's ambush, and as Jeffords rides off into the future, his heart full, violins play their nonmodal romantic theme. When push comes to shove, Friedhofer seems to suggest, local color must cede to *real* musical language.

Friedhofer's soundtrack for *Broken Arrow* is nuanced and expressive, well ensconced in the late-romantic tradition of the classical film score. Other liberal westerns, with rare exceptions such as David Raksin's modernist sound for *Apache* (1954), treat Indians in much the same way, with only slight variations on the musical stereotypes described.[23]

The basic set of conventions continues to characterize "Indian music" of the 1950s and 1960s. Toward the end of a thousand-mile trek upriver in *The Big Sky* (Howard Hawks, 1952), the frontiersmen's boat becomes entangled in brush and trees. Hope wanes; and as if this misfortune did not already spell doom, Indians appear on shore. Low bass notes and a drumming in fours supply the menace music. The Indians do not attack immediately; over the tom-tom rhythm we hear a minor-modal melody. Then the moment of recognition occurs: the Indians are friendly Blackfeet, coming to aid the travelers and trade with them. Triumphantly the melody switches into major, then segues into happy western frontier music. The same melodic motif thus works

Example 8.3 Romance themes from *Broken Arrow* (1950)

for both moods; instrumentation, mode, and presence or absence of the tom-tom musically define the difference between friend and foe.

THE 1970S

We have noted that the humanizing of the Indian occurred more slowly in musical scoring than in on-screen characterization, and it is intriguing to speculate on reasons for Hollywood music's conservatism. Composer Dimitri Tiomkin (responsible for scoring some of the most famous westerns of the 1940s to 1960s), when asked in the 1950s why less stereotypical music should not be used to represent Indians, responded that audiences simply wouldn't understand who was who on the screen. Indeed, one constantly has to wonder why the neoromantic style persisted as long as it did in Hollywood's musical language—as well as the stereotypes for actions, ethnic groups, gender, geography, and social class that evolved within it. The classical model was driven by the desire to cement musically the meanings onscreen, and thus became highly codified, calling on a style of music that antedated the musical modes of the day. Not until a series of structural shifts—the Paramount decree and the reallocation of capital in the film industry;[24] the gradual transition to younger generations of composers influenced by television, jazz, and rock 'n' roll; and the entry of film studios into the recording industry and their consequent strategy of marketing soundtracks as commodities in themselves—did the unity, redundancy, and stylistic conservatism of the traditional western score begin to loosen its grip. Beyond 1960 it is difficult to make generalizations about musical coding of Indians in westerns. To be sure, the Indian stereotypes continued to prevail in all the audiovisual media, but new scoring solutions arose as well—especially in the liberal westerns where the Indian was no longer the faceless enemy.

In the late-1960s western, the Indians' floating symbolic significance moored itself onto both Vietnam and the hippie generation, notably in the cluster of films including *A Man Called Horse* (Elliot Silverstein, 1970), *Little Big Man* (Arthur Penn, 1970), and *Soldier Blue* (Ralph Nelson, 1970).

Soldier Blue stars Candice Bergen as Cresta Lee, a tough, wisecracking beauty who has lived with the Indians. Ultimately, despite her efforts to warn the Cheyenne, the Army invades the Indian village and slaughters everyone there (historical referent: the Sand Creek massacre of 1864), in a thinly veiled evocation of the 1968 My Lai massacre. By the end, both Cresta and her companion, Soldier Blue, converted to pacifism by witnessing the carnage, look like hippies fresh from Woodstock. The inept score by Roy Budd is a study in repetitiveness, in a minimalist folk-inflected form of classical Hollywood-era hurry music.

A Man Called Horse is richer both dramatically and musically. Richard Harris plays a bored English nobleman on a hunting trip in the American frontier in the 1820s. A party of Sioux capture him with a lasso, and thus name him Horse as they bring him to their encampment. He is awarded as a slave to old Buffalo Crow (Dame Judith Anderson), chief Yellow Hand's mother. Little by little, Horse gains respect in the village, and also wins the love of Running Deer, the chief's sister. He marries Running Deer after his initiation and purification by the excruciating Sun Vow ritual. A devastating Shoshone attack kills many in the village, including Yellow Hand and Running Deer, and only through the British military strategy and prowess of Horse do the Sioux remain unconquered. His wife dead, he is resigned to return to the world of white society.

A Man Called Horse has a unique tone among the liberal westerns; one might call it faux ethnographic. The Sioux are depicted as primitively violent, and they define family and community in a decidedly foreign way. The film strains to give us the feeling of shocking immersion in an alien culture. Sioux language is not translated by the use of English-speaking actors (as in *Broken Arrow*) or by subtitles (as in *Soldier Blue* or *Dances with Wolves*); occasionally, but not always, Horse's French sidekick Baptiste will translate into broken English.

But of course the viewer does understand everything that needs to be understood, through a combination of mediating forces: Baptiste's occasional oral translations, the meanings embedded in the mise-en-scène and editing themselves, the Indians' frequent expressive use of hand signals instead of speech, and their body language. The film is predicated, it seems, on the notion that body language is universal. The best "speakers" of it are the old woman—played not by a Sioux but by a famous British actress—and Horse's bride—played by Corinna Tsopei, a Greek heiress and Miss Universe of 1964.

But beyond the undeniable fact that the film is a white self-idealizing fantasy—after all, it has a white protagonist who rises to greater success as a warrior than any Sioux in the story[25]—there persists the novelty of its effort to preserve the Indians' otherness by means of the hero's trajectory through it. Jeff Chandler would have no role here as the eloquent and earnest statesman he plays in *Broken Arrow*. The acceptance James Stewart acquires through politeness in *Broken Arrow*, Richard Harris acquires only through the passage of time, tests of courage, and great physical pain in *Horse*.

Leonard Rosenman's music matches this pseudoanthropological project.

For the first time, a relationship is drawn between onscreen chanting/drumming and the composer's background score. Rosenman cast his score in a distinctly twentieth-century idiom, well beyond conventional tonality (with the exception of a major-key choral theme). For the most part, the filmgoer has no easy tonal language to fall back on; the score alternates between Indian chanting and modernist choral/orchestral music. Furthermore, key sounds from the Indian chanting carry over into the background score: singing voices, and the Indian flute, rattle, drum, and high-pitched whistle.

In short, Rosenman's score *translates* the Indian music. Take for example a scene early in Horse's life among the Sioux. The hobbled Frenchman Baptiste has agreed to teach Sioux ways to Horse in hopes that the two might eventually escape together. A montage shows the passage of summer to winter, during which we see villagers drumming, singing, and dancing, animals in nature, Horse at work, and Baptiste teaching warrior skills to Horse. The authentic diegetic chant heard at the beginning of this montage, over the images of chanting tribesmen and women, segues into Rosenman's background score, here featuring the orchestra with a male chorus singing a modal melody in unison. The instrumentation includes the Indian drum, rattle, and flute heard previously in crowd scenes of Sioux music-making. The strings play a chord using the first, second, and fifth tones of the scale, in an interesting repeated rhythm. A women's chorus joins the men's, singing a modal melody in counterpoint to the men's. They sing in "ha-ya" syllables, and the men's line imitates the Sioux tradition of vocal pulsation on the longer notes. The sequence is therefore predicated on an audition of the actual chant, then segueing into a westernized "version" that retains some original features. It de-alienates the Indians (on white terms).[26]

What is lost in this musical translation, and what is gained? Rosenman falsifies the original, but not as flagrantly as did the tom-tom formulae that held sway in film music from the 1920s to 1960s. His music represents the Sioux chants through a western filter, making it readable for viewers. Reading a translation is, of course, a far cry from learning the original language itself, and the cultural translation necessary to make a linguistic translation readable is always political. But given that a translation is always itself a reading, Rosenman's score is new in being a reading at all, rather than a series of clichés. Perhaps this is the farthest a Hollywood score of the era could go without becoming incoherent and unreadable.

Once the film has identified with the Sioux via Horse's relationship with them, the Shoshone come to fill in as the racial other. Rosenman's musical treatment of the two Shoshone raids is interesting in this regard. In the first, just outside the village, Horse jumps from a rock and surprises an attacker. An Indian whistle trills, and stridently dissonant sounds from the orchestra are heard. The high point has yet to come: once he has killed the second marauder, a number of Sioux spectators have arrived from the village, and he knows he must scalp the victim to show his membership in the tribe. As he does so in emotional agony, we hear a climactic blare of trumpets in parallel fourths sound a descending motif. Thus, in representing the other, Rosenman reverts to two tried-and-tested kinds of musical language: the parallel-fourths technique from the classical western, and strident atonality (thus the Shoshone as other is represented by clichéd modernist tropes). This scene signals a turning point: for when Horse triumphantly reenters the village to general acclaim, we hear not the usual orchestral pomp befitting the conquering hero, à la Korngold, but Indian whistles and drumming and above all the shouting and chanting of the Sioux villagers.

As the tribe mourns their dead after the climactic battle near the end, a similar wonder occurs. No war requiem plays here, no 120-piece orchestra in a minor key externalizing the grief of a people. Instead, we hear the big Indian drum being beaten, and the sound of the medicine man's chanting and his rattle. The real Indian music has been allowed to carry the emotion of the scene, and does so effectively, since the score has accustomed us to that music and its performers. We have learned to read a bit in a foreign language which has become ours. It no longer acts as sound effect but as music.

THE 1980S TO PRESENT

Following a period of hibernation, a spate of westerns on film and television revived the genre beginning in the mid- to late 1980s. *Lonesome Dove, Dances with Wolves, Tombstone, Unforgiven, Wyatt Earp, Posse, The Ballad of Little Jo*, and others have continued to examine and revise the myths through the lenses of contemporary concerns. *Dances with Wolves* (Kevin Costner, 1990) owed its box-office success to its combination of political correctness, compelling story, stunning cinematography, star actor-director, and lavish score by John Barry, which became a best-selling soundtrack CD. The film draws on precisely the same strategies as any liberal western since *Broken Arrow*. The white protagonist—the film's liberal—comes to know the nobility and wisdom of the Indians, mourning their vulnerability in the face of advancing white civilization. As in *Broken Arrow* and *A Man Called Horse*, the hero of *Dances with Wolves* virtually becomes an Indian but, in the end, leaves the doomed tribe to wander the white world.

Dances with Wolves offers itself to a variety of different readings, ranging from current American preoccupations with gender roles and masculinity to dwindling natural resources and environmental quality, multiculturalism, the encroachment of big business and government on daily life, the loss of community in American life, and, incidentally, Native American rights. It pits the meaningless, bureaucratic, greedy, wasteful, stupid culture of the U.S. Army against the unified culture, generosity, intelligence, gentle humor, and respect for the earth that characterize the Sioux. In an ironic reversal of their position in classical westerns, the Indians here represent traditional American community and values. They discuss important matters in town meetings; the chief listens to their reasoned arguments and makes decisions that reflect a consensus. Unlike the Sioux in *A Man Called Horse,* these Indians are reasonable and well groomed—the original small-town conservatives.

John Barry's score hails from the grand, lush, neoromantic 1930s tradition of Korngold and Steiner, which continues into contemporary movies with John Williams, recent work of Thomas Newman, and others. It is replete with beautiful themes that bestow narrative clarity and emotional force on the story. *Dances with Wolves*'s host of themes include the main title, an expansive motif for Dunbar's travel through the west, a 3/4 melody for the wolf Two-Socks, a lush "vista" theme (heard when Dunbar first beholds the Sioux village below him, and also on first sight of the huge buffalo herd), a theme for the buffalo, a theme for the romance with Stands-with-a-Fist, and a theme for the Pawnees.

The most striking difference between Barry's score and the music for liberal westerns of the 1950s is that the compulsive depiction of Indians as other through the standard background "Indian-music" techniques seemingly disappears. The Sioux receive a musical treatment free of tom-tom and modal-melody clichés. Dunbar's new allies are graced with occasional real Lakota chants on one hand (to establish their authenticity on the musical level) and a set of lovely western-sounding themes on the other.

Theme A (example 8.4, theme A) enters only after Dunbar has befriended the Sioux. At first, when the hero still is unsure of the Indians' motives, we hear a more conventionally modal "Indian"-sounding accompaniment, complete with an attenuated tom-tom rhythm in the bass. But soon the Sioux are treated to the same musical language as Dunbar. The accessibility of this musical language is a key to understanding that the Sioux are "us." In fact, late in the film, when the hero is captured by the newly arrived white soldiers, they ask him his name. He answers in Lakota, "I am Dances-with-Wolves"— and the Sioux theme plays![27] The film has completed the protagonist's metamorphosis, and the musical score has completed the shift in spectator identification by identifying Costner's character with the Indians.

The Sioux may be assigned Euro-American music, but there is another racial other: the Pawnee tribe, whose visual representation (negroid features, mohawk and other fanciful hairdos) strongly evokes blacks and skinheads of 1990. In contrast to the romanticism of the rest of the score, the Pawnees' theme is angular and nonmelodic, and though it is based firmly on the tonal center of E, it is clearly more harmonically indeterminate than the rest of the score (see example 8.4, theme B). The motif is heard at each appearance of the Pawnee. As noted, this isolated use of musical modernism is itself a Hollywood cliché, connoting danger and otherness in contrast to the

Example 8.4 Contrasting treatment of Sioux and Pawnee in *Dances with Wolves* (1990)

standard tonal conventions of the rest of the score.[28] Thus Barry has found a less hackneyed means to replicate Indian otherness in the context of an otherwise traditional musical language, achieving a newly displaced racism.

Once "we" perceive the Army as the second enemy, the music announcing them conveys a number of associations above and beyond their threat. Trombones play a sustained minor triad while a snare drum beats out a simple 4/4 rhythm—not the DUM-dum-dum-dum denoting the tom-tom, but a regular pulsation nevertheless. Is it a coincidence that the score's depiction of the ugly Americans combines conventions of military music with those of savage Indians?

Barry's decision to depict the Sioux in *Dances with Wolves* in the same lush musical language as the good white protagonist is a political one. It turns the tables on the traditional distinctions between self and other—although not completely, as we have seen in noting that the Pawnees are musically scapegoated as the new focus of racism, and also in the sense that the diegetic Sioux singing and drumming remain distinctly alien, "untranslated," more irreducibly exotic than in *Horse,* which effectively trains us to understand it. But in general, the depiction of the Sioux as subjects rather than objects reinforces a reading of *Dances with Wolves* that sees the Indians as the traditional Americans. They stand in nostalgically for the American values that prevailed before meaningful physical communities were replaced by the ersatz community of telecommunications and by intrusive big government. From this perspective, the film expresses dark pessimism about Americans' ability to retain a sense of self-determination at the end of the twentieth century, just as the film's fiction recounts the end of the Sioux as a self-determining nation at the end of the nineteenth.

CONCLUSIONS

The political rehabilitation of the Indians in many westerns since 1950 by no means shifts the central focus on American masculine identity worked out against a mythologized landscape. But the Indians' position changes in this landscape in relation to the hero, and film music's status in the background of consciousness inflects this relation in subtle and forceful ways.

Walter Hill's *Geronimo: An American Legend* (1993) illustrates the suggestive power of music. This film takes up roughly where Jeffords and Cochise
left off in *Broken Arrow.* Its white liberal is Lieutenant Gatewood (Jason Patric),
saddled with the task of negotiating with the legendary Apache leader Geronimo (Wes Studi) for his surrender. The villainous force is the Army, this time
in the person of the Machiavellian General Miles. Gatewood carries out his
duty with distaste, aware that Miles is deceiving Geronimo. An Indian-
hunter (Robert Duvall) sums up Gatewood's predicament: "You don't love
who you're fighting for, and you don't hate who you're fighting against."

Ry Cooder's score creates a global dimension to this chapter in American
history by means of an eclectic selection of folk and "world" musics. In the
context of world music, diegetic Apache chanting takes on an avant-garde
mystique; it sounds *interesting.* Cooder's score, punctuated with reverb and
other electronic effects, includes zither, Indian flutes and/or recorders, the
high-pitched Indian whistle, a plucked stringed instrument like the Chinese
lute, the very low vocal productions of Tuvan throat-singing, period brass
band music, snare drums, Scottish bagpipes, a solo cello playing "Wayfaring
Stranger," traditional American shape-note singing, and the Boston Camerata
intoning a hymn.

How can we make sense of such music in such a setting? First, independent of narrative meaning, this movie was calculated to sell CDs, as commercial films are these days. In the 1980s, as exotic ethnic musics became
raw materials to pass through the mills of global media commodification and
consumption by western markets, a world-music soundtrack began to stand
for a style in itself, defining the film audience as much as the film. Whereas
by the 1930s neoromantic orchestral underscoring took hold as a "universal" language whose effects depended in large part on not being attended
to, the song score of the 1980s and 1990s enables a more immediate social
identification. Hence the success of such movie soundtracks in the 1990s as
Dead Man Walking (1995, a drama with music by Nusrat Fateh Ali Khan and
Tom Waits) and *Addicted to Love* (1997, a comedy that includes a song by the
Malian world-music star Ali Farka Toure in collaboration with Ry Cooder).

Second, if it is still indeed a valid exercise to read textually, Hill's *Geronimo* becomes a meditation on the nineteenth-century nationalistic way of
conceiving identity (the Apaches) in conflict with the twentieth-century dissolution of nations through U.S. imperialistic assimilation and domination
(the Army). Like the Indian in liberal westerns of the last fifty years, Geronimo stands for what America has lost: virility, purity of spirit, community,
commitment.

The liberal western seems to be more and more elegiacal with respect to
this perceived loss. The classical western's Heroic West has ceded to images
of an Aging America, increasingly limited by technological progress, cor-

porate capitalist interests at the expense of people, and ethical relativism. Whereas the prewar Indian was an obstacle to overcome, the postwar Indian has emerged as the ideal American. As we have seen, film music has responded to this changing repository of cultural meanings in a number of ways. For the moment, it seems, the prettiest music belongs to the Indian.

NOTES

1. "Throughout the twentieth century, popular western novels by Zane Grey, Ernest Haycox, Max Brand, Luke Short, and Louis L'Amour have sold hundreds of millions of copies. . . . Western radio shows in the thirties and forties were followed by TV shows in the fifties and sixties. In 1959 there were no fewer than thirty-five Westerns running concurrently on television, and out of the top ten programs eight were Westerns." Jane Tompkins, *West of Everything: The Inner Life of Westerns* (New York: Oxford University Press, 1992), 5.

2. Philip French, "The Indian in the Western Movie," originally in *Art in America* 60 (July-August 1972), reprinted in *The Pretend Indian: Images of Native Americans in the Movies,* ed. Gretchen Bataille and Charles Silet (Ames, Iowa: Iowa State University Press, 1980), 99.

3. A few examples among many are the pop song "Running Bear" (1960), the 1960s TV cartoon song "Powwow, the Indian Boy," the Hamm's Beer publicity campaign of the 1980s, the motif for the Apaches in *Stagecoach* (1939), or Max Steiner's motifs for the Sioux in *They Died with Their Boots On* (1942) and for the Seminoles in *Key Largo* (1949).

4. Cooper's Leatherstocking Tales, five novels written between the 1820s and 1841 (including *The Last of the Mohicans* and *The Deerslayer*), and Longfellow's epic poem *The Song of Hiawatha* (1855) are perhaps the best-known embodiments of this image.

5. Surely the movies contain other Indian types, but these are individual characters: the town drunk, the comical Indian (e.g., the squaw in *The Searchers*), the old sage, the sidekick (e.g., the Lone Ranger's Tonto).

6. Michael V. Pisani, "'I'm an Indian Too': Creating Native American Identities in Nineteenth- and Early Twentieth-Century Music," in *The Exotic in Western Music,* ed. Jonathan Bellman (Boston: Northeastern University Press, 1998), 218–57.

7. Among these composers are Charles Wakefield Cadman, Charles Sanford Skilton, Henry Gilbert, and Amy Beach.

8. See his article "Music in America," *Harper's,* February 1895, 428–34, reprinted in *Dvořák in America, 1892–1895,* ed. John C. Tibbetts (Portland, Ore.: Amadeus Press, 1993), 370–80.

9. Fletcher, an active voice for Indian culture in the late nineteenth century, collaborated with an Omaha Indian, Francis La Flesche, in collecting songs among Plains Indians. Her published collections and studies of 1893 and 1900 (in addition to transcriptions by others such as the musicologist Theodore Baker) were invaluable resources for Indianist composers. Fletcher's songs were transcribed and harmonized with hymnlike piano accompaniments by music historian and theorist John C. Fillmore, who elsewhere wrote "how monophonic Indian music could be harmonized and made more palatable to cultured tastes" (Pisani, "'I'm an Indian Too,'" 242).

10. Farwell's passion for Indian tribal music continued all his life. Some of his later compositions are remarkably daring in their departure from Euro-American convention and their exploration of tribal song patterns. The most "authentic" of his works is a "Navajo War Dance" (Op. 102, no. 1, 1937) for unaccompanied chorus. A recording exists on "Farwell, Orem, and Cadman," *Recorded Anthology of American Music* (New World Records NW 213, 1977).

11. Arthur Farwell, *American Indian Melodies* (Wa-Wan Press, 1901; reprint, ed. Maurice Hinson, Chapel Hill, N.C.: Hinshaw Music, 1977).

12. Charles Wakefield Cadman, for example, had a gift for facile expression, and achieved popular success beyond the reach of the more accomplished composer Farwell. Cadman won fame with his song "At Dawning," which was taken up by the celebrated tenor John McCormack and eventually sold more than a million copies. Another song, "From the Land of the Sky-Blue Water," did comparably well.

13. Richard Crawford, *The American Musical Landscape* (Berkeley: University of California Press, 1993), 86.

14. Anthologies of selections for silent-film musical accompaniment provide evidence. *Sam Fox Moving Picture Volumes* of 1913, 1914, and 1923, composed by J. S. Zamecnik, include sections on American Indian music. Some of this material is difficult to distinguish from the Chinese and Arabic entries. All include pentatonic composition, and some open fifths; moreover, some of the "Indian" cues do not use the stereotypes outlined here. (The cue "Indian Attack" cited by Pisani does, however, have the standard devices.) The selections under "Indian: West" in Erno Rapee's piano scores in the later 1910s are musically more sophisticated and complex, and also include but are not limited to the stereotypes described. Rapee's selections from various composers include dances, war songs, and scenics.

15. In film noir, the woman is the force that troubles the hero's masculinity. She becomes the displaced focus of investigation, and is often quite literally *fatale*. Very few fascinatingly ambivalent women characters populate the landscape of the postwar western; in fact, with exceptions like *Johnny Guitar*, the woman is nothing if not supportive of her man. (Burt Lancaster beats, drags, and starves Jean Peters in the 1954 *Apache*, until he is finally convinced that she will stand by him.)

16. Yves Kovacs, *Le Western* (1963; reprint, Paris: Gallimard, 1993), 167.

17. I have taken this apt remark out of its original context; it comes from a review, by a Vietnamese-born writer, of Oliver Stone's *Heaven and Earth*. Lan Cao, "The Details Are Vietnamese, the Vision, Guilty American," *The New York Times*, 23 January 1994, H13.

18. Georges-Henri Morin, *Le Cercle brisé: L'Image de l'indien dans le western* (Paris: Payot, 1977), 254. See also Philip French's essay on the changing cultural meanings of Indians in westerns from 1950 to 1970, "The Indian in the Western Movie."

19. "Directors, fearful of censorship if they denounced contemporary injustices (social, economic, or resulting from the United States' imperialist policies in Korea, then Cuba, Santo Domingo, and Vietnam), found in their depiction of outlaws and redskins new ways to construct a satisfactory means of criticism." Ralph E. and Natasha A. Friar, *The Only Good Indian . . . : The Hollywood Gospel* (New York: Drama Book Specialists, 1972), 162.

20. Thomas Cripps, *Making Movies Black: The Hollywood Message Movie from World War II to the Civil Rights Era* (New York: Oxford University Press, 1993).

21. Some films in this cycle include *Devil's Doorway* (Mann, 1950), *The Big Sky* (Hawks, 1952), *Apache* (Aldrich, 1954), *The Last Hunt* (Brooks, 1956), *Run of the Arrow* (Fuller, 1957), *The Unforgiven* (Huston, 1960), *Flaming Star* (Siegel, 1960), and even some of John Ford in the 1960s—*Two Rode Together* (1961) and *Cheyenne Autumn* (1965).

22. Personal communication.

23. Even Raksin's score ultimately invokes the stereotypes. His main theme can sound warlike when accompanied by rhythmically repeated fifths in the bass, and romantic when the strings bring out its lyricism.

24. The Paramount decree was the 1948 Supreme Court decision that brought about the beginning of the end of the Hollywood studio system by forcing the studios to separate their production and distribution arms from their exhibition arms. The aim of the decree was to break oligopolistic control of the film industry.

25. Native American singer Buffy Sainte-Marie said in 1970: "It's the writers' fault. That's what I object to. Hollywood keeps using the same old white writers over and over again. They don't say anything important and they don't know what they're writing about. There's no empathy. Even the so-called authentic movies like *A Man Called Horse*—that's the whitest of movies I've ever seen. Everything they do, everything they write has to go through layers and layers of white cheesecloth and it's all bound up in rolls and rolls of white tape. And it's the audience that ends up getting gypped. . . ." Friar, *The Only Good Indian*, 124.

26. Rosenman's music here bears comparison to Arthur Farwell's 1937 piece, the "Navajo War Dance" cited above (cf. n. 10).

27. In *Dances with Wolves*, dialogue in Lakota is subtitled.

28. Except where a composer has written an entire score in this idiom, in which case the music can become perfectly expressive of moods, emotions, and actions within its own language.

The Poetics and Politics of Pygmy Pop

Steven Feld

Stories begin when a beginning is chosen . . .

Colin Turnbull's death, on July 28, 1994,[1] hurtled me back into lengthy day-dreams about the classes in anthropology I took with him from 1969–71 as a college junior and senior, classes that featured patiently detailed story after story drawn from his years of living with the Mbuti pygmies in the Ituri forest of Congo. Colin was a humanist who came into anthropology from studies in philosophy and religion, and from a substantial background as a skilled keyboardist as well. He was my first model of an anthropologist whose understanding of sociability was nurtured by a deep musical engagement.

Although the anthropology Colin learned at Oxford in the 1950s was largely functionalist and oriented toward the understanding of social institutions and organizations, the anthropology he taught was principally focused on issues of morality and conflict. He was deeply moved by the need to chronicle the experiential ravages of change in a world of rapidly escalating inequalities. What his critics called the romanticism in books like *The Forest People* (1961), *The Lonely African* (1962), or *The Mountain People* (1972) came through somewhat differently in Colin's teaching, as a passionate discussion of why neither Western nor African societies had morally superior claims to the most humane ways of imagining and treating others.[2] As a way of promoting debate on these issues Colin began each of our classes with a reading and critique of the ideas about exchange and reciprocity in Marcel Mauss's *The Gift*.[3]

My story begins with wanting to read and critique *The Gift* yet again, for and with Colin, from the standpoint of the schizophonic mimesis of pygmy music. My reading is about the turbulent morality of today's increasingly blurred and contested lines between forms of musical invasion and forms of cultural exchange. I want to critique Mauss by indicating how acts of schizophonic exchange simultaneously create powerful bonds and produce equally powerful divisions. This is a story about the musical discourses and practices that link colonial and postcolonial Africa to worlds of music, particularly via the new ubiquitous global pop sales genre: "world music."

just as when, without warning,
reading an ethnography opens a space for allegory . . .

It's hard for me to start with thoughts of Colin without opening up a significant moment in the ethnography and ethnomusicology of the Central African forests, namely his exposition, in *The Forest People* and *Wayward Servants,* of the moral vicissitudes of sound in Mbuti cosmology and habitus.[4] Perhaps a brief ethnographic recounting can form a ground against which we can figure some of the complexities of new representational histories, like the ones emergent in the world music subgenre of "pygmy pop."

Turnbull explicates the Mbuti saying *akami amu ndura,* "noise kills the forest," and the parallel saying *akami amu mukira,* "noise kills the hunt," by insisting that they are central to understanding the connection between social organization and ritual in Mbuti life. To draw out this assertion, he elaborates on how Mbuti imagination and practice construct the forest as both benevolent and powerful, capable of giving strength and affection to its "children." For this to happen Mbuti must attract the attention of the forest, must soothe it with the strength of sound that is fully articulated in the achievement of song. "Song is used to communicate with the forest, and it is significant that the emphasis is on the actual sound, not on the words" (259). "The sound 'awakens' the forest . . . thus attracting the forest's attention to the immediate needs of its children. It is also of the essential nature of all songs that they should be 'pleasing to the forest.'" (257). As a cooperative social activity, singing fosters heightened sociability both directed to and in the presence of the forest. The positive position of song in pleasing and awakening the forest ties it to the notion of *ekimi,* of "quiet," central to Turnbull's interpretation of a Mbuti idealization of a benevolent forest that provides all.

This quiet, which Turnbull interprets as the coolness of songs and the highly cooperative process of singing them to awaken and rejoice the forest, directly opposes the force of noise, *akami.* As quiet pleases the forest, so noise displeases it, and Turnbull reads the opposition of *ekimi* and *akami* as indexical to the polarities of sociability. Thus quiet is social cooperation, embodied in good hunting, singing, dancing, feasting. And noise embraces "laziness and aggressiveness and disputatiousness" (278), embodied in ill humor, shouting, crying and anger, bad hunting and death. This noise resonates between human action and a forest that "stops 'talking' . . . a sign that something is very wrong" (259) or becomes silent, *kobinengo,* "an indication of great and imminent danger" (287). The crises announced by noise and silence, where poor hunting, social disintegration, sickness, or death emerge and linger, indicate that the forest is "sleeping." These crises are typically countered by singing; singing both opposes noise and silence and stimulates the forest to resume "talking." More importantly, singing opposes death, the strongest and most destructive form of noise and silence.

which quickly blurs to another point of crossing . . .

I am riding the ferry across Hong Kong Harbor on a bright afternoon in October of 1994. Somewhat distracted by vibrant motions and sounds all around, I am reading Jon Pareles's *International Herald Tribune* review of Madonna's brand new CD, *Bedtime Stories.*[5] In conversation with Pareles, Madonna reveals her artistic desire du jour, a makeover from feisty eroticist to gentle whisperer. "There's lots of ways to get your point across and lots of ways to try and influence people," she says. "You can be aggressive and loud and you can shock people and you can hit them over the head. But then there are other ways. You can subliminally seduce someone. . . . " Pareles tells how Madonna practices this subliminal seduction: of one track he writes, "In 'Sanctuary' pygmylike hoots and throbbing low bass notes frame Madonna's declaration 'It's here in your heart I want to be carried.' "[6]

"Pygmylike hoots?" My mind goes racing ahead, and as soon as the boat lands at Star Ferry I find the first record shop, listen to the just-arrived *Bedtime Stories,* and realize that the material girl—"virtuoso of the superficial" in Pareles's memorable phrase, which Madonna ever so strongly approved of—has once again outdone herself. But before I even hear the song I see that the songwriting credit for "Sanctuary" is shared by Madonna, Dallas Austin, Anne Preven, Scott Cutler, and Herbie Hancock. Herbie Hancock, the famous African American jazz pianist? Yes, his presence is right there in the song's early moments, but soft, in the understructure, the repeating digital sample of musical lingerie swaying gently beneath the satin sheets of Madonna's bedtime voice.

Listeners familiar with jazz recordings of the last twenty-five years will quickly recognize the Herbie Hancock connection upon hearing "Sanctuary." The short digital sample introduced early in the song comes directly from Hancock's 1973 Columbia LP *Headhunters,* the first jazz recording to go gold and until quite recently the biggest-selling jazz album in history. The LP included a remake of Hancock's best-known composition, "Watermelon Man," whose opening is the obvious source material for Madonna's looped samples.

where signatures, careers, and more stories are joined . . .

Herbie Hancock's reputation and the song "Watermelon Man" are closely connected. Hancock's career was launched forcefully by his first LP date as a leader, the 1962 Blue Note album *Takin' Off,* featuring veteran saxophonist

Dexter Gordon. The LP included the first recording of the gospel-tinged "Watermelon Man," a tune that came into much greater circulation and popularity when it was recorded the following year by the Afro-Latin ensemble of Cuban percussionist Mongo Santamaria.

By the early 1970s Hancock's playing extensively involved soul-funk-rock-fusion forms, and he increasingly performed on electric and electronic pianos and synthesizers. His stylistic reorientation to more commercial music was signaled by *Headhunters*. Within a year of that reorientation Hancock's new success was clear: he had three albums on *Billboard*'s pop LP charts, and in the following ten years he recorded numerous commercially successful pop-funk hits, in addition to film scores and more mainstream jazz work. The hit song on *Headhunters* was a composition called "Chameleon." But the surprise of the LP, probably second in airplay, was the remake of "Watermelon Man," cocredited to Hancock as author and Harvey Mason, the band's drummer, for arrangement.

But why does Pareles refer to the sample of this song so indirectly, as Madonna's use of "pygmylike hoots?" In Scott Thompson's liner notes to the 1992 CD reissue of *Headhunters*, Hancock talks about the remake of "Watermelon Man:" "The beginning of the tune, that was Bill Summers' idea. The intro was actually from Pygmy music with Bill blowing in a beer bottle. . . . " Bill Summers, the band's percussionist, is credited on the LP's instrumentation list for playing "hindewho." But this is not the name of an instrument, but rather the onomatopoeic term of the BaBenzélé pygmies of the Central African Republic for the alternation of voice with the sound of a single-pitch papaya-stem whistle. The introduction for "Watermelon Man" was clearly copied from a performance of this instrumental and vocal interplay heard on the opening track of an ethnomusicological LP of 1966, Simha Arom and Geneviève Taurelle's *The Music of the Ba-Benzélé Pygmies*.

Hindewhu announces the return from a hunt, and can be performed solo or duo or multiple, in all cases with or without a group of accompanying singers. Track A-1 of Arom and Taurelle's LP is a solo performance, and this is obviously the recording that Bill Summers heard, and the one he imitated using a beer bottle version of the papaya whistle for the opening of "Watermelon Man."

like "a brothers kind of thing" . . .

In 1985 I called Herbie Hancock and asked him if he felt any legal or moral concern surrounding the *hindewhu* copy on *Headhunters*. He was quite cordial, and quick with his comeback. "You see," he answered, "you've got to understand, this is a brothers kind of thing, you know, a thing for brothers to work out. I mean, I don't actually need to go over there and talk to them, I could do it but I know that it's OK 'cause it's just a brothers kind of thing."

I then asked if musicians could sidestep the music industry and copyright conventions to directly remunerate the sources of their inspiration. "Look," he replied, "we're the people who've lost the most, who've had the most stolen from us. We know what it means to come up with, you know, a sound or a tune, then to have it copped and turned into a big hit or something like that. We've been through all of that. But this isn't like that. This is a different thing, you see, brothers, we're all making African music, that's what I'm talking about."[7]

Comments like these are now routine grounds of political attack. But in what follows my concern is with how such standard polemics might be held aside for a moment so that we might more subtly scrutinize the complexity of Herbie Hancock's subject position. In other words, how else might we inquire about the musical-political-industrial habitus in which particular acts of schizophonic mimesis take place, how might we locate and interpret the discourses which surround their circulation? For in the case of *Headhunters* Hancock obviously did not think he was hunting anyone's head. Besides, his action was hardly unique.

The *hindewhu* appropriation for "Watermelon Man" took place in a Western music industry context where hundreds of performers rather closely "adapt" (the masking yet legally correct term) and thereby come to own other sounds, compositions, and styles without directly crediting the source material or paying the original performers or owners.[8] But, quite significantly, Hancock didn't invoke music copyright law (even as of 1973) on "traditional" songs and their adaptation as his rationale. Nor did he cite industrywide common practice as his justification. Rather, he positioned himself as an actor in a particular moral universe, one that authorizes him to take certain actions and to promote or defend them as politically and culturally acceptable. His statement basically claims the recycling of oral tradition as an African American ethic and aesthetic. This approach is historically consistent with a wide variety of African American citation practices, of which the best-known and most currently discussed is the dramatic copy-and-splice self-referentiality of rap and hip hop.[9]

While Hancock's Afrocentrism was certainly on display, Columbia (now Sony Music) clearly does not operate on the level of "a brothers kind of thing," and it is with this distinction that another set of stories begins. As Herbie Hancock's record company, Columbia/Sony is in the business of musical ownership and financial growth and protection. The specific property that concerns them here is not the cultural property of people in the forests of Central Africa, and the commodity that concerns them is not the out-of-print, high-priced, hard-to-get, UNESCO-sponsored German import LP that happened to be incorporated by one of their artists. This is obviously why my repeated inquiries to various offices at Columbia and Sony about copyright clearance or acknowledgment of the *hindewhu* sound on the Hancock LP and song went unanswered. Ten years later, reflecting both legal and social changes, Madonna's label, Warner Brothers, clearly licensed and paid for the sample used on "Sanctuary" and openly acknowledged the source LP and its owner, Sony Music, and gave Herbie Hancock a coauthor credit in the liner notes to *Bedtime Stories*. Warner Brothers also faxed back to me almost instantly in response to my request for information on their current practice for fair compensation and credit related to use of digital samples.

in a chain of imitation and inspiration . . .

Significantly, Hancock's prototypic pygmy pop was not entirely unique in its time or musical context. Juxtaposing it with two other late-1960s to mid-1970s examples of pygmy-inspired mimetic practices in the jazz arena might allow us to scrutinize more closely how appropriations are neither musically nor politically singular, even when they copy the same source or claim to honor or acknowledge similar cultural heritage.

For example, there is the case of Leon (a.k.a. Leontopolis, Leone) Thomas. Jazz listeners know the power of his big full voice and six-foot-two-inch frame; his sound signature is immediately reminiscent of both Joe Williams's blues delivery and the warm velvety intonation of Billy Ekstine or Arthur Prysock, with tinges of 1960s soul and gospel shouting filling out the mix. Although Thomas crooned the Joe Williams role with Count Basie's band in the early 1960s, he is more closely associated with the Afrocentric jazz avant-gardes of the late 1960s and early 1970s, particularly the ensembles of Rahsaan Roland Kirk and Pharoah Sanders. In these groups Thomas sang some conventionally texted lyrics, but more often vocally improvised untexted solos. In these solos Thomas freely mixed a modified rapid-alternation yodel technique with a kind of vocabalic scat singing that sounded more glottal than the dominant King Pleasure or Eddie Jefferson male jazz scat style typical of the era. These stylizations were set in a larger performance context which included African clothing and frequent references to Afro-Islamic humanism and African American nationalism.

Thomas credited the source of his yodel techniques to Central African pygmy recordings, and he spoke often of his experiences listening to pygmy music on record, including listening with John Coltrane and other 1960s jazz avant-garde icons.[10] Like Hancock, his African connection was imagined as a "brothers kind of thing." A 1970 interview has the following exchange:

Q: Have you been to Africa?

A: Naw. Africa is where *I* am. Africa is here. The most primitive people in Africa sing like me.[11]

Among the most often played examples of Thomas' pygmy-inspired yodeling is the lengthy scat improvisation over an ostinato on "The Creator Has

a Master Plan," a composition coauthored with Pharoah Sanders and performed on Sanders's 1969 LP *Karma.*

subtly spanning oppositional ideology and lyrical romanticism . . .

The Afrocentrism of African American artists did not constitute the only
arena in which jazz musicians expressed an affinity for Central African pygmy
musics in the 1960s and 1970s. From another portion of the jazz spectrum,
take Jimmy Rowles, the well-known pianist who moved from the West Coast
to New York in 1973. Rowles performed and recorded backing Peggy Lee,
Carmen McRae, Billie Holiday, Sarah Vaughan, Frank Sinatra, Ella Fitzger-
ald, and many other singers and instrumentalists on both coasts. Noted by
jazz writers as a favorite accompanist,[12] he was also known for impressionist
improvisatory stylings, marked by touches of Debussy and Ravel.[13] An example is Rowles's jazz ballad "The Peacocks," written in the early 1970s after hearing a Central African LP on the radio. This song has become part
of the repertory of many jazz musicians. The best-known rendition is still the
one Rowles recorded with tenor saxophonist Stan Getz on the 1977 LP *Stan
Getz Presents Jimmy Rowles: The Peacocks.*

Instantly evoking the melodic material and vocal techniques of Central
African forest music, the introductory motif of three tones begins by spring-
ing up a fifth and then a minor third to sound a minor seventh. It then returns by rapidly alternating the tones of the opening fifth to evoke the flut-
tering sound of echoed yodel. This phrase repeats and leads to a second part
of the A theme, using a cascading, descending pentatonic pattern to develop
the initial evocation of the yodel patterns so familiar to listeners of Central
African forest musics.[14]

On the surface Hancock's appropriation, Thomas's imitation, and Rowles's
inspiration are distinct. Yet, as all jazz musicians know, the bounds of mimesis are wide open, and what constitutes a small imitative mutation in one
instance appears more as artistic transformation in another. These examples are united by the way they all take place and make sense within a tradition which is deeply oral, despite a long history of music writing and arranging. It is also a tradition with a long history of celebrating Africa,
including parts of Africa to which it has no direct historical connection. And
because the jazz aesthetic of citation can be orally constituted at any point
in improvisation and composition, the term "theft" doesn't apply when taking from oneself, when revitalizing one's own tradition. Or at least that's
the way almost all jazz players, white and black, young and old, have
phrased it to me when I've played these three examples back-to-back with
source materials from LPs of BaMbuti and BaBenzélé song. While players
clearly recognize that some copies are closer to the source than others, or
that some texts copy pieces while others copy processes, textures, or grooves,

all tend to either nonchalantly note or defensively argue that this is just "in the tradition," which is presumably similar to Herbie Hancock calling it "a brothers kind of thing."

in a global space of circulating commodities . . .

These stories would be a lot less interesting did they not represent a small portion of a much larger pattern, one that has intensified considerably in the last thirty years. I'll later return to some of the current tokens of the pattern. But first I want to locate the Hancock-Thomas-Rowles inventions within another world of recordings. That "other" world is the extraordinary popularity and commercial viability of recordings of Central African forest peoples, particularly the BaMbuti LPs recorded by Colin Turnbull in the Ituri forest of Zaïre in the 1950s and 1960s, and the BaBenzélé and Baka LPs recorded by Simha Arom in the Central African Republic during the 1960s and 1970s.[15]

Although these recordings were made by scholars and were realized specifically as anthropological and ethnomusicological documents, they have reached an unusually large and diverse audience. The space of imagining that encompasses the great popularity of these recordings also reveals their role in allowing academics to characterize the elements of the music they contain. Such analyses mediate a claim to "pygmy music" as a distinct cultural invention, as signaled, for example, by the specific entry under that title in the *New Grove Dictionary of Music and Musicians* as well as the attention to "pygmy music" in the Zaïre and Central African Republic entries by Alan P. Merriam and Simha Arom.[16]

But the story is more complicated in this specific case because we have another connection to explore, one linking the tremendous popularity of Turnbull's *The Forest People* (1960), a literary classic in the ethnographic genre, and the popularity of the Turnbull and Arom recordings, including, in the case of Arom's *Centrafrique: Anthologie de la Musique des Pygmées Aka* an audio classic in the ethnomusicological genre. The existence of all of this research and publication clearly relates to a cumulative historical imaginary, which is historically connected to a colonial past that created a hierarchy of racialized others in which the radical physical distinctiveness of "pygmies" figured prominently.[17] Wedded to this is a less anticipated narrative: the enormous appeal of pygmy music as music—that is, as an extraordinary form of cultural invention in its own right, whether in the eyes of ancient Egyptians, of African villagers, of colonials and missionaries, of anthropologists and ethnomusicologists, of African and Western pop stars, or the accumulation of all of the above in the current world-music marketplace. This fascination and appeal, this history of pygmyphilia, has been manifest, unevenly, both within and outside Africa.

like where Madonna says, "let's get physical" . . .

Taking in portions of the current Congo, Republic of the Congo, Gabon, Cameroon, and Central African Republic, the equatorial forest is home to perhaps two hundred thousand people. Locally circulating names like Mbuti, Aka, Mbenzélé, Binga, Ngombe mask the fact that these original forest dwellers are lumped together by outsiders under the term "pygmy," in reference to the once-common height of under 150 centimeters. More than commonality of physical stature, the people in question share, across geographical region and languages, striking historical commonalties in their hunting and gathering practices, their relatively egalitarian and nonhierarchical social patterns, their aesthetic expressions, and their long-standing patterns of exchange, symbiosis, and accommodation with surrounding Bantu agriculturists.[18]

Schizophonic makeovers of musics originating from Central Africa's rainforest peoples are particularly striking because the small physical stature of the people involved resembles their unempowered and disempowered material position. I say "unempowered" because they have been historically dominated by various outsiders to their forest homes—Bantu agriculturists, European colonizers, national states, and, increasingly, transnational extractors of rainforest resources.[19] But they also are disempowered, precisely because they have never gained control over how they are discursively represented. I refer to the reproduction of the term "pygmy" as their generic name.[20] Slightness in height is what historically tied the notion of "pygmy" to the childlike and chimplike representations emanating from diverse observers, from Egyptians to Greeks, social Darwinists to social scientists. Halfway to adult, halfway to human, "pygmy" remains a specific physical essence, a primordial diminutive other.

Lest one worry about the drama in this phrasing, recall for a brief moment one of its historical consequences—namely, the dehumanization endured by Ota Benga, the first Central African forest hunter to take up residence in the United States. "Residence" is merely an ironic reference here, for Ota Benga was brought from Africa for display at the 1904 World's Fair in St. Louis. He showed his filed teeth for a nickel per smile. His next home was a cage at the Bronx Zoo with a pet chimpanzee. His story, from capture to suicide, is told in detail in Phillips Verner Bradford and Harvey Blume's *Ota Benga: The Pygmy in the Zoo*.[21] It is a chilling account of the complicity of scientists and museums in turn-of-the-century racism and freak-show commerce.

But most of the world did not encounter pygmies at the fair and zoo. And this is why the varieties of schizophonia that emerge from the colonial encounter are particularly important to map: they mark the historical moments and contexts where oral performance and cultural participation are transformed into material commodity and circulable representation. Ethnomusicologists and anthropologists could once claim innocence about the activities of recording and marketing what was variously called tribal, ethnic, folk, or traditional music. Now there is little doubt that this whole body of work, since the time of the invention of the phonograph, has been central to complex representations and commodity flows that are neither ideologically neutral, unfailingly positive, or particularly equitable.

which brings us to schizophonic mimesis . . .

A serious by-product of the popularity of the recordings by Turnbull, Arom, and others is their heightened mediating positions in new chains of schizophonic mimesis. I coin the phrase "schizophonic mimesis" here to point to a broad spectrum of interactive and extractive practices. These acts and events produce a traffic in new creations and relationships through the use, circulation, and absorption of sound recordings. By "schizophonic mimesis" I want to question how sonic copies, echoes, resonances, traces, memories, resemblances, imitations, and duplications all proliferate histories and possibilities.[22] This is to ask how sound recordings, split from their source through the chain of audio production, circulation, and consumption, stimulate and license renegotiations of identity.[23] The recordings of course retain a certain indexical relationship to the place and people they both contain and circulate. At the same time their material and commodity conditions create new possibilities whereby a place and people can be recontextualized, rematerialized, and thus thoroughly reinvented. The question of how recordings open these possibilities in new, different, or overlapping ways to face-to-face musical contacts, or to other historically prior or contiguous mediations, remains both undertheorized and contentious.

Nonetheless, nobody questions the way in which musical commodification is now dominated by acceleration and amplification.[24] The critical factors—the omnipresent possibilities for musical mixing and synthesis, and the rapid transit speeds at which such musical interchanges routinely occur—are themselves part of a broader set of focal conditions in what Arjun Appadurai links as global ethnoscapes and mediascapes.[25] I want to question the role schizophonic mimesis plays in this "scaping," this acceleration, and to ask what kinds of meanings are thus circulated by the resulting commodities.

In a recent essay on discourses and practices of world music and world beat I tried to historicize the idea of schizophonia by recalling Walter Benjamin's 1936 essay on "The Work of Art in the Age of Mechanical Reproduction."[26] Benjamin's concern with the transformation from unique to plural existences invoked the idea of "aura," that which is lost from an original once it is reproduced. This aura frames the consequent status of the copy, particularly as regards contestation of its authenticity or legitimacy vis-à-vis an original. Against this earlier and somewhat monolithic anxiety about the jeopardy to primal originality, I urged that schizophonia needs now to be imagined as more varied and uneven, as practices located in the situations, flows, phases, and circulation patterns that characterize how recordings move in and out of short- and long-term commodity states.

This perspective on schizophonia comes as part of a general debate developed in dialogue with Charles Keil[27] concerning how celebrations of global musical heterogeneity marketed as "world music" are now dynamically interdependent with the parallel musical homogeneity marketed as "world beat." I imagine this tension and interaction between world music and world beat as a rapidly reciprocating and symbiotic traffic, one that links schizophonia to schismogenesis. By this I mean that the cultivation of a transnational arena of global musical discourses and practices is now characterized by a mutualism of splitting and escalation. This escalation—of difference, power, rights, control, ownership, authority—politicizes the schizophonic practices artists could once claim more innocently as matters of inspiration, or as a purely artistic dialogue of imitation and inspiration.

just as when, without warning, reading
an allegory opens a space for ethnography . . .

Jacques Attali's *Noise: The Political Economy of Music*[28] opens another window onto this space of giving and taking, splitting and copying. He provides a sweeping allegorical remove for rereading the BaMbuti metaphor of *akami*, "noise," in the current audio-enviro-cosmology linking rainforest to record factory.

Attali imagines music as a succession of networks, the third and current of which he calls the network of "repetition," the network that emerges with recording technology. He sees this network as heralding the "repetitive mass production of all social relations."[29] And he views this kind of repetition as dominated by processes of unification, of centralization, of molding, of depersonalization, of integration, of systems—a cybernetic matrix of programming and control he calls "imperial universality."[30] It is here that he locates elite musicians as ideologues, working alongside powerful technocrats and a knowledge-rich minority to manage the flow of sound.

"Today the repetitive machine has produced silence, the centralized political control of speech, and more generally, noise. Everywhere, power reduces the noise made by others and adds sound prevention to its arsenal. Listening becomes an essential means of surveillance and social control."[31] If, within Attali's network of repetition, "identity . . . creates a mimicry of desires,"[32] how are we to imagine the contestation over a silence that mutes difference and the "conquest of the right to make noise" that affirms it? In what ways does schizophonic mimesis heighten the stakes in identity politics?

Obviously, discourses on mimesis—on copies, on resemblance, on duplication—have been central to Western aesthetics since Plato's warning, in the *Republic,* that the depiction of likeness is a dangerous subversion of art's essential quest for truth. Aristotle's reply, that mimetic production involved creative impulses no less complex than those in nature to which they are a response, set in motion a debate that has reverberated endlessly into our times.[33]

To turn directly to the contemporary positions: under modernism, the notion of representation often appears transformed into the notions of reflection and revelation—a direct appeal to the senses to imagine an interconnected world of objects. The process of mimetic production thus elides the problem of the split original, the split resemblance of a simultaneous unity and multiplicity. This rupture is precisely the linchpin of postmodern discourse, where the appropriation born of mimesis is both the official bastard of social hierarchy and the living mark that every relationship of copy to copied is an icon of unequal power relations. Jacques Derrida, in particular, was persuasive in rephrasing this critique toward questioning whether a truth is mimicked by a fiction, or a fiction by a truth.[34] This deconstructive view tends toward a discourse on mimesis that makes it about crisis, about destabilizing ideas about authenticity and truth, about disrupting presumptions about primal reference or originality.[35]

This is curiously close to another theorization of mimesis at the double edge of affirmation and critique, namely the one found in Theodor Adorno's final project, on aesthetic theory.[36] Here mimesis makes a theatrical appearance cloaked as the warped logic of domination, dialectically unleashing repressed desire, a longing for the other, while regressively controlling it so as to bury its history forever. Adorno repeatedly insists that as distance, separation, and isolation are illuminated as the products of domination, so too do they glow as signals of a desire to reach out of subjection and into connection. Thus the Janus face of social history central to Adorno, that of liberation and repression, always smiles and smirks through mimetic expression.

If these ideas seem eerie and even local to anthropologists and ethnomusicologists, it is no doubt because a parallel dialectic historically links their fields to mimesis. This is the process of continually subverting and inverting what is familiar and what is strange. Like aesthetic mimesis, anthropology or ethnomusicology's own involves an erotic embrace of the other framed by the negative potential of dominating love. That is perhaps why they often acknowledge mimesis as memory. In Adorno's own phrasing: "Longing, which posits the actuality of the non-existent, takes the form of remembrance."[37]

but meanwhile, an avant-garde techno-jungle kind of thing . . .

The jazz avant-gardes of the 1960s and 1970s extended well beyond New York. One connection was to Brazilian guitarist and composer Egberto Gismonti, well known internationally for his eight-string-guitar virtuosity and his performances with percussionists and jazz improvisers like Airto Moriera, Paul Horn, Nana Vasconcelos, and Charlie Haden. Trained in composition in Paris with Nadia Boulanger and Jean Barraqué, Gismonti devoted 1977 to the study of Xingu Indian music.[38] This project was directly reflected by his LP released in the following year, *Sol Do Meio Dia* (*Midday Sun*). The album features Gismonti with percussionists Nana Vasconcelos and Collin Walcott, guitarist Ralph Towner, and saxophonist Jan Garbarek. The LP was recorded in Oslo for the ECM label, which released it internationally in 1978 to enthusiastic reviews.

ECM developed a technological aesthetic significant to global improvisational avant-gardism in the late 1970s, a transparently brittle if ice-clear sound, marked by hauntingly stark reverberation. It is in this context that we can hear the deep fundamentals and open overtones of a moment in Gismonti's "Sapain." Here, in a densely layered Villa-Lobos to global-village interlude featuring bottles and wood flutes, the same musical material from both the Arom/Taurelle and Hancock presentations of the BaBenzélé *hindewhu* is merged with an evocation of the overlapping echo-phonies of Amazonian Indian flutes. Gismonti joins the Amazonian rainforest and its inhabitants together with an imagined parallel world in Central Africa, producing an interconnected space of primal musical otherness. He writes: "The music on this album is dedicated to Sapain and the Xingu Indians, whose teachings were so important to me during the time I spent with them in the Amazon jungle: the sound of the jungle, its color and mysteries; the sun, the moon, the rain and the winds; the river and the fish; the sky and the birds, but most of all the integration of musician, music and instrument into an undivided whole."

An interesting and immediate contrast similarly traversing art and pop avant-garde lineages is Jon Hassell and Brian Eno's 1979 LP *Fourth World Vol. 1: Possible Musics*, which has a track titled "Ba-Benzélé," credited to Hassell. The source material was obviously the same BaBenzélé *hindewhu* recording, but the transformative techniques and media employed are concrète and electronic, yielding a muted, mysterious, muzaklike quality, a cross between synthesized panpipes and speeded-up tape loops. Like Gismonti's, Hassell's work is framed by his impeccable international avant-garde credentials: jazz trumpeting, a European Ph.D. in musicology, composition studies in Cologne with Karlheinz Stockhausen, and performance studies in India with renowned vocalist Pran Nath.[39] These experiences create the elements for Hassell's work in the jungle garden of primitive futurism. *Fourth World Vol. 1*, like Hassell's other projects from the same period, *Earthquake Island* and *Dream Theory in Malaya,* helped create a global avant-garde space whose sound is equally futuristic and primitivistic, ethnic and electronic.

But there is an additional appropriation to consider. "Ba-Benzélé": a people are now a song title owned by another. And upon hearing the song the connection to a place or people is in every way sonically distant, while a human specificity is called into immediacy. For Hassell, Eno, and their listeners, ambient music was an other world of the imagination and illusion. Electronic synthesis—always low-key, ambient, repetitive, minimal, vaguely reminiscent but definitely nonreferential—was its mode of techno-transport. The listener who has heard BaBenzélé music must strain to insert a memory trace, must imagine the original pattern in the wavy, watery, wishy-washy dissolution of its elements.

Fourth World Vol. I and the ambient electrosynthesis of Hassell and Eno's "Ba-Benzélé" can be further contextualized in a larger body of avant-garde art and pop music. Hassell was clearly influenced by the high electromodernism of Stockhausen, whose experiments in "found objects" and "international gibberish" (e.g., *Hymnen*, using 137 national anthems), East-West cutups (*Stimmung*), and global forecasting (*Telemusik*) are detailed in an important background text of 1973, his *Towards a Cosmic Music*, especially a chapter titled "Beyond Global Village Polyphony."[40] In parallel, Eno's formative 1960s influences were John Cage and Cornelius Cardew. He took up multitrack tape recorder as his instrument, and through the 1970s had a string of extraordinary pop collaborations and credits from Roxy Music to Robert (King Crimson) Fripp, John Cale, Velvet Underground, and David Bowie. By the end of the 1970s Eno focused on his soundtrack and *Ambient* volumes, including *Music for Airports,* and the extremely popular (and later highly contested for its appropriation politics) 1981 project with David Byrne, *My Life in the Bush of Ghosts.*[41]

On these margins two additional Eno-pygmy connections come to mind. One is Louis Sarno, an American who has spent more than ten years living with the BaBenzélé and has recently collaborated on a soundscape and music recording project, *Bayaka,* with acoustic ecologist Bernie Krause.[42] He has also written a popular book, *Song from the Forest,* a romantic and lyrical travelogue which mentions a commission from Eno to collect music and sounds for a rainforest environment Eno was to produce for a New York art festival.[43] This "collecting" is part of a pattern in Eno's avant-gardism, which involves a particular use of and attitude toward Africa. As Eno expresses it in a recent interview: "Do you know what I hate about computers? The problem with computers is that there is not enough Africa in them. . . . Do you know what a nerd is? A nerd is a human being without enough Africa in him or her . . . You know why music was the center of our lives for such a long time? Because it was a way of allowing Africa in."[44]

Yet another Eno-pygmy connection is renowned filmmaker Wim Wenders. Eno produced (with Daniel Lanois) the U2 song "Until the End of the World," which is featured in Wenders's 1991 film of the same name; he also influenced the design direction of the soundtrack.[45] Pygmies are featured in a major symbolic role in this film, which is an allegorical treatment of the history of vision, film, and dreaming. Wenders's vehicle is an apocalyptic, around-the-world chase thriller mixed with a mad scientist tale. At its center is a camera that can record brain impulses, which once decoded can permit a blind person to see. Ultimately this technology creates the possibility for people to record and replay their own dreams. The last part of the film is set in the scientist's lab in the Central Australian desert. Aboriginal Australians are deployed in numerous ways to suggest the links between past and future, between x-ray art and futurist mental telepathy. They are represented as uniquely able to see back into the Dreamtime and ahead into the end of the world. Wenders uses the trope of Aboriginal empathy for and adoption of the visionary scientist and his blind wife to tell a story about memory as forecasting in a world which has become addicted to dreams.

The pygmies fit into this grand scheme as the aural, childlike foil to the Aboriginals, who are clearly the embodiment of ancient and futurist visual wisdom. To bring the pygmies into the narrative, composer Graeme Revell used digital samples of Aka children's songs in the film's soundtrack, beginning with the titles. These samples were taken from and credited to Simha Arom's *Centrafrique: Anthologie de la Musique des Pygmées Aka*. More significant is an important on-screen referential use of an Aka lullaby track to signify aural past echoes of simple, joyous, childlike, uncomplicated life (i.e., what Europeans presumably must once have been like). After hearing the pygmy lullaby on a cassette in the car, the heroine goes into a deep trancelike slumber for five hundred kilometers of Euro-highway. "I haven't slept so long in weeks," says Claire as she awakes in Paris.

and a hybrid sisters kind of thing . . .

Jon Hassell isn't the only musician to name a song "Ba-Benzélé." So did (with a different spelling) Zap Mama, an a capella group comprised of women of mixed African and European heritage. The U.S. release of their 1993 (originally 1991) debut CD, *Zap Mama: Adventures in Afropea*, was curated by former Talking Heads leader David Byrne, whose Luaka Bop label (in the Warner Brothers family) has taken an important entrepreneurial role in global pop. The recording commanded the number one position on *Billboard*'s World Music Albums chart for four months that year.

In the CD's liner notes Zap Mama leader Marie Daulne says: "Thanks to my dual cultural background—Walloon and Bantu, Belgian and Zaïrean— I discovered (and would like others to discover by listening to this record) the richness and diversity of the musics that are the foundation of our African and European repertoire." Daulne goes on to acknowledge "the ethnomusicologists whose records inspired me," but saves her strongest words of admiration for "the Pygmies of Central Africa."

Daulne's pygmy connection was regularly taken up by the pop press, who used it for their own exoticizing spins,[46] barely mentioning that she had studied at the Antwerp School of Jazz, or that other tracks on the CD draw on Spanish, Syrian, Cuban, Congolese, and other idioms and influences. The Zap Mama track "Babanzélé" is an eight-voice adaptation of a complex polyphonic piece featuring whistles and voices, originally recorded on the same 1966 Arom and Taurelle LP as the solo *hindewhu*. What is striking about this Zap Mama performance is that it is a far more detailed, nuanced, and complete vocal mimesis of BaBenzélé vocalization than anything previously recorded. Treating BaBenzélé music as music, as fully articulated practices and pieces, Zap Mama copies the repertory object and develops its techniques of ostinatos and variations to closely duplicate the multiple layering of voices, *hindewhu*, clapping, and percussion on the 1966 LP. An authenticity is guaranteed to mimesis here in light of Daulne's invocation of her own physical, cultural, and historical hybridity. In other words, invoking hybridity as one's own identity position, one then becomes licensed to claim the full spatiotemporal terrain of that identity as an artistic palette.

maybe even a magic flute kind of thing . . .

Cameroonian novelist, poet, and composer Francis Bebey was born and educated in Douala, then went to Paris to study music and broadcasting. He has many times toured the world as a classical guitarist, and is also well known as a prolific poet and novelist.[47] He has worked for UNESCO in Paris since 1972. Bebey is widely credited as the first Cameroonian musician to transcend specific local styles of music and to successfully mix elements of different African instrumental and vocal repertoires with European music. Although Cameroon is better known on the international pop scene since the early 1970s for the Makossa beat of saxophonist and bandleader Manu Dibango, Bebey was equally important as an early inspirational model for Cameroonian and other African musicians who wanted to blend musical sources and styles.[48]

Cameroon has forests populated by Baka, but Bebey is well aware of pygmy musics from the recorded sources of the 1960s, and wrote about them in his 1975 (French original 1969) general book, *African Music: A People's Art*. Now the BaBenzélé *hindewhu* sound has emerged in Bebey's own concert repertory. His 1993 CD *Lambaréné Schweitzer,* a tribute to Dr. Albert Schweitzer, features *'ndewhoo* (his spelling) sounds, developing the vocal-instrumental interplay with overdubbed percussion. Like Zap Mama, Bebey takes a BaBenzélé technique and extends it. In his liner notes he refers to the *'ndewhoo* as "a magical flute" due to its ability to produce a whole melody from a single note.

Bebey apparently began to incorporate the *hindewhu* sound in the early 1980s, following his success using the *sanza*. He has performed the technique live in concerts from Elysée Palace in Paris to New York's Carnegie Hall. In addition to *Lambaréné Schweitzer,* two other recordings document his compositional history with *hindewhu* techniques: *Akwaaba* (1985) and *Nandolo/ With Love* (1995). The back jacket of the latter mentions that Bebey has just finished a commission, "a piece for Pygmy flute and string quartet, 'Kasilane' for the Kronos Quartet. . . . " Listening to these three recordings makes it clear that Bebey has mastered all the techniques of rapid blown/sung and falsetto/open voice alternations, using a bamboo panpipe imitation of the papaya stem whistle.

Yet there is still, as with Zap Mama, not to mention Herbie Hancock or Leon Thomas, a lingering issue, which is the place of condescension, even subjugation, within a sphere overtly marked by inspiration and musically coded as homage. Which is to say that polemics of race and cultural theft do not feature in critical discourses surrounding Zap Mama, Frances Bebey, or the African American musicians' pygmy kind of thing the way they feature more immediately in relation to Gismonti or Hassell and Eno's pygmoid kind of thing. Clearly the subject positions of African Americans, Afropeans, and Africans tend to discourage a particular kind of moral and political scrutiny here, instead foregrounding an aesthetic reading of schizophonic mimesis as musical ambassadorship. Nonetheless, the power differentials separating cosmopolitan African Americans, Afropeans, and Africans from their forest pygmy muses cannot be elided. Such differentials are no less striking here than anywhere in imagining how commodity circulation reproduces the place of givers and takers, sources and users. While avant-gardes know no bounds, some have differential recourse to roots. Respect, as Aretha Franklin taught us, carries a complicated burden.[49]

or a folkie and green you-can-have-it-both-ways kind of thing . . .

Martin Cradick's 1993 *Spirit of the Forest* combines digital sampling and studio overdubs with tracks of his live guitar and mandolin playing, along with the percussion of Baka forest people in Southeast Cameroon. Some of the Baka sounds, in their original live form, appear on the companion CD *Heart of the Forest*. Thus spoken for simultaneously is the authenticity of the original—the "Heart"—and the sincerity of the copy—the "Spirit." Here the documentary world music genre completely blurs with its world beat jam-session remix.

While there are numerous divergences between the two CDs, the immediate impression of their close connection is overwhelming. Not only is the cover art for the two extraordinarily similar, but their beginnings stake out an auditory kinship. "Yelli," track 1 of *Heart of the Forest*, consists of untexted yodels sounded deep in the forest. "Spirit of the Forest," track 1 of *Spirit of the Forest*, begins with a digital sample of this sonic material, which then gives way to a mandolin and guitar reworking of the yodeled melody line. This track is credited to Martin Cradick and performed by Martin Cradick (guitar, mandolin, digital samples), accompanied by Baka percussionists and vocalists. This technique, in a variety of forms and transformations, characterizes the relationship between the Baka "heart" and the "spirit" known as Baka Beyond, Cradick's band name. Following the success of these two recordings, Cradick continued the approach with new field recordings to create a second CD, *The Meeting Pool*, in 1995.

Aside from the "have it both ways" authenticity of this form of production, there is another complicated connection between the two recordings. In the liner notes to *Spirit of the Forest*, Cradick writes: "All performance and compositional royalties due to the Baka for this album will be collected for them to use to protect their forest and to develop in a sustainable way without losing their knowledge and culture." And in the liner notes to *Heart of the Forest*, Cradick also notes that the royalties will all go to the Baka. In both instances Cradick indicates clear concern for the current cultural and environmental survival issues faced by Baka and their forest home. In the *Spirit of the Forest* liner notes this concern takes the form of romantic notes that border on a deep nostalgia. But in the conclusion of the *Heart of the Forest* notes, Cradick's collaborator Jeremy Avis directly articulates how this is perhaps but a fantasy, lightly floating above the realities of nation-states who marginalize their remote others in harmony with global capitalist expansion:

> African governments crippled by debts owed to Western development banks are forced to "mine" their natural resources, such as the Baka's rainforest homeland, to get badly needed foreign capital. This short term financial gain does not reach the Baka, and the long term effects on their culture of this loss of habitat will have destructive and far-reaching consequences. Proceeds from the sale of this album will go back to the rainforest and go a small way to reversing the flow of resources exploitatively removed from the South to the North. The rest is up to you.[50]

and finally, an international disco dance megahit kind of thing . . .

As a final contrast, there is the international disco multimillion seller, *Deep Forest*. Released in 1992, in a bilingual edition produced by Dan Lacksman and "based on an original idea by Michel Sanchez," *Deep Forest* features digitally sampled and manipulated African sounds mixed with synthesized contemporary percussion and melody tracks. Arranged and adapted by Eric Mouquet and Michel Sanchez using synthesizer keyboards and other MIDI programming devices for synchronization, the African materials come from several ethnographic recordings of musics from Ghana, Senegal, Cameroon, Central African Republic, and Burundi. Some of the pygmy sources are credited to a recent CD, *Polyphony of the Deep Rain Forest;* others come from earlier recordings by Simha Arom.

Deep Forest's liner notes, publicity, video, art packaging (childlike scrawls, forest symbols), and audio design are a treasure textbook of every essentializing, romanticizing, exoticizing trope available. The pygmy other is particularly equated with spirituality, the natural world, solidarity with the earth, balance, and timelessness. As the introductory song puts it (in deep tones): "Somewhere deep in the jungle are living some little men and women. They are your past; maybe they are your future." The musical correlates of this stance are clear. In "Hunting," for example, the main melody is a direct digital sample from the first track of *Polyphony of the Deep Rain Forest.* The opening loop which creates a continuous response is a repeated sample metrically fixing a three-pitch yodel—up a minor seventh, down a minor third to sound the fifth—to create the key figure and refrain for a dance groove.

In addition to extraordinary success in the international marketplace (at least 2.5 million copies sold worldwide in the three years following its release in April 1992), *Deep Forest*'s lead song was also heard widely as the soundtrack to TV commercials where a nude mermaid splashed through lush mountain streams advertising Neutrogena skin care products. Material from the CD was also licensed for other TV commercials, such as for Sony's Trinitron TV, and by clients as diverse as the Body Shop and Porsche; "it is truly the Benetton of music-marketing concepts."[51] The publicity has been massive, the press response overwhelmingly positive, and the Deep Forest production team has gone on to apply the same technique to Gypsy and Celtic musics.[52] The Gypsy CD, *Bohême,* won the 1996 World Music Grammy award.[53] In an interview about this new recording Deep Forest's Eric Mouquet displays his technocratic attitude toward music: "They say, 'Ah, no. You have no right to do that, put synthesizers on our music.' I say 'Why? Why can't I do that? Give me a good reason.' And of course they have no good reason."[54]

Like the *Heart of the Forest* and *Spirit of the Forest* CDs, *Deep Forest* prominently advertises its social altruism, asking listeners to help contribute to the Pygmy Fund, a California-based charity managed by Jean-Pierre Hallet, who grew up near the Ituri forest and won a Presidential End Hunger award for his agricultural work with the Efé.[55] Hallet's Pygmy Fund is specifically designed to help the Efé, a group whose music was not sampled on the *Deep Forest* CD. As it turns out, inspection of the Pygmy Fund's tax returns for the years since the *Deep Forest* debut reveals little change in their contribution base. One can only surmise that the fund has received little money from *Deep Forest.* My own letters and phone calls to Passionate Entertainment (the *Deep Forest* production company) about this have gone unanswered for the last two years.

telling what kinds of stories?

Do these scattered moments and manifestations form a narrative? If so, is it as coherent as (or more or less so than) what I've hunted and gathered here? How are these stories speaking to critical postmodern themes about disjunctions in a global sphere of popular commodity circulation? How are they promoting anger and respect at the same time? In what ways are they forcing listeners to choose sides both aesthetically and politically? To these questions, and across the range of engagements—who enjoys and embraces, or who regrets and detests the music objects circulating in the pygmy pop genre—I'd propose four critical ostinatos underlying world beat's pygmy pop.

From Afronationalism to Euro-avant-gardism, from electroacoustic modernism to digital postmodernism, from highbrow to low, there's a pygmy product to fit every viewpoint on authenticity and collaboration, every celebration of roots and hybridity.

Whether the groove is pop sweet-talk, jazz scat, funk, or ballad; whether it is transforest acoustic or transworld ambient; whether it is the hybridity of Afropea, the concertizing of Euroafrique; whether it is a folkie mandolin play-along eco-jam or ethno-techno sampling, there's a pygmy for any and all consumer positions and tastes.

Everyone—no matter how exoticizing, how patronizing, how romanticizing, how essentializing in their rhetoric or packaging—declares their fundamental respect, even deep affection, for the original music and its makers.

Concern for the future of the rainforests and their inhabitants is now central to the genre. This heightening is paralleled by romantic and patronizing renditions of an old theme, the pygmy as timeless primal other. A complex humanity is thus fixed as a tape loop in the machine of both postcolonial devastation and primitivist fantasy.

For anthropologists and ethnomusicologists the most profoundly ironic and complicated aspect of the situation is the contrast between the musical stories told by pygmy pop and those told by the documentary recordings upon which these copies draw and depend. The documentary records emphasize a vast repertory of musical forms and performance styles, including complex and original polyphonic and polyrhythmic practices. Yet what of this diverse musical invention forms the basis for its global pop representation? In the most popular instances it is a single untexted vocalization or falsetto yodel, often hunting cries rather than songs or musical pieces. This is the sonic cartoon of the diminutive person, the simple, intuitively vocal and essentially nonlinguistic child. Why, in the face of such a varied and complex corpus of musical practices, does global pygmy pop reproduce the most caricatured image of its origin?

There is a further irony. Some critics and contemporary pygmy pop artists like Zap Mama and Frances Bebey thank ethnomusicologists for recording the sounds in the first place and for bringing them to the world's attention. Yet others position ethnomusicology as the discourse of musical regression, and its practitioners merely as purist romantics and apologists. For example, *Village Voice* critic Randall Grass states his initial pessimism upon reading Marie Daulne's liner notes about the source of her inspiration: "Don't get me wrong—the Pygmies' genuinely awesome vocal polyphony can be magical; it was the academic aesthetic of the recordings themselves [i.e., those by ethnomusicologists] that undermined their beauty." But upon listening he was won over by the group's performance: "Zap Mama uses Pygmy tradition as a base to create something personal and—dare we say it?—novel."[56] Likewise, *Melody Maker* columnist Ben Turner praises the Deep Forest duo by positioning them opposite academic voyeurs: " . . . *Deep Forest's* mystical sound is not, however, that of two musicologists who have hidden in the forest and eavesdropped on the conversations of the Pygmies."[57] Other writers attempt to position what's exciting about hybrid world beat in opposition to what's moldy about world music roots. *Creem's* Brooke Wentz writes:

> What's the ethnic flavor of the month? Pygmies. Like this year's contemporaries—the Belgian/Zaïrian *a capella* group Zap Mama and the French techno duo Deep Forest—the Afro-Euro instrumental melange Baka Beyond incorporates the voices and water drums of Cameroon's Baka pygmies with western music. The result is a marvelous combination of crystalline rhythms—a modern listener's wet dream, and an ethnomusicologist's worst nightmare.[58]

Whatever one's judgment on the purism of ethnomusicology or the fun of the record studio, pygmy pop's schizophonia involves a rapid escalation of amplification and diminution. The primary circulation of small-scale, low-budget, and largely nonprofit ethnomusicological records is now directly linked to a secondary circulation of several million dollars' worth of contemporary record sales, copyrights, royalties, and ownership claims, many of them held by the largest music entertainment conglomerates in the world. Hardly any of this money circulation returns to or benefits the originators of the cultural and intellectual property in question. It is this basic inequity, coupled with the reproduction of negative caricature, that creates the current ethnomusicological reality: discourses on world music are inseparable from discourses on indigeneity and domination. As elsewhere, this means increasingly that aesthetic practices and choices are being deeply felt and portrayed as markedly political ones.

Fans and marketers of contemporary world beat want the world to listen and dance to musics they imagine to be contemporary, vital, and profoundly transcultural. They are selling celebrations of hybridity; for them pygmy pop rejoices the forest. But for critics, whether world-music purists, pastiche haters, nostalgia apologists, or advocates for indigeneity and intellectual property rights, this rejoicing is burdened. The worry is that Jacques Attali's *Noise*, however dramatic and freewheeling, might be more correct than not: "Mimesis eliminates all obstacles to murder, all scapegoats."[59] Either way, readers of Colin Turnbull's ethnographies are now inevitably forced to consider a more nuanced, ironic, or cynical reading of his exegesis of the Mbuti saying *akami amu ndura*, "noise kills the forest."

DISCOGRAPHY

Aka Pygmy Music, Auvidis D8054 (1973; reissue 1994).

Baka Beyond, *Spirit of the Forest*, Rykodisc/Hannibal HNCD 1377 (1993).

Baka Beyond, *The Meeting Pool*, Rykodisc/Hannibal HNCD 1388 (1995).

Bayaka: The Extraordinary Music of the BaBenzélé Pygmies and Sounds of their Forest Home, Ellipsis Arts CD 3490 (1995).

Frances Bebey, *Akwaaba*, Original Music OMCD 005 (1985).

Frances Bebey, *Lambaréné Schweitzer*, Disques Ceddia (Amaya No. 2) CED 001 (1993).

Frances Bebey, *Nandolo/With Love (Works 1963–1994)*, Original Music OMCD 027 (1995).

Cameroon: Baka Pygmy Music, Auvidis D8029 (1977; reissue 1990).

Centrafrique: Anthologie de la Musique des Pygmées Aka, Ocora C559012 13 (1978; reissue 1993).

Congo: Cérémonie du Bobé, Ocora C 560010 (1991).

Deep Forest, 550 Music/Epic BK 57840 (1992).

Echoes of the Forest: Music of the Central African Pygmies, Ellipsis Arts CD 4020 (1994).

Brian Eno, *Music for Airports*, Editions EG, EGS 201 (1979).

Brian Eno and David Byrne, *My Life in the Bush of Ghosts*, Sire 6093-2 (1981).

Gabon: Musique des Pygmées Bibayak, Ocora C559 053 (1989).

Egberto Gismonti, *Sol Do Meio Dia*, ECM 1116 (1978).

Herbie Hancock, *Takin' Off*, Blue Note BLP 4109 (1962).

Herbie Hancock, *Headhunters*, Columbia/Sony CK 47478 (1973; reissue 1992).

Jon Hassell, *Earthquake Island*, Tomato TOM 7019 (1979).

Jon Hassell/Brian Eno, *Fourth World vol. 1: Possible Musics*, Editions EG EEGCD 7 (1980).

Jon Hassell, *Fourth World vol. 2: Dream Theory in Malaya*, Editions EEGCD 13 (1981).

Heart of the Forest: The Music of the Baka Forest People of Southwest Cameroon, Rykodisc/Hannibal HNCD 1378 (1993).

Madonna, *Bedtime Stories*, Maverick/Sire/Warner Bros. 9 45767-2 (1994).

Mbuti Pygmies of the Ituri Rainforest, Smithsonian Folkways SF CD 40401 (1992).

Music of the Ba-Benzélé Pygmies, Bärenreiter Musicaphon BM 30 L 2303 (1966).

Music of the Ituri Forest, Folkways 4483 (1957).

Music of the Rainforest Pygmies, Lyrichord 7157 (1961; reissue 1992).

Polyphonies Vocales des Pygmées Mbenzélé, République Centrafricaine, Auvidis W 260 042 (1992).

Polyphony of the Deep Rain Forest: Music of the Ituri Pygmies, JVC VICG-5015-2 (1990).

Pygmeés du Haut-Zaïre, Fonti Musicali, fmd 190 (1991).

The Pygmies of the Ituri Forest, Folkways 4457 (1958).

Jimmy Rowles, *Stan Getz Presents Jimmy Rowles, The Peacocks,* Columbia/Sony CK52975 (1977; reissue 1994).

Pharoah Sanders, *Karma,* Impulse/MCA MCAD-39122 (1969; reissue 1992).

Until the End of the World (motion picture soundtrack), Warner Bros. W2 26707 (1991).

Zap Mama, *Adventures in Afropea 1,* Luaka Bop/Warner Bros. 9 45183-2 (1993).

NOTES

This is a shortened version of a paper first published in the *Yearbook for Traditional Music,* vol. 28 (1996), 1–35. It is dedicated to the memory of Colin Turnbull.

1. See Eric Pace, "Colin M. Turnbull, 69, Anthropologist and Author," *New York Times,* 1 August 1994.

2. Colin Turnbull, *The Forest People* (New York: Simon and Schuster, 1961); *The Lonely African* (New York: Simon and Schuster, 1962); *The Mountain People* (New York: Simon and Schuster, 1972).

3. Marcel Mauss, *The Gift* (1929; reprint, New York: W. W. Norton, 1976).

4. Colin Turnbull, *Wayward Servants: The Two Worlds of the African Pygmies* (New York: Natural History Press, 1965), especially 254–67, 286–91. All page references in the next paragraph are from Turnbull, *Wayward Servants.*

5. Jon Pareles, "Madonna Makes Her Next Career Move: Innocence," *International Herald Tribune,* 25 October 1994, 20.

6. Both quotations from ibid., 20.

7. Herbie Hancock, phone conversation with author, April 1985.

8. For historical perspectives on this issue see Roger Wallis and Krister Malm, *Big Sounds from Small Peoples: The Music Industry in Small Countries* (New York: Pendragon, 1984), 165–215; Anthony Seeger, "Singing Other People's Songs," *Cultural Survival Quarterly* 15, no. 3 (1991): 36–39; Seeger, "Ethnomusicology and Music Law," *Ethnomusicology* 36, no. 3 (1992): 345–59; and the essays in Simon Frith, ed., *Music and Copyright* (Edinburgh: Edinburgh University Press, 1993).

9. On some of the dimensions of African American citation ethics and recycling across genres and styles, see Amiri Baraka, "The Blues Aesthetic and the Black Aesthetic," *Black Music Research Journal* 11, no. 2 (1991): 101–9; Paul Berliner, *Thinking in Jazz: The Infinite Art of Improvisation* (Chicago: University of Chicago Press, 1994); Henry Louis Gates Jr., *The Signifying Monkey* (New York: Oxford University Press, 1988); Dick Hebdige, *Cut 'n' Mix* (New York: Methuen, 1987); Leroi Jones, *Blues People* (New York: William Morrow Monson, 1963); Tricia Rose, *Black Noise* (Hanover, N.H.: Wesleyan University Press, 1994). Especially provocative in this regard is Paul Gilroy's *The Black Atlantic: Modernity and Double Consciousness* (Cambridge, Mass.: Harvard University Press, 1993). Gilroy takes up the politics of authenticity in black music, approvingly citing Houston Baker, *Modernism and the Harlem Renaissance* (Chicago: University of Chicago Press, 1987), on the trope of "family" in African American consciousness: see Gilroy, *The Black Atlantic,* 72–110.

10. See for example the Thomas interviews in Joe H. Thomas, "Avant-Garde with Roots," *Down Beat,* 10 December 1970, 18–19; and Tyson Rawlings, "Africa Is Where I Am: Interview with Leon Thomas," *Jazz and Pop* 9, no. 11 (1970): 5–18.

11. In Rawlings, "Africa Is Where I Am," 18.

12. Peter Watrous, "Jimmy Rowles, 77, Lyrical Jazz Accompanist," *New York Times,* 30 May 1996.

13. Len Lyons, *The Great Jazz Pianists, Speaking of Their Lives and Music* (New York: William Morrow, 1983).

14. The full lead sheet is published in Chuck Sher, *The World's Greatest Fakebook* (Petaluma, Calif.: Sher Music, 1991), 303.

15. See Richard Henderson, "Born of Dreams: The Music of the Pygmies," *The Beat* 14, no. 5 (1995): 46–49; and see the discography appended above for a sampling of popular Central African recordings.

16. *The New Grove Dictionary of Music and Musicians,* ed. Stanley Sadie (New York: Macmillan, 1980), 15:482–83. See also Simha Arom, "The Use of Playback Techniques in the Study of Oral Polyphonies," *Ethnomusicology* 20, no. 3 (1976): 483–519; and Arom, *African Polyphony and Polyrhythm* (Cambridge: Cambridge University Press, 1991).

17. John Haller, *Outcasts from Evolution: Scientific Attitudes of Racial Inferiority 1859–1900* (New York: McGraw-Hill, 1975); Leslie Fiedler, *Freaks: Myths and Images of the Secret Self* (New York: Simon and Schuster, 1978); Stephen Jay Gould, *Mismeasure of Man* (New York: Norton, 1981); Robert Bogdan, *Freak Show: Presenting Human Oddities for Fun and Profit* (Chicago: University of Chicago Press, 1988); Robert Farris Thompson and S. Bahuchet, *Pygmées?* (Paris: Editions Dapper, 1991); Phillips Verner Bradford and Harvey Blume, *Ota Benga: The Pygmy in the Zoo* (New York: Dell/Delta, 1992); Jan Nederveen Pieterse, *White on Black: Images of Africa and Blacks in Western Popular Culture* (New Haven, Conn.: Yale University Press, 1992); Susan Stewart, *On Longing: Narratives of the Miniature, the Gigantic, the Souvenir, the Collection* (Durham, N.C.: Duke University Press, 1993), 108–11.

18. L. L. Cavalli-Sforza, ed., *African Pygmies* (New York: Academic Press, 1986); Thompson and Bahuchet, *Pygmées?*

19. Marvine Howe, "Pygmies, Many Owned by Planters, Are Central Africa's Second-Class Citizens," *New York Times,* 8 July 1972; S. Bahuchet and H. Guillaume, "Aka-Farmer Relations in the Northwest Congo Basin," in *Politics and History in Band Societies,* ed. Eleanor Leacock and Richard B. Lee (Cambridge: Cambridge University Press, 1982); Colin Turnbull, *The Mbuti Pygmies: Change and Adaptation* (New York: Holt Rinehart Winston, 1983); S. Bahuchet, *Les Pygmées Aka et la Forêt Centrafricaine* (Paris: SELAF, 1985); Cavalli-Sforza, *African Pygmies;* Barry Hewlett, *Intimate Fathers: The Nature and Context of Aka Pygmy Paternal Infant Care* (Ann Arbor: University of Michigan Press, 1991); Roy Grinker, *Houses in the Rainforest: Ethnicity and Inequality among Farmers and Foragers in Central Africa* (Berkeley: University of California Press, 1992); Louis Sarno, *Song from the Forest: My Life among the Ba-Benjellé Pygmies* (New York: Penguin, 1993) and *Bayaka: The Extraordinary Music of the BaBenzélé Pygmies* (Roslyn, New York: Ellipsis Arts, 1995); Joan Mark, *The King of the World in the Land of the Pygmies* (Lincoln: University of Nebraska Press, 1995); Douglas Chadwick, "Ndoki: Last Place on Earth," *National Geographic* 188, no. 1 (1995): 2–45.

20. Turnbull, *The Mbuti Pygmies,* 1; Thompson and Bahuchet, *Pygmées?*

21. Op. cit.

22. Michael Taussig, *Mimesis and Alterity: A Particular History of the Senses* (New York: Routledge, 1993).

23. R. Murray Schafer, *The Tuning of the World* (New York: Knopf, 1977), 90–91; Steven Feld, "From Schizophonia to Schismogenesis: On the Discourses and Practices of World Music and World Beat," in Charles Keil and Steven Feld, *Music Grooves* (Chicago: University of Chicago Press, 1994), 258–60.

24. Veit Erlmann and Deborah Pacini Hernandez, "The Politics and Aesthetics of 'World Music,'" *The World of Music* 35, no. 2 (1993): 3–15.

25. Arjun Appadurai, "Global Ethnoscapes: Notes and Queries for a Transnational Anthropology," in *Recapturing Anthropology*, ed. Richard Fox (Santa Fe, N.M.: School of American Research Press, 1991), 191–210.

26. Feld, "From Schizophonia to Schismogenesis." Benjamin's essay is in *Illuminations* (1934; reprint, New York: Schocken, 1969).

27. Keil and Feld, *Music Grooves*, 290–330.

28. Jacques Attali, *Noise: The Political Economy of Music* (1977; Minneapolis: University of Minnesota Press, 1985).

29. Ibid., 32.

30. Ibid., 113.

31. Ibid., 122.

32. Ibid., 121.

33. A thorough review is Gunter Gebauer and Christoph Wulf, *Mimesis: Culture, Art, Society* (Berkeley: University of California Press, 1995).

34. Jacques Derrida, *Of Grammatology* (1967; Baltimore: Johns Hopkins University Press, 1976).

35. Theodor Adorno, *Aesthetic Theory* (London: Routledge, 1983).

36. For the anthropology of art two rather different evaluative discourses have historically applied to these traffics. One is a discourse about the degree of artfulness marking the contact; the other is a discourse about the degree of power differences opened up by the split image. For some it is the discourse on artfulness that most characterizes the embrace of primitivism and the fetishization of "authenticity" in modernist art history. For others it is the discourse on power differences and the fetishization of "hybridity" that most characterizes the naturalization of appropriation in the postmodern era. For more on these developments, see James Clifford, *The Predicament of Culture* (Cambridge, Mass.: Harvard University Press, 1988); Sally Price, *Primitive Art in Civilized Places* (Chicago: University of Chicago Press, 1989); Marianna Torgovnick, *Gone Primitive: Savage Intellects, Modern Lives* (Chicago: University of Chicago Press, 1990); Shelly Errington, "What Became Authentic Primitive Art?" *Cultural Anthropology* 9, no. 2 (1994): 201–26; and the essays in George Marcus and Fred Myers, eds., *The Traffic in Culture: Refiguring Art and Anthropology* (Berkeley: University of California Press, 1995).

37. Adorno, *Aesthetic Theory* (London: Routledge, 1983), 192.

38. Chip Stern, "Egberto Gismonti: Finding the Avant-Garde in the Jungles of Brazil with an Eight-String Jazz Guitar," *Guitar Player* 12 (November 1978): 45, 114–20.

39. Robert Palmer, "Jon Hassell and the 'Fourth World,'" *Rolling Stone*, 4 September 1980.

40. Karlheinz Stockhausen, *Towards a Cosmic Music* (1973; reprint, London: Element Books, 1989).

41. Jon Pareles, "Eno Uncaged," *Village Voice*, 4 May 1982, 77–78; David Toop,

Ocean of Sound: Aether Talk, Ambient Sound, and Imaginary Worlds (London: Serpent's Tail, 1995), 122–23.

42. Sarno, *Bayaka.*

43. Sarno, *Song from the Forest,* 80. Also see Toop, *Ocean of Sound,* 130–31.

44. Kevin Kelly, "Eno: Gossip Is Philosophy," *Wired* 3, no. 5 (1995): 146–51, 204–9.

45. On the Lanois, Hassell, and Eno connections see Toop, *Ocean of Sound,* 146–48.

46. David Sinclair, "Global Music Pulse: Belgium," *Billboard,* 20 June 1992, 47; Melinda Newman, "Artist Developments: Breaking Zap Mama," *Billboard,* 20 March 1993, 20; Thom Duffy, "Zap Mama Rides World Wave: Afro-European Quintet Bridges Cultural Gaps," *Billboard,* 7 August 1993, 1, 77; Gould Hall, "A Belgian-African Quartet Mixes Traditions in Many Ways," *New York Times,* 11 June 1994, 16.

47. See, for example, Francis Bebey, *Agatha Moudio's Son* (1968; reprint, Nairobi: Heinemann, 1971); *African Music: A People's Art* (1969; reprint, London: Harrap, 1975); *King Albert* (1976; reprint, Westport: L. Hill, 1981).

48. Manu Dibango, *Three Kilos of Coffee* (Chicago: University of Chicago Press, 1994), 15, 79.

49. Keil and Feld, *Music Grooves,* 218–26, 304–11.

50. Cradick might be the first of the pygmy pop artists to recognize the complexities of actually returning money—see Andrew Means, "In the Field: Ethno-Phonography in the Late 20th Century," *Jazziz* 13, no. 5 (1996): 72–77. Cradick says that since music is communal in Baka villages, the performance and composition royalties must be treated as communal property. This led to the creation of a fund which collects the royalties and allows Baka to democratically decide how to disburse them. He notes, "To simply give them cash would be the easiest thing to do . . . but it would be the most irresponsible since they would not keep it for long. They have a poor understanding of figures and money, compared to some of their neighbors (particularly the liquor sellers), who would very quickly end up with all the money" (ibid., 75).

51. Jon Pareles, "Pop View: A Small World After All," *The New York Times,* 24 March 1996.

52. Andrew Ross, "Ecoculture," *Artforum* 32, no. 4 (1993): 11.

53. David Sprague, "Deep Forest Mines Globe for Second Set," *Billboard,* 18 March 1995, 14; Erik Goldman, "In Deep with Deep Forest," *Rhythm Music* 4, no. 8 (1995): 36–39, 53.

54. Ibid., 39.

55. Jean-Pierre Hallet with Alexandra Pelle, *Pygmy Kitabu* (New York: Random House, 1973).

56. Randall Grass, "Zap Mamas," *Village Voice,* 29 December 1992, 84.

57. Ben Turner, "Bushwhackers!" *Melody Maker,* 12 February 1994, 37.

58. Brooke Wentz, "Baka Beyond," *Creem* (January/February 1994).

59. Attali, *Noise,* 130.

International Times:
Fusions, Exoticism, and Antiracism
in Electronic Dance Music

David Hesmondhalgh

In memory of Jim Osborne (1965–1998)

Plagiarism as a cultural tactic should be aimed at putrid capitalists,
not potential comrades.

HAKIM BEY

New technologies of sampling—the transfer of sounds from one recording
to another—allow contemporary musicians unprecedented access to the
global memory banks of recorded sound. The resulting ethical and political questions about the authorship and ownership of sounds are tangled
enough in the case of rap, where it can be argued that a distinctively African
American form of cultural production, centered on intertextuality and recontextualization, has been systematically discriminated against by intellectual copyright law.[1] But these questions become even more controversial
when "Western" musicians sample "non-Western" musicians. What are the
implications for our understanding of the ethics of cultural appropriation
when the sound of a Pacific island women's choir becomes the hook of a
club hit in Europe, without reward, recompense, or credit for that choir?
And when that hook is then lifted into a Coke commercial? To what extent
does the act of recontextualization, the placing of the sample next to other
sounds, mean that authorship (and the resultant financial rewards) should
be attributed to those sampling, rather than those sampled? How, in other
words, are issues of cultural "borrowing" and appropriation reconfigured in
the era of digital sampling technologies? This chapter investigates these issues via a case study of a West London–based record company, Nation
Records, which specializes in forms of electronic dance music[2] in which the
sampling of non-Western sounds plays a prominent part.

A theme of this chapter, then, is the interpenetration of racial inequality,
cultural ownership, new musical technologies, and the commodification of

entertainment. However, the case of Nation adds another layer to previous debates on these issues. When "world music" superstars make their well-intentioned forays into non-Western sounds and release the resulting albums through the subsidiaries of multinational entertainment corporations, a sense of exploitation is tangible to many people, however generously the musicians are paid and however sincerely Paul Simon or David Byrne seek to raise awareness of their traditions. But Nation is that rare thing, a successful black-owned British independent record company. Its staff and musicians, black and white, are aware of issues of racial inequality and are committed to antiracist political struggle. Does the political awareness of record company staff and musicians make a difference? How might the ownership of the record company by black entrepreneurs affect debates about ownership of musical styles?

An issue of wider relevance raised by the case study is that it allows a close look at the aspirations of politically oriented musicians and record company staff. The examination of a particular site where the recording, distribution and marketing of music are organized allows us to scrutinize the production practices and ideologies of musicians and record company staff at a micro level, and to assess the discursive, commercial, and technological contexts of their work. How do musicians and music industry workers see the issues of ethics, identity, and commerce involved in musical exchange and borrowing? There has been relatively little space in popular music studies for the views of musicians and industry staff. This is perhaps because of a worry among researchers that a focus on musicians' conceptions of the creative process would risk reproducing the banalities of publicity interviews. This is indeed a danger, but what emerged in my interviews with Nation musicians and staff was something more than a set of naïve complaints about the tainting of pure creative impulses by commercial imperatives. Instead, I found that musicians and staff at Nation had long been involved in complex political, aesthetic, and ethical debates over their own practices. I outline such debates at Nation to indicate the tangled ethical and political issues surrounding new musical technologies such as sampling in 1990s music-making. But I also suggest how independent record companies can serve as sites of struggles over meanings, messages, and rewards for labor.[3]

I. TWO TYPES OF DANCE FUSION

Nation has been an unusually successful black-owned British record company. It was established, owned, and managed by a black woman of Caribbean descent (Kath Canoville) and a Pakistani man (Aki Nawaz). Nation's development in the period 1988–93 reflects the partners' attempts to fulfill two avowed aims of the company. The first was to develop careers for British-Asian musicians. By the late 1980s, the partners were moving away from their earlier interests in postpunk music and becoming increasingly involved in British variants of South Asian musical styles, including bhangra.[4] They enjoyed some success promoting bhangra events, but as a manager Canoville experienced great frustration in attempting to work with major and large independent record companies on signing and developing British-Asian acts. In interview, she attributed the reluctance of the established industry to take on bhangra to institutional racism:

> It has to be racism, because I don't know of any indie acts who would be sell-ing 50,000 albums and wouldn't be signed up. It's just a complete impossibil-ity. And there was the evidence there that these albums were being sold. And at the end of it, each company would say, "It sounds really good, but I don't see how we could get involved, this is their market," as opposed to "This is some-thing we could get into."[5]

Nation, according to Canoville, was set up in order to combat such inequities. The second aim of the company was almost pedagogical: to introduce young listeners to unfamiliar, non-Western sounds via the fusion of global music with posthouse dance music culture. Canoville put it in the following way: "The idea initially was, basically, if we could introduce the younger genera-tion who were into fusion to this type of music, they may actually look be-yond that, and delve into the sources and actually find out [that] this Mo-roccan fusion is actually a fusion of Algerian rai, and rai music is really good music in its own right."

Since 1993, Nation has been mainly associated with two types of music which attempt to fulfill these aims. The first juxtaposes various non-Western musical styles with "Western" dance rhythms and is produced, for the most part, by white musicians with a strong commitment to multiculturalism (Transglobal Underground, Loop Guru, and others). Among a number of terms for such music, "world dance fusion" was the most widely used.[6] The second fusion genre prevalent at Nation has been Asian hip hop, produced by Fun-da-mental and Hustlers HC, plus Asian Dub Foundation, whose mu-sic is not strictly hip hop and who aim toward a more ambitious and complex fusion music that includes jungle influences. I shall introduce these two sub-genres via discussion (here in section I) of the two biggest-selling bands on Nation, Transglobal Underground and Fun-da-mental, before going on to assess debates at the label about the politics and ethics of sampling (II), about multiculturalism (III) and about black identity in popular music (IV).

The "hybrid" forms produced at Nation have been seen by musicians, mu-sic journalists, and others as politically progressive interventions which offer new models of cultural interaction in (contemporary Western European) so-cieties marked by racial inequality and violence. The favorable treatment of Nation acts in the relatively politicized British music press has been striking. In what follows, I ask whether such positive interpretations are justified, or whether these multiculturalist practices actually serve to confirm and reinforce existing racial divisions and inequalities, against the explicit intentions of the musicians and staff responsible for their production and distribution.

a) Transglobal Underground: "World Dance Fusion"

Kath Canoville and Aki Nawaz knew, through their contacts, a generation of white musicians who, in the 1980s, had gradually turned away from the post-punk scene, where the momentum of innovation was slowing down, toward "world music" and non-Western sounds. Early singles on Nation give a flavor of the work of these musicians.[7] The tracks combine the pulsating house rhythms popular in clubs at the time with some gentler, ambient tracks, and they feature widespread use of sampled extracts from non-Western music. But it was only with the release in 1991 of "Temple Head" by Transglobal Underground, a band based around a core of three white musicians with a postpunk pedigree, that Nation's world dance fusion gained particular attention from the music press.[8]

The track features a steady looped dance beat, combined with live tabla-playing, acid house–style piano chords, and a number of samples, interspersed with a rap (by guest rapper Sheriff) on the familiar theme of global unity via music. The relative eclecticism of the track compared with other club music at the time is indicated by a rock-style electric guitar solo. But the most striking features of the track are two samples taken from recordings of Tahitian gospel choirs. The real hook, and one much commented upon in reviews and among audiences, was the first, often referred to as the "na na na" sample.[9] The sample is picked up by the rap ("learn to say peace and na na na") and the sampled choir effectively act as backing singers for the rapper Sheriff. Their "na na na" is constructed as the prototypical unity chant, a model of music as a universal language. Yet the singers in the choirs are effectively without a voice: catchy though the mixing of contemporary rap with "ancient" voices may be, the samples act as an exotic backing for the message of the song. The pastoral innocence of the non-Western voices serves for the song-text as the "other" which the West can use to redefine itself. While this appears to pay respect to the music sampled, it denies the complexity of the identities of these others. In terms of the production of the track, the singers were merely virtual presences, voices transferred via ethnomusicological recordings to the Western music market. They were neither consulted about nor paid for the use of their work in the track.

The representational work being carried out in the track—and by extension in Nation's work generally—is not innocent of the kind of exoticism and primitivism which the music press, in the early 1990s, was beginning to criticize in world music multiculturalism. Yet the same music press continued to distinguish the cultural politics of world music from that of Nation's world dance fusion. Indeed, their approval of the Nation aesthetic intensified as Transglobal Underground began to promote their records by playing live concerts, and quotations from various reviews will indicate the ways in which world dance fusion was constructed as a more valid and progressive form of "hybrid" cultural product than world music—often on the grounds that it avoided world music's earnest quest for authenticity in favor of a more playful pastiche:

> The new movement offers global sounds a second chance after the half-hearted World Music hype of the mid-80s. . . . The endless CDs of Eskimo, Tibetan and Asian virtuosi bypassed both the pop and underground music scenes to lurk in a ghetto of right-on vegans and Sunday supplement readers.

> Transglobal Underground's Natacha Atlas: true "world" music.

> Thankfully, we've long since passed that wanky stage where, cough, World Music had to *mean* something, or be authentic. . . . [10]

b) Fun-da-mental: Asian Hip Hop

In some respects, the music of the second major act to emerge on Nation, Fun-da-mental (see figure 10.1), set up by Nation owner-manager Aki Nawaz in 1992, is consistent with the fusion aesthetic practiced by the company and praised by the music press. Fun-da-mental sample from non-Western sources: Hindi film music, muezzin wails, *qawwali* singing. But the generic conventions around which Nawaz and his various collaborators in Fun-da-mental have organized such borrowings are those of hip hop, in particular black American political rap, rather than the posthouse dance music favored by Transglobal Underground and other acts such as Loop Guru. Hip hop techniques such as scratching (the manipulations of turntables to produce rhythms) and breaks (when all other instruments other than the looped percussion track drop out) are adopted: no previous Nation record had used them. MC Bad-Sha Lallaman, meanwhile, adopted a (Jamaican) ragga style for his vocals. And, crucially, Fun-da-mental demonstrated an explicit allegiance to African American Islamic radicalism, and to the black separatist politics of groups such as the Black Panthers. [11]

Although they used a mixture of African American and Caribbean musical and political influences, all the original members of Fun-da-mental came from British Asian backgrounds. Three, including Nawaz, were Moslems, while the group's tabla player, Goldfinger, was Sikh. Many young British Asians were involved in breakdancing and graffiti from the early 1980s on, but relatively few were rapping and scratching. Fun-da-mental were innovative in bringing these elements into music aimed in part at Asian communities. While African American radicalism provided political inspiration, the raps and spoken samples in Fun-da-mental tracks were concerned with Asian and British-Asian issues. The band's name reflects this—a controversial in-

Figure 10.1 Leading British hip-hop act Fun-da-mental in their post-1994 incarnation, featuring Dave Watts (left) and Nation Records owner Aki Nawaz (right). Photo by Matt Bright.

vocation of Islamic fundamentalism, even while the hyphens in the name indicate another purpose, that of combining pleasure ("fun") with thought ("mental"). The band's symbol is a crescent, to evoke Islam, but also the Pakistani flag. (Aki Nawaz's mother was a leading British activist for Benazir Bhutto's Pakistan People's Party.) And Fun-da-mental's first single, "Righteous Preacher," contained lyrics which supported the Ayatollah Khomeini's "fatwa" against Salman Rushdie. An interview in *Melody Maker* at the time of the release of the single caused great controversy. Goldfinger made the following statement: "Even though I'm Sikh, I agree with my Muslim brothers that Rushdie has to face the consequences of what he has done. . . . Until you understand the importance of religion in our culture, you will not understand how much this man has hurt us. And Rushdie's actions haven't just affected Asians. Who do you think is paying to house and protect the bastard?"[12] In making such controversial and problematic statements, Fun-da-mental were attempting to puncture the complacency of the white music press, and to address the Asian community.

Nation also attempted to move beyond the predominantly white audience for fusion in other ways. Deals were arranged for a series of singles by Fun-da-mental (and another Nation band, Hustlers HC) to be distributed by British-Asian firms in the parallel cassette market, away from record shops, in the Asian stores where traditionally many Asian Britons bought their music. But a key distributor went bankrupt, owing Nation money, and margins were extremely low in any case, compared with the mainstream market. Ultimately, Nation abandoned their attempt to intervene in the separate Asian cassette market. The feeling at the label was that there were other ways to reach Asian youth without going through the separate Asian system. As one Nation insider, Simon Underwood, put it, "The problem isn't about specialist shops. These kids go to HMV and Our Price. They *work* there, and get discounts."[13]

In spite of such setbacks, the use of African American and Caribbean-influenced forms by Asian British bands, initiated by Fun-da-mental, was to become increasingly important at Nation over the following years, as Hustlers HC and Asian Dub Foundation began to record for the label. From this point on, there was an increasing division at the label between the work of Asian musicians and the world dance fusion of white multiculturalists.

II. THE POLITICS AND ETHICS OF SAMPLING

From 1993 onwards, the multiculturalist aesthetics prevailing at Nation were to become more controversial among the musicians and staff based there. A significant event was the arrival of Simon Underwood at the company in that year. Like many of the fusion musicians associated with Nation, Underwood came into the music business in the wake of punk, having founded a political postpunk act, The Pop Group, and a later funk-fusion band, Pig-bag. Like many musicians in the early 1980s, Underwood had been excited and fascinated by the vitality of early New York City hip hop and its use of sampling. But during the 1980s, he had grown increasingly suspicious of the use of sampling in house music, and of the borrowing of African forms by world music figures such as Peter Gabriel. In particular, he felt that non-Western music was being treated "as if it was a natural thing that came out of these countries just like cocoa beans . . . just flew off trees and suddenly landed in our shops via some miraculous thing. There was no idea that there was a trade. Just like there was a trade in resources, a trade in bodies from Africa." These views meant that Underwood brought a new perspective to bear on sampling. As Nation acts such as Transglobal Underground, Fun-da-mental, and Loop Guru achieved greater success, Canoville and Nawaz began to take Nation out of the more underground twelve-inch-single dance niche, and toward the risky but potentially more prestigious and lucrative album market. In this more mainstream sector, copyright infringements are much more closely monitored by owners, and so musicians using samples of other recordings need to "clear" them—to obtain permission for their use, usually by agreeing to pay a fee or a percentage of royalties. Underwood's interest in the global political economy of sampling led him to take on the job of obtaining permissions from copyright-owners for Nation acts. Because the ownership of copyright in the music industry usually falls to companies rather than musicians, this involves some difficult ethical issues: "We've got to clear our samples, you know. I don't always agree with a lot of it because if we can, we'd rather pay the artist, but usually most of these samples the artists have sold out to labels somewhere down the line anyway." Many of the copyrights on the ethnomusicological recordings used by Nation acts belong to public institutions such as the Smithsonian Institute[14] or have been sold *en bloc* to major corporations, who are keen to buy even such seemingly obscure catalogues in an era when television and film companies may well pay thousands of dollars for music which creates the right ambience to accompany visual images.

Underwood saw a strong distinction between the practices of major corporate and independent copyright owners:

> I tried to clear some Bulgarian sample for Loop Guru last year. They [a major publisher, subdivision of a multinational entertainment corporation] didn't even know they *had* it. They won't start talking to you under two and a half thousand dollars. It's all centralized, they've got one person in LA who's got a pile this big, and they're dealing with requests from platinum-selling artists, so you're on the bottom of the pile.[15]

According to Underwood, smaller labels and publishing companies are more committed to protection of the artists whose copyright they administer than corporate publishers. One particular story illustrates the sensitivity with which Nation and a small independent publisher attempted to handle a copyright clearance issue, and suggests that music-industry practices are not monolithic with regard to sampling ethics. Transglobal Underground wanted to use a sample from a track by the Mauritanian vocal artist Dimi Mint Abba, whose album was on a North London label called World Circuit. The usual procedure in copyright clearance is for cassettes to be sent to the publisher and to the record company, who generally own the rights to the underlying composition and to the recording of it, respectively. The publisher is usually responsible for forwarding the cassette to the artist, so the artist can give her permission for the extract to be used, if her contract with the publisher so requires. But Dimi Mint Abba was touring Bedouin communities in the Sahara and could not be contacted. World Circuit carried out the publishing deal on her behalf, but in order to ensure that the sample used by Transglobal Underground did not appear in a context defamatory to the artist, Nation, Transglobal Underground, and World Circuit made an arrangement. Underwood had the lyrics sung on the track translated into the dialect used by Dimi Mint Abba; he signed a statement to the effect that the lyrics would not be changed in any way, that no other lyrics would be transposed over the top, and that nothing defamatory to Islam would be used. The matter was resolved to the satisfaction of all concerned.

David Muddyman, a key member of another Nation world dance fusion act, Loop Guru, echoed some elements of Simon Underwood's sentiments about copyright, but differed significantly from Underwood in his views. Muddyman was much more reluctant to make payments:

> Having had intimate relations with a lot of musicians from all over the world, I wouldn't wish to cheat them, but the one thing I'm completely against is the fact that in a lot of big companies, none of the money will get back to the original musicians because they're field recordings.[16] They may go to the guy who recorded it and they will most certainly go to the record companies, but the musicians will not get any more money.

A key issue in debates about sampling ethics concerns the *citation* of sampled musicians on CD and record sleeves. For David Muddyman, such naming, while desirable, leaves them open to the accumulation of further charges for borrowed samples:

> Another thing is that I would love to thank and give credit to the people we sampled—not the labels, but the *people* we sampled—but if say we did it on *Duniya* [Loop Guru's album for Nation], where there was absolutely no money to clear the samples, then obviously we're letting ourselves open to an influx of record companies hunting for money, so it's a case of if . . . when you've got money, yes, clear it, but if you haven't, what can you do?

But for Simon Underwood, the lack of citations on album sleeves was a source of deep unease, and a factor which he felt reinforced the generalized exoticism of the musical "borrowings." Because of his concerns over the ethical and financial implications of sampling, Underwood has increasingly come to advocate the use of live musicians in the studio, in preference to the digital sampling techniques which caught his imagination in the wake of hip hop. (His objection, he was often at pains to point out, was not to sampling but to the particular uses to which sampling was put). The problem for a small record company, though, is that such collaboration is expensive. This is particularly the case at Nation, because of the nature of the music they are seeking to incorporate into the fusions. To substitute real musicians for sampled recordings would involve paying session rates as well as incurring significant expenses in locating suitable musicians in the first place.

The story of the "na na na" sample on Transglobal Underground's "Temple Head" reveals some of the complex issues facing politically committed musicians and staff when they choose to sample from non-Western musicians. Early coverage of "Temple Head" claimed that one of the band members "taped the chorus to 'Temple Head' ten years ago when he came across some women singing it."[17] In fact, Transglobal's drummer Hamilton Lee (variously known as DJ Man Tu and Hamid under the band's pseudonym strategies—see below) later admitted that David Muddyman of Loop Guru passed the sample to him when they were sharing a house together.[18] In interview, Muddyman confirmed that the sample came from a well-known series of recordings of South Seas music. The original evasion was presumably so that the owners of the copyright on the Tahitian sample would not have their suspicions raised. The financial significance of these issues should not be underestimated. Coca-Cola adopted the "na na na" section of "Temple Head" for their 1996 Summer Olympics advertising campaign in the UK. Under Nation and Transglobal Underground's deal, BMG have kept the "circle-p" copyright to the recording, which means that they will gain the public performance royalties.[19] One thing is fairly certain in all this: the women of the Tahitian gospel choir are unlikely to receive any money. These issues of rewards for less powerful musical creators have been ignored in previous discussions of sampling ethics, which have tended to concentrate on the sampling of earlier pop and soul hits by African American artists.

Transglobal Underground have, partly in response to Underwood's interventions (and appeals to their own preexisting political inclinations against racism and exploitation), changed their recording practice, and their recent work has made extensive use of live musicians.[20] Even from their earlier days, Transglobal Underground adopted a loose, flexible structure which has enabled collaboration and cooperation around a core of three members. Other musicians are hired, often at generous rates. One key collaborator who eventually became a fourth core member was the singer Natacha Atlas. Atlas was less interested in the aesthetic possibilities of sampling than the original three-man core of the band, but she was keen to bring in some of the network of musicians she had come to know. At first, however, there were pragmatic limitations to overcome:

> *DH:* Was the intention from the beginning to use sampling?
>
> *Natacha Atlas:* I think that was the other three's idea more than it was mine. My idea was more to replace a lot of the samples with other Arabic and Indian musicians that I actually know. So that idea came in that we were going to mix samples with real playing. They wanted to do that too. But at the time, it was about what was financially possible.

What made "real playing" by specialist non-Western musicians possible, in line with the shift away from sampling, was Nation's licensing deal with Sony for the second Transglobal Underground album, *International Times*.[21] Such extra finances, combined with a deal signed with the larger independent Beggars Banquet, enabled the band to bring in an Egyptian classical musician based in Southall (in South West London), Essam Rashad, to arrange the strings on the track "Taal Zaman." Natacha Atlas's own first solo album for Nation (licensed through Beggars Banquet) involved considerable collaboration with non-Western musicians.[22]

Loop Guru, however, did not move toward such collaboration with actual musicians; rather, they continued to employ sampling. This was the source of some tension at Nation. Loop Guru did not achieve anything like the same sales as Transglobal Underground, and their preference for samples over collaboration with live musicians was in part financial. In fact, though, *cleared* samples can cost almost as much as studio work with outside musicians.[23] The preference for sampling over collaboration on the part of Loop Guru was primarily ideological, stemming from an attachment to certain modernist forms of aesthetic, such as collage, and a sense that copyright law favors record companies rather than musicians. David Muddyman asked me: "Is collage a legitimate art form? If pieces of photographs appear in an art collage, do the original photographers get money out of it? I very much doubt it. So in a sense I think a lot of sampling debates are organized by record companies who clearly see an instant profit for doing bugger all." No doubt Muddyman is correct to recognize the record companies' economic interests. But some at Nation were disquieted by what they felt was an evasive attitude toward issues of authorship and creativity by Loop Guru. In one interview, bandmember Salman Gita appealed to a notion of music as a medium which eternally invites exchange and influence:

Music has been thievery since the beginning of time. Ultimately when you sample something it takes on a life of its own. You can have a 20 minute piece of music, and you find one little gem in there, and loop it, and it becomes your own idea. They [the original musicians] didn't think of doing it like that, otherwise they'd have done it. I don't want to start originating too much of our own samples. You're just playing with a machine, or taking apart a singer's voice when you do use real musicians, and it gets rid of the ego thing.[24]

Gita here implicitly appeals to a critique of individual authorship which is prevalent among many dance musicians and which perhaps owes something, indirectly, to the poststructuralist analysis of authorship. But there are unfortunate implications here: the evacuation of the ego of the non-Western musician from the studio, so that the Western musician, immersed in his or her technology, can go about the task of collaging non-Western sounds, unfettered by any objections that might be made. Simon Underwood expressed his doubts about such views in the following faux-sympathetic manner: "I can respect their ideas. It's their music, and their music is sample-based in the William Burroughs cut-up sense. They want to work with samples because they can manipulate samples whereas they don't want to manipulate human beings. [A pause]. Or they don't want the person around when they're manipulating them [laughs]."

The two musicians at the core of Loop Guru do sometimes work with other musicians, as opposed to using samples. David Muddyman's solution to the "collaboration" problem is to record non-Western musicians "in the field":

Ethically, I do have problems with sampling. Wherever I go, I meet lots of musicians and I hire them for a session to come and play in my room or whatever. They go away happy, they know what I want to do with them and you know I pay them, because it's impossible to pay royalties on things like that, so if they go away happy, and I'm happy, then there's no problems on either side. And I hope that if the records continue to sell, then I'll be able to fund more trips to go away.

It is hard not to hear echoes in Muddyman's language of tourists who feel sure that there could never be a problem for the people of the places they visit, on the basis of friendly transactions in the restaurant or the crafts market.

Aki Nawaz, leader of Fun-da-mental, has chosen not to clear his samples at all. His reasons reveal further levels of difficulty in the ethics of sampling:

A lot of the things I steal are from Indian folk, Indian classical music, a lot of that is like bootleg tapes. . . . I know where I've got them from. There's no point in me clearing it. All over the Third World, music doesn't work like it works here, it's a lot tighter here. If I was to ring up somebody in EMI India and say "I've taken a sample," he'd say "So what?" . . . 'cos people copy their music all the time. And the artist would never see any reward anyway.

To others at Nation, this was a disingenuous way of justifying nonpayment. Nawaz's solution to the ethical and political problems raised by sampling is a radical one: to make payments directly to the "people."

> All we want to do if we make any money out of [a record], is to put it some-where where it really matters, and that's into kids' mouths. . . . We make do-nations to active, humanist groups. I'd like to do something more. Even Trans-global have mentioned it, that they'd like to set up some sort of fund. But it's like what do you do? Where do you send the money to? You can send money to Pakistan, but you know that fucking 75 percent of it is put into somebody's back pocket. There's no point in sending it to charities here, 'cos you know that 95 percent is put away in administration costs. Charity is big business here. Eventually we'll come to something.

The sleeve to Fun-da-mental's second album, *With Intent to Pervert the Cause of Injustice*,[25] also makes reference to such donations, and also fails to stipu-late which groups will receive them. I do not wish to imply that Fun-da-mental and Nation have failed to make such payments. But by omitting to name these groups, they have failed to specify their support for the projects they feel de-serve it.

Even more problematically, Nawaz has also appealed to a dubious notion of racial ownership of musical intellectual property to resolve some of the issues about sampling. Simon Underwood recalled:

> Aki had sampled someone from an independent label [Indipop] that was do-ing very similar stuff to Nation, particularly with Indian music, but that was run by . . . an Englishman, and Aki had sampled from him, and the man had written to him, and said "Listen, you've sampled from us, you can't do this, you've got to pay." And Aki had written to him and said "I've got more right to use this music than you have."

Aki Nawaz's claim about his greater right to use Indian music than the white copyright holder rested on the grounds that he, like the musicians who orig-inated the sample, came from Asia, and that he shared their history of vic-timization by racism and imperialism. This recalls arguments made by rap and hip hop musicians and their advocates about "citation ethics." Various commentators have remarked on how the use in hip hop culture of first DJ-ing and then sampling draws on the longstanding African American tradi-tion of "Signifyin"—using and referring to previous texts while transform-ing them into new ones—and how the validity and creativity of this tradition have not been adequately recognized in copyright law.[26] However, there is a considerable difference between the issues involved in the exclusion of a cul-tural tradition in a hegemonic legal system and the ownership of a sample by another independent company. Nawaz's claim was presumably intended as a clever way of evading a demand for payment for a sample, by appealing perhaps to liberal guilt; but, in his argument, he invokes a powerful, essentialist notion of cultural ownership.

III. DEBATES ABOUT MULTICULTURALISM

The range of positions within Nation toward the crucial issue of due payment for creative labor is striking. These differences can be seen to derive not only from the ideological and economic differences outlined, but also in large part from the various political views within the label about multiculturalism and responses to contemporary racial division. A new generation of Asian musicians who came to work at Nation in the mid-1990s brought with them a political critique of the multiculturalism of the world dance fusion acts at the label, such as Loop Guru and Transglobal Underground. A track by one such act, Asian Dub Foundation, summarizes this critique nicely:

> We ain't ethnic, exotic or eclectic
> The only E we use is electric . . .
> But this militant vibe ain't what you expected
> With your liberal minds, patronise our culture
> Skimming the surface like vultures
> With your tourist mentality, we're still the natives
> You're multicultural, we're antiracist.[27]

The pun on "E" (the name commonly used in Britain for ecstasy, the drug central to rave culture) makes it clear that it is the exoticism of dance music culture, typified by the Nation world dance fusion acts and their audiences, which is the primary target here. Anirhudda Das, who penned these lines and who played in rave acts for many years before forming Asian Dub Foundation, spoke in interviews of a number of ways in which he became dissatisfied with dance music culture. There was, he felt, an "unspoken censorship" about certain political issues, because of dance music's focus on drug experience. Das was careful not to define political music in terms of lyrics, though: "I'd always resented not being able to express political ideas, and not just in terms of lyrics, but in terms of the sounds that you could use." But while world dance fusion acts such as Transglobal Underground were incorporating this wider range of textures, Das was suspicious of the motives of audiences drawn toward such fusions:

> We've done a lot of gigs with Transglobal, we've seen the audience, and we think, "Right, you're getting into all this music, and Asian music, and hippies have done it from the time of George Harrison or whatever, but how many Asian people do you know? How many black people do you know? Do you have any contact? Do you make any effort?" We just want basics like that. They might talk about

South Africa and all of that shit, because it's far away, but on the basic local and
personal level, are these people making any contact with black people?

And while Das praised the way that the core members of Transglobal Underground have been prepared to engage in debate and dialogue with Asian
musicians, and for their awareness of issues of racial inequality, he felt that
they "haven't taken this discussion out to their audience enough. If that was
happening, then that would change the nature of those sounds being regarded as exotic."

This criticism of exoticism extends to *visual* aspects of world dance fusion
as a subgenre. When ADF played a gig with Nation's other key white multiculturalist dance fusion act, Loop Guru, at London's Astoria 2 venue, Das
felt there was a sharp and ironic contrast between the "militant" combat and
jungle clothing worn by ADF and the Asian dress worn by the white members of Loop Guru for their set. Whereas Das seems to have engaged in dialogue with members of Transglobal Underground, he indicated that the
gap he and ADF felt between themselves and Loop Guru made dialogue impossible: "We didn't have to say much, us just being there, we had to share
the same space. We didn't say to their face. . . . We didn't have to say anything, but people have said that they've brought stuff up with Loop Guru,
and that they're obliv . . . either oblivious, or not prepared to discuss it."

From time to time, in interview, Transglobal Underground have been confronted with charges that they are appropriating exotic cultural identities for
their own purposes. A riposte commonly made by the group is that in the
contemporary world identities are unstable. Natacha Atlas, from 1994 the
group's lead singer and most public face, often refers to her own mixed origins (she is mixed-race Jewish and Arabic and was brought up in Northamp-
ton, in the English Midlands, and in Brussels, Belgium) as evidence that the
group reflects such hybrid and diverse cultural identities.[28]

One journalist put the issue in the following way: "Could Transglobal
Underground be guilty of the very imperialism they loathe? After all, if
they wanted an African tribal chant, why didn't they go to Africa and record
it? Isn't that theft?"[29] Atlas's response to the question was: "I have to be a
hybrid—that's what I am; a hybrid of those cultures, those bloods. That's why
the music has to be a hybrid as well." But this is a response to an assertion
that musical styles should not be mixed, rather than to the point the journalist is making about working directly with (nonsampled) musicians. In addition, Transglobal Underground were involved in a significant fudging of
issues of ethnic identity. Of the four permanent members of the band, only
Natacha Atlas's face appeared in publicity photographs for their first two albums. The other three core band members wore copies of Nepalese temple
masks to cover their faces (see figure 10.2). They also adopted pseudonyms,
which have shifted over the years, further confusing who is who in the band.

Figure 10.2 A publicity photograph for Transglobal Underground that mixes
a number of exotic visual signs. The white male musicians wear Nepalese masks,
while (as was usual in publicity photos) singer Natacha Atlas is the only band
member unmasked. Photo by Mick Hutson.

This is a deliberate strategy, and the band often explain it as a way of challenging what they feel is an excessive focus on personality in popular music—
recalling the quasi-poststructuralist critique of authorship invoked by Loop
Guru. However, the pseudonyms they adopt carry strong suggestions that
they are black. But while they collaborate with Atlas and black musicians such
as rapper TUUP, the three core members are white. Bass player Nick (who
left the band in 1997) used the pseudonym Count Dubulah, recalling the
Caribbean and African American naming tradition of parodying aristocratic
names (e.g, Prince Buster, Prince Far-I, Duke Ellington, Count Basie). The
hint of "dub," appropriate for a bass player, reinforces the sense of this lin-

eage. Drummer Hamilton Lee calls himself Hamid Mantu, which has a distinctly Arabic ring. Keyboardist Tim Whelan sometimes goes under the name Attiah Ahlan (at other times, he uses the more Germanic Alex Kassiak). Publicity photographs, rather than representing a "hybrid" cultural identity, flirt with various exotic signifiers. (See figure 10.2.)

A limited amount of controversy has surrounded Natacha Atlas's use of belly dancing and of Arabic costume. When, in interview, I raised the issue of whether dancing in belly dancer costume might draw on certain stereotypical representations of Arabic women, Atlas responded vigorously:

> It seems to be more of a problem to everyone else than it is to me. I do get rather sick of some sort of feminist . . . almost like coming from one area where they want to present things in this very worthy way, certain dancers and certain journalists, some of them happen to be Asian—whatever. They have this very hard line—"Well, it's just in a belly dance costume, and it's just exoticizing it again." But that is the actual reality, if you go to Cairo in an actual Arabic nightclub, it's what you're gonna fucking well see, so what is the problem? . . . So people say, "It's exoticizing it, exploitation. . . . " Bollocks! It's not my problem, it's theirs. I've worked in Arabic nightclubs, I know the reality.

In fact, it seems that criticism of this aspect of Natacha Atlas and Transglobal Underground's work has been remarkably muted. The music press have proved unsurprisingly willing to reproduce publicity photographs featuring a scantily clad Atlas surrounded by the men of the band encased in their exotic masks, hiding their whiteness.

Criticisms of exotica at the label by no means came only from black musicians like Ani Das. Simon Underwood was a particularly vigorous critic of world dance fusion, as I have already explained. Like Ani, Underwood was loyal to Transglobal Underground. He was gently satirical of their pseudonyms and masks, but he put their case about "playing" with ethnic identity in order to undermine essentialism. He reserved special venom for Loop Guru, however, and often expressed outright impatience with their refusal to collaborate, rather than sample, and with their Orientalist garb and music.

> I just kind of draw a blank about these things when I see them, I just get so sort of wound up by them. I'm so pissed off. As far as I'm concerned, Loop Guru are still following the same path as they've always done. They're not interested in collaborating with artists. They're interested in taking snippets of music and making it to create an *Arabian Nights* kind of picture book . . .

But the impatience with which some staff at Nation talked about Loop Guru seemed to me, at times, to be a way of avoiding having to confront similar problems in the musical and visual strategies of Transglobal Underground. We should not, perhaps, discount the influence of the fact that Transglobal Underground have been by far the biggest-selling act on the label. But there is no doubt that even the most critical insiders felt that Transglobal have been willing to engage in a dialogue with criticism and to move toward greater collaboration with diasporic artists. Loop Guru, on the other hand, were increasingly felt to be beyond the pale. In early 1995, they left the label. When I interviewed him, David Muddyman said that he felt that other projects were receiving priority over Loop Guru, and he hinted at the special interest that Canoville and Nawaz, the label owner-managers, had as manager of Transglobal Underground and artist in Fun-da-mental, respectively.

IV. MODALITIES OF BLACK IDENTITY AT NATION

Until now, I have concentrated on the differences between two strands of musical/political/aesthetic strategy present at Nation Records: that of the label's world dance fusion acts on the one hand and of its Asian acts on the other. But it would be wrong to portray these Asian groups as homogeneous and united in their approach to musical politics. I can only briefly sketch here some of the conflicts and contradictions which black musicians working at the label have faced, but two main issues emerge: differences over religion and nationalisms, and differences over appropriate political-aesthetic strategies, particularly as regards the legacy of hip hop.

Sikh hip hop duo Hustlers HC (who disbanded in 1997) at times found Fun-da-mental's use of religious (and nationalistic) imagery divisive. This was particularly apparent at certain Nation events, where Hustlers HC often found themselves opening for Fun-da-mental. Fun-da-mental use the star and crescent (the Pakistani flag) as a backdrop for their live performances, and Hustlers were frequently asked by Sikh youths why Hustlers did not likewise play under the flag of Khalistan, the area of India where Sikhs form a majority and which Sikh separatists wish to make an independent state. At one particular Asian event, because they came on immediately before Fun-da-mental and because there was no time to change set decor between performances, Hustlers ended up playing under the star and crescent hanging on the stage in anticipation of Fun-da-mental's appearance. Sikh youths approached them after the gig to ask them why they did this. For Hustlers, such uncomfortable experiences were a reminder of the ethnic divisions between British Asians that they experienced in tertiary education. Aki Nawaz of Fun-da-mental belongs to an older generation and has never directly experienced the way in which the intense religious conflicts of South Asia, North Africa, and elsewhere have translated into British campuses during the 1980s and 1990s.

Just as significant as the bands' different attitudes toward religious politics were the very different uses they made of the legacy of hip hop. Aki Nawaz had been a punk and discovered rap relatively recently. He was drawn to hip hop because it could act as a vehicle for certain ideas about political expression through music, ideas which owed a great deal to punk, and Fun-da-mental adopt an agit-prop style common to early versions of both punk and political rap. (Nawaz's alias for record credits was Propa-Ghandi.) Fun-da-mental found a space within white music institutions for messages which are defiantly and positively antiracist. They figured prominently in music-press coverage of a revival in antiracist campaigning following the election of a neo-Nazi to a local government seat in London's Isle of Dogs in 1993.[30] But whereas Nawaz discovered rap late, and found "its politics more sorted than its music," Hustlers HC's longstanding allegiance to hip hop culture predated that culture's pedagogical turn in the mid- to late 1980s.[31] One of the duo, Ski, joined a West London breakdancing crew in the early 1980s—a common way in which young British Asians expressed their allegiance to black American hip hop culture at the time. His partner, Paul, was involved in the running of an electro sound system in the mid-1980s.[32] Like many other hip hop fans, they were drawn to musical-aesthetic and cultural features of the form as much as to the direct expressions of political anger contained within certain versions of it. Given the greater allegiance of Fun-da-mental to black nationalism, it is ironic that Fun-da-mental have found greater recognition among white audiences and institutions while Hustlers HC gained much more positive reactions from British Caribbean hip hop crowds.[33] Such crowds tend to have a strong sense of hierarchy about who can best perform and play rap: African Americans tend to be most favored, followed by British African-Caribbeans. So for a British Sikh band to gain the respect of an African-Caribbean hip hop crowd was no mean feat. Fun-da-mental, while seemingly respected by many Asian young people, draw a mainly white audience to their gigs. Aki Nawaz was frank about the fact that the audience for Fun-da-mental's politics is primarily white youth: "And I think it's a good thing that there are a lot more white kids being influenced by things like that. . . . I'm a firm believer that more dissent and subversion has to come from the West; it's actually more oppressed in its vocalness and its rebelliousness than anywhere else." But the acceptance of forms of hip hop with explicitly "political" raps at the expense of other forms raises crucial and difficult issues concerning the acceptance of black cultural forms. Although in the United States a wide range of rap acts sell well among white audiences, in Europe rap is still granted very little prestige and critical attention outside diasporic communities, except where the music is felt to express an "authentic" political anger. Are white radicals finding in bands like Public Enemy and Fun-da-mental a reflection of their own political agendas and thereby denying the validity of the wide range of musical expression and themes in hip hop as a whole?[34] Might the exclusive acceptance of political versions of rap be a refusal to engage in real dialogue with the greater diversity of African American concerns and voices to be found in hip hop culture? This view might be confirmed by the fact that Fun-da-mental were granted considerably more coverage in the British rock press than any other British rap act.

There is a danger, then, that hip hop and the music of diasporic groups might be valued primarily in terms of a white left-liberal agenda. The story of Asian Dub Foundation may add another twist to this situation. Disillusioned by the lack of promotional push at Nation, the band left the label in 1996. There were conflicts over a change of name. Apparently, Nation felt that keeping the word "Asian" would always limit their appeal in "middle England," according to Rich McLean, Nation's press officer. Having gained a solid audience in France, where Nation had licensed their records to an offshoot of Virgin, in 1997 the band were signed to dance label ffrr, part of the multinational entertainment conglomerate PolyGram (which since 1998 has been owned by Seagram). The album they had released on Nation in 1995, *Facts and Fictions*, was remixed and re-released. By 1998, as they released their second album, *Rafi's Revenge*, the band was gaining enormous press and media coverage (though, at time of writing, it is too early to assess whether the publicity has translated into sales). The band became caught up in the phenomenon of "New Asian Cool," the media's label for its own coverage in 1997 and 1998 of a number of newly fashionable British-Asian acts which, besides Asian Dub Foundation themselves, included Talvin Singh (at one time managed by Kath Canoville and closely associated with Nation in its early days), Cornershop, and Nitin Sawhney. A number of Asian commentators, including the musicians themselves, worried that the label New Asian Cool would make the bands merely an item of fashion, and thus more prone to being discarded once the next media phenomenon arrived. Commentators have rightly applauded the way that recent British-Asian acts have transcended stereotypes of Asian people as "submissive, hard-working, passive and conformist."[35] But the shadow of exoticism is never far away when the primary audience for Asian acts comes mainly from the white middle class.[36] Indeed, the argument that such acts as Asian Dub Foundation represent the "real" face of contemporary British-Asian youth, against prevailing stereotypes, has quickly become a cliché in itself, asserted routinely in nearly all coverage. As with Fun-da-mental, it seems that much of Asian Dub Foundation's audience was made up of the mainly white, college constituency associated with the British indie/alternative rock press. Asian Dub Foundation can hardly be blamed for this situation; nor, indeed, can their audiences. But the situation suggests that, unfortunately, "hybrid" acts may be relatively limited in their cultural effects.

Hustlers HC, who seemed far removed from the two principal defining features of Nation, its agit-prop punk roots and its use of musical fusions to express aspects of contemporary cultural identity, received very little coverage and eventually disbanded. As their main associate at Nation, Simon Underwood, put it while they were still at the label: "The problem is—where do you go with them? I think the racism in the music industry is so thick and institutionalized that it's invisible. And it's smothered by the fact that the record industry makes most of its money out of exploiting black artists, and it sets the standards of what's hip and not hip."[37] And Hustlers HC did not, ultimately, count as hip, either for the white audience, uninterested in most forms of hip hop, or for the hip hop audience, unimpressed by non-U.S. acts.

CONCLUSION: CAN THE SUBALTERN SING?

The critical acclaim (and, for a while, corporate support, from Sony) that has greeted the music of Transglobal Underground suggests that there is certainly room for multiculturalist aesthetics in the contemporary popular music marketplace; and it seems that even explicitly antiracist messages, in the work of Fun-da-mental and Asian Dub Foundation, can find a significant audience. In many respects, this picture supports the orthodox view of hybrid forms of popular music culture in much recent writing. Commentators have celebrated musical-subcultural movements and moments which allow for interaction between black and white youth. A series of fine studies has portrayed popular music culture optimistically as a space where ethnic difference can be negotiated and even temporarily overcome.[38] In addition, many aspects of the work of Nation demonstrate that independent record companies can provide a relatively democratic forum for cultural production: debate about musical and political ideologies was healthy and lively at the company, and resulted in considerable changes in practices there, including a move toward a much more reflexive view of the ethics of sampling. Black musicians were given a platform for an articulate questioning of assumptions about the nature of contemporary black cultural identity, via the determined efforts of Nation's owners and staff to intervene in existing social relations. Dialogue and cooperation were rife, alongside the misunderstandings and allegations which are a feature of so many cultural enterprises.

But much of what happened suggests that there are limits to the political potential of hybridity in recent popular music culture and that racial inequality continues to make its consequences felt in cultural production. The well-intentioned uses of sampling among some Nation acts were politically problematic in terms of how non-Western sounds were represented in the texts; and the authorship of the musicians sampled was often erased, via lack of citation and lack of payment. Exoticist discourses and visual representations added insult to injury. Hybrid musical forms falling outside the categories acceptable to cultural intermediaries, such as the indie music press and the larger companies which have worked with Nation, struggle to be heard.

At present, then, even among the "alternative" institutions of British popular music, black musicians can find a space only on certain terms. This is a result of continuing racial inequality and division. The problem is made worse by a refusal to recognize the situation among many who work in the British music industry, which has led to the neglect of some difficult musical-political issues: the "whiteness" of indie and rave culture; the lack of respect accorded to black British musicians working within the hip hop tradition by both black and white audiences; the racialized tripartite division of the press, with the (white) rock and dance press thriving and the (black) r&b press barely surviving; and the difficulties faced by black music radio stations, to name a few key points. There are limits to what an independent record company like Nation can achieve, within prevailing institutional conditions, in the way of raising consciousness and challenging prevailing structures of cultural production (the company's avowed aims). The independent record company is not a refuge of ethically motivated creativity set apart from, and autonomous of, the nasty world of big business. But only through an adequately critical perspective on such brave but flawed attempts to provide an alternative can any headway be made in transforming the conditions of music-making.

NOTES

1. This is the case made by Thomas G. Schumacher's superb piece, "'This Is a Sampling Sport': Digital Sampling, Rap Music and the Law in Cultural Production," *Media, Culture and Society* 17, no. 2 (1995): 253–73. Legal doctrine is contradictory, he argues, as it assigns copyrights to corporate subjects but defines originality as origin in the individual author. But this contradiction is "consistently resolved in the interests of copyright holders" (ibid., 259). See also Thomas Porcello, "The Ethics of Digital Audio-Sampling," *Popular Music* 10, no. 1 (1991): 69–84.

2. For my purposes here, electronic dance music includes hip hop but also the various genres associated with the massively increased importance of club and dance music culture in the wake of the rave and acid house phenomena of the late 1980s: house, garage, techno, jungle, and drum and bass among them. Dance music culture has been central to debates about popular music in Europe in a way which still seems alien to many U.S. readers. For introductory surveys which attempt to outline the political importance of rave/dance music culture, see my "The Cultural Politics of Dance Music," *Soundings* 5 (1997): 167–78, and "Club Culture Goes Mental," *Popular Music* 17, no. 2 (1998): 247–53. For an impressive history and analysis, see Simon Reynolds, *Energy Flash: A Journey through Rave Music and Dance Culture* (London: Picador, 1998), published in the United States as *Generation Ecstasy* (New York: Routledge, 1999). On the complex relations between hip hop and dance music, and the particular importance of jungle as a diasporic form, see Reynolds, *Energy Flash*, and David Hesmondhalgh and Caspar Melville, "Urban Breakbeat Culture: Repercussions of Hip Hop in the UK," in *Global Noise: Rap and Hip Hop Outside the USA,* ed. Tony Mitchell (Hanover, N.H.: Wesleyan University Press, forthcoming).

3. This chapter is based on research carried out in 1994 and 1995. I am very grateful to the staff at Nation for their friendly cooperation, especially Kath Canoville, Rich McLean, and Simon Underwood. Canoville and Underwood have left Nation since I carried out my fieldwork.

4. Aki Nawaz had been the drummer for the postpunk "goth" band Southern Death Cult, and Kath Canoville had worked as promoter and manager. Sabita Banerji and Gerd Baumann, "Bhangra 1984–8: Fusion and Professionalization in a Genre of South Asian Dance Music," in *Black Music in Britain*, ed. Paul Oliver (Milton Keynes: Open University Press, 1990), 137, offer the following definition of bhangra: "Bhangra music, in all its widely divergent styles, represents the fusion of a rural Punjabi dance and its songs with sounds, social forms, and production strategies associated with disco music and pop. In its more adventurous styles, it has further come to take up influences from hip hop and house, as well as dance techniques such as spinning, body-popping, and breaking."

5. Unless otherwise indicated, all the quotations below are from recorded interviews carried out by me in 1994–95 in research funded by the Economic and Social Research Council.

6. Others included "ethnic techno," "radical global pop," and "world dance music." The company itself encouraged the use of such terms in its marketing and packaging, in order to distinguish its work from "world music," which was becoming unfashionable among younger audiences in Britain in the early 1990s.

7. Most of these singles were collected on two compilations released in 1989 and 1991, *Fuse* and *Fuse 2*. These vinyl compilations were combined on a double CD in 1993: Various Artists, *Fuse I & II* (Nation NATCD35). The best-known of these musicians was Jah Wobble, but others included Harri Kakoulli (formerly of Squeeze) and David Harrow.

8. Transglobal Underground, "Temple Head" (Nation NR008T, 1991), re-released in remixed form on BMG/Deconstruction Records later that year, and then again when the band returned to Nation in 1993 as "Temple Head '93/I, Voyager" (NR020T/CD). The track is most easily available on Transglobal Underground, *Dream of 100 Nations* (Nation NR021, 1993).

9. A listen to the track will make it obvious why. I discuss this track in more detail in David Hesmondhalgh, "Nation and Primitivism: Multiculturalism in Recent British Dance Music," in *Music on Show: Issues of Performance*, ed. Tarja Hautamäki and Helmi Järviluoma (Tampere, Finland: University of Tampere Department of Folk Tradition, 1998), 138.

10. The sources of these quotations are, respectively, Tony Marcus, "Ethno Trance," *Mixmag*, May 1994, 44; photo caption accompanying a review of a gig by Transglobal Underground at the *New Musical Express*'s "On into '94" event, *NME*, 22 January 1994, 25; Peter Paphides, review of Transglobal Underground single, "Earth Tribe," *Melody Maker*, 9 April 1994, 12. Although their influence is waning now, as a new generation of glossy monthly music magazines are beginning to dominate, the weekly *New Musical Express* and *Melody Maker* have for many decades been the mainstays of the British music press.

11. Their third single, "Wrath of a Black Man" (Nation NR017T/C, 1993), for example, is built around a sample of a speech by Malcolm X. It is worth pointing out here that other Asian hip hop crews were also emerging in the early 1990s, notably Kaliphz, from Rochdale.

12. Quoted in Push, "Turban Warriors," *Melody Maker*, 9 May 1992, 7. The subeditor's heading is typical of the jokey exoticism in liberal music press coverage of Nation bands.

13. HMV and Our Price are two of Britain's leading entertainment retail chains.

14. The U.S. national ethnological and zoological museum, which has made many thousands of ethnomusicological recordings.

15. Another source told me that the publishers initially asked for £6,000, and eventually came down to £4,000. The track ("The Bird Has Flown") was never released because of the clearance problem.

16. This of course suggests that ethnomusicological recordings themselves have a problematic history of not fully respecting or rewarding authorship in non-Western cultural contexts.

17. Lee Harpin, "Head Cases," *The Face*, September 1991, 10.

18. Lee's account appeared in *Muzik*, June 1995, 98.

19. The publishing rights are owned jointly by Quickfire, BMG, and Warner-Chappell, meaning that Nation, via its publishing arm Quickfire, should receive some performing rights payments.

20. Their most recent album, *Rejoice, Rejoice* (Nation NR1073CD, 1998) features over forty musicians, including Hungarian "gypsy" bands and Bengali and Rajasthani groups.

21. Transglobal Underground, *International Times* (Nation NATLP/CD/C38, 1994), which Sony distributed and marketed internationally.

22. Natacha Atlas, *Diaspora* (Nation NAT47LP/CD, 1995).

23. Such smaller publishers apparently charge much lower rates than the major publishers. Even at the lower rates charged by smaller publishers such as World Circuit and Globestyle, though, administration costs and copyright advances can together make a substantial fee.

24. Salman Gita (a pseudonym for David Muddyman's collaborator, Sam Dodgson), quoted in Jakubowski, "Global Pillage," *The Wire*, November 1994, 18.

25. Nation NAT 56, 1995.

26. See Schumacher, "'This Is a Sampling Sport,'" which uses Henry Louis Gates's work on the distinctive intertextuality of African American expressive traditions (*The Signifying Monkey: A Theory of African-American Literary Criticism* [New York: Oxford University Press, 1988]) to argue that judgments in sampling cases have "been consistently resolved in favour of copyright holders," at the expense of "more dialogic forms of cultural production" (259). See also Porcello, "The Ethics."

27. Asian Dub Foundation, "Jericho," from *Facts and Fictions* (Nation NR54T/CD, 1995). Lyrics reproduced by kind permission of Nation Records.

28. E.g. in Tim Marsh, "Never Mind the Warlocks," *Select*, June 1994.

29. Steve Sutherland, "Nile's House Party," *NME*, 12 March 1994, 32–33. Note that Sutherland thinks that the "na na na" sample comes from Africa, not Tahiti.

30. See Iestyn George, "Let Sleeping Dogs Lie," *NME*, 7 May 1994, a feature on Fun-da-mental which features an alarming still from the promotional video for "Dog Tribe," showing Aki made up as the victim of a racist beating. The most prominent coverage of antiracist struggle in the light of the neofascist British National Party election victory, though, was a special issue of the *NME* (18 October 1993) devoted to music and antiracism, timed to coincide with a march near BNP headquarters in an outer London suburb. *NME*'s coverage featured Transglobal Underground rather than the black groups on Nation. "Count Dubulah" (Nick) made the following claim (13): "Just by existing, we are winding the likes of the BNP up. We're their worst night-

mare, a mini-multi-cultural society getting along, throwing everything into the melting pot and making beautiful music!"

31. See David Toop, *The Rap Attack* 2 (London: Serpent's Tail, 1991): the early rappers were primarily *entertainers,* however political the implications of the emergent culture.

32. A sound system is a massive hi-fi, operated as a small business, where recorded music can be mixed with live vocals. It is taken from venue to venue by its operators to play music for dancing at youth clubs, "blues parties," and all manner of community events, from weddings and christenings to "sound clashes," where two or more systems compete in front of a crowd to produce the most original selection of records, and the loudest sound. The sound system originated in Jamaica and developed new forms in Britain. See Les Back, "Coughing Up Fire: Soundsystems in South-East London, *New Formations* 2 (1988): 141–52, and *New Ethnicities and Urban Culture: Racisms and Multiculture in Young Lives* (London: UCL Press, 1996) for vivid ethnographic detail and contextualization.

33. See Pat Reid, "Turban Species," *Hip Hop Connection,* September 1994.

34. For a treatment which recognizes this range, see the many references to hip hop in Paul Gilroy, *The Black Atlantic* (London: Verso, 1993).

35. Rupa Huq, "Asian Kool? Bhangra and Beyond," in *Dis-Orienting Rhythms: The Politics of the New Asian Dance Music,* ed. Sanjay Sharma, John Hutnyk, and Ashwani Sharma (London: Zed Books, 1996), 63. This valuable collection provides much useful context and analysis of contemporary British-Asian popular music, including a number of the Nation acts discussed here.

36. See Burhan Wazir, "Asian Pop Is Cool—with Everyone Except Asians," *The Observer* Review Section, 31 January 1999, 7.

37. A South African hip hop crew, Prophets of da City, brought to Britain by Nation in association with Beggars Banquet in 1995, encountered similar problems, in spite of some good press. They were ignored by black British hip hop fans, who prefer U.S. acts, and the white indie crowds were alienated by Prophets' attachment to aspects of hip hop culture such as graffiti and breakdancing, which have only formed a relatively marginal part of the way that rap was received in Britain.

38. E.g., Dick Hebdige, *Subculture: The Meaning of Style* (London: Methuen, 1979); Simon Jones, *Black Music, White Youth* (Basingstoke: Macmillan, 1988); George Lipsitz, *Dangerous Crossroads: Popular Music, Postmodernism and the Poetics of Place* (London: Verso, 1994); Back, *New Ethnicities and Urban Culture.*

The Discourse of World Music

Simon Frith

When was the last time an ethnomusicologist went out to discover sameness rather than difference? When did we last encourage our students to go and do fieldwork not in order to come back and paint the picture of a different Africa but of an Africa that, after all the necessary adjustments have been made, is the "same" as the West?

KOFI AGAWU

The pioneers of [our] native rock did not step down here from a flying saucer, they emerged from the grain of the people, like the folklorists and the tangoists before them. Our rock is already part of the Argentinean musical tradition, despite those who view it solely as "foreign penetration." The [acoustic] guitar and the bandoneon were also imported to these pampas and it occurs to nobody to consider them aliens.

MIGUEL GRINBERG

"World music" is an unusual pop genre in that it has a precise moment of origin.[1] In July 1987 eleven independent record companies concerned with "international pop" began meeting at a London pub, the Empress of Russia, to discuss how best to sell "our kind of material." As a press release issued at the end of the month explained: "The demand for recordings of non-Western artists is surely growing. This is where problems can start for the potential buyer of WORLD MUSIC albums—the High Street record shop hasn't got the particular record, or even an identifiable section to browse through, it doesn't show on any of the published charts, and at this point all but the most tenacious give up—and who can blame them?" The world music tag (and subsequent sales campaign) was designed "to make it easier to find that Malian Kora record, the music of Bulgaria, Zairean soukous or Indian Ghazals—the new WORLD MUSIC section will be the first place to look in the local record shop." From the start, therefore, world music described the commercial process in which the sounds of other people ("diverse forms of music as yet unclassifiable in Western terms") were sold to British record buyers, and the record companies involved were well aware of the descriptive problems involved: "Trying to reach a definition of WORLD MUSIC provoked much lengthy discussion and finally it was agreed that it means practically any music that isn't at present catered for by its own category, e.g.:

Reggae, jazz, blues, folk. Perhaps the common factor unifying all these WORLD MUSIC labels is the passionate commitment of all the individuals to the music itself."[2]

This story has by now the status of a myth. It is told by academic analysts to show that the very idea of world music was an assertion of Western difference, with core—Anglo-American—musics being protected from the encroachment of other sounds, and peripheral—non-Western—musics being assigned to their own shop display ghetto.[3] But this reading of the myth is misleading. The record companies involved were in the business of persuading consumers to distinguish themselves from the mainstream of rock and pop purchasers, to be different themselves. World music wasn't a sales category like any other; these record labels claimed a particular kind of engagement with the music they traded and promised a particular kind of experience to their consumers. As Jan Fairley notes, world music records were, on the one hand, sold as individual discoveries, the record company as musical explorer bringing back a gem to share with the discriminating public; and, on the other hand, exchanged as a currency to link together a community of enthusiasts—record company bosses being at the same time promoters, journalists, deejays, musicians.[4]

Two aspects of this interest me. First, as an ideological category, world music can only be understood by reference to the rock world from which it emerged. The eleven independent labels at the famous meeting had histories. Hannibal Records was run by Joe Boyd, pioneer producer since the 1960s of folk rock; Globestyle Records was a subsidiary of Ace, a specialist in small label rock and roll and r&b reissues; Oval Records was co-owned by deejay Charlie Gillett, whose influential 1970s Radio London show, *Honky Tonk,* had specialized in regional American music (and its British pub rock tributes). The world music house journal, *Folk Roots,* had, as *Southern Rag,* developed an eclectic but militant line on the state of contemporary folk music. World music was launched with an anthology cassette, *The World at One* (available only through the indie-rock-oriented journal *NME*), and with live performances at such roots-rock venues as the Town and Country Club and the Mean Fiddler. As live music it was initially subsidized through the multicultural policy of the socialist Greater London Council and sustained by WOMAD festivals, outdoor musical celebrations clearly modelled on similar rock events.

World music, in short, might have come from elsewhere but it was sold in a familiar package—not as global pop but as roots rock, as music like that made by British and American bands who had remained true to rock and roll's original spirit. This was music for grown-ups not adolescents, unashamedly functional (for dancing, courting), expressive of local community, emotionally robust. It featured guitars, drums, voices, sweat. Many academic commentators have since observed that while "world music" sounds like an inclusive term it is, in practice, systematically exclusive. Timothy Taylor, just to give one example, draws our attention to the exclusion of Cantopop and karaoke from *World Music: The Rough Guide*.[5] But given the rock origins of world music this is hardly surprising. Indeed, as a rock critic in the late 1980s on most world-music mailing lists, I was always more aware of the authenticity claims of the music sent to me than of its exoticism. The difference at stake wasn't between Western and non-Western music but, more familiarly, between real and artificial sounds, between the musically true and the musically false, between authentic and inauthentic musical experiences. As the back cover blurb of the book of the 1989 BBC TV series *Rhythms of the World* put it: "During the late 1980s, rock and pop have become increasingly predictable and nostalgic and an appetite has developed for stronger stuff."[6]

Note, secondly, the way in which world music depended from the start on a displayed expertise. This is most obvious in record sleeve notes (and WOMAD Festival program notes), in the explanations and descriptions of particular musical forms and their roots in local traditions and practices, their well-researched biographies of the artists involved. International pop as world music was thus marketed quite differently from international pop as tourist music (as was most obvious when old releases were reissued); proper appreciation of world music meant, it seemed, ethnomusicological knowledge rather than tourist memories. World music discourse drew here on the collecting ideology that had given most of these labels their original market niche. Folk song and rock record collecting, with its equation of obscurity and significance, its obsession with fact, its pursuit of the original, its hierarchy of experts, had long been a key route through which African American music, from jazz and r&b to soul and Motown, had been appropriated by Europeans. And such collectors' expertise had always involved a kind of academicism.[7]

The relevant academic expertise for world music marketing was ethnomusicology, and if one result was the scholar as deejay, anthologist, journalist, and writer of blurbs,[8] another was the record company boss as scholar, engaged in his or her own fieldwork, developing his or her own theories of musical movement and exchange. The coming together of academic and commercial concerns was reflected in the late 1980s development of the International Association for the Study of Popular Music (which even recruited Peter Gabriel for a while), and can be seen in the list of contributors to *World Music: The Rough Guide*.[9]

If ethnomusicologists thus helped define world music, the subsequent relationship between academic and commercial expertise has not been straightforward. World music record companies may have had little difficulty justifying their activities in terms of their musical enthusiasm, but academic enthusiasts were soon anxious about the assumptions behind and effects of world music as a sales category. The very fact that ethnomusicological expertise was needed to guarantee the authenticity of what was being sold called into question the notion of authenticity itself. It was soon clear, for example, that "the authentic" worked in retail terms as a redescription of the exotic. International pop music in the 1990s may be packaged quite differently from international pop music in the 1950s, with greater respect shown to its formal qualities and local history, but what's on offer to the consumer, the musical pleasures promised, aren't so different: in the context of the denunciation of Western pop artifice and decadence, the authentic itself becomes the exotic (and vice versa). This move is familiar enough from the long European Romantic celebration of the native (the peasant and the African) as more real (because more natural) than the civilized Westerner. The implication is that world musicians can now give us those direct, innocent rock and roll pleasures that Western musicians are too jaded, too corrupt to provide. World music thus remains a form of tourism (as *World Music: The Rough Guide* makes clear), just as "world travellers" are still tourists, even if they use local transport and stay in local inns rather than booking package tours and rooms in the national Hilton. Indeed, this musical equation of the exotic and the authentic can be traced back at least to Capitol Records' *Capitol of the World* series, launched in 1956: "*Recorded in the country of the music's origins * Captured in flawless high fidelity * A remarkable series of albums for world music-travellers.*"[10] As Keir Keightley notes, already the search for the exotic and the authentic is going hand in hand. He cites a *Holiday* magazine ad in 1957 headlined "The Real Stuff":

> The spicier Paris haunts where tourists go, and the more genuine quarters where Frenchmen go, have now been captured in pure melody by famed French conductor-composer Andre Colbert. It's the most authentic and lovely album of Parisian listening that'll come your way in a month of Tuesdays . . . here is the real stuff, the real music of Paris—romantic melody that can never be copied.[11]

From the academic point of view this equation of the authentic with the exotic calls into question the meaning of authenticity. On the one hand it can be doubted whether there is such a thing as an "authentic"—autonomous— musical form in the first place; on the other hand it is apparent that authenticity here functions as an ideological construct—a construction of commercial (and academic) discourse. It describes a process of music appropriation rather than music-making. And this leads us to a second kind of academic anxiety: the lurking problem of cultural imperialism, the suspicion that what "world music" really describes is a double process of exploitation: Third World musicians being treated as raw materials to be processed into commodities for the West, and First World musicians (in the back cover words of *Rhythms of the World*) putting "new life into their own music by work-ing with artists like Ladysmith Black Mambazo, Youssou N'Dour and Celia Cruz."

As I write, Ladysmith Black Mambazo's *Greatest Hits* is riding high in Britain's Top Ten Album charts, following the use of the group's music in a Heinz TV advertisement; world musicians' international success is clearly an effect of global capitalism, and if by the beginning of the 1990s there was general academic agreement that "cultural imperialism" was no longer a term that clarified the workings of leisure corporations, it was also agreed that these workings did need critical analysis.[12] World music labels are highly infor-mative about the musical source of their releases, about local musical tradi-tions, genres, and practices, but they are highly uninformative about their own activities—the process through which music from Mali reaches a record store in Middlesborough is not explained. On the one hand, there is re-markably little information available about the licensing and publishing deals involved, about copyrights and contracts, about the money flow.[13] On the other hand, world music sleeve notes systematically play down the role of record producers in shaping non-Western sounds for Western ears, in de-scribing Western markets to non-Western artists. When the sales emphasis is on local musical authenticity, the creative role of the international record producer is best not mentioned.

In academic popular music studies the suggestion that the producer some-how interferes (whether for commercial or colonialist reasons) with the free flow of sounds from artist to audience has by now been challenged by a more sophisticated reading in which popular music is an effect of the relationship between musician and producer, between musical and market considera-tions.[14] This is, again, to challenge the concept of authenticity, and by the early 1990s academic discussions of world music were being organized around a different term, the hybrid. Hyunju Park summarizes current aca-demic thinking:

> Musicians are blending together musical elements from everywhere and adding to them the musical possibilities afforded by new technologies. This process of global bricolage is still intertwined with, but no longer entirely de-pendent on, the core industry. In observation of this new eclecticism, the core industry itself has begun to look to all cultures for potential raw materials and consequently its former rock centre has splintered into many subgenre frag-ments. Even if centre dominance diminishes, however, local musicians will not work in a less commercialized environment. The process of hybridity is not one of absolute free choice but one of constant compromise between what might be desired creatively and what will be accepted commercially.[15]

In introducing the concept of hybridity into the discussion ethnomusicolo-gists were not simply pointing at the value of detailed local work on music-making processes, or trying to follow the movement of particular musics through the international trade in sounds and symbols; they were also drawing on broader academic concerns about globalization, concerns inflected by postmodern theory. On the one hand, then, world music could be seen as a site on which new sorts of (hybrid) identity are being performed.[16] On the other hand, world music could be seen as a site on which new sorts of cultural theory could be developed, new futures glimpsed. The academic concern is no longer to apply some general theory of development (the cultural imperialism thesis, say) to music as an example, but, rather, to read the meaning of globalization through world music. Jocelyne Guilbault thus claims that "world music seems far ahead of other fields of activity in its use of active social forces that are diverse and contradictory as agents of change and in its reliance on both local and international forces in the shaping of individual and social identities."[17] Edwin Seroussi writes, about popular music studies in Israel:

> The study of the forces that shaped Israel's popular music industry or the description and classification of Israeli music according to genres is certainly not the ultimate goal of this field of research. Although interpretative analysis of social and musical processes from the past will continue to guide much future research, it is also necessary to pay attention to the power of popular music to predict. Just as the emergence of *musikah mizrahit* predicted the rise of political consciousness among the second generation of North African and Middle Eastern Jewish immigrants in the early 1970s, the rich palette of popular music expression in Israel today may forecast new social configurations still in their formative stages.[18]

If for world music record companies the concept of authenticity was a way of condensing a series of arguments about how music works and why it matters, drawing on potential listeners' understandings of rock and folk, so for world music scholars hybridity has become a way of condensing a number of arguments about globalization and identity, drawing on potential readers' understandings of postmodern theory. For Seroussi, for instance, to study popular music in Israel is to study "the struggle to create a new, local culture," to examine the dialectical relationships between past Jewish cultures and present Middle Eastern cultures, between Israeli national identity and the "threatening influence" of global, Americanized dreams. And it is this sense of struggle to which the concept of hybridity draws our attention.

In using this term scholars have adopted two different analytic approaches— detailed studies of local practice on the one hand, grand theories of the global condition on the other. Local studies start from established accounts of musical syncretism, of the ways in which musical styles develop through a constant process of borrowing and quotation. As Nancy Morris suggests in a review of recent work on Latin American and Caribbean music, ethnomusicologists have long assumed that "neither identities nor traditions are static; both change with changing circumstances, and with the continuous interaction of peoples."[19] From this perspective, hybridity is a new name for a familiar process: local musics are rarely culturally pure (a genre as nationally distinct as Dominican *bachata* can thus be shown to draw on Mexican, Colombian-Ecuadorian, and Puerto Rican as well as Dominican sources). As Morris suggests such music is made in local contexts of mobility, migration, the constant writing out and blurring of class and ethnic difference; tradition is always a matter of invention and reinvention, and what's at issue here is not simply commercialization (rural music becoming urban commodity, say) but also legitimation, as styles initially despised for their association with the lower classes become nationally and internationally popular. This is not a process without tensions—it is still difficult for the Jamaican cultural establishment, for example, to come to terms with the fact that reggae is the country's most successful cultural export—but the point is that world music is shaped by responses to national/political as well to commercial/global conditions.[20]

In local studies the most important conclusion to draw from this is that musical traditions are only preserved by constant innovation. In his study of Peruvian panpipe music, Thomas Turino quotes the charter of the Federation of Puno Musicians in Lima. These musicians, children of urban immigrants, started out by asserting that their music was "the creation of our ancestors. It is a free and natural manifestation of community that expresses the living history of our Quechua and Symara nations."[21] This sense of tradition inspired these students to teach themselves to play a music that articulated an imagined regional identity even as their urban experience shaped the way in which they conceived and played that music, and it can be contrasted to the artificial preservation of tradition by state edict, exercised through the control of radio outlets, local recording studios, education, and performance. The impact of international pop, in other words, may be as important for the preservation of music traditions as for their destruction. In the books Morris discusses, this is probably best brought out by Deborah Pacini Hernandez's study of *bachata* in the Dominican Republic. Local musicians there are clear that traditional Dominican sounds have only developed freely since the end of the thirty-year Trujillo dictatorship in 1961: "We can't forget how significant it has been to merengue as a popular music to have come into contact with the popular music of other countries."[22]

The fieldwork of Turino, Hernandez, and many other contemporary ethnomusicologists makes clear, in Morris's words, that "urbanization, modern transportation, and electronic media" have speeded up "the age-old process of musical mixing" and "with fewer intermediaries than ever before," but it does not suggest that the underlying dynamic of musical change has become qualitatively different. Today Peruvian *chicha* combines electric rock instruments, highland-mestizo *wayno* melodies and phrasings, and the rhythms of Colombian *cumbia,* musical elements absorbed by the Lima-born children of rural-born parents as much from radio, records, and *MTV Internacional* as from neighborhood performers, tutors, and rituals. In the early 1960s Jamaican popular musicians brought together the musical resources of African drumming, Afro-Protestant Revivalist hymns, European ballroom dance, Caribbean calypso and rumba, and United States rhythm and blues, pilfering from local musical events and internationally distributed and broadcast records alike. The media of global musical communication may change; the ways in which music is a mobile life form do not.

This is the optimistic view of world music: musical creativity always involves cultural borrowing; changes in musical tradition don't mean the loss of cultural identity but articulate the way it changes with circumstance. The fact that such hybrid forms become popular internationally, are traded in the global marketplace, is analytically irrelevant; the meaning of local musics must be referred to local conditions of production. This is the academic argument that best suits (and is most used by) world music companies; it defines hybridity as authenticity and implies that musical creativity depends on a free trade in sounds; "uncorrupted" music can now be seen as stagnant music, music constrained by reactionary political and cultural forces.

This argument is developed most systematically and critically in Jocelyne Guilbault's study of *zouk.* Guilbault describes the local effect in the Antilles of the international success of the *zouk* group Kassav:

> As it has acquired power through fame, Kassav has contributed to some significant changes: a revolution in local show business practices and in record production in the French Antilles; the development of ties for the first time with international markets; new collaboration between local and commercial entrepreneurs and music groups; and a transformation of social consciousness. . . . Kassav's financial success has led to the recognition that cultural changes brought about through popular music can bring economic changes, that the process of cultural identification awakened by mass-distributed music in general and zouk in particular informs new attitudes, which in turn affect the economy through consumer choices and production methods.[23]

But Guilbault also makes clear the difficulty of confining "local conditions of production" to a locality. As live music-making in the Antilles was replaced by the use of records, by mobile discos and deregulated radio stations, "Antillean music groups of the early eighties were forced to develop a 'sound' that could compete with imported foreign music," and such competition in itself transformed the frame of musical expectations. If local ethnomusicological studies tend to see the dynamics of musical change as somehow organic, Guilbault argues that once musicians enter the international music market their music is shaped by new kinds of nonlocal forces:

Popular local dance musics that reach the international market are subject to the paradox inherent in the transnational recording industry. They must comply with what is often referred to as the "international sound," that is, the use of preponderant Euro-American scales and tunings, harmony, electronic instruments now seen as standards, accessible dance rhythms, and a Euro-American-based intonation. They are also obliged to deal with subjects that are accessible to a wide audience. . . . But in contrast to the standardization of the songs' sounds and content, these musics must, at the same time, distinguish themselves from the others by featuring elements unique to their cultural elements. They must utilize in a specific way their dependence on the international markets by and through a continual process of creation/adaptation.[24]

And this has its own local effects. Kassav's choice to sing in Creole rather than French "was certainly and unapologetically a marketing device to attract attention and to be clearly identified [in the international French music market] as *Antillais*," but "it was also unmistakeably a way to show solidarity with compatriots at home and in exile," and therefore both to nurture a sense of collectivity among all Creole speakers in the Islands and to legitimate the use of Creole in public Antillean institutions.[25] Guilbault concludes,

As do all other world musics, zouk creates much stress in its countries of origin by underscoring how its relation with the international market reformulates local traditions and creative processes. As it emphasises the workings of world political economy at the local level, zouk renders more problematic for Antilleans the definition of the "we" as a site of difference. It challenges in fact the traditional way of thinking about the "we" as a self-enclosed unit by highlighting its relational character.[26]

A similar argument has been proposed by cultural sociologists writing from the opposite direction, studying not world music as the other of Western culture but rock music as the other of non-Western cultures. Motti Regev thus argues that for many musicians and fans in the last twenty-five years,

the presence of rock music in their own local cultures and its influence on local music is hardly seen as a form of cultural imperialism. On the contrary, they perceive rock as an important tool for strengthening their contemporary sense of local identity and autonomy. Anglo-American sub-styles of rock as they are, imitations that put local-language lyrics to the same styles, or hybrids that mix rock elements with local music traditions, proliferate in countries around the world. Italian hip hop, Polish reggae, Chinese *xibei-feng*, Algerian *pop-rai*, Israeli *musica mizrahkit*, Argentinian *rock nacional*, Zimbabwean *chimurenga* or *jit*, are a few of these sub-styles. Producers of and listeners to these types of music feel, at one and the same time, participants in a specific contemporary global-universal form of expression *and* innovators of local, national, ethnic and other identities. A cultural form, associated with American (US) culture and with the powerful commercial interests of the international music industry, is being used in order to construct a sense of local difference and authenticity.[27]

Regev is partly arguing here that rock, as a "local authentic" music, is important for resolving the postmodern condition of occupying global/mediated and local/immediate space simultaneously. But his more specific point is that rock is a modern rather than postmodern form. Rock, that is, stands for a certain kind of self-consciousness, a particular mode of individual expressivity. "Rock music," in his words, "is used to declare a 'new'—modern, contemporary, young, often critical-oppositional—sense of local identity, as opposed to older, traditional, conservative forms of that identity."[28] Rock, to put this another way, can be seen as the authentic articulation of a local identity in its very recognition of the complexity of that identity, of the global in the local and the local in the global.

On the one hand, then, rock is a vernacular lower class version of the expressive modernity that has always "transcended" local conditions (not least in the spread of Western classical music); on the other hand, it exemplifies, in Regev's words, "one of the cultural logics of globalization"—"instead of being disparate, relatively independent musical languages, local styles of music become part of one history, variations of one cultural form—without necessarily losing a sense of difference."[29] From this postmodern perspective hybrid music is the necessary expression of a hybrid condition. This condition is partly technological. David Toop thus concludes an essay on "Exotica and World Music Fusions" with the observation:

> It is all too probable that one of the endearing, perhaps enduring, clichés of the end of the twentieth century will be the postmodern/electronic age concept of image chaos: the progressively unshocking shocks of overloaded layers, bizarre juxtapositions and oppositions, forgeries and thefts, wrenches of time and location, and dislocations of function and meaning. There are tangible models everywhere: the streetsounds of a modern Fourth World, *retronuevo* city like Miami; the recording studios of the Bombay film industry with its indiscriminate pile-ups of world music bites; the traverse of historical and religious divides and levels of technology in the music of Mali and Senegal.... Music history has become, to a remarkable extent, a record and tape collection. Music is composed or performed with knowledge gleaned from recordings; records are made with fragments of music lifted from other records. Unnecessary, at the end of the twentieth century, to bring forty marines and a brass band [as the Prussian ambassador brought to Japan in 1860]; a single cassette, arriving in a new geographical location, can upturn musical traditions for good.[30]

And Peter Manuel argues, also with reference to the cassette, that "the lower costs of production enable small-scale producers to emerge around the world, recording and marketing music aimed at specialized, local grassroots audiences rather than at a homogenous mass market. The net result is a remarkable decentralization, democratization, and dispersal of the music industry at the expense of multinational and national oligopolies."[31] Either way, technology makes for a new music culture, organized around neither local traditions nor global corporate trends. In Manuel's words about India, "while obscure, specialized traditional genres have come to be marketed on cassette, new syncretic styles have also emerged in close association with cassette dissemination. Such genres have been able to bypass the disapproving or indifferent control of state bureaucracies and/or formerly dominating majors."[32]

The postmodern condition is reflected both in the collapse of grand musical narratives and authorities and in the blurring of musical borders and histories. World music can thus be treated as the sound of postmodern experience, following Stuart Hall's suggestion that "the aesthetics of modern popular music is the aesthetics of the hybrid, the aesthetics of the crossover, the aesthetics of the diaspora, the aesthetics of creolization."[33] Timothy Taylor analyzes the way the British musician Apache Indian exploits "free-floating signifiers," and suggests that if Apache Indian is, as Peter Manuel suggests, "a quintessential postmodern musician," this is not just a matter of style or irony but articulates, rather, a particular experience of—and emotional response to—what Taylor calls (following Hall) "the global postmodern." In Taylor's words, "new technologies and modes of musical production allow musicians to occupy different subject positions in a kind of simultaneity never before possible; they don't move from one to the next but rather employ and deploy several at once."[34] Or as Veit Erlmann argues more abstractly:

> For the contradiction that characterizes our historical moment is this: if the truth of an individual or collective identity, the experience of an authentic rooting in a time and a place, is now inextricably bound up with the truths of other places and times, then the desire to account truthfully for this very fact in some kind of macro model amounts to missing the individual experience. But if the systemic notion of a cultural totality is to be of any value and if it is to avoid the dangers of Eurocentric monolithic representations, it must precisely capture this dilemma as one of the deepest motivating forces for a global aesthetic production.[35]

Erlmann's interest is the "wholesale disappearance of the social and of difference as such" and "the rapid loss of referentiality." World music thus "does away with time and space altogether." Developing Fredric Jameson's concept of pastiche, Erlmann suggests that in world music "difference itself becomes the signified," while global music pastiche describes the "attempt at coating the sounds of a commodified present with the patina of use value in some other time and place."[36]

The contrast between these positions is clear enough: Erlmann is considering the weight world music has to carry for its listeners in the West, Taylor the meaning it has for the musicians themselves. Either way, the difference between the West and its other is preserved: Erlmann sees it in the constantly reinstated nostalgia of the world music consumer; Taylor suggests that only world musicians express the postmodern condition authentically. Their music is, paradoxically, a critique of Erlmann's postmodern despair: "Just as the subordinate groups in US culture have always done more than the dominant groups to make radical positions available through new sounds, new forms, new styles, it looks as though it is the subordinate groups around the world who are doing the same, perhaps even showing us how to get along on this planet. If we would only listen."[37] Taylor's argument draws here from cultural, or rather subcultural, studies of "resistance," of the ways in which "subordinate" consumers turn commodities back on themselves, and marginalized communities define their own social spaces, their own centers and peripheries, in the process of stylization.[38] The problem here (as in the original youth subcultural studies) is that "resistance" describes such a variety of activities, from day-to-day communal sociability to full scale political mobilization. In his study of a typical hybrid youth form, German hip hop, Dietmar Elflein distinguishes between the music made by "Krauts with attitudes," German rappers using the German language to express (however ironically) a nationalist resistance to U.S. leisure culture, and the music made by the children of "guest workers," rap used to explore critically the complexities of German immigrant experience. But he also cautions against reducing either kind of rap simply to an ideological or ethnic position (a position of more interest to the record companies marketing the music than to the musicians making it):

> The music these bands produce is hip hop and nothing more. There is no need to propose different ethnically defined subgenres on the basis of the origin of particular musical samples. . . . In the end, the issue is this: anyone who wants to gather up musicians under an ethnically defined flag (as did *Cartel* and *Krauts with Attitude*) is, in practice, trying to become the dominant musical, political and commercial power in a scene which is, by its nature, various and pluralistic.[39]

To treat world music as postmodern resistance is to beg questions about music's significance for identities and social mobilization, questions that are better answered in the particular than the general.[40] A rich source of such particular discussion can be found in *Retuning Culture,* a collection of essays on "musical changes in Central and Eastern Europe" edited by Mark Slobin.[41] What concern these authors are the ways in which "music shapes politics and economics and social life as well as being shaped by them."[42] The question is how does such shaping work?

Effectively, according to these studies, through processes of social identity formation. On the one hand, music plays a role in turning a class-in-itself into a class-for-itself. Vague feelings of ethnic affiliation become a self-conscious ethnic identity, as shared myths and memories are articulated musically, given instrumental, rhythmic and lyric form. On the other hand, people are mobilized by music materially, as crowds brought together to make events; concerts offer, in themselves, the experience of collective power. Under certain circumstances, then, music becomes a source of collective consciousness which promotes group cohesion and social activities that in turn have political consequences.

These Eastern European studies suggest first (unsurprisingly) that music is particularly significant for the politics of national and ethnic identity; music becomes politically significant, that is, when issues of national and ethnic identity are the prime sites and sources of political dispute —whether at moments in the creation and dissolution of states or in terms of diasporic mobilization around the rights of minorities and migrants. Secondly (and more tellingly), these studies suggest that the music at issue in these situations is "folk" music, music precisely defined in terms of collective identities. It is when the validity of a social group is in dispute that music becomes politically important, as a way of authenticating it. It follows that aesthetic arguments—what makes for good music?—are ethical arguments—what makes for the good life? In this context, music articulates a way of being-in-society both representationally (in its subject matter) and materially (in its lived-out relationships between musicians and between musicians and audience). This is a process of idealization both in formal terms (the way in which music provides a narrative, an experience of wholeness and completion) and as a matter of staging, in events in which solidarity is made physical.

Catherine Wanner thus describes a Ukrainian nationalist song festival which took place (shortly before the collapse of the Soviet empire) in a football stadium in Zaporizhzhia. This was a rock concert that began with a religious procession ("A stream of priests solemnly entered the stadium walking along the track in long black robes carrying candles and crosses. In this way, twenty chanting priests introduced, so to speak, the first rock band") and mixed the lineup of rock bands with folk singers. If the (local) rock bands indicated that Ukrainian culture was contemporary, and not confined to officially sanctioned folklore, the folk singers (groups from the Ukrainian communities of Canada, the U.S.A., France, and Australia) suggested that the Ukraine's authentic cultural tradition had been protected from Soviet incursions.

> During the third song of the opening ceremony of the festival, as the feeling of solidarity and euphoria accelerated, most of the audience poured down from the bleachers onto the soccer field to dance. They broke the traditional segregation of performer and audience and joined hands or elbows in a human chain, encircling the singers on stage and each other. . . . The soccer stadium became the central town square as the "imagined community" of Ukrainians, at least for one night, was reified and celebrated in music and dance.

"Why," asks Wanner, "did advocates of Ukrainian independence turn to music to recast the critical relationship between Russia and Ukraine?"

> The demarcations between musical styles, genres, and performances, while nonetheless reflective of a cultural tradition, are infinitely more porous than other avenues of culture that also inform identity. Other cultural elements . . . such as religious affiliation, historical memories and myths, and language, do not command the immediate acceptance and visceral reactions that music has the power to trigger.[43]

The importance of Eastern European studies for accounts of world music is that they address questions of identity and musical change in a situation in which identity is the central political issue. In doing so they make clear that the way we feel music—respond to it emotionally and viscerally—must be analyzed as a grounded experience, grounded in a particular time and place, grounded in a particular form. Musical response involves recognition, sympathy, and commitment; it is at once free and necessary. Following a stay in Bulgaria, Tim Rice writes:

> Studying music as social life and symbolic system would have taken more time than I had, but I did observe the extraordinary staying power of tradition, which speaks if not to the autonomy of music, then to its power to make claim on us—to force us to engage with its rules—even as social, economic, and political conditions change. . . . Musicians were undoubtedly using music to construct notions of ethnic and national identity, but precisely how that is working itself out in the details of musical style will have to be studied in more careful future analyses.[44]

Meanwhile, Rice notes three developments: Gypsy musicians appropriating African American rap in the Romany language; radio programs mixing the previously segregated genres of "authentic folklore," "arranged folklore," and "wedding music"; and a new folk radio station "broadcasting a large amount of Macedonian music, along with a fair dose of Bulgarian *narodna, svatbarska* and *starogradska* ("old city") *muzika,* and Gypsy, Greek, Serbian and even Latin American music."[45] Whatever new forms of Bulgarian identity are being constructed musically, then, they are being constructed through a series of explorations of the non-Bulgarian, and to describe the resulting sounds (Romany rap, for example) as hybrid may be to miss the point: what's involved here is less a sense of subjective instability than the negotiation of new cultural alliances.

Rice concludes his essay on Bulgaria with the observation that "when viewed from the point of view of the individual practitioners, music can be understood as economic practice, as social behavior, and as a symbolic system with the powerful ability to make aesthetic sense while hiding meaning; to reference existing worlds; and to imagine new, utopian worlds."[46] When world music is viewed from this perspective the most commonly imagined utopia seems to be one in which issues of identity do not even arise. "'Stick to African music!'" writes Manu Dibango. "How many times have I heard this *diktat,* from critics as much as musicians from the continent. I have found myself stuck, labeled, locked in behind prison bars. . . . " Dibango accepts that "Weight comes from tradition. . . . But you need rhythm to move forward. . . . Talent has no race; there simply exists a race of musicians. To be part of it, you have to have knowledge. Musicians—and composers even more so—perceive pleasant sounds around them and digest them. They like the sounds; the sounds become part of them."[47]

But such a view—commonly expressed by world musicians—is not simply utopian. It reflects too the realities of the world musical life.[48] Jocelyne Guilbault has analyzed in detail how the Caribbean superstars of Calypso and Soca live as "transnationals."

> In this respect, the production of a typical album by the calypsonian Arrow offers a telling example. Arrow is a calypsonian from Montserrat, who does most of his recordings in New York City, often at the recording studio owned by Frankie McIntosh, a musician from St. Vincent. For each track, Arrow often uses two arrangers who do not necessarily originate from the same country—one for the brass parts and another for the rhythm and brass arrangements. Regularly, Arrow asks Trinidadian Leston Paul, one of the most sought-after arrangers in the English Caribbean, to fly to New York to write and direct horn parts for his songs. Arrow always uses a mix of musicians from the United States and the Caribbean to produce a special sound in the horn section. . . . The production of Caribbean recordings typically involves musicians from different nationalities and territories, and various stages of the recordings often take place in different locales.[49]

The recording process described here is familiar enough in other musical worlds, whether rock or classical, but the juxtapositions of friendship and influence seem more accidental in international pop. Take, for example, the musical background of the Ethiopian musician Mulatu Astatqé. As a teenager he studied clarinet, piano, and harmony at London's Trinity School of Music and music theory at Berklee College of Music in Boston. In London he played with the calypso musician Frank Holder and in Edmundo Ros's Latino big band; in New York he founded the Ethiopian Quintet to record an album of "Afro-Latin Soul" (the other group members were Puerto Rican); back in Ethiopia, as band leader, arranger, and teacher of "Ethio-jazz," he remains after thirty years the country's only vibraphone player, a musician regarded simultaneously as a guru and a novelty.[50]

Such lives are the stuff of world music biographies and suggest, finally, that the concept of globalization, with its intimations of the inexorable forces of history and/or capital, should be replaced in the discussion of world music by an understanding of networks—globalization from below, as it were. And this is where we came in. Those record company bosses who orginally met in a pub to define world music were, self-consciously, networking; world music promoters (European radio deejays, for example), continue to pass sounds around semiformal organizations of knowledge and friendship; the World Circuit (the name of an influential world music label) is, it is implied, different from the global pop market because it is a community, its authenticity guaranteed less by the music circulated than by the relationship between the people (including the musicians) doing the circulating. And here we have the final irony: academic music studies look to world music for clues about the postmodern condition, for examples of hybridity and lived subjective instability, but to understand this phenomenon we also have to recognize the ways in which world music has itself been constructed as a kind of tribute to and a parody of the community of scholars.

NOTES

1. I'm referring here to the British music market term. In the U.S.A. the retail label is "world beat," first used by the musician Dan Del Santo as the title for an album released in 1982—see Andrew Goodwin and Joe Gore, "World Beat and the Cultural Imperialism Debate" *Socialist Review* 20, no. 3 (July-September 1990): 65.

The epigraphs to this chapter are from Kofi Agawu, "The Invention of 'African Rhythm'" *Journal of the American Musicological Society* 48, no. 3 (1995): 389–90, and Motti Regev, "Rock Aesthetics and the Musics of the World," *Theory Culture and Society* 14, no. 3 (1997): 131.

2. Quotes taken from the first WORLD MUSIC press release (n.d.).

3. See, for example, Jocelyne Guilbault: "On Redefining the 'Local' through World Music," *The World of Music* 35, no. 2 (1993): 36; Timothy D. Taylor, *Global Pop: World Music, World Markets* (London: Routledge, 1997), 2–3.

4. Jan Fairley, "The 'Local' and the 'Global' in Popular Music," in *The Cambridge Companion to Rock and Pop,* ed. Simon Frith, Will Straw, and John Street (Cambridge: Cambridge University Press, forthcoming). Fairley is commenting in particular here on Ian Anderson's editorial arguments about world music in *Folk Roots* magazine—Anderson had been involved in the original world music discussions in his capacity as boss of Rogue Records. And see Peter Jowers, "Beating New Tracks: WOMAD and the British World Music Movement" in *The Last Post: Music after Modernism,* ed. Simon Miller (Manchester: Manchester University Press, 1993), 71.

5. Taylor, *Global Pop,* 16–17.

6. Francis Hanly and Tim May, eds., *Rhythms of the World* (London: BBC Books, 1989).

7. Charlie Gillett's classic *Sound of the City,* the first systematic account of the 1950s emergence of rock and roll, which put in place the ideology of rock as roots music, locally based, the product of independent rather than major record companies, was originally written as a master's thesis at Columbia University.

8. I'm thinking here of people in Britain like Latin music expert Jan Fairley and African music expert Lucy Duran.

9. Simon Broughton et al., eds., *World Music: The Rough Guide* (London: Rough Guides Ltd, 1994).

10. Cited in Keir Keightley, "Around the World: Musical Tourism and the Globalization of the Record Industry, 1946–66," unpublished paper (1998).

11. Keightley, "Around the World."

12. See Goodwin and Gore, "World Beat and the Cultural Imperialism Debate," and Reebee Garofalo, "Whose World, What Beat: The Transnational Music Industry, Identity, and Cultural Imperialism," *World of Music* 35 (1993): 16–32.

13. One of the few detailed accounts of world music as trade, Rick Glanvill's "World Music Mining—The International Trade in New Music" was removed from the BBC book of *Rhythms of the World* following threats of libel action.

14. Roger Wallis and Krister Malm's concept of "transculturation" has thus been more influential on studies of world music than those models in which indigenous local music cultures are celebrated for "resisting" international cultural forces. Compare Roger Wallis and Krister Malm, *Big Sounds from Small Peoples: The Music Industry in Small Countries* (London: Constable, 1984) with Deanna Robinson et al., eds., *Music at the Margins* (London: Sage, 1991).

15. Hyunju Park, *Globalization, Local Identity and World Music: The Case of Korean Popular Music* (M.Litt thesis, John Logie Baird Centre, Strathclyde University, 1998).

16. See, for example, Jocelyne Guilbault, "Interpreting World Music: A Challenge in Theory and Practice," *Popular Music* 16, no. 1 (1997): 31–44.

17. Jocelyne Guilbault, *Zouk: World Music in the West Indies* (Chicago: University of Chicago Press, 1993), 210.

18. Edwin Seroussi, *Popular Music in Israel: The First Fifty Years* (Cambridge, Mass.: Harvard College Library, 1996), 25–26.

19. Nancy Morris, "Cultural Interaction in Latin American and Caribbean Music," *Latin American Research Review* 34, no. 1 (1999): 187–200. And see also Jorge Duany, "Rethinking the Popular: Caribbean Music and Identity," *Latin American Research Review* 17, no. 2 (1996): 176–92.

20. See Kiki Marriott, *Communications Policy and Language in Jamaica* (Ph.D. thesis, John Logie Baird Centre, Strathclyde University, 1998).

21. Thomas Turino, *Moving Away from Silence: Music of the Peruvian Altiplano and the Experience of Urban Migration* (Chicago: University of Chicago Press, 1993), 188.

22. Deborah Pacini Hernandez, *Bachata: A Social History of a Dominican Popular Music* (Philadelphia: Temple University Press, 1995), 78–79.

23. Guilbault, *Zouk*, 30.

24. Ibid., 37, 150.

25. Ibid., 166. Compare Kiki Marriott's discussion of reggae's impact on the use of patois in Jamaica—Marriott, *Communications Policy and Language in Jamaica*.

26. Guilbault, *Zouk*, 209–10.

27. Regev, "Rock Aesthetics and Musics of the World," 125–26.

28. Ibid., 131.

29. Ibid., 139.

30. David Toop, "Into the Hot—Exotica and World Music Fusions," in Hanly and May, *Rhythms of the World*, 126.

31. Peter Manuel, *Cassette Culture: Popular Music and Technology in North India* (Chicago: University of Chicago Press, 1993), xiv.

32. Ibid., 33.

33. Quoted in Taylor, *Global Pop*, xxi.

34. Ibid., 155–65, 203, 94.

35. Veit Erlmann, "The Politics and Aesthetics of Transnational Musics," *The World of Music* 35, no. 2 (1993): 7.

36. Ibid. 8, 11, 13.

37. Taylor, *Global Pop*, 204.

38. See, for example, Sanjay Sharma et al., eds., *Dis-Orienting Rhythms: The Politics of the New Asian Dance Music* (London: Zed Books, 1996); Tony Mitchell, *Popular Music and Local Identity: Rock, Pop and Rap in Europe and Oceania* (London: Leicester University Press, 1996).

39. Dietmar Elflein, "From Krauts with Attitudes to Turks with Attitudes: Some Aspects of the German Hip Hop History" *Popular Music* 17, no. 3 (1998), 255–65.

40. For a good survey of the issues involved here see Martin Stokes, ed., *Ethnicity, Identity and Music: The Musical Construction of Place* (Oxford: Berg, 1994).

41. Mark Slobin, ed., *Retuning Culture* (Durham, N.C.: Duke University Press, 1996).

42. Carol Silverman, "Music and Marginality: *Roma* (Gypsies) of Bulgaria and Macedonia" in Slobin, *Retuning Culture*, 231.

43. Catherine Wanner, "Nationalism on Stage: Music and Change in Soviet Ukraine," in Slobin, *Retuning Culture*, 139–44, 148.

44. Timothy Rice, "The Dialectic of Economics and Aesthetics in Bulgarian Music," in Slobin, *Retuning Culture*, 195–96.

45. Ibid., 196.

46. Ibid., 198.

47. Manu Dibango, *Three Kilos of Coffee* (Chicago: University of Chicago Press, 1994), 125–26.

48. Compare the musicians' views recorded in Rehan Hyder, *Indie Bands and Asian Identity: Negotiating Ethnicity in the UK Music Industry* (Ph.D. thesis, University of Staffordshire, 1998), with the arguments made on their behalf in Sharma, *Dis-Orienting Rhythms*.

49. Jocelyne Guilbault, "World Music," *The Cambridge Companion to Rock and Pop*, ed. Frith, Straw, and Street.

50. Information taken from Francis Falceto's sleeve notes for *Ethiopiques 4: Ethio Jazz & Musique Instrumentale 1969–1974*.

CONTRIBUTORS

Philip V. Bohlman is Professor of Music and Jewish Studies at the University of Chicago. He has held guest professorships at the Universities of Vienna, Freiburg im Breisgau, Bologna, and California, Berkeley, and was awarded the Dent Medal of the Royal Music Association in 1997. His research ranges broadly in the field of ethnomusicology and includes Jewish music, the Middle East, ethnic and folk musics in North America, and the interrelation of music and religion. Among his books are *The Study of Folk Music in the Modern World* (1988), *"The Land Where Two Streams Flow"* (1989), *The World Centre for Jewish Music in Palestine 1936–1940* (1992), *Central European Folk Music* (1996), and *"Jüdische Volksmusik": Eine europäische Geistesgeschichte* (forthcoming). Bohlman is currently at work on several historical projects devoted to Jewish music and European modernity, and on a book on music in the New Europe.

Georgina Born trained as an anthropologist and is Lecturer in the Sociology of Culture, Faculty of Social and Political Sciences, University of Cambridge, and a Fellow of Emmanuel College, Cambridge. She was previously Senior Research Fellow of King's College, Cambridge. As a musician, she has worked professionally in avant-garde jazz and rock and in experimental and improvised music. She is the author of *Rationalizing Culture: IRCAM, Boulez, and the Institutionalization of the Musical Avant-Garde* (1995) and writes on cultural production, the politics of culture, and sociology and aesthetics in relation to music, television, and new technologies. Essays have appeared in *Cultural Anthropology, Social Anthropology, New Formations, Screen, Journal of Material Culture, American Anthropologist,* and several edited books. She is now writing on the transformation of public service broadcasting through an ethnographic study of the BBC.

Julie Brown is Lecturer in the Department of Music at Royal Holloway College, University of London; and she taught previously at King's College, London, St Peter's College, Oxford, and the University of Southampton. From 1992–95 she held a research fellowship at Emmanuel College, Cambridge. Her publications have appeared in *Music Analysis, Cambridge Opera Journal, Music and Letters,* and the *Journal of the American Musicological Society,* and she is currently completing two books. *Re-reading Schoenberg,* forthcoming with Cambridge University Press, stems from her doctoral dissertation on Schoenberg's *Das Buch der hängenden Gärten. Bartók's Third String Quartet: Interpretative Perspectives* is forthcoming with the RMA Monographs Series.

John Corbett is an adjunct professor in the Sound Department at the School of the Art Institute of Chicago. A regular contributor to *Down Beat, Pulse!,* and the *Chicago Reader,* he has published widely on jazz, improvised music, and audio art for journals including *Discourse, October, TDR,* and *Stanford Humanities Review.* He is the author of *Extended Play: Sounding Off from John Cage to Dr. Funkenstein* (1994), and the host of weekly radio programs on WHPK-FM and WNUR-FM in Chicago.

Steven Feld is Professor of Anthropology at New York University. His writings include *Sound and Sentiment* (1982; 2d ed. 1990; J. I. Staley Prize, 1991), *Music Grooves* (with Charles Keil, 1994; Chicago Folklore Prize, 1995), *Senses of Place* (edited with Keith Basso, 1996), and *Bosavi-English-Tok Pisin Dictionary* (with Bambi Schieffelin and five Bosavi collaborators, 1998). He also produced, with Grateful Dead drummer Mickey Hart, the CD *Voices of the Rainforest* (1991).

Peter Franklin is Reader in Music at the University of Oxford, and a Fellow of St Catherine's College, Oxford. His published work includes *The Idea of Music: Schoenberg and Others* (1985), *Mahler Symphony no. 3* (1991), and *The Life of Mahler* (1997). He also writes on early twentieth-century opera and Hollywood film music.

Simon Frith is Professor of Film and Media Studies at the University of Stirling, Scotland. From 1995 to 1999 he was Research Director of the Economic and Social Research Council's Programme in Media Culture and Media Economics. A rock columnist for *The Scotsman* newspaper, he was previously a rock critic for the New York *Village Voice.* His publications include *Sound Effects* (1983), *Music For Pleasure* (1988), *World Music, Politics and Social Change* (1989), *On Record: Rock, Pop, and the Written Word* (1990), and *Performing Rites: On the Value of Popular Music* (1997).

Claudia Gorbman is Professor of Film Studies in the Interdisciplinary Arts and Sciences program at University of Washington, Tacoma. She is the author of *Unheard Melodies: Narrative Film Music* (1987), the editor and translator of Michel Chion's *Audio-Vision: Sound on Screen* (1994) and of Chion's *The Voice in Cinema* (1999), and the editor of *Film Music II* (forthcoming). Her scholarly writing focuses on film sound and film music theory and criticism. She has contributed essays to *Quarterly Review of Film Studies, Cine-tracts, Yale French Studies, Screen,* and the *Oxford Guide to Film Studies;* elsewhere she has written on French cinema, music in the films of Fellini, pop music in film, women directors, and music in films from *Mildred Pierce* to *The Piano.*

David Hesmondhalgh is Research Fellow in Sociology at the Open University, U.K. He is the author of articles in *Media, Culture and Society, Popular Music, British Journal of Sociology, Soundings,* and *Cultural Studies,* and of chapters in a number of edited collections. He was international treasurer of the International Association for the Study of Popular Music (IASPM) from 1997 to 1999. He is currently writing a book called *The Cultural Industries.*

Richard Middleton is Professor of Music at the University of Newcastle Upon Tyne and taught previously at the Open University. He is the author of *Pop Music and the Blues* (1972), *Studying Popular Music* (1990), and numerous articles on popular music topics. He was a founding editor of the journal *Popular Music* (Cambridge University Press). His current research interests are in discourses about popular music, analytical and interpretative strategies, and the concept of a historical transatlantic vernacular music-culture area.

Jann Pasler is Professor of Music at the University of California, San Diego and earned her Ph.D. from the University of Chicago in 1981. Musicologist, pianist, and documentary filmmaker, she has been awarded three NEH fellowships and a Senior Fellowship at the Stanford Humanities Center. She organized the International Stravinsky Symposium at UCSD in 1982. In Paris at the CNRS in 1983–84 she helped found the Centre d'Information et de Documentation "Recherche musicale," and in 1994 she ran with Philip Brett a research group at the UC Humanities Research Center called "Retheorizing Music." Her publications have focused on French music and cultural life, contemporary American music, and modernist, postmodernist, and cross-cultural issues in music. She is currently completing *Useful Music, or Why Music Mattered in Paris, 1870–1903* for the University of California Press.

Martin Stokes is Associate Professor in the Department of Music at the University of Chicago. He earned a D.Phil. in Social Anthropology from the University of Oxford, and previously taught ethnomusicology and anthropology at the Queen's University of Belfast, as well as holding a visiting appointment at Bogazici University, Istanbul. His main publications include *The Arabesk Debate* (1992), *Ethnicity, Identity and Music: The Musical Construction of Place* (ed., 1994), *Nationalism, Minorities and Diasporas: Identities and Rights in the Middle East* (1996, co-edited with Kirsten Shulze and Colm Campbell), a special issue of the journal *Popular Music* on the Middle East (1996, co-edited with Ruth Davis), and articles in *New Formations* and the *Journal of the Royal Anthropological Institute.*

INDEX

Abba, Dimi Mint, 288
Abdelwahhab, Mohammed, 220
aboriginals, Australian, role in film *Until the End of the World*, 268
acculturation theory, 25, 30
acı (pain), in arabesk, attempt to remove in the 1980s, 227
acid house music culture, 301n2
acoustic effects, importance in materialist minimalism, 174–75
Addicted to Love (film score), 250
ADF. *See* Asian Dub Foundation
Adorno, Theodor, 16, 17, 44, 66–67, 155; on mimesis, 214, 230n7, 265; on modernism, 143–44, 151
Adventures of Robin Hood, The (film score), 155, 156
Ady, Endre, 125
aesthetics, 21, 24, 41–42, 61, 315; idealism as an instrument of patriarchal domination in *Deception*, 158–59; mimesis, 214, 230n7, 265, 278n36
Africa, 12, 29 (*see also* South Africa)
  music, 170, 173–74, 176, 208n12, 305, 319; of Central African forest peoples, *see* pygmy music; ethnomusicological recordings of used by African American musicians, 25–26, 28, 256–60; Tiersot on, 89; use by Bebey, 269–70
  peoples, "pygmies" seen as the primal other, 261–62, 268, 272–73
African American music(s), 22–24, 52n52,

53nn54, 55, 63, 83n66, 307 (*see also individual genres and performers*); Afrocentrism, 258, 259–61; and conflation of black and low, 66; Gershwin's portrayal of in *Porgy and Bess*, 67–70 (*see also Porgy and Bess*); pan-Africanist discourse's influence on, 34; as source of inspiration for an American school of composition, 169, 236; strategies of "Signifyin(g)," 73–78, 292; use of ethnomusicological recordings of traditional African music, 25–26, 28, 256–60
African Americans, 22, 24, 49n11, 55n93, 298; American Indians seen as representing in 1950s movie westerns, 240; black separatist politics, Fun-da-mental's allegiance to, 284, 302n11; depiction in post–World War II films, 240; legacy of "double consciousness," 71, 77; strategies of "Signifyin(g)," 24, 73–78, 83n62, 84n78, 292, 303n26
African Music: A People's Art (Bebey), 269
"Afro-Latin Soul," recorded by the Ethiopian Quintet, 319
Agawu, Kofi, 78n2, 305
Age of Discovery, construction of external others, 189–90, 191, 208n12
agency, 3, 7, 36, 38–39, 45, 46
agit-prop style, adopted by Fun-da-mental, 298
Ahlan, Attiah (Alex Kassiak; Tim Whelan), 296

Text:	10/12 Baskerville
Display:	Baskerville
Composition:	Integrated Composition Systems, Inc.
Printing and binding:	Data Reprographics